no100F

FINANCING AND EXTERNAL DEBT OF DEVELOPING COUNTRIES

1992 SURVEY

ORGANISATION FOR ECONOMIC CO-OPERATION AND DEVELOPMENT

ORGANISATION FOR ECONOMIC CO-OPERATION AND DEVELOPMENT

Pursuant to Article 1 of the Convention signed in Paris on 14th December 1960, and which came into force on 30th September 1961, the Organisation for Economic Co-operation and Development (OECD) shall promote policies designed :

— to achieve the highest sustainable economic growth and employment and a rising standard of living in Member countries, while maintaining financial stability, and thus to contribute to the development of the world economy;

— to contribute to sound economic expansion in Member as well as non-member countries in the process of economic development; and

— to contribute to the expansion of world trade on a multilateral, non-discriminatory basis in accordance with international obligations.

The original Member countries of the OECD are Austria, Belgium, Canada, Denmark, France, Germany, Greece, Iceland, Ireland, Italy, Luxembourg, the Netherlands, Norway, Portugal, Spain, Sweden, Switzerland, Turkey, the United Kingdom and the United States. The following countries became Members subsequently through accession at the dates indicated hereafter: Japan (28th April 1964), Finland (28th January 1969), Australia (7th June 1971) and New Zealand (29th May 1973). The Commission of the European Communities takes part in the work of the OECD (Article 13 of the OECD Convention).

In order to achieve its aims the OECD has set up a number of specialised committees. One of these is the Development Assistance Committee, whose Members have agreed to secure an expansion of aggregate volume of resources made available to developing countries and to improve their effectiveness. To this end, Members periodically review together both the amount and the nature of their contributions to aid programmes, bilateral and multilateral, and consult each other on all other relevant aspects of their development assistance policies.

The Members of the Development Assistance Committee are Australia, Austria, Belgium, Canada, Denmark, Finland, France, Germany, Ireland, Italy, Japan, Luxembourg, the Netherlands, New Zealand, Norway, Portugal, Spain, Sweden, Switzerland, the United Kingdom, the United States and the Commission of the European Communities.

Publié en français sous le titre :
FINANCEMENT ET DETTE EXTÉRIEURE DES PAYS EN DÉVELOPPEMENT
Étude 1992

This Survey has been compiled by the OECD
Development Co-operation Directorate and is
published on the responsibility of the Secretary-General.

ALSO AVAILABLE

Development Assistance Manual DAC: Principles for Effective Aid (1992)
(43 92 06 1) ISBN 92-64-13779-3   FF75   US$19.00   DM31

Development Co-operation: Efforts and Policies of the Members of the Development Assistance Committee. 1992 Report *by R. Alexander Love* (1992)
(43 92 05 1) ISBN 92-64-13772-6   FF160   US$34.00   DM65

Geographical Distribution of Financial Flows to Developing Countries. 1988-1991: Disbursements – Commitments – Economic Indicators (1993)
(43 93 01 3) ISBN 92-64-03717-9   FF295   US$68.00   DM115

Table of Contents

Chapter I

Introduction and Overview

The recovery in resource flows to the developing countries, which has been progressing steadily since the mid-1980s, took a quite dramatic turn in 1992 with total net resource flows surging to $175 billion. Since their low point in 1986, total resource flows have increased by over 60 per cent in real terms. Private flows in general and international bank lending in particular were responsible for most of the growth of resource flows in 1992. However, most of the 1992 expansion was captured by a relatively small number of countries.

Progress on the debt front was maintained in 1992. Debt stocks continued to expand, but at a slow pace, and service payments were stable. Recent debt creating flows are on a sounder footing – from both creditor and borrower perspectives – than was previously the case, as new loans are increasingly going to those countries putting them to productive use and whose debt is sustainable or is approaching sustainability. While the pace of action by the main creditor groups on debt reorganisation has continued and taken on important new dimensions, for many of the poorer developing countries undertaking economic stabilization and reform, debt burdens still prevent the attainment of financial viability.

The main highlights of developments in resource flow patterns and debt are presented below, followed by a commentary on their significance and on the outlook for resource flows. The remainder of this annual survey provides a comprehensive picture covering aggregate financial flows (Chapters II and III), and debt (Chapters IV and V), including breakdowns by continents and income groups. The debt situation of some 140 individual countries is presented in Annex 2, while Chapter VI reviews current technical issues and definitions concerning the external financing situation of developing countries.

1. Recent developments: the highlights

A. *Resource flows*

- Total net resource flows to developing countries increased in 1992 by a massive $40 billion to a record of $175 billion. On the basis of constant prices and exchange rates, they increased by 23 per cent on their 1991 level.
- Most of this expansion was due to the surge in international bank lending which increased from $11 billion in 1991 to $40 billion in 1992. Other components of private flows (direct and portfolio investment and bonds) also witnessed important growth.

Official Development Finance (ODF)

- ODF, at $72 billion, increased by $2 billion on its 1991 level, but in real terms fell by nearly 3 per cent. Since 1984, ODF has expanded by an average of about $4 billion per annum, but in real terms it was more or less flat until 1990, after which it declined.
- In real terms, the upward trend in total DAC ODA (bilateral plus multilateral) has continued (averaging 2.7 per cent per annum during 1989-92), but much of this has been offset by the decline in aid from the former Soviet bloc and from Arab donors.
- Although the share of ODF in total flows fell to 41 per cent as a result of the expansion in private flows, ODF remains very much the backbone of financial flows to the vast majority of developing countries.

Particular features of 1992 ODF patterns were:

- Bilateral ODA remained at its 1991 level in nominal terms, while ODA from multilateral sources rose by $1 billion. Other ODF recovered by $1.3 billion due to an increase in bilateral official loans.
- ODF continues to be provided on highly concessional terms; the share of official grants in ODF now stands at 69 per cent.
- ODF from non-DAC donors, at less than $2 billion, continues to dwindle.

Export credits

- Export credits recovered in 1992 to $3.5 billion, but still only account for a small proportion (2 per cent) of total flows.

Private flows

- Private flows, which had been growing steadily in absolute and relative terms since 1987 surged by 60 per cent in 1992 to $100 billion representing 57 per cent of total flows.

Although dominated by a major jump in international bank lending, the expansion of private flows in 1992 was nevertheless broad-based, with all other components also reaching record levels in 1992:

- Bond lending maintained its recent expansion, up by over $1 billion to $14 billion;
- Foreign direct investment also continued its upward trend, increasing by $4 billion to over $30 billion in 1992 – a particularly notable development in that total outward investment from the OECD area has been falling recently;
- Other private flows (essentially portfolio equity and supplier credits) increased by $3 billion to over

$9 billion, reflecting improved investor interest in the equity of developing country corporations.

The developments in overall resource movements referred to above were, however, not at all equally shared between income groups and regions.

At the level of the *income groups*:

- While there was some growth in resource inflows to the LIC and LMIC groups in 1992, most of the expansion went to the UMICs, where 1992 levels were over 50 per cent above 1991 inflows. Resource flows to the LLDCs actually fell in 1992.
- The LICs continue to be highly aid dependent, with ODF accounting for 72 per cent of total flows in 1992. For the LLDCs, private flows in 1992 were at negative levels.

At the level of the *regions*:

- Asia still receives the largest share of resource inflows, although there was an upsurge in Latin America's share in 1992 as improved economic prospects caused private flows to double.
- Resource flows to North Africa and the Middle East doubled in 1992 as bank lending, particularly to the Gulf states, recovered.

Table I.1. **Recent trends in total net resource flows to developing countries**

Current $ billion and percentage

	1989	1990	1991	1992
Total net resource flows	115.5	131.9	136.0	175.3
1. Official Development Finance (ODF)	60.8	71.0	71.9	72.0
of which: Concessional	(79.9)	(76.2)	(82.3)	(80.1)
– Bilateral	(59.7)	(57.3)	(59.9)	(56.9)
– Multilateral	(20.2)	(18.9)	(22.4)	(23.6)
Non-concessional	(20.1)	(23.8)	(17.6)	(19.4)
– Bilateral	(8.5)	(9.4)	(6.8)	(8.3)
– Multilateral	(11.5)	(14.4)	(10.8)	(11.1)
2. Export Credits	9.5	4.4	1.7	3.5
3. Private Flows	45.2	56.5	62.4	99.8
of which: Foreign direct investment	(59.1)	(47.6)	(42.3)	(30.7)
International bank lending	(23.2)	(26.5)	(17.6)	(41.0)
Bond lending	(2.9)	(8.0)	(20.8)	(14.2)
Other private	(6.0)	(8.8)	(10.6)	(9.5)
Memorandum item:				
Distribution of total net resource flows by income group (%)[a]:				
LICs	42.5	45.6	39.2	33.1
of which: LLDCs	12.8	13.9	11.1	8.3
LMICs	18.5	23.4	21.5	19.2
UMICs	26.2	22.5	31.3	36.1

Note: Figures in parenthesis are percentages of sub-totals.
a) Percentages do not add up to 100 per cent due to amounts unallocated and unspecified.

- Flows to Africa as a whole have been static in real terms recently, but have fallen considerably since the mid-1980s due to increasing unattractiveness to private investors and lenders. The situation for Sub-Saharan Africa is worse; total resource inflows have fallen continuously in real terms since 1986, even though an increased share of aid from DAC donors has been channelled to this region.

B. Debt and debt service payments

- The *external debt* of developing countries increased by 3 per cent to $1 534 billion in 1992, on the basis of provisional data.

The clear slowing down of the pace of growth of the stock of debt which had been evident since 1987 continued both for the developing countries as a whole, as well as for each of the main income groups.

- Asia in particular, but also Latin America, have been responsible for most of the growth of the stock of external debt in 1992; the external debt of Africa as a whole actually fell slightly, reflecting the concessionality of lending and the effects of debt reorganisation.
- There has been a quite fundamental change in the distribution of total external debt between the regions over the last decade; Latin America's share has fallen steadily from 41 per cent in 1982 to 29 per cent in 1992. Asia's debt more than doubled over the decade such that its share has increased

considerably, especially since 1987, reaching 34 per cent in 1992.
- At the level of the income groups, it is the low-income countries which have registered the highest rate of expansion of debt stocks since 1987 (related to the growth of lending to countries such as China, Indonesia and India). LLDC debt stocks have expanded much more slowly, thanks to accelerating debt reorganisation since the end of the 1980s.

Particular developments in the structure of debt stocks are:

- The stock of *multilateral debt,* the main component of which is non-concessional, continues to expand, accounting for 17 per cent of total external debt.
- *Financial market debt,* which had been falling since 1988, is now growing again.
- *Short-term debt* grew by 11 per cent in 1992 reflecting in particular the accumulation of arrears in countries such as Argentina (which has since been cleared), Brazil and Peru, and a more cautious approach by lenders.
- While the debt owed to *non-OECD creditors,* notably the former Soviet Union, has changed little over the last five years, it is increasingly problematic for certain countries as there is no established forum in which to deal with it.

Aggregate *debt service payments,* at $150 billion, were unchanged on their 1991 levels. This "no change" situation held for all of the main developing country income groups, except for the UMICs, where service

Table I.2. **Recent trends in developing country external debt and debt service**

Current $ billion and percentage

		1989	1990	1991	1992
Total external debt		1 353	1 428	1 485	1 534
1. Long-term		1 071	1 094	1 133	1 146
of which:	ODA	(10.7)	(11.6)	(12.0)	(12.3)
	Export credits	(16.9)	(17.7)	(17.8)	(16.7)
	Financial markets	(34.7)	(31.4)	(30.8)	(31.4)
	Bilateral	(64.0)	(62.4)	(62.2)	(62.0)
	Multilateral	(20.3)	(22.4)	(23.1)	(23.7)
2. Short-term		255.0	301.0	318.0	354.0
Total debt service		160.2	156.4	150.2	150.0
Memorandum item:					
Regional distribution of total external debt (%)					
Sub-Saharan Africa		11.6	11.9	11.6	11.0
Asia		28.8	31.0	33.2	33.6
Central & South America		33.2	31.1	30.0	29.6

Notes: Figures in parenthesis are percentages of sub-totals. Percentages do not add up to 100 per cent due to amounts unallocated and unspecified.

payments increased by $3 billion. In general, the trend in service payments has been downward since 1989; over the period 1989-1992, service payments fell by 6 per cent while the stock of debt increased by 15 per cent. This trend in debt service payments reflects:

- the growing pace of debt reorganisation;
- the accumulation of arrears;
- changes in the composition and concessionality structure of debt.

Looking back at changes in the structure of debt service payments over the last five years:

- *Multilateral service payments* have expanded considerably, now accounting for a quarter of total debt service payments.
- Payments to *non-OECD creditors* as well as on *export credit* debt have fallen in both absolute and relative terms.
- Payments related to *long-term debt* as well as to *financial market* debt have remained stable over the period.

The changing structure of debt service payments differs between the regions in a number of important respects:

- In Sub-Saharan Africa, the relative importance of service payments related to multilateral and financial market debt has increased while the share of official bilateral debt service has declined.
- The significance of payments on financial market debt in Latin America has been reduced but has been offset by the expansion of multilateral service payments.
- In Asia, service payments to export credit debt have declined in importance, but short-term debt service payments have grown.

Recent years have also witnessed important developments in debt reorganisation activity by the major groups of creditors. Since the late 1980s, there has been a decisive movement away from an approach based on rescheduling and refinancing towards *debt and debt service reduction*. Most recently:

- The application of the enhanced Toronto terms for the poorest developing countries provides greater concessionality through the Paris Club. It also now allows for the review of the total stock of debt after a given period if adjustment policies for the restoration of viability have been implemented and maintained.
- The IDA Debt Reduction Facility has permitted the poorer developing countries to enter into the commercial debt reorganisation process.

- Middle- and low-income countries can now engage in a certain amount of debt conversion through Paris Club rescheduling.

The combination of debt reorganisation and the pursuit of sound macroeconomic management has permitted a small but growing number of developing countries to put their debt on a sustainable basis, to regain financial viability and to improve their prospects for attracting and keeping new international finance.

While an increasing number of countries are moving in this direction, the debt situation for many developing countries continues to remain critical due to inappropriate adjustment efforts at home and/or because debt reorganisations have still not been sufficient for them to exit from the process of repeat rescheduling. Issues that may well merit increasing attention on the debt agenda include:

- the growing burden of multilateral debt;
- the official debt situation not only of the poorest countries but also those of the low middle-income group;
- debt owed to non-OECD creditors;
- co-ordination between debt and debt service reduction and other donor efforts.

2. Commentary and outlook

Despite the modest growth of world output and the still uncertain outlook in the OECD countries, the most recent economic performance of the developing countries, seen in aggregate terms, displayed a certain resilience in the face of slackness in the global economy. While external factors have played some part in this, the major force behind their improving outlook has been the very considerable progress achieved with stabilization and reform policies which have resulted in more outward and market-oriented development strategies. Endorsement of this progress is clearly reflected in the growth of private flows to the developing countries in recent years. Total net resource flows have expanded significantly with the 1992 level 50 per cent in real terms above that of five years ago.

Progress with reform and stabilisation policies is being endorsed by expanding private inflows.

The very striking jump in resource flows in 1992, up by 23 per cent on 1991 levels in real terms, is heartening. While the history of resource flows to the developing countries has been one of surges followed by curtailment, present prospects suggest that these new inflows may be more sustainable. In the past, the resources going to the developing countries were too often misused by an over-expanded and inefficient public sector or by a protected private sector, but significant policy changes on these fronts suggest that resources are now being used for more productive purposes and are yielding returns that are captured by the recipient economies. While some of these inflows are debt creating, this is also likely to be less of a concern today than in the past as they help to create a genuine debt-servicing capacity. Loans are better provisioned by creditors, terms are more concessional on average and they are increasingly used to finance investment rather than consumption.

Growing divergence and aid dependency

The expansion of resource flows to the developing countries is particularly welcome. But, at a more disaggregated level, it is immediately clear that by no means all of the developing countries have shared in better economic prospects or the growth of external resources for development. The largest part of the growth of private flows has been captured by the UMIC group of countries as well as by China, Indonesia and India. The poorer and smaller developing countries have made little progress in attracting external, particularly private finance.

While the external economic environment may not have been too kind to the poorer developing countries, the principal cause has been the lack of sufficient progress in the countries themselves. Institutional rigidities, too much government involvement, weak administrative capacity, poor infrastructure and social and political instability reflect slow progress with economic reform and good governance that continue to make countries unattractive to badly needed external capital. Some developing countries report that although they are making progress on economic and political fronts, this has not led to any noticeable improvement in the flow of resources from abroad. However, such views should be placed in the perspective of the recent experience of other countries, where commitment to economic and political progress has been clearly matched by greater attractiveness to external finance. For example, investor interest is expanding in countries such as Ghana and Uganda as a result of their efforts since the mid-1980s to pursue sound development policies.

The growth of resource flows has been captured by only a few countries – many of the poorest are increasingly aid dependent.

The external resource situation of many of the low-income countries is critical. Apart from China, Indonesia and India, they have benefited little from the recent expansion of private sector inflows. They are increasingly, if not already totally, dependent on aid and their debt burdens continue to be a major hindrance to development. This is particularly problematical for a number of reasons. Most of the growth of financial flows is from private sources, for which these countries are singularly unattractive. Aid has increased relatively slowly in real terms and no significant positive change in this trend can be realistically expected in the coming years. Aid from non-DAC donors has dwindled to next to nothing. Leaving aside the issue of possible resource diversion to the countries of Central and Eastern Europe and the countries of the former Soviet Union (for which there is no supportive evidence at present), aid resources are subject to other claims within the developing countries themselves in light of growing demands for humanitarian, peacekeeping and emergency aid over and above the need for aid to provide the foundation for long-term sustainable economic growth.

Key issues in the development dialogue are therefore how to help the poorer countries break out of this situation and how ODA can be used to catalyse efforts to attract private capital. As a growing number of countries achieve a sounder pattern of external finance and use this to foster development, there is a possibility that their progress could free more aid for the poorer countries, although the amount of aid going to the UMICs (less than 8 per cent of total ODA) is not substantial. Other countries outside the UMIC group, which will continue to require ODA, are now able to attract significant levels of private flows. However, if the poorer countries are to attract more aid they will certainly first have to demonstrate that it can be used effectively and productively and in a manner that will complement and not replace private flows or domestic savings.

Attracting private finance

While the role of increased bank lending was predominant in the major expansion of private sector flows in 1992, the fact that the growth of private flows was broad-based, covering all of the components of private sector flows, is also of considerable importance. The recent growth of foreign direct investment, for example, has occured at a time when outward investment from

OECD countries has been falling off. The developing countries are therefore now getting a growing share of a declining total, the reverse of the situation just a few years ago when their share of expanding outward investment was falling. The expansion of portfolio investment is also an encouraging sign of the interest shown by investors in the equity of developing country corporations.

The significance of growing private sector inflows lies not only in the fact that they bring additional finance. Over the past few years, the structure of private inflows has also been improving. There has been a move from debt to equity and from bank to non-bank finance. The importance of these inflows for development is disproportionate to their volume in that they are associated with integration into world markets, they facilitate the absorption of external shocks and sustain adjustment efforts, they lower the cost of capital and they bring with them the transfer of technology and management practices. In many ways, the growth of private inflows can be seen as the seal of approval from the international financial community on the reform efforts of the countries receiving them. In fact, it is estimated that an important part of these flows is return flight capital, the owners of which are perhaps best placed to judge the outlook for their countries. This is of particular interest given the vast amounts of flight capital that are estimated to have left not just Latin America but also Asia and Africa.

Recent experience in Latin America has shown that both internal and external forces are behind expanding private inflows. Domestic economic reform and a reorientation towards more productive use of capital have certainly been the main factors. The significance of the role of external factors, such as a fall in world real interest rates and recession in the OECD area, lies in the fact that these may change, sometimes abruptly, causing a reversal. If the inflows due to external forces are to be retained it means that the countries concerned must pursue credible economic policies.

The credibility of governments' commitment to sound economic management and good governance is crucial for external development finance.

The availability of external (and domestic) financing for development depends essentially on the prospects for sustainable growth. External suppliers of finance, both private and official, will make their own assessments of political and economic prospects. The credibility of the government's commitment to sound market-oriented policies and good governance, basic requirements for sustainable development, is therefore crucial. The experience of a small but growing number of countries shows that such commitment works, as witnessed by renewed access to international lending, growing foreign direct investment and the return of flight capital.

A dynamic private sector is a key prerequisite for viable development. Financing private sector growth will create both a need and a basis for a more diversified pattern of development finance. As the private sector emphasis is pursued, private capital inflows must and do increase as a share of total external financing. The link between private sector financing and the pattern of external finance is therefore an increasingly central element in policy thinking about the pattern of development finance.

Central strategic elements for a viable domestic private and financial sector, which bear importantly on the ability to attract external finance, include:

- Financial sector: a *sine qua non* for private sector development is the parallel evolution of intermediation services on a market basis catering to a wide range of enterprises. Comprehensive reform and rehabilitation of the financial sector are especially important in countries with serious dysfunctions in their banking systems.

- Regulatory environment: review and reform of regulatory systems are necessary to clear away costly and obstructive laws and administrative requirements and to strengthen competition and prudential supervision of the financial sector. On the international front, the best way to attract foreign investment is to create a climate conducive to domestic private investment. The additional requirements needed to attract foreign investment are an open investment regime, equal treatment of foreign and domestic companies, allowing full foreign ownership, and liberalising foreign exchange and repatriation regimes.

- Public sector: an excessive size and role of the public sector has crowded out private and financial sector development in many countries. Downsizing the public sector is therefore a necessary, if difficult, priority. Privatisation programmes will constitute important components of private sector strategy in many cases. At the same time, there is a need to strengthen the role of the state in providing public goods, investing in human capital, and creating an enabling environment through a sound policy and legal framework, along with the efficient provision of administrative and physical infrastructure.

The role of policies in the OECD countries:

- Macroeconomic and trade policies: while recipient country policies are the principal determinants of their ability to attract external resources, there are nevertheless a number of areas where actions by the developed countries could significantly improve the prospects for developing countries. Clearly, an improvement in macroeconomic and trade policies would be beneficial. OECD countries have yet to adjust their public sector deficits to a level compatible with an overall savings surplus available to finance development outside the OECD area at reasonable rates of interest. OECD countries have also yet to finalise the Uruguay Round, which has created uncertainty about the stability of the world trading system at a time when many developing countries are liberalising their trade regimes and moving towards more open and outward looking strategies.
- Facilitating capital outflows to developing countries: there is considerable scope to improve efforts to promote outward investment and to target this to developing countries, including greater co-ordination with counterpart promotion agencies in capital export and recipient countries. There may also be supply side restrictions unduly impeding the flow of other investment funds to the developing countries. For example, institutional investors in the OECD area may be a major source of potential future funds for the developing countries. Such investors have a traditional home bias in investing funds, but while the share of foreign assets in their portfolios has been increasing, they hold only a very small fraction of their assets in the emerging markets of the developing countries. The significance of institutional investment funds is that even a small expansion of their assets in the developing countries would represent a major capital flow. It may therefore be worthwhile to look into regulatory regimes to see where impediments might exist and be relaxed without jeopardising the prudential and fiduciary objectives they are intended to achieve.

There is, therefore, a need on the side of the capital exporting countries to ensure that they pursue coherent policies and investigate possible impediments to financial flows to the developing countries. However, and this point should not be overlooked, while such actions may increase the potential for resource flows to the developing country, the principal way of ensuring that they can actually attract and keep such resources is for them to provide a sound and stable environment by pursuing policies for sustainable development and good governance.

Debt relief

Recent trends and developments in the external debt situation of developing countries have been highlighted above and are dealt with in detail in Chapter IV. In particular, the present rate of expansion of debt stocks has to be seen in the light of the economic situation of countries, the growth of their exports and the structure and concessionality of debt-creating flows. In these respects there have been quite positive developments.

While these improvements should not be underplayed, it is increasingly apparent that for many developing countries there is a major mismatch between the terms of debt reorganisation and their ability to exit from the cycle of repeat reschedulings. As was identified above in respect of ability to attract resource flows, there is also a growing differentiation between developing countries in terms of their ability to put their debt burdens on a sustainable basis. In some cases, the heart of the problem lies in the lack of commitment to pursuing necessary policy changes at home. But other countries, which have adopted major adjustment and policy programmes, continue to face difficulties in making progress with private and financial sector reforms due to debt burdens which are not compatible with becoming creditworthy in the near future.

In this connection, the growing importance of certain categories of debt is noteworthy. For example, short-term debt, including arrears, has been expanding and its non-repayment hinders or blocks the disbursement of new loans. For some countries, debt to the former Soviet Union (FSU) is a major burden. Given its economic situation, Russia (which has taken over the claims of the FSU) is putting increasing pressure on its debtors to repay. But a variety of political and technical factors hinder negotiation. At present there is no forum, other than bilateral, to deal with such issues for countries such as Mozambique and Ethiopia. One possibility might be to bring debt owed to the FSU into the negotiations in the Paris Club when it discusses the debt of Russia.

Most significant is the growing importance of debt owed to multilateral agencies, which is not renegotiable and, on average, relatively expensive, given the level of real interest rates. While the non-negotiability principle pertaining to such debt cannot be relaxed, a problem is potentially building up. The situation creates a need for facilities to clear up arrears to the multilateral institutions (such as the *ad hoc* arrangements made for a number of countries under the so-called "fifth dimension"). It also means that the international financial institutions have to pay stricter attention to the future debt-servicing capacity of their clients. In other words, multilateral lending must, more imperatively than ever, be based on sound economic policies.

For many of the poorer countries, debt obligations, even after restructuring, are still beyond their ability to repay.

For a large number of countries, and not just the poorest ones, debt obligations are still beyond their ability to repay, even after Paris Club restructuring. The situation in Africa illustrates the nature of the problem. Debt has expanded considerably over the last decade, but largely as a result of the build-up of unpaid interest. Africa as a whole now meets roughly only half of its debt service obligations and even those countries which meet their obligations struggle to do so.

Some recent initiatives reflect the concern with this situation. For example, in 1992 France created a scheme for a number of African countries, previously excluded from debt forgiveness, where forgiveness is linked to use of freed funds for sound development projects aimed at combating certain short-run effects of adjustment programmes. Most recently, the United States, which had previously always chosen the "non-concessional" option in the Paris Club, has proposed to Congress a programme through which it will cancel an important part of its claims on the poorest African countries. Other countries, notably the United Kingdom, continue to press for the multilateral application of the more concessional Trinidad Terms for the poorest developing countries.

The debt burdens of a number of countries in the middle-income group continue to depress their medium-term prospects, but they still do not benefit from the more concessional treatment accorded to the poorer countries. The commitment to consider the total stock of debt of the poorest countries if adjustment policies for the restoration of viability are carried through is indeed welcome. But there will be a need to ensure – and this is not yet evident – that the reduction of the debt stock is sufficient to allow exit from a perpetual cycle of reorganisation. The task facing Paris Club creditors is to ensure decisive debt relief for the poorest countries, which provides the means to pursue sustainable development policies.

With the realisation that debt problems are not just a matter of liquidity but of solvency, debt reorganisation has moved on from an approach dominated by rescheduling, to one based on the reduction of debt stocks and service; in other words, from managing the situation to resolving it. Further progress, however, may require a broadening of the perspective from which the debt situation is analysed. The present financing gap/balance-of-payments approach and the requirement for an IMF-backed adjustment strategy need to be maintained to ensure that debtor countries undertake the necessary reforms to ensure a sound base for future loans. But more definitive debt reorganisation "up front" could enhance the prospects for sustainable adjustment and the early resumption of growth.

Chapter II

Resource Flows to Developing Countries

This chapter reviews recent trends in net resource flows to developing countries (LDCs), namely: official development finance (bilateral and multilateral ODF, including grants and concessional and non-concessional loans), officially supported export credits, and private flows (including direct investment, international bank finance, equity and bond issues, suppliers credits and private grants). This survey covers net resource flows to developing countries from OECD Member countries and other sources.

The chapter should be read in conjunction with the tables in Chapter III (Resource Flow Tables). The first section briefly recapitulates the overall trends in resource flow patterns and volumes in 1992. The following section takes up the individual components of resource flows in turn, describing changes that have occurred both over the past year and from a longer-term perspective (see Table III.1). The third section comments on resource flows channelled to major LDC regions (see Tables III.2 to III.5), followed by a review of recent trends and magnitudes of resource flows directed to LDCs grouped according to income levels (see Tables III.6 to III.11).

1. Introduction

Net resource flows to the developing countries surged from $134 billion to over $175 billion in 1992, growing faster than at any time in the past decade and attaining levels – in real terms – not seen since the onset of the 1982 debt crisis. Virtually all of the growth in net resource flows in 1992 was due to private capital inflows, which jumped a spectacular 60 per cent to almost $100 billion over the past year, reflecting a boom in international bank lending, solid growth in foreign direct investment, sustained recourse to international bond markets and a sharp rise in equities issued by developing country sovereign and corporate borrowers.

Aside from the extraordinary growth of international bank lending, the broader pattern of resource flows to developing countries in 1992 was consistent with trends established during the latter half of the 1980s. Official Development Finance (ODF) increased by $2 billion to $72 billion (in current terms) despite budget duress, the unsettled economic outlook in several OECD countries and the virtual cessation of aid from non-DAC donors. Export credits doubled in volume over the year but, at 2 per cent of total net resource flows, continued to play a marginal role. Private flows consolidated recent growth due to a combination of lack-lustre economic growth in the industrialised nations, low interest rates on international capital markets and the improved growth performance of those developing countries which have opened their economies to international trade and investment. The most recent trends seem to confirm what other market phenomena – such as the re-entry of several Latin American countries on international capital markets and renewed streams of foreign investment – have been suggesting: the overall decline in external financial flows to the developing world and the limited range of funding sources that characterised much of the 1980s now appears, at least for a number of countries, to be rapidly reversing (see Chart II.1).

Underlying these resource flows are a number of notable events and trends. International bank lending, which rose from $11 billion to $40 billion over the year, climbed to heights not seen for more than a decade. Greater numbers of developing countries tapped international capital markets, some for the first time ever, for their funding needs. 1992 was also a year that saw unprecedented growth and diversification of portfolio flows to developing countries, particularly to middle-income Latin American countries that only recently re-entered international securities markets. Breakthroughs were achieved in debt negotiations for some nations, easing financial burdens and releasing new resource flows. And liberalisation of trade, investment and foreign exchange regimes quickened in a large number of developing countries, prompting capital flows in search of opportunities created by economic reform, invigorated business climates and active privatisation programmes.

Chart II.1. **Breakdown of total net resource flows to developing countries**
1982-1992, $ billion
At 1991 prices and exchange rates

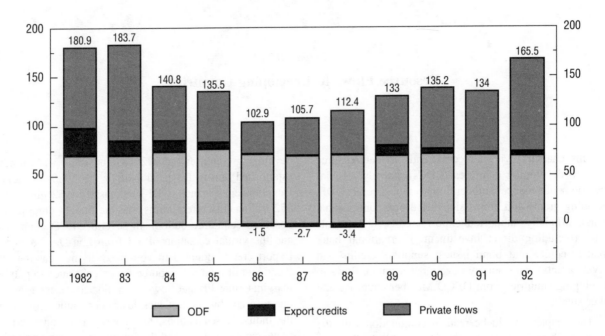

Note: Data for 1992 are provisional.

The resurgence of private flows in 1992 is an important development, since renewed commercial bank finance and international capital market acceptance of developing country securities has been slow to materialise and hard-won. Further, if access to private funding sources is maintained, it will ultimately result in a more balanced and diversified external financing base for the countries concerned.

It remains to be seen, however, whether private flows, especially of the magnitudes registered in 1992, will prove to be stable and sustainable in the future. More importantly, only a few Asian and Latin American countries have benefited from the bulk of the growth of private flows. For the vast majority of developing countries, especially the poorer ones, 1992 saw a continuation of well-entrenched trends in relation to net resource flows: aid flows provided the bulk of external resource flows and dependence on such flows grew, access to bank and bond markets remained out of reach or very expensive, debt repayments consumed large amounts of foreign exchange, and overall private flows were scant and often limited to grants from non-governmental organisations and to some foreign direct investment.

A different approach to finance has taken hold during recent years: external capital is being deployed with increasing frequency for productive investment and bankers are assessing more realistically investment project viability and the creditworthiness of borrowers.

1992 also marked ten years that have passed since the debt crisis first flared, inviting reflection on how, and to what extent, this event affected international capital flows to the developing world. In effect, the volume, composition and character of external financial flows to developing countries went through radical changes over the decade. Capital flows, which dropped sharply at the outset of the 1980s, have only now recouped their pre-debt-crisis levels. Non-debt-creating flows (*e.g.* grants provided by bilateral donors and non-governmental organisations, equity issues and foreign direct investment) have steadily bitten into the share once held by debt flows, which themselves have undergone considerable transformation over the decade, shifting from being voluntary, to more

16

concerted, back to voluntary again. Private lenders, who ceded their important intermediation role to official public lenders as from 1982, have now reassumed their dominance, while public sector borrowers in developing countries have been increasingly supplanted by private sector borrowers, with important implications for the efficiency with which capital is used. More fundamentally, a different approach to finance is taking hold: external capital is being deployed with increasing frequency in productive investment projects and there is keener interest on the part of bankers to assess realistically the overall viability of investment projects and the creditworthiness of borrowers, and to adjust risk premiums accordingly. This emerging pattern, while welcome, is still quite fragile, as witnessed by the fact that an important part of the growth of international bank lending has been in the form of short-term credits. If these present positive trends persist, however, they will eventually result in a more balanced and diversified pattern of external resource flows to the developing world, one where greater economic efficiency can be achieved and

where risks are more evenly shared between investors and borrowers.

2. Overall trends in resource flows

A. *Official Development Finance*

Official Development Finance from bilateral and multilateral donors increased by $2 billion to over $72 billion in 1992 but in real terms it fell by 3 per cent to $68 billion, its lowest point in nearly a decade. The trend towards a falling share of ODF in total net resource flows (see Chart II.2) was particularly marked in 1992 due to the major growth of private flows.

By contrast, development finance provided by DAC countries to the developing world – including direct disbursements as well as contributions to multilateral institutions – rose in real terms to $57 billion in 1992. In fact, total DAC ODA has grown in real terms by an annual average of 1.7 per cent over the past five years.

Chart II.2 **Total official development finance (ODF) as a percentage of total net resource flows
1984-1992
At 1991 prices and exchange rates**

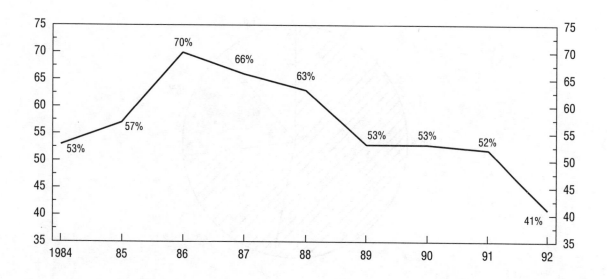

Note: Data for 1992 are provisional.

ODF continues to be highly concessional – with ODA grants representing two-thirds of the total – and represents the backbone of external finance for the development of the poorest countries.

Almost 70 per cent of ODF flows in 1992 were channelled to the poorer countries (LICs), and out of this more than a third went to the least-developed countries (LLDCs), where concessional finance accounted for the only positive source of external finance secured in 1992. Approximately 90 per cent of ODF channelled to the poorer countries was extended on highly concessional terms, two-thirds of it in the form of grants, continuing the trend towards greater ODF concessionality.

Bilateral donors continue to provide the largest share of ODF: in 1992 they supplied two-thirds of total net ODF flows, a share which has remained relatively stable over the past decade. In comparison to bilateral ODF, a large proportion of multilateral aid (32 per cent in 1992) is non-concessional: interest rates on multilateral loans are closer to market rates as these loans are funded on international capital markets.

Resource flows from non-DAC bilateral donors

Development finance provided by non-DAC bilateral donors to the developing world totalled $1.9 billion in 1992. This represents a sharp drop from the $6 billion provided in 1990, when non-DAC donor flows reached their highest point during the past decade. The total for 1990, however, was exceptionally high, since it reflected extraordinary flows from the Arab world to countries directly affected by the dislocation and destruction wrought by the Gulf War. Arab donors, which provided large amounts of development assistance to developing countries throughout the 1970s and early 1980s, have progressively reduced these flows since the latter part of the 1980s. Concessional flows provided by Central and Eastern European Countries and the former Soviet Union have virtually ceased since 1989 due to changing political priorities and the lack of available finance: residual support still being provided is confined to technical assistance. Intra-LDC development finance in the form of concessional export credits, technical assistance, food

Chart II.3 **Breakdown of total ODF by income groups 1992**

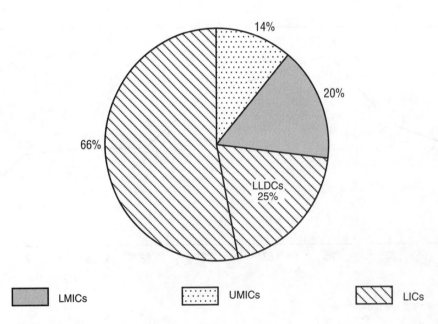

Notes: Unallocated amounts by income group excluded.
Data are provisional.

aid, emergency assistance and project lending continues to be an additional, though marginal, source of external finance.

B. Export credits

Officially supported export credits recovered from a low of $1.8 billion in 1991 to $3.5 billion in 1992, but despite this rise they continue to account for a minimal share (just 2 per cent) of total resource flows to the developing world. This was not always the case: in the decade prior to the debt crisis, export credits accounted for roughly 15 per cent of total net resources. Throughout the 1980s, cashflow problems of Export Credit Agencies (ECAs) became increasingly acute as a result of economic distress in a large number of developing countries and, as a result, the volume of loans and guarantees fell. More recently several ECAs have strengthened their institutional capacity and revised their policies and pro-cedures in an effort to increase cashflow and generate profits.

C. Private flows

In 1992, for the first time in more than a decade, private resource flows – which consist primarily of direct investment, bank lending (including suppliers credits and export credits that are not officially guaranteed) and bond and equity issues – exceeded official resource flows to developing countries.

The various elements of private flows as set out in Chart II.4 below illustrate the recent sharp growth of private flows and overall trends characterising these flows over the past decade. Direct investment recouped relatively quickly from debt crisis lows and has registered steady gains since 1985. All other private flows embodying an element of risk-taking have recovered only very recently but in every case this growth has

---

Recent Growth in Private Flows to Developing Countries

Borrowing on international markets by developing countries (*e.g.* gross announced loans, bonds and equities) has grown considerably over the past four years. Gross debt and equity flows from OECD capital markets to developing countries more than doubled over the period from $22 billion to $47 billion, while total global borrowing increased by a more moderate 30 per cent. A combination of low interest rates on some international markets and vibrant growth and privatisation in several developing countries have attracted both borrowers and investors. But the most telling factor giving rise to this phenomenon has been resurging investor confidence in the growth prospects and creditworthiness of those countries which have successfully accessed voluntary capital markets abroad. Confidence levels have been bolstered by both wide-ranging economic reforms and the resolution of outstanding commercial debt problems by the countries in question.

The role that structural reform plays in relation to strengthened investor confidence levels cuts several ways. Countries that have liberalised trade and investment regimes create more competitive, export-oriented productive sectors that can generate the foreign exchange needed to service external obligations. Better fiscal discipline and monetary restraint have diminished inflationary pressures which, in combination with more rational and predictable exchange rate policies, have reduced the spectre of devaluation. Policies to reform public sector finances (including phasing out price subsidies and more effective and equitable tax collection), to curtail the role of the state in the economy and to establish a supportive enabling environment for private initiative have improved overall economic efficiency and created incentives for putting burgeoning capital inflows to productive use.

Borrowing on international capital markets by groups of borrowers[1]

	1989	1990	1991	1992
OECD area	426.5	384.4	457.9	535.7
LDCs	21.8	28.6	36.2[2]	47.3
Central and Eastern Europe	4.7	4.6	1.8	1.5
Others[3]	13.5	17.3	19.0	25.2
Total	**466.5**	**434.9**	**524.9**	**609.7**

1. Figures cover gross announced bond (both public and private placements) and equity issues, gross announced commitments for medium- and long-term bank loans and gross announced medium-term bank facilities (committed and uncommitted).
2. Excludes syndicated credits totalling $10 billion granted to Gulf States for reconstruction costs arising from the Gulf War.
3. Includes securities issued by international organisations (constituting the bulk of this category) and unallocated.
Source: OECD Financial Market Trends.

19

Chart II.4. Private flows from OECD countries to developing countries
1984-1992, $ billion
At 1991 prices and exchange rates

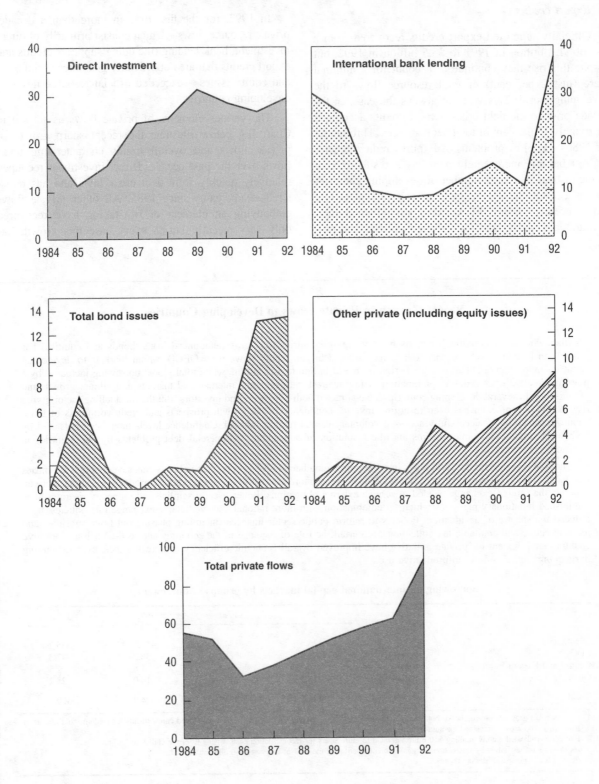

Note: Data for 1992 are provisional.

surpassed previous peaks – quite substantially in the case of bond and equity issues (see Box). Total private flows have more than tripled since falling to a low of $33 billion in 1986 (in constant terms).

International bank lending

Asia accounted for more than 60 per cent of total net bank finance going to developing countries in 1992, followed by Latin America with 27 per cent and North Africa and the Middle East (NAME) at 13 per cent. Africa maintained its growing deficit on net bank financial inflows in 1992. Once again short-term credits accounted for a large share of bank lending, reflecting commercial bank preferences for trade finance, the cautious stance of creditors and a number of structural factors related to regional trends and changes in the underlying status of developing country debt positions.

The volume and direction of bank flows changed considerably between 1991 and 1992: Asia was the only region in 1991 to receive net positive inflows of bank finance (all other continents registered deficits). In 1992 all of the main regions, except Africa, received positive and substantial bank inflows. The $25 billion obtained by Asia in international credit markets in 1992 was roughly equivalent to amounts it received in both 1990 and 1991. On the other hand, capital inflows to the NAME region from banking sources reversed from a deficit of $6.1 billion to more than $5 billion between 1991 and 1992. Substantial bank inflows (totalling $11 billion) to Latin America – after years of low and declining net inflows that culminated in high net outflows of $7.7 billion and $2 billion in 1990 and 1991 – indicate reviving interest in the region among international bankers after almost a decade of careful distancing. Of particular note in this regard is Mexico, which was the sole Latin American country to access long-term credit through a bank syndication in 1992, heralding the definitive normalisation of its relations with external creditors.

Rising bank finance in 1992 was in part linked to active privatisation programmes in Mexico, Argentina and Brazil, continued economic expansion and capital investment in Asia, accelerating economic reform in India and China and reconstruction finance in the Middle East.

A large share of bank flows in 1992 was lent at short-term maturities, continuing the more generalised shift towards a shorter-term structure apparent over the past decade. A variety of factors explain this trend. Many international banks have preferred to extend short-term trade credit to developing countries as opposed to medium- or long-term credit: this is especially true for lending to Latin America, where memories of previous lending problems are slow to dissipate. Part of the short-term shift can also be explained by the bunching of residual maturities of long-term loans falling due, by debt sales or write-offs, by the preference of Middle East borrowers for short-term money or by debt conversion operations. In Asia, interbank borrowing by domestic banks for onlending to local customers (*i.e.* maturity transformation) could account for some of the recent shift in maturity structure.

Patterns in bank finance over the past decade

Recent trends, which are strongly reinforced by the 1992 outcome, suggest that commercial bank lending to the developing world is on the rise: its share of total net resource flows has recouped from a low of 8 per cent in 1987-88 to 23 per cent in 1992, a level roughly equivalent to its pre-debt-crisis level. This development is all the more impressive in view of the relatively depressed activity on international credit markets throughout 1992, as pressures for banks to align balance sheets in conformity with the Basle guidelines on capital adequacy (*i.e.* by improving portfolio quality or increasing equity) and to increase provisioning in accordance with national requirements have more generally led banks to make cautious, more selective lending decisions. In general, bank finance today is sounder than it was in the early 1980s *vis-à-vis* risk assessments, the use to which such finance is put, and improved economic conditions generated by economic reforms.

Chart II.5 shows that between 1982 and 1987 bank finance plummeted from $63 billion to less than $9 billion in constant terms. Every region experienced a sharp contraction in bank lending until 1990, when lending to Asia rose sharply in response to high economic growth and related capital investment. Bank lending to Latin America and NAME in 1992 has pushed total bank flows closer to the historic – but unsustainable – levels attained in 1982.

The ebb and flow of international bank finance over the past decade has had a major impact on the overall volume of private flows (measured in constant terms), but its predominant role diminished over the period. The share of bank lending in total private flows (measured in constant terms) fell from almost 80 per cent in 1982 to less than 20 per cent in 1988, accounting for all of the drop-off in private flows over the period. Since then, the resumption of bank finance – in part related to debt and debt service reduction operations – has had a telling impact on the recent growth of overall private flows.

Chart II.5. International bank lending by continent
At 1991 prices and exchange rates, $ billion

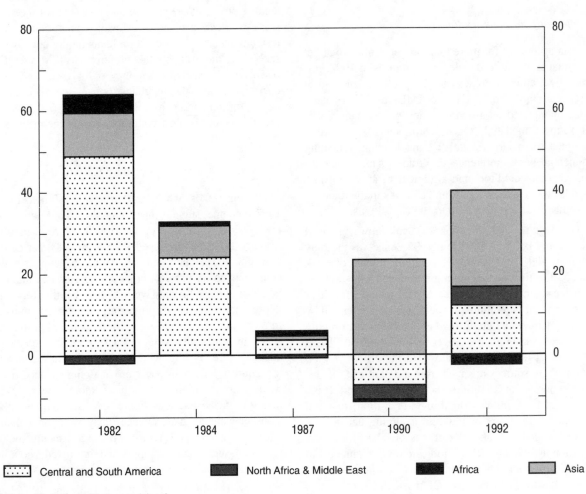

Central and South America   North Africa & Middle East   Africa   Asia

Note: Data for 1992 are provisional.

Table II.1. **Bank flows *vis-à-vis* total net private inflows to developing countries**

At 1991 prices and exchange rates

	1982	1984	1986	1988	1990	1992
			$ billion			
Bank flows	62.7	30.3	9.8	8.9	15.5	37.7
Total private flows	81.0	55.1	32.9	45.2	56.5	94.0

Recent Growth and Diversification of LDC Portfolio Flows

Portfolio flows to developing countries are not only growing in absolute terms – they are also diversifying rapidly among a broad range of financial instruments. This shift has had a marked impact on the composition of private flows: the dominant share accorded to syndicated credits throughout the 1980s has been progressively supplanted by bonds, equities and short-term credit facilities (certificates of deposit and commercial paper). Figures reflecting gross announced borrowing indicate that syndicated credits fell from 74 per cent of total gross portfolio flows to developing countries in 1989 to 35 per cent in 1992, while bonds more than doubled to 30 per cent and equities soared from less than 1 per cent to 15 per cent.

Solid growth in LDC bond issues can be attributed to low international lending rates, greater institutional capacities by developing country issuers to meet information and regulatory requirements and stronger demand by potential investors for such securities to diversify portfolio holdings (*i.e.* reduce overall risk levels) and generate high returns. The sharp increase in short-term committed and uncommitted borrowing facilities granted to LDCs is due to the lower risk levels associated with short-term maturities, the greater flexibility afforded by such arrangements and the relative ease with which borrowers can comply with information requirements.

One outcome of the recent spate of borrowing by developing countries is that international markets for their securities have rapidly matured: spreads have narrowed, maturities have gradually lengthened, market liquidity has been enhanced, new market segments (currencies and financial instruments) have been successfully breached and a range of derivative products have become available.

LDC borrowing on international capital markets[1]
$ billion

Instruments	1989	1990	1991	1992
Bonds	2.6	4.5	8.3	14.0
Equities	0.1	1.0	5.0	7.2
Syndicated loans	16.2	19.8	16.7	16.4
Committed back-up facilities	0.9	2.1	4.5	1.8
Uncommitted borrowing facilities	2.0	1.2	1.7	7.9
Total	**21.8**	**28.6**	**36.2**[2]	**47.3**

1. Figures cover gross announced bond (both public and private placements) and equity issues, gross announced commitments for medium- and long-term bank loans and gross announced medium-term bank facilities (committed and uncommitted).
2. Excludes syndicated credits totalling $10 billion granted to Gulf States for financing reconstruction costs arising from the Gulf War.
Source: OECD Financial Market Trends.

International bonds

The substantial growth in net bonds issued by developing countries in 1991 (which trebled from $4.5 billion to $13 billion) was consolidated in 1992 at over $14 billion. This underscored the return in force of recently re-admitted Latin American nations (principally Mexico, Argentina and Brazil) to international bond markets and continued recourse by Korea. International securities markets were especially buoyant for developing country borrowers in 1992: several nations (Trinidad and Tobago, Uruguay, Morocco, Tunisia, Zimbabwe and Vietnam) entered for the first time or regained access after a lengthy hiatus.

For the second year in a row – and with increasing frequency – several Latin American borrowers resorted to the short-term Europaper markets (certificates of deposits and commercial paper). Most of the growth in this market segment in 1992 took place in the second half of the year, when growing concerns about possible market saturation began to push spreads on new straight bonds issued by Latin American borrowers higher.

The accelerating pace of LDC bond issues since 1990 stands in vivid contrast to the 1980s, when very little borrowing was channelled through bond issues due to high perceived sovereign risk levels. Bond issues fell to zero in 1984 and averaged $1.1 billion per year up through 1989, at which point the market began to recover. (See Box)

Direct investment

In line with its generally upward growth path in real terms over the past decade, direct investment flows from

Chart II.6. **Direct investment flows**
Current $ billion

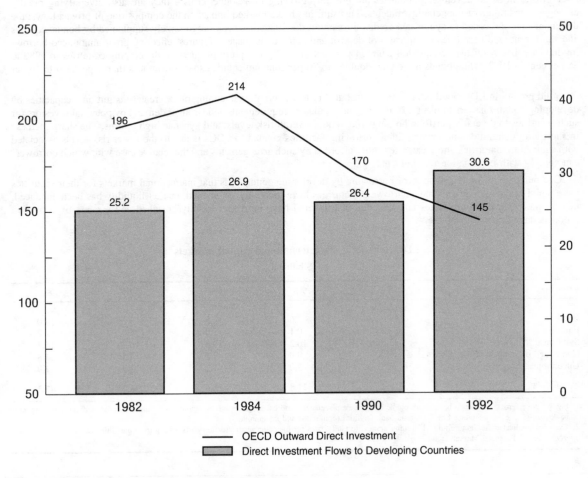

Source: OECD outward direct investment, OECD Secretariat.
Direct investment flows to LDCs, Table III.1.

OECD countries to developing countries increased by $4 billion to $30.6 billion in 1992, accounting for 17 per cent of total resource flows and more than 30 per cent of total private flows. Against the backdrop of declining OECD outward direct investment flows (from $214 billion to an estimated $145 billion between 1990 and 1992), this emphasizes the growing attractiveness of a number of developing countries for foreign investors (see Chart II.6). Nonetheless, the benefits of these flows are not evenly distributed since a relatively small number of developing countries attract the predominant share of direct investment inflows.

Developing countries, particularly where structural reforms are well advanced, are attracting a growing share of outward investment from OECD countries.

The sharp drop in total outward investment from OECD countries after 1990 can be traced to their generally weak economic performance. In addition, the expansion of direct investment into the European Community, with firms preparing for the Single European Market, has now fallen off. The bulk of direct investment flows to the developing world is directed to those countries where structural reforms are well advanced and is based on investor perceptions that future returns will be high. As such, foreign direct investment to Latin America, at over $13 billion in 1992, has expanded to a level comparable to that for Asia. In Asia, China has emerged as a major recipient of foreign direct investment because of the size of its domestic market, low labour costs and a more attractive regime governing inward investment.

The growing globalisation of industry is also contributing to increased direct investment in developing countries. The creation and consolidation of regional trade and investment arrangements are pushing multinational enterprises to secure a firm foothold in certain regions for strategic purposes, such as establishing market presence, rationalising production, creating regional supply networks, penetrating larger, ultimately more homogeneous markets or capitalising on geographical or logistical opportunities.

Other private flows

Other private flows include suppliers credits and equity issues. In 1992 the growing tendency of developing country corporations to issue equities in international markets intensified, lifting this category of resource flows to a high of $9.5 billion, up $3 billion from 1991. More frequent issues of equity shares on international capital markets by developing country corporations – a novel development – have been facilitated by more widespread use of depository receipts (negotiable instruments traded on industrialised country markets representing LDC company shares), active privatisation programmes and liberalisation in both source and recipient country stock markets.

The buoyancy of equity offerings in 1992 was strongly influenced by a number of large placements by Latin American countries in foreign and international markets in connection with ongoing privatisation programmes (the largest being the $1 billion Telecom Argentina programme). Several Chinese corporations also floated equities on United States markets. A modest revival took place in the closed country funds market, particularly those targeted at Latin America and Asia: a total of five country funds were floated in China during the year and two African funds – the first African regional fund and one targeting Nigeria – were also launched.

While the number of developing country corporate equities sold and traded on OECD capital markets is still very small, interest in acquiring such securities is growing and the market is rapidly maturing. For example, in 1992 the Chicago Board Options Exchange launched a number of options on American Depository Receipts trading on United States markets to help investors hedge price risks.

Suppliers credits, which have expanded roughly in parallel with the growth of international trade over the past decade, registered slight growth over the year as OECD exporters extended credit facilities to more developing country importers in response to lower perceived risk levels.

3. Recent trends by region and income group

Resource flows by region

On the basis of allocable flows (by region and income group the proportion of flows that are unallocated can be important, particularly for the most recent years), overall rankings among the regions in terms of their ability to attract resource flows was unchanged in 1992. Asia continued to receive the largest amount of finance (38 per cent of total resource flows) followed by Latin America (29 per cent), Africa (14 per cent) and NAME (10 per cent). Private flows remain the dominant and most dynamic component of overall resource flows for both Asia and Latin America, while official development finance continues to be the mainstay of external finance for African countries and an important source of financing for Asia and NAME countries. In 1992, African countries received 39 per cent of total ODF flows, followed by Asia with 29 per cent, NAME with 17 per cent and Latin America with 14 per cent.

The decline in total resource flows experienced by all of the major developing country regions at the beginning of the decade has not been recouped across the board. Total flows to Africa, the region where development challenges and financing needs are the greatest, have still not recovered from the steep decline between 1982-84 (although at the height of the debt crisis Africa received more net resources in constant terms than any of the other regions, in large part due to the sharp fall in private flows at that time which impacted particularly strongly on Latin America and Asia – see Chart II.7).

Africa's difficulties in accessing external resources have become more acute over the past decade, and since 1990 flows have stagnated at approximately $23 billion in constant 1991 terms. Private flows, which contributed to overall flows up to the end of the 1980s, have fallen dramatically of late: since 1990 Africa has registered a deficit on net private flows. Recent trends in private flows to Africa are in part explained by the greater attractiveness of other regions as well as its difficulty in consolidating and carrying forward economic reforms.

Chart II.7. Total net resource flows by component & by continent
1982-1992, in $ billion
At 1991 prices and exchange rates

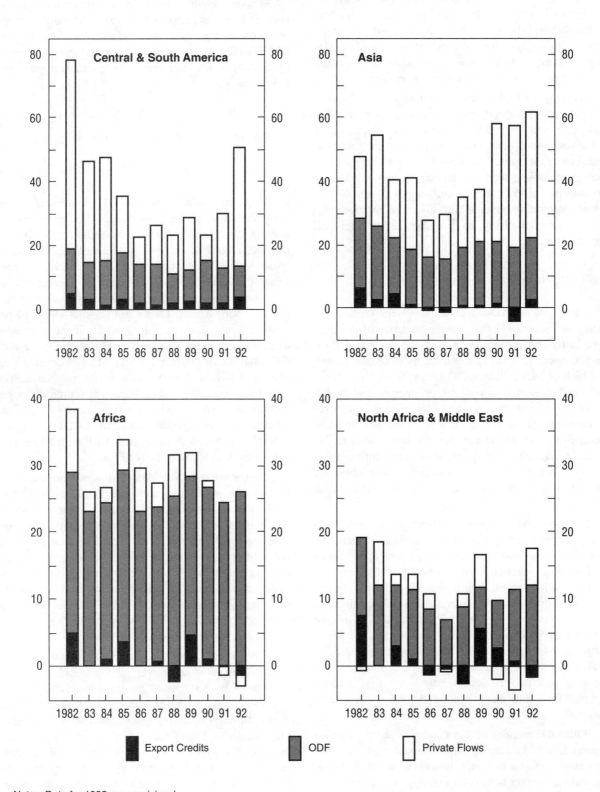

Note: Data for 1992 are provisional.

26

By contrast, in Asia and Latin America, which together account for two-thirds of total resource flows to developing countries, the trend since 1982 has been characterised by a steady drop in flows between 1983 and 1986 followed by a recovery, although for Asia the upturn was earlier (due to the absence of a debt "crisis" in the region and better overall economic conditions) and resource flows have been consistently stronger. Starting from relatively similar bases in 1986, total flows (in constant terms) to Latin America had doubled by 1992, while the growth of resource flows to Asia has been even stronger. The resurgence in resource flows to NAME countries that began in 1987 faltered in 1990 due to uncertainties created by the Gulf War, but momentum has recently picked up.

Bank flows

Asian nations, which in general maintained good working relationships with international commercial banks throughout the 1980s, have relied heavily on international bank loans for financing since 1990. India and China (both of which have recently announced far-reaching liberalisation measures) together drew in $9.5 billion on a net basis in 1992, more than two-thirds of which went to China. The Chinese economy continues to lead the Asian region in terms of GNP growth (almost 13 per cent in 1992) and is considered a good credit risk by major international lenders. Bank lending to Indonesia in 1992 matched that of China. Thailand ($4.8 billion), Korea ($4 billion) and Malaysia ($1.9 billion) also received significant bank flows. For the third consecutive year, the Philippines registered a deficit ($1.3 billion in 1992).

In Latin America, Brazil received net loans totalling $3.1 billion, accounting for almost a third of total bank finance extended to the region in 1992. Some of this inflow was linked to privatisation activities. Aside from Chile, which returned to the market for loans totalling $2.1 million, most of the remainder of bank finance secured by the region was shared among Mexico ($1.1 billion) and Colombia and Uruguay ($0.6 billion each).

Post-Gulf War reconstruction finance continued to be a major factor contributing to strong lending to the Middle East, with Kuwait accessing $5.2 billion and Saudi Arabia $1.3 billion. These inflows alone caused NAME net resource flows to more than double between 1991 and 1992. Iran continued to source large amounts of cash abroad ($3 billion in 1992) in its bid to consolidate relations with the international banking community in order to finance reconstruction and development. Since mid-1989, it has netted a total of $6.5 billion from international commercial banks. Egypt and Algeria posted large negative net balances on bank borrowing in 1992 (–$1.2 billion and –$0.5 billion, respectively), partly due to political uncertainties.

Africa's net deficit position on bank finance continued in 1992. Africa in general still labours under large accumulated debt burdens and, apart from some concerted lending in connection with previous debt rescheduling, little fresh bank finance has been forthcoming. Nigeria, which signed a Brady agreement in January 1991 (the only African country to have done so), continues to register large net bank capital outflows (averaging $1 billion per year between 1990-92).

International bonds

Latin America accounted for the bulk ($8 billion) of net allocated bonds issued by developing countries in 1992, led by Brazil (where flows doubled to $2.6 billion) and Argentina ($1.5 billion). Bond issues now account for 17 per cent of all external capital going to Latin America. Net bond issues by Asian borrowers totalled $1.4 billion in 1992, just 2 per cent of total resources, although on a gross basis fund-raising activities by certain countries (China, Malaysia, Indonesia) on international securities markets were not inconsiderable. Zimbabwe, the only Sub-Saharan African nation to float an international issue in recent years, returned to the market for the second time in as many years. The Middle East region showed marginal net outflows in 1992, with Algeria accounting for most of the deficit.

Central and Eastern European Countries and the New Independent States

Substantial financial resources are required to support the transformation of Eastern Europe and the former Soviet Union. Both official and private sources are being mobilised to this end. Efforts to quantify such resource flows have only recently been undertaken and there are many problems regarding data quality, coverage and comparability. Initial figures indicate that both aid flows and private flows contributed importantly to overall capital inflows in 1991. The short-term outlook remains uncertain despite large commitments of official finance: both bilateral and multilateral disbursements are complicated by the unstable economic and political climate currently prevailing in many of these countries (see Box).

Resource flows by income group

Most of the changes in resource flow patterns at the level of income groups are due to movements in private flows, the most dynamic component of resource flows. For example, Latin American countries which have regained access to international capital markets have boosted totals for the upper middle-income countries

External Resource Flows to Eastern Europe and the Former Soviet Union in 1991

Aid to the Central and Eastern European Countries (CEECs) and the NIS (New Independent States) totalled $7.5 billion in 1991, of which 29 per cent financed contributions to multilateral programmes (e.g. the EC and EBRD), 28 per cent supported debt forgiveness (Poland) and almost 19 per cent was accounted for by food grants. Approximately 70 per cent – virtually all ODA except that allocated to multilateral programmes – was provided in the form of grants or debt forgiveness.

The former Soviet Union and Poland received the largest amounts of aid in 1991, each with $2.3 billion. Eighty per cent of official aid to the former Soviet Union was provided by Germany in the form of food aid, emergency and medical assistance and the construction of housing facilities for returning soldiers. Most of the aid to Poland involved debt relief granted by the United States. Hungary and the Czech and Slovak Federal Republics (CSFR) were the next largest recipients of aid flows.

Preliminary figures suggest that net private flows totalled approximately $3.4 billion (of which $1.7 billion entered as foreign direct investment) in 1991. IMF lending operations, which totalled $3.7 billion, were extended (in descending order of magnitude) to the CSFR, Hungary, Romania, Bulgaria and Poland. Net loan disbursements by the World Bank amounted to some $800 million in 1991 and were extended mainly to Poland, Hungary and the CSFR.

As regards private capital flows, preliminary figures for 1992 indicate that no bank finance was provided to the region (although the former Soviet Union accumulated substantial arrears over the year) and that net bond issues were limited to $0.3 billion for the former CSFR and $2 billion for Hungary. Foreign direct investment flows have been targeted mainly at Hungary, the Czech Republic and Poland. The NIS may experience a considerable expansion in foreign direct investment in the oil, gas and mineral sectors before the end of the decade, but it is unlikely that foreign investment will rise appreciably in the short-term.

(UMICs) to all-time highs, and heavy private banking flows to certain Asian countries pushed totals for low-income countries (LICs) and low middle-income countries (LMICs) up in 1992. As a result of the concentration of the growth of private flows in a few countries, figures for income groups mask the fact that for most developing countries there has been very little change in recent years in the volume and composition of resource flows.

For all but a small number of developing countries, there has been very little change in recent years in the volume and composition of resource flows.

Chart II.8 compares total resource flows for the different income groups over the past decade. The LICs have consistently accounted for the largest share of resource flows (averaging $54 billion throughout the period), and the substantial share of ODF – which has remained relatively stable in the total – has tended to smooth overall flows, buffering to some extent yearly changes in other components of overall resource flows. Flows to the LLDCs have been static since 1982, due to the virtual absence of private flows. By contrast, the LMICs and the UMICs have experienced sharp and frequent fluctuations in overall resource flows over the past decade due in particular to oscillations in the volume of

private flows. Policy reforms that have created a more hospitable environment for private initiative and established a framework for sustainable growth have been a key determinant for the recent expansion of private capital flows to the LMICs and UMICS. Large private inflows since 1990 have reduced the share of ODF in total resources quite dramatically for UMICs (from 41 per cent in 1991 to 14 per cent in 1992) and more moderately for LMICs (from 44 per cent to 38 per cent).

International bank loans to the developing world were fairly evenly split between the UMICs (38 per cent of total net bank flows), the LMICs (33 per cent) and the LICs (30 per cent) in 1992. This rather "balanced" outcome is due to the fact that within each major income group there are a few countries which have received substantial bank flows. Large net loan flows to Korea, Brazil, Argentina, Saudi Arabia, Kuwait and Hong Kong vaulted the UMIC group from a moderate $0.5 billion bank inflow in 1991 to $15 billion in 1992. Heavy banking flows to Indonesia, China and India accounted for most of the $12 billion sourced by LICs.

Private flows to UMICs in 1992 were further bolstered by strong direct investment targeted to these countries by OECD investors: UMICs attracted 50 per cent of allocated OECD outward investment flows to the developing world, while LMICs and LICs attracted substantially smaller shares (22 per cent and 12 per cent, respectively). A growing share of foreign direct investment in

Chart II.8.   Official development finance
and total net resource flows by income group
1982-1992, in $ billion
At 1991 prices and exchange rates

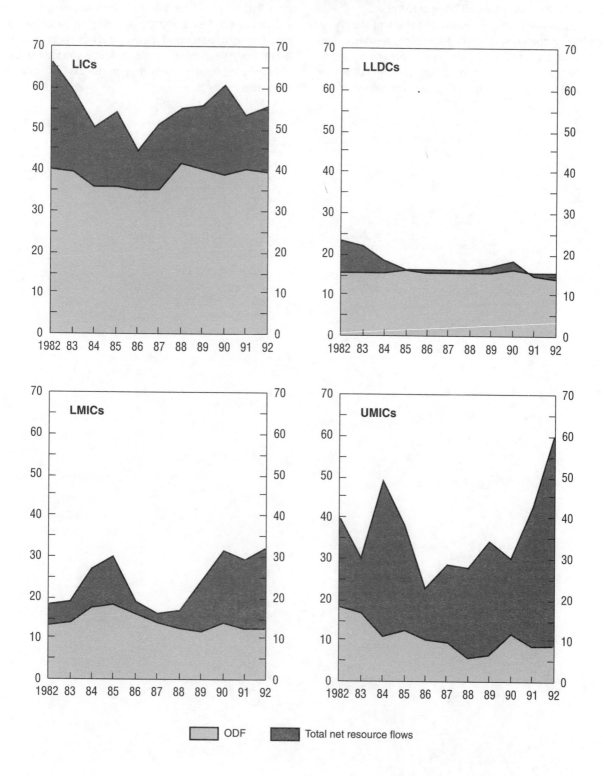

ODF   Total net resource flows

Note: Data for 1992 are provisional.

Asian LICs and LMICs originates from UMICs within the region, as corporations from Korea, Taiwan, Singapore and Hong Kong set about relocating labour-intensive production in lower-wage countries as a way of enhancing their international competitiveness.

The external resource situation of many of the poorer developing countries remains disquieting. Resource flow patterns and trends for the LICs as a whole can be deceptive, as the recent ability of countries such as China, India and Indonesia to attract greater private flows masks the deteriorating situation for other countries in the group, for whom concessional aid funds are virtually the only source of external finance for development. Demands for these funds in recipient countries are very high, but they will have to be used increasingly to provide a basis for attracting the private flows necessary for sustainable development and to permit them to move away from near total aid dependency towards a more balanced structure and higher levels of external financing.

Chapter III

Resource Flow Tables

List of Tables III.1 to III.11

Total Resource Flows, 1984-92 to:

Table III.1. Total net resource flows to developing countries

Major expansion in resource flows in 1992 following a surge in bank lending

	Current $ billion									Per cent of total		
	1984	1985	1986	1987	1988	1989	1990	1991	1992ᵖ	1984	1988	1992
I. OFFICIAL DEVELOPMENT FINANCE (ODF)	**42.1**	**44.4**	**50.9**	**56.9**	**61.4**	**60.8**	**69.4**	**70.1**	**72.3**	**52.6**	**62.3**	**41.2**
1. Official Development Assistance (ODA)	30.0	32.9	39.1	43.8	47.5	48.6	52.4	57.4	58.3	37.5	48.2	33.2
of which: Bilateral disbursements	22.4	24.8	29.8	33.8	36.4	36.3	39.2	41.3	41.3	28.0	37.0	23.5
Multilateral disbursements	7.6	8.1	9.3	10.0	11.0	12.3	13.2	16.1	17.0	9.5	11.2	9.7
2. Other ODF	12.1	11.5	11.8	13.1	13.9	12.2	17.0	12.7	14.0	15.1	14.2	8.0
of which: Bilateral disbursements	4.0	3.8	3.8	6.3	7.3	5.2	6.8	4.9	6.0	5.0	7.5	3.4
Multilateral disbursements	8.1	7.7	8.0	6.8	6.6	7.0	10.2	7.8	8.0	10.1	6.7	4.6
II. TOTAL EXPORT CREDITS	**6.6**	**3.7**	**-1.1**	**-2.2**	**-2.5**	**9.5**	**4.5**	**1.8**	**3.5**	**8.3**	**-2.5**	**2.0**
of which: Short-term	1.3	3.2	3.0	4.1	2.0	4.8	4.4	-0.8	0.5	1.6	2.0	0.3
III. PRIVATE FLOWS	**31.3**	**30.1**	**23.4**	**31.6**	**39.6**	**45.2**	**56.6**	**62.2**	**99.8**	**39.1**	**40.2**	**56.8**
1. Direct Investment	11.2	6.5	10.8	19.6	21.9	26.7	26.9	26.4	30.6	14.0	22.2	17.5
of which: Offshore centres	3.8	3.7	5.8	10.9	8.9	6.5	7.0	6.5	6.7	4.8	9.1	3.8
2. International bank lending	17.2	15.2	7.0	7.0	7.8	10.5	15.0	11.0	40.0	21.5	8.0	22.8
of which: Short-term	-6.0	12.0	-4.0	5.0	4.0	8.0	7.0	12.0	25.0	-7.5	4.1	14.3
3. Total bond lending	x	4.2	1.0	-0.1	1.5	1.3	4.5	13.0	14.2	0.0	1.5	8.1
4. Other private	0.3	1.3	1.3	1.1	4.2	2.7	5.1	6.6	9.5	0.4	4.3	5.4
5. Grants by non-governmental organisations	2.6	2.9	3.3	4.0	4.2	4.0	5.1	5.2	5.5	3.3	4.3	3.1
TOTAL NET RESOURCE FLOWS (I + II + III)	**80.0**	**78.2**	**73.2**	**86.3**	**98.5**	**115.5**	**130.5**	**134.0**	**175.6**	**100.0**	**100.0**	**100.0**
Memorandum items:												
Total net credits from IMF	5.3	0.5	-2.0	-4.9	-4.4	-2.1	-2.2	1.0	-0.2			
Acquisition of assets by LDCs, net	-20.0	-8.7	-13.1	-9.0	-22.5	-18.4	-25.5	-27.5	..			
Interest and dividends paid by LDCs, gross	-89.5	-83.3	-75.8	-76.6	-91.8	-93.2	-89.1	-78.5	..			
Total official grants	23.0	25.0	28.9	30.9	33.7	34.4	45.5	48.2	49.6			
At 1991 prices and exchange rates												
Total Net Resource Flows	140.8	135.5	102.9	105.7	112.4	133.0	135.2	134.0	165.5			
Total Official Development Finance	74.1	76.9	71.5	69.7	70.1	70.0	71.9	70.1	68.1			
Total ODA receipts from: DAC Countries, CEEC, Arab Countries and IFIs	59.0	61.9	60.1	57.1	56.6	56.9	61.8	60.6	57.3			
Total DAC ODA (bilateral and multilateral)	49.5	49.9	50.4	49.7	53.7	52.9	54.8	56.7	57.3			

Note: The tables in Chapter III cover essentially resource flows from OECD countries to developing countries. See technical notes (Chapter VI) for details.

Table III.2. **Total net resource flows to low-income countries (LICs)**

Modest growth of ODF and private sector finance to the poorer developing countries in 1992

	Current $ billion									Per cent of total		
	1984	1985	1986	1987	1988	1989	1990	1991	1992p	1984	1988	1992
I. OFFICIAL DEVELOPMENT FINANCE (ODF)	**20.2**	**20.5**	**24.8**	**28.7**	**36.5**	**34.9**	**37.5**	**40.3**	**42.2**	**70.6**	**75.7**	**71.9**
1. Official Development Assistance (ODA)	15.8	17.1	21.2	23.4	27.1	27.6	32.3	34.5	36.7	55.2	56.2	62.5
of which: Bilateral disbursements	10.1	11.2	14.1	15.6	18.5	18.8	22.3	23.5	24.7	35.3	38.4	42.1
Multilateral disbursements	5.7	5.9	7.1	7.8	8.6	8.8	10.0	11.0	12.0	19.9	17.8	20.4
2. Other ODF	4.4	3.4	3.6	5.3	9.4	7.3	5.2	5.8	5.5	15.4	19.5	9.4
of which: Bilateral disbursements	1.8	0.9	1.1	1.9	5.1	2.6	0.7	1.5	1.2	6.3	10.6	2.0
Multilateral disbursements	2.6	2.5	2.5	3.4	4.3	4.7	4.5	4.3	4.3	9.1	8.9	7.3
II. TOTAL EXPORT CREDITS	**2.9**	**1.5**	**1.0**	**2.0**	**0.0**	**6.2**	**2.2**	**0.7**	**0.9**	**10.1**	**0.0**	**1.5**
of which: Short-term	0.7	1.4	0.9	1.9	1.5	2.6	2.5	0.5	0.7	2.4	3.1	1.2
III. PRIVATE FLOWS	**5.5**	**9.3**	**6.1**	**11.3**	**11.7**	**7.2**	**18.7**	**12.0**	**15.6**	**19.2**	**24.3**	**26.6**
1. Direct investment	0.7	0.1	0.5	1.7	0.9	3.7	1.4	2.7	3.6	2.4	1.9	6.1
2. International bank lending	3.1	6.0	4.8	5.8	6.8	0.1	14.0	4.5	12.0	10.8	14.1	20.4
3. Total bond lending	0.2	1.2	-1.9	0.9	1.0	0.7	0.3	1.5	-1.1	0.7	2.1	-1.9
4. Other private	x	0.3	0.7	0.5	0.7	0.5	0.2	0.6	1.1	1.0	1.5	1.9
5. Grants by non-governmental organisations	1.5	1.7	2.0	2.4	2.3	2.2	2.8	2.7	..	5.2	4.8	0.0
TOTAL NET RESOURCE FLOWS (I + II + III)	**28.6**	**31.3**	**31.9**	**42.0**	**48.2**	**48.3**	**58.4**	**53.0**	**58.7**	**100.0**	**100.0**	**100.0**
Memorandum items:												
Total net credits from IMF	0.7	-0.5	-0.9	-1.5	-2.5	-1.2	-2.5	2.0	1.4			
Acquisition of assets by LDCs, net	-1.3	-5.2	-1.3	-3.7	-3.5	-5.8	-6.9	-6.8	..			
Interest and dividends paid by LDCs, gross	-18.7	-19.1	-17.8	-19.8	-23.0	-25.2	-25.6	-23.7	..			
Total official grants	10.7	11.3	13.3	14.2	16.8	17.4	22.4	25.0	..			
At 1991 prices and exchange rates												
Total Net Resource Flows	50.3	54.2	44.8	51.4	55.0	55.6	60.5	53.0	55.3			
Total Official Development Finance	35.6	35.5	34.8	35.2	41.6	40.2	38.9	40.3	39.8			
Total ODA receipts	29.2	31.0	31.6	29.9	32.1	32.2	35.9	34.5	33.6			

Note: See Technical Notes.

Table III.3. **Total net resource flows to least-developed countries (LLDCs)**

Aid dependent poorest countries unable to attract private flows

	Current $ billion									Per cent of total		
	1984	1985	1986	1987	1988	1989	1990	1991	1992^p	1984	1988	1992
I. OFFICIAL DEVELOPMENT FINANCE (ODF)	**8.8**	**9.4**	**11.0**	**12.5**	**13.6**	**13.4**	**15.9**	**15.1**	**16.0**	**90.7**	**93.2**	**104.6**
1. Official Development Assistance (ODA)	7.4	8.6	10.3	11.9	13.1	13.3	15.1	14.8	15.7	76.3	89.7	102.6
of which: Bilateral disbursements	4.4	5.3	6.5	7.5	8.6	8.0	9.3	8.8	9.2	45.4	58.9	60.1
Multilateral disbursements	3.0	3.3	3.8	4.4	4.5	5.3	5.8	6.0	6.5	30.9	30.8	42.5
2. Other ODF	1.4	0.8	0.7	0.6	0.5	0.1	0.8	0.3	0.3	14.4	3.4	2.0
of which: Bilateral disbursements	1.3	0.5	0.6	0.5	0.4	0.1	0.7	0.5	0.6	13.4	2.7	3.9
Multilateral disbursements	0.1	0.3	0.1	0.1	0.1	x	0.1	-0.2	-0.3	1.0	0.7	-2.0
II. TOTAL EXPORT CREDITS	**-0.4**	**-0.3**	**-0.8**	**-0.6**	**-0.5**	**-0.1**	**-0.3**	**-0.6**	**0.1**	**-4.1**	**-3.4**	**0.7**
of which: Short-term	0.3	0.2	x	0.1	-0.1	x	0.2	-0.3	-0.1	3.1	-0.7	-0.7
III. PRIVATE FLOWS	**1.3**	**0.6**	**0.9**	**1.7**	**1.5**	**1.5**	**1.9**	**0.7**	**-0.8**	**13.4**	**10.3**	**-5.2**
1. Direct investment	x	-0.1	-0.1	0.1	0.3	0.7	0.5	0.2	..	x	2.1	0.0
2. International bank lending	0.6	x	0.2	0.6	0.2	-0.2	0.2	-0.8	x	6.2	1.4	0.0
3. Total bond lending	x	x	x	-	x	x	x	x	-0.8	x	x	-5.2
4. Other private	x	x	x	x	x	x	x	0.1	..	x	x	0.0
5. Grants by non-governmental organisations	0.7	0.7	0.8	1.0	1.0	1.0	1.2	1.2	..	7.2	6.8	0.0
TOTAL NET RESOURCE FLOWS (I + II + III)	**9.7**	**9.7**	**11.1**	**13.6**	**14.6**	**14.8**	**17.5**	**15.2**	**15.3**	**100.0**	**100.0**	**100.0**
Memorandum items:												
Total net credits from IMF	0.2	-0.1	-0.3	x	-0.2	-0.3	-0.4	0.1	0.2			
Acquisition of assets by LDCs, net	-0.1	-0.5	x	x	-0.6	-0.4	-0.1	-0.2	..			
Interest and dividends paid by LDCs, gross	-2.4	-2.4	-2.7	-2.6	-2.5	-2.7	-2.6	2.2	..			
Total official grants	5.8	6.5	7.4	8.0	9.5	9.5	11.1	12.2	..			
At 1991 prices and exchange rates												
Total Net Resource Flows	17.1	16.8	15.6	16.7	16.7	16.9	18.1	15.2	14.4			
Total Official Development Finance	15.5	16.3	15.5	15.3	15.5	15.3	16.5	15.1	15.1			
Total ODA receipts	14.3	16.1	15.9	15.4	16.0	15.7	15.9	14.8	14.8			

Note: See Technical Notes.

Table III.4. **Total net resource flows to low middle-income countries (LMICs)**

Resource flows to LMICs grow by 10 per cent in real terms in 1992

	Current $ billion									Per cent of total		
	1984	1985	1986	1987	1988	1989	1990	1991	1992ᵖ	1984	1988	1992
I. OFFICIAL DEVELOPMENT FINANCE (ODF)	**10.1**	**10.4**	**11.5**	**11.4**	**10.8**	**10.3**	**13.3**	**12.2**	**12.9**	**66.4**	**73.0**	**37.7**
1. Official Development Assistance (ODA)	6.6	6.7	7.3	8.5	8.2	8.2	10.4	9.4	9.8	43.4	55.4	28.7
of which: Bilateral disbursements	5.8	6.0	6.4	7.6	7.1	7.0	9.0	7.7	8.0	38.2	48.0	23.4
Multilateral disbursements	0.8	0.7	0.9	0.9	1.1	1.2	1.4	1.7	1.8	5.3	7.4	5.3
2. Other ODF	3.5	3.7	4.2	2.9	2.6	2.1	2.9	2.8	3.1	23.0	17.6	9.1
of which: Bilateral disbursements	0.9	0.5	1.3	0.4	0.7	0.7	1.0	0.9	1.2	5.9	4.7	3.5
Multilateral disbursements	2.6	3.2	2.9	2.5	1.9	1.4	1.9	1.9	1.9	17.1	12.8	5.6
II. TOTAL EXPORT CREDITS	**1.8**	**1.9**	**-1.7**	**-0.5**	**0.5**	**4.1**	**4.4**	**1.8**	**1.0**	**11.8**	**3.4**	**2.9**
of which: Short-term	0.6	0.8	x	0.9	0.3	1.2	2.4	-0.5	..	3.9	2.0	0.0
III. PRIVATE FLOWS	**3.3**	**5.0**	**3.6**	**2.0**	**3.5**	**6.6**	**12.4**	**15.1**	**20.3**	**21.7**	**23.6**	**59.4**
1. Direct investment	1.5	0.7	2.1	3.0	2.6	5.6	4.0	5.2	6.7	9.9	17.6	19.6
2. International bank lending	1.0	0.8	0.8	-2.2	-3.6	1.4	7.3	7.0	13.0	6.6	-24.3	38.0
3. Total bond lending	0.2	2.6	x	0.2	2.5	-2.0	0.3	1.1	-0.2	1.3	16.9	-0.6
4. Other private	0.1	0.3	x	0.2	1.2	0.8	-0.2	0.8	0.8	1.4	8.1	2.3
5. Grants by non-governmental organisations	0.5	0.6	0.7	0.8	0.8	0.8	1.0	1.0	..	3.3	5.4	0.0
TOTAL NET RESOURCE FLOWS (I + II + III)	**15.2**	**17.3**	**13.4**	**12.9**	**14.8**	**21.0**	**30.1**	**29.1**	**34.2**	**100.0**	**100.0**	**100.0**
Memorandum items:												
Total net credits from IMF	0.7	x	-1.0	-1.3	-1.0	-0.1	-1.2	-1.0	0.2			
Acquisition of assets by LDCs, net	-3.1	-0.5	0.2	-1.3	-1.6	x	-1.5	-3.0	..			
Interest and dividends paid by LDCs, gross	-19.6	-18.6	-18.5	-20.2	-21.2	-23.4	-25.4	-23.1	-13.9			
Total official grants	3.0	4.2	3.6	4.1	4.3	4.5	5.4	6.7	..			
	At 1991 prices and exchange rates											
Total Net Resource Flows	26.8	30.0	18.8	15.8	16.9	24.2	31.2	29.1	32.2			
Total Official Development Finance	17.8	18.0	16.2	14.0	12.3	11.9	13.8	12.2	12.2			
Total ODA receipts	14.3	14.4	12.6	12.6	10.4	10.0	11.7	10.5	9.2			

Note: See Technical Notes.

Table III.5. Total net resource flows to upper middle-income countries (UMICs)

Better-off developing countries attract most of the expansion in total flows in 1992

	Current $ billion									Per cent of total		
	1984	1985	1986	1987	1988	1989	1990	1991	1992 p	1984	1988	1992
I. OFFICIAL DEVELOPMENT FINANCE (ODF)	**6.3**	**7.1**	**7.2**	**8.1**	**5.0**	**6.0**	**11.4**	**9.1**	**9.2**	**22.7**	**20.6**	**14.4**
1. Official Development Assistance (ODA)	2.4	3.2	3.6	3.2	3.0	3.2	4.2	4.9	4.5	8.7	12.3	7.0
of which: Bilateral disbursements	2.2	3.0	3.4	3.0	2.8	2.9	4.0	4.5	4.0	7.9	11.5	6.2
Multilateral disbursements	0.2	0.2	0.2	0.2	0.2	0.3	0.2	0.4	0.5	0.7	0.8	0.8
2. Other ODF	3.9	3.9	3.6	4.9	2.0	2.8	7.2	4.2	4.7	14.1	8.2	7.3
of which: Bilateral disbursements	0.9	2.0	1.1	3.9	1.4	1.8	3.5	2.6	3.0	3.2	5.8	4.7
Multilateral disbursements	3.0	1.9	2.5	1.0	0.6	1.0	3.7	1.6	1.7	10.8	2.5	2.7
II. TOTAL EXPORT CREDITS	**1.1**	**1.8**	**0.5**	**-0.1**	**0.5**	**4.0**	**1.5**	**1.7**	**2.6**	**4.0**	**2.1**	**4.1**
of which: Short-term	x	1.0	2.1	1.3	0.2	1.0	-0.5	-0.8	-0.2	0.0	0.8	-0.3
III. PRIVATE FLOWS	**20.3**	**12.9**	**8.3**	**15.6**	**18.8**	**19.8**	**16.0**	**31.5**	**52.3**	**73.3**	**77.4**	**81.6**
1. Direct investment	6.5	3.4	5.7	13.6	13.2	10.6	12.6	14.8	15.4	23.5	54.3	24.0
2. International bank lending	13.7	8.4	1.0	3.4	4.6	9.0	-6.3	0.5	15.0	49.5	18.9	23.4
3. Total bond lending	-0.4	0.4	0.8	-2.1	-1.6	-1.4	3.7	10.4	14.7	-1.4	-6.6	22.9
4. Other private	-0.1	0.1	0.1	-0.1	1.6	0.6	4.7	4.6	7.2	-0.4	6.6	11.2
5. Grants by non-governmental organisations	0.6	0.6	0.7	0.8	1.0	1.0	1.3	1.2	0.0	2.2	4.1	0.0
TOTAL NET RESOURCE FLOWS (I + II + III)	**27.7**	**21.8**	**16.0**	**23.6**	**24.3**	**29.8**	**28.9**	**42.3**	**64.1**	**100.0**	**100.0**	**100.0**
Memorandum items:												
Total net credits from IMF	3.7	1.1	-0.1	-2.0	-1.0	-0.5	1.5	-0.9	-1.4			
Acquisition of assets by LDCs, net	-15.6	-3.0	-12.0	-4.0	-17.4	-12.5	-17.0	-17.7	..			
Interest and dividends paid by LDCs, gross	-61.6	-50.8	-41.1	-33.8	-42.2	-53.4	-53.5	-34.8	..			
Total official grants	2.2	3.1	3.2	2.8	3.0	3.0	3.3	4.1	..			
At 1991 prices and exchange rates												
Total Net Resource Flows	48.8	37.8	22.5	28.9	27.7	34.3	29.9	42.3	60.4			
Total Official Development Finance	11.1	12.3	10.1	9.9	5.7	6.9	11.8	9.1	8.7			
Total ODA receipts	4.6	5.7	5.1	4.0	3.5	3.8	4.0	4.7	4.3			

Note: See Technical Notes.

Table III.6. **Total net resource flows to Africa**

African resource flows totally dominated by ODF

	Current $ billion									Per cent of total		
	1984	1985	1986	1987	1988	1989	1990	1991	1992ᵖ	1984	1988	1992
I. OFFICIAL DEVELOPMENT FINANCE (ODF)	**13.4**	**14.7**	**16.4**	**18.9**	**22.2**	**20.4**	**24.8**	**24.6**	**27.9**	**87.6**	**86.0**	**113.4**
1. Official Development Assistance (ODA)	10.0	11.4	13.3	15.1	16.9	17.6	22.1	22.8	24.8	65.4	65.5	100.8
of which: Bilateral disbursements	7.2	8.1	9.3	10.7	12.0	12.1	16.0	16.7	17.5	47.1	46.5	71.1
Multilateral disbursements	2.8	3.3	4.0	4.4	4.9	5.5	6.1	6.1	7.3	18.3	19.0	29.7
2. Other ODF	3.4	3.3	3.1	3.8	5.3	2.8	2.7	1.8	3.1	22.2	20.5	12.6
of which: Bilateral disbursements	2.2	2.1	1.6	2.3	4.3	1.2	0.8	0.1	1.0	14.4	16.7	4.1
Multilateral disbursements	1.2	1.2	1.5	1.5	1.0	1.6	1.9	1.7	2.1	7.8	3.9	8.5
II. TOTAL EXPORT CREDITS	**0.5**	**2.1**	**-0.1**	**0.5**	**-2.1**	**4.1**	**0.9**	**0.2**	**-1.6**	**3.3**	**-8.1**	**-6.5**
of which: Short-term	-0.6	1.3	0.8	2.8	0.9	2.5	2.4	-0.4	-0.6	-3.9	3.5	-2.4
III. PRIVATE FLOWS	**1.4**	**2.8**	**5.0**	**3.3**	**5.7**	**3.3**	**1.0**	**-1.5**	**-1.7**	**9.2**	**22.1**	**-6.9**
1. Direct investment	x	0.5	0.5	0.4	1.2	2.8	0.2	0.5	0.6	1.6	4.7	2.4
2. International bank lending	0.5	0.8	3.3	1.5	2.3	-1.1	-0.8	-4.0	-2.5	3.3	8.9	-10.2
3. Total bond lending	-0.1	0.4	x	-0.1	0.3	0.1	x	..	..	-0.7	1.2	0.0
4. Other private	0.1	0.1	0.1	0.1	0.5	0.1	-0.1	0.3	0.2	0.7	1.9	0.8
5. Grants by non-governmental organisations	0.9	1.0	1.1	1.4	1.4	1.4	1.7	1.7	..	5.9	5.4	0.0
TOTAL NET RESOURCE FLOWS (I + II + III)	**15.3**	**19.6**	**21.3**	**22.7**	**25.8**	**27.8**	**26.7**	**23.3**	**24.6**	**100.0**	**100.0**	**100.0**
Memorandum items:												
Total net credits from IMF	0.7	x	-0.6	-0.5	-0.2	0.1	-0.6	0.2	-0.1			
Acquisition of assets by LDCs, net	-1.2	-3.5	0.4	0.2	-2.6	-4.5	-7.2	-5.8	..			
Interest and dividends paid by LDCs, gross	-4.7	-12.8	-12.3	-12.9	-14.5	-15.7	-13.8	-13.1	..			
Total Official Grants	7.2	8.7	9.6	10.4	12.4	13.1	18.2	18.6	..			
At 1991 prices and exchange rates												
Total Net Resource Flows	26.9	34.0	29.9	27.8	29.4	32.0	27.7	23.3	23.2			
Total Official Development Finance	23.6	25.5	23.0	23.1	25.3	23.5	25.7	24.6	26.3			
Total ODA receipts	19.5	21.5	20.0	19.5	19.9	20.7	26.1	24.7	23.3			

Note: See Technical Notes.

Table III.7. Total net resource flows to Sub-Saharan Africa

Resource flows to Sub-Saharan Africa declining in real terms since 1989

	Current $ billion									Per cent of total		
	1984	1985	1986	1987	1988	1989	1990	1991	1992p	1984	1988	1991
I. OFFICIAL DEVELOPMENT FINANCE (ODF)	**9.9**	**9.7**	**12.4**	**15.1**	**16.0**	**16.6**	**20.0**	**18.9**	**20.0**	**115.1**	**75.5**	**102.2**
1. Official Development Assistance (ODA)	7.4	8.4	10.5	12.1	14.0	14.7	17.1	17.1	17.7	86.0	66.0	92.4
of which: Bilateral disbursements	4.9	5.6	7.0	8.2	9.6	9.7	11.5	11.0	11.2	57.0	8.0	59.5
Multilateral disbursements	2.5	2.8	3.5	3.9	4.4	5.0	5.6	6.1	6.5	29.1	20.8	33.0
2. Other ODF	2.5	1.3	1.9	3.0	2.0	1.9	2.9	1.8	2.3	29.1	9.4	9.7
of which: Bilateral disbursements	1.7	0.7	1.1	2.1	1.6	1.1	2.0	1.3	1.5	19.8	7.5	7.0
Multilateral disbursements	0.8	0.6	0.8	0.9	0.4	0.8	0.9	0.5	0.8	9.3	1.9	2.7
II. TOTAL EXPORT CREDITS	**-0.7**	**3.1**	**3.7**	**2.9**	**1.8**	**3.1**	**-0.8**	**-0.5**	**-1.0**	**-8.1**	**8.5**	**-2.7**
of which: Short-term	0.2	0.9	0.5	1.5	1.1	1.2	1.0	-0.3	x	2.3	5.2	-1.6
III. PRIVATE FLOWS	**-0.6**	**1.6**	**4.2**	**4.0**	**3.4**	**2.1**	**0.8**	**0.1**	**-1.0**	**-7.0**	**16.0**	**0.5**
1. Direct investment	-0.3	-0.2	0.6	1.2	0.5	2.5	0.3	0.4	-3.5	2.4	2.2	-10.8
2. International bank lending	-1.0	0.8	2.5	1.7	1.8	-1.6	-1.0	-2.0	-1.0	-11.6	8.5	-10.8
3. Total bond lending	x	x	x	x	-0.1	x	x	x	x	0.0	-0.5	0.0
4. Other private	x	0.1	0.1	0.1	0.1	x	x	0.2	:	0.5	0.5	1.1
5. Grants by non-governmental organisations	0.7	0.9	1.0	1.0	1.1	1.2	1.5	1.5	:	8.1	5.2	8.1
TOTAL NET RESOURCE FLOWS (I + II + III)	**8.6**	**14.4**	**20.3**	**22.0**	**21.2**	**21.8**	**20.0**	**18.5**	**18.0**	**100.0**	**100.0**	**100.0**
Memorandum items:												
Total net credits from IMF	0.5	x	-0.4	-0.5	-0.2	-0.4	-0.3	x	:			
Acquisition of assets by LDCs, net	-1.7	-3.3	0.6	-2.0	-1.7	-3.3	-3.8	-3.0	:			
Interest and dividends paid by LDCs, gross	-5.7	-5.1	-6.0	-6.8	-7.6	-7.8	-7.1	-6.7	:			
Total official grants	5.4	6.0	7.7	8.3	10.4	10.8	14.2	13.9	:			
At 1991 prices and exchange rates												
Total Net Resource Flows	15.1	24.9	28.5	26.9	24.2	25.1	20.7	18.5	17.0			
Total Official Development Finance	17.4	16.8	17.4	18.5	18.3	19.1	20.7	18.9	18.8			
Total ODA receipts	14.3	15.9	16.0	15.6	16.5	17.2	18.1	17.2	16.7			

Note: See Technical Notes.

Tableau III.8. Total net resource flows to Asia

From similar starting points in 1989, private flows expand to double the level of ODF

	Current $ billion									Per cent of total		
	1984	1985	1986	1987	1988	1989	1990	1991	1992 p	1984	1988	1992
I. OFFICIAL DEVELOPMENT FINANCE (ODF)	**9.9**	**9.9**	**11.4**	**12.7**	**16.6**	**17.8**	**18.7**	**19.5**	**20.6**	**41.9**	**52.7**	**31.1**
1. Official Development Assistance (ODA)	7.3	7.6	9.7	10.6	12.6	12.8	13.6	14.1	14.6	30.9	40.0	22.1
of which: Bilateral disbursements	4.4	4.6	6.2	6.9	8.5	8.8	9.2	9.5	9.8	18.6	27.0	14.8
Multilateral disbursements	2.9	3.0	3.5	3.7	4.1	4.0	4.4	4.6	4.8	12.3	13.0	7.3
2. Other ODF	2.6	2.3	1.7	2.1	4.0	5.0	5.1	5.4	6.0	11.0	12.7	9.1
of which: Bilateral disbursements	0.2	0.3	0.2	0.2	1.5	1.8	1.9	1.7	2.0	0.8	4.8	3.0
Multilateral disbursements	2.4	2.0	1.5	1.9	2.5	3.2	3.2	3.7	4.0	10.2	7.9	6.0
II. TOTAL EXPORT CREDITS	**2.6**	**0.7**	**-0.3**	**-1.5**	**0.5**	**0.6**	**1.4**	**-4.6**	**3.2**	**11.0**	**1.6**	**4.8**
of which: Short-term	0.7	0.9	0.3	0.7	1.2	-0.4	x	-3.0	x	3.0	3.8	0.0
III. PRIVATE FLOWS	**11.1**	**13.6**	**8.6**	**12.1**	**14.4**	**14.7**	**36.7**	**39.2**	**42.4**	**47.0**	**45.7**	**64.0**
1. Direct investment	3.9	0.5	2.2	8.3	7.4	10.0	10.0	10.8	12.6	16.5	23.5	19.0
2. International bank lending	4.5	6.2	1.2	0.7	4.0	0.9	23.0	21.3	25.0	19.1	12.7	37.8
3. Total bond lending	1.1	4.6	2.4	0.9	x	0.7	0.4	3.0	1.4	4.7	0.0	2.1
4. Other private	0.4	1.0	1.3	0.6	1.4	1.2	0.9	1.8	3.4	1.7	4.4	5.1
5. Grants by non-governmental organisations	1.2	1.3	1.5	1.6	1.6	1.9	2.4	2.3	..	5.1	5.1	0.0
TOTAL NET RESOURCE FLOWS (I + II + III)	**23.6**	**24.2**	**19.7**	**23.3**	**31.5**	**33.1**	**56.8**	**54.1**	**66.2**	**100.0**	**100.0**	**100.0**
Memorandum items:												
Total net credits from IMF	0.4	-0.8	-0.8	-2.4	-2.4	-1.1	-2.5	1.9	1.3			
Acquisition of assets by LDCs, net	-0.6	-3.7	-3.3	-1.8	-5.3	-3.8	-5.8	-9.4	..			
Interest and dividends paid by LDCs, gross	-22.5	-20.9	-19.3	-21.8	-23.5	-26.8	-28.0	-26.0	..			
Total official grants	4.8	4.2	6.9	6.9	6.6	6.8	7.0	8.0	..			
At 1991 prices and exchange rates												
Total Net Resource Flows	41.5	41.9	27.7	28.5	35.9	38.1	58.9	54.1	62.4			
Total Official Development Finance	17.4	17.2	16.0	15.6	18.9	20.5	19.4	19.5	19.4			
Total ODA receipts	17.8	17.0	20.2	18.2	17.7	17.4	15.6	14.5	13.8			

Note: See Technical Notes.

Table III.9. **Total net resource flows to Asian low-income countries**

Growth of bank lending responsible for the expansion of resource flows to Asia's poor countries in 1992

	Current $ billion									Per cent of total		
	1984	1985	1986	1987	1988	1989	1990	1991	1992p	1984	1988	1992
I. OFFICIAL DEVELOPMENT FINANCE (ODF)	**8.1**	**8.6**	**10.5**	**11.8**	**16.7**	**16.8**	**16.8**	**17.9**	**18.5**	**51.6**	**65.7**	**53.3**
1. Official Development Assistance (ODA)	6.4	6.7	8.7	9.3	11.4	11.5	11.8	12.5	13.0	40.8	44.9	37.5
of which: Bilateral disbursements	3.7	3.9	5.5	5.9	7.6	7.8	7.7	8.2	8.5	23.6	29.9	24.5
Multilateral disbursements	2.7	2.8	3.2	3.4	3.8	3.7	4.1	4.3	4.5	17.2	15.0	13.0
2. Other ODF	1.7	1.9	1.8	2.5	5.3	5.3	5.0	5.4	5.5	10.8	20.9	15.9
of which: Bilateral disbursements	0.2	0.3	0.2	x	1.4	1.6	1.4	1.3	1.5	1.3	5.5	4.3
Multilateral disbursements	1.5	1.6	1.6	2.5	3.9	3.7	3.6	4.1	4.0	9.6	15.4	11.5
II. TOTAL EXPORT CREDITS	**2.2**	**1.0**	**0.7**	**1.4**	**0.3**	**2.0**	**1.9**	**2.1**	**0.7**	**14.0**	**1.2**	**2.0**
of which: Short-term	0.7	0.7	x	0.6	x	-0.2	0.2	0.8	0.6	4.5	4.5	1.7
III. PRIVATE FLOWS	**5.4**	**9.0**	**4.2**	**9.7**	**8.4**	**5.2**	**19.2**	**9.4**	**15.5**	**34.4**	**33.1**	**44.7**
1. Direct investment	0.8	-0.2	-2.0	1.0	0.3	2.4	1.6	1.5	0.0	5.1	1.2	0.0
2. International bank lending	3.3	6.5	2.3	5.9	5.1	-0.1	14.9	7.3	14.5	21.0	20.1	41.8
3. Total bond lending	0.2	1.2	1.9	0.9	1.0	0.7	0.4	-1.5	1.0	1.3	3.9	2.9
4. Other private	x	0.3	0.7	0.5	0.6	0.5	0.2	..	..	x	2.4	0.0
5. Grants by non-governmental organisations	1.1	1.2	1.3	1.4	1.4	1.7	2.1	2.1	..	7.0	5.5	0.0
TOTAL NET RESOURCE FLOWS (I + II + III)	**15.7**	**18.6**	**15.4**	**22.9**	**25.4**	**24.0**	**37.9**	**29.4**	**34.7**	**100.0**	**100.0**	**100.0**
Memorandum items:												
Total net credits from IMF	0.2	-0.5	-0.4	-1.0	-1.6	-0.8	-2.2	1.9	1.3			
Acquisition of assets by LDCs, net	-1.0	-1.9	-1.3	-0.6	-1.8	-1.4	-1.7	-1.5	..			
Interest and dividends paid by LDCs, gross	-11.1	-10.8	-9.7	-11.0	-12.8	-14.7	-15.7	-15.5	..			
Total official grants	3.6	3.5	4.5	4.8	5.6	5.7	5.7	6.8	..			
	At 1991 prices and exchange rates											
Total Net Resource Flows	27.6	32.2	21.6	28.0	29.0	27.6	39.3	29.4	32.7			
Total Official Development Finance	14.3	14.9	14.8	14.5	19.1	19.3	17.4	17.9	17.4			
Total ODA receipts	11.3	11.6	12.2	11.4	13.0	13.2	12.2	12.5	12.3			

Note: See Technical Notes.

Table III.10. **Total net resource flows to North Africa and the Middle East**

Resource flows to North Africa and the Middle East more than double in 1992 as bank lending recovers

	Current $ billion									Per cent of total		
	1984	1985	1986	1987	1988	1989	1990	1991	1992 p	1984	1988	1992
I. OFFICIAL DEVELOPMENT FINANCE (ODF)	**5.2**	**6.1**	**6.2**	**5.8**	**7.7**	**5.5**	**7.2**	**10.8**	**12.4**	**65.8**	**106.9**	**72.5**
1. Official Development Assistance (ODA)	4.2	5.1	5.0	4.8	4.6	4.6	7.3	10.8	11.6	53.2	63.9	67.8
of which: Bilateral disbursements	3.7	4.6	4.5	4.3	4.1	3.9	6.4	9.1	9.8	46.8	56.9	57.3
Multilateral disbursements	0.5	0.5	0.5	0.5	0.5	0.7	0.9	1.7	1.8	6.3	6.9	10.5
2. Other ODF	1.0	1.0	1.2	1.0	3.1	0.9	-0.1	0.0	0.8	12.7	43.1	4.7
of which: Bilateral disbursements	0.5	0.4	0.5	0.4	2.6	0.2	-1.1	-1.1	-0.5	6.3	36.1	-2.9
Multilateral disbursements	0.5	0.6	0.7	0.6	0.5	0.7	1.0	1.1	1.3	6.3	6.9	7.6
II. TOTAL EXPORT CREDITS	**1.7**	**0.6**	**-1.0**	**-0.4**	**-2.5**	**4.8**	**2.6**	**0.9**	**-1.8**	**21.5**	**-34.7**	**-10.5**
of which: Short-term	-0.7	x	x	0.4	-1.8	2.7	2.3	-0.6	0.3	-8.9	-25.0	1.8
III. PRIVATE FLOWS	**1.0**	**1.5**	**1.7**	**-0.2**	**2.0**	**4.6**	**-2.2**	**-3.8**	**6.5**	**12.7**	**27.8**	**38.0**
1. Direct investment	1.0	1.0	0.7	-0.2	0.6	0.3	0.9	1.2	1.4	12.7	8.3	8.2
2. International bank lending	x	x	0.8	-0.2	0.7	3.6	-3.0	-6.1	5.0	0.0	9.7	29.2
3. Total bond lending	-0.1	0.4	x	x	0.3	0.2	-0.3	0.8	-0.1	-1.3	4.2	-0.6
4. Other private	x	x	x	x	0.2	0.3	-0.1	0.1	0.2	0.0	2.8	1.2
5. Grants by non-governmental organisations	0.1	0.1	0.2	0.2	0.2	0.2	0.3	0.2	..	1.3	2.8	0.0
TOTAL NET RESOURCE FLOWS (I + II + III)	**7.9**	**8.2**	**6.9**	**5.2**	**7.2**	**14.9**	**7.6**	**7.9**	**17.1**	**100.0**	**100.0**	**100.0**
Memorandum items:												
Total net credits from IMF	0.3	0.1	-0.2	x	x	0.5	-0.3	0.2	0.1			
Acquisition of assets by LDCs, net	-8.2	1.1	-8.8	2.9	-6.8	-5.0	-5.7	-4.2	..			
Interest and dividends paid by LDCs, gross	-17.7	-15.2	-14.3	-14.0	-15.7	-16.8	-15.3	-13.1	..			
Total official grants	3.1	4.1	4.0	4.5	3.6	3.7	6.2	8.2	..			
At 1991 prices and exchange rates												
Total Net Resource Flows	13.9	14.2	9.7	6.4	8.2	17.2	7.9	7.9	16.1			
Total Official Development Finance	9.2	10.6	8.7	7.1	8.8	6.3	7.5	10.8	11.7			
Total ODA receipts	10.6	11.8	9.3	7.7	5.9	5.5	12.0	12.0	10.9			

Note: See Technical Notes.

Table III.11. Total net resource flows to Central and South America

Improved economic prospects and debt reorganisation cause private flows to Latin America to double in 1992

	Current $ billion									Per cent of total		
	1984	1985	1986	1987	1988	1989	1990	1991	1992ᴾ	1984	1988	1992
I. OFFICIAL DEVELOPMENT FINANCE (ODF)	**7.8**	**8.5**	**9.1**	**10.1**	**8.2**	**8.2**	**13.4**	**10.8**	**10.2**	**28.7**	**39.4**	**19.8**
1. Official Development Assistance (ODA)	3.0	3.4	3.7	4.3	4.3	3.9	5.3	6.0	6.2	11.0	20.7	12.0
of which: Bilateral disbursements	2.2	2.6	2.9	3.5	3.4	3.8	4.2	4.9	5.0	8.1	16.3	9.7
Multilateral disbursements	0.8	0.8	0.8	0.8	0.9	0.1	1.1	1.1	1.2	2.9	4.3	2.3
2. Other ODF	4.8	5.1	5.4	5.8	3.9	4.3	8.1	4.8	4.0	17.6	18.8	7.8
of which: Bilateral disbursements	1.1	1.8	1.4	3.2	1.1	1.9	3.5	2.5	2.0	4.0	5.3	3.9
Multilateral disbursements	3.7	3.3	4.0	2.6	2.8	2.4	4.6	2.3	2.0	13.6	13.5	3.9
II. TOTAL EXPORT CREDITS	**0.7**	**1.7**	**0.9**	**1.0**	**1.3**	**2.0**	**1.3**	**1.6**	**3.8**	**2.6**	**6.3**	**7.4**
of which: Short-term	0.1	1.4	1.6	1.5	1.0	0.8	0.9	0.6	0.8	0.4	4.8	1.6
III. PRIVATE FLOWS	**18.7**	**10.6**	**6.3**	**10.6**	**11.3**	**15.1**	**8.0**	**17.9**	**37.6**	**68.8**	**54.3**	**72.9**
1. Direct investment	5.9	5.1	5.9	8.9	9.7	9.7	8.8	12.0	13.4	21.7	46.6	26.0
2. International bank lending	13.7	6.2	1.6	3.7	1.5	6.0	-7.7	-2.0	11.0	50.4	7.2	21.3
3. Total bond lending	-1.0	-0.8	-1.4	-2.1	-1.4	-1.2	3.2	5.0	8.0	-3.7	-6.7	15.5
4. Other private	-0.3	-0.3	-0.3	-0.4	0.8	-0.1	2.8	2.1	5.2	-1.1	3.8	10.1
5. Grants by non-governmental organisations	0.4	0.4	0.5	0.5	0.7	0.7	0.9	0.8	..	1.5	3.4	0.0
TOTAL NET RESOURCE FLOWS (I + II + III)	**27.2**	**20.8**	**16.3**	**21.7**	**20.8**	**25.3**	**22.7**	**30.3**	**51.6**	**100.0**	**100.0**	**100.0**
Memorandum items:												
Total net credits from IMF	3.9	1.5	0.2	-0.8	-0.5	-0.2	1.2	-1.0	-1.6			
Acquisition of assets by LDCs, net	-7.2	-1.6	1.0	-7.3	-5.3	-4.9	-7.4	-6.7	..			
Interest and dividends paid by LDCs, gross	-37.2	-34.6	-29.8	-28.3	-36.5	-32.7	-29.1	-24.8	..			
Total official grants	2.2	2.6	2.8	3.3	3.5	3.8	4.2	6.1	..			
At 1991 prices and exchange rates												
Total Net Resource Flows	47.9	36.0	22.9	26.6	23.7	29.1	23.5	30.3	48.6			
Total Official Development Finance	13.7	14.7	12.8	12.4	9.4	9.4	13.9	10.8	9.6			
Total ODA receipts	6.9	5.9	5.2	5.3	4.9	4.5	5.5	6.0	5.8			

Note: See Technical Notes.

Chapter IV

External Debt of Developing Countries:
Trends and Policy Developments

Introduction

The past decade saw a sharp reversal in the rate of growth of the external debt of the developing countries. The slowdown, which started in 1987, continued to be accompanied by marked changes in the composition of debt stock. Debt service has been falling since 1988, as a result of:

- the slower growth of debt stocks;
- lower international interest rates;
- a higher degree of concessionality on some loans;
- major developments in the policies and instruments for restructuring developing country debt.

Bilateral debt forgiveness initiatives increased considerably from 1990, and starting in 1988 there were major developments in multilateral debt relief policies. Official and bank debt restructuring packages started to include mechanisms for debt and debt service reduction. Coupled with continuing efforts to promote adjustment, these approaches helped to restore some countries to financial viability and improved their growth prospects. Such was the case for Mexico, whose announcement in 1982 that it was no longer able to service its debt, triggered the deep and widespread debt crisis in the developing countries. But despite these positive developments, the external debt situation of many countries is still a source of concern because their adjustment policies have been inappropriate and/or restructurings agreed with their creditors have been inadequate.

This chapter is divided into two parts. The first outlines the external debt situation of the developing countries since the onset of the debt crisis. The second describes the main features of the policies implemented by the various actors involved – debtor countries, creditor governments, commercial banks and multilateral institutions – in response to the indebtedness of the developing countries.

The tables in the accompanying chapter V show aggregated debt and debt service data up to 1992. These data were compiled from the country tables in Annex 1.

The data for 1992 are Secretariat estimates. Tables V.1 to V.8 contain aggregated data by major income groups. Tables V.9 to V.16 show aggregated data for Africa, Central and South America, and Asia. Table V.17 gives details of multilateral restructurings of developing countries' official debt.

1. Trends in the stock, composition and service of developing country debt

A. Debt stock

Preliminary data show that the total external debt of the developing countries in 1992 was $1 534 billion, an increase, measured in current prices and exchange rates, of 3.3 per cent on the previous year. Most of this increase was attributable to the Asian countries, while there was a slight fall in the debt of the African countries.

The growth of external debt has slackened since 1987, due in part to debt reorganisation and the growth of grants in overall resource flows.

This increase was in line with the average annual increase of about 3 per cent from 1987. It contrasts with the relatively high growth of external debt from the early 1980s, when it averaged 8 per cent, well above the rate of GDP growth in these countries. The change in trend from 1987 affected all income groups and regions, and had several causes. The first two relate to changes in the supply of, and demand for, finance, while the latter two reflect changes in donor policies:

- Some developing countries adopted more cautious debt policies; non-debt-generating flows of resources gradually came to account for a larger share of total flows to the developing countries;
- Private creditors reconsidered their lending policies to developing countries, either because their

own lending capacity had decreased or because they restructured their asset portfolios in the light of the financial difficulties of certain developing countries. From 1987, the combined effects of a decrease in new loans and of debt conversions resulted in a fall in the stock of developing country long-term bank and bond debt, although it increased slightly in 1991-1992;

- ODA flows from the OECD countries included a growing share of non-debt-generating grants. At end-1992, official grants accounted for about 85 per cent of total ODA flows to the developing countries, compared with 70 per cent in 1987;

- In recent years, a growing fraction of debt was cancelled bilaterally, and through the Paris Club from 1988.

Debt stocks by region and income group

Asia was the region whose external debt stock increased the most over the past ten years (by an annual average of almost 9 per cent). This was due in large part to the rapid growth of the debt of India, Indonesia and especially China. Whereas in 1982 Central and South America had been the most heavily-indebted region, in 1992 Asia accounted for the largest share of developing country debt (33.6 per cent). As Chart IV.1 shows, Africa's share of the developing countries' total debt remained fairly stable. However, because of exchange rate fluctuations (the sterling, peseta and lira devaluations), the current values understate the growth of Africa's debt. By income group, the low-income countries (LICs) had the highest growth of debt stocks. Within this group, however, the least-developed countries experienced slower growth of their debt stocks on account of the debt cancellations that they received from the end of the 1980s.

B. *Debt structure*

The growth of the debt stocks of the developing countries, which was relatively high up to 1987 and moderate thereafter, was accompanied by major changes in debt structure. The most salient developments were:

- a large increase in short-term claims after 1987;
- a steep rise in the relative share of multilateral debt between 1982 and 1988, and a smaller increase thereafter;

Chart IV.1. **Regional breakdown of debt, 1982-87-92**
At current prices and exchange rates in $ billion

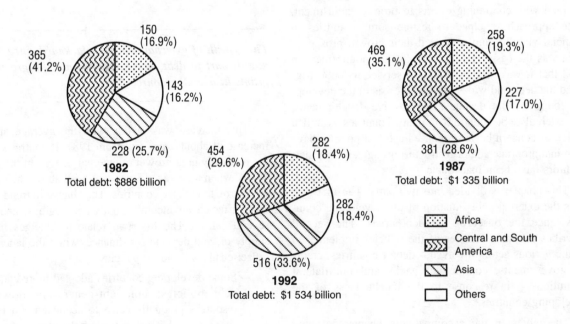

1982
Total debt: $886 billion

1987
Total debt: $1 335 billion

1992
Total debt: $1 534 billion

Africa

Central and South America

Asia

Others

Note: Data for 1992 are provisional.

Chart IV.2. Composition of external debt by category and region
(in percentage)

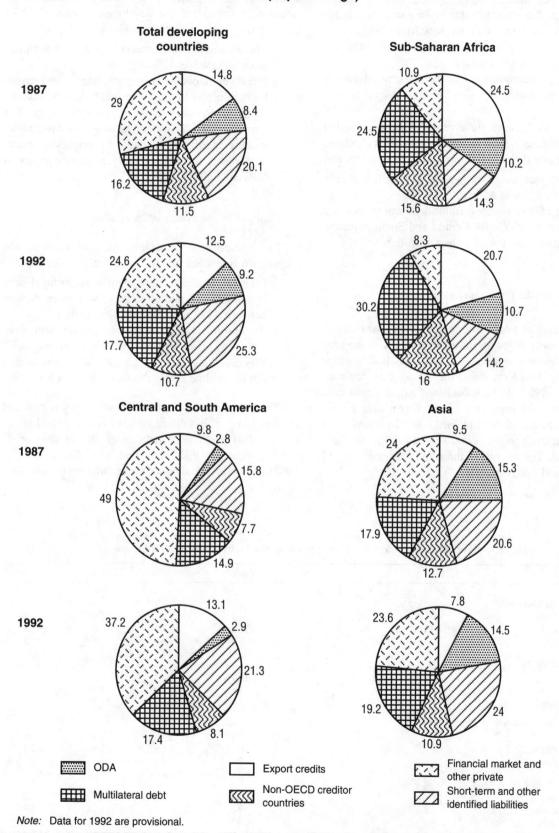

Total developing countries

1987

14.8
8.4
20.1
11.5
16.2
29

1992

12.5
9.2
25.3
10.7
17.7
24.6

Sub-Saharan Africa

1987

10.9
24.5
10.2
14.3
15.6
24.5

1992

8.3
20.7
10.7
14.2
16
30.2

Central and South America

1987

9.8
2.8
15.8
7.7
14.9
49

1992

13.1
2.9
21.3
8.1
17.4
37.2

Asia

1987

9.5
15.3
20.6
12.7
17.9
24

1992

7.8
14.5
24
10.9
19.2
23.6

ODA	Export credits	Financial market and other private
Multilateral debt	Non-OECD creditor countries	Short-term and other identified liabilities

Note: Data for 1992 are provisional.

- a reduction in the share of long-term bank and bond debt after 1988;
- a fall in the absolute value of long-term credits for exports of goods and services from 1987; up to then, they had been increasing steadily from the beginning of the decade;
- a sharp increase in the degree of concessionality for some loans.

As Chart IV.2 shows, the changes in the composition of debt were more marked in some regions than in others. The main regional changes over the past five years were:

- a steep increase in the weight of multilateral debt for Sub-Saharan Africa;
- a sharp fall in private creditor debt, and an increase in short-term debt for Central and South America;
- an expansion of Asia's short-term debt.

Changes in the term structure of debt

The change of trend in total debt stocks was due to the slow growth of long-term debt. Whereas at the start of the decade the growth of long-term debt had outstripped that of short-term debt, this trend was reversed sharply after 1987. As both bank and export credit debt were affected, the expansion of short-term debt for all income groups cannot be explained solely by a revival of international trade in goods and services in the developing countries. The reversal of this trend was most marked in Central and South America.

The relatively large increase in short-term debt stocks is disquieting. In principle, it is likely to increase the future debt service of the developing countries. Other explanations and implications can also be drawn:

- The accumulation of arrears impedes the disbursement of new loans;
- Private creditors, and especially banks, are increasingly reluctant to grant long-term loans on account of the over-indebtedness of some countries. The terms of such loans are usually less favourable, making it difficult to draw up long-term investment plans, and, consequently, impairing prospects for economic growth.

Changes in the composition of debt

The composition of developing country debt displayed two important trends during the past decade:

- Bilateral, and especially multilateral, official debt increased. The rate of increase was more marked between 1982 and 1987 than thereafter;
- An absolute fall in long-term private debt from 1987 was offset by an increase in short-term debt. Whereas long-term bank debt and export credits fell in absolute terms, short-term debt grew rapidly.

The composition of debt varies widely by region and income group. Sub-Saharan Africa has a large and growing share of multilateral debt (over 30 per cent of its external debt in 1992, compared with 20 per cent in 1982). However, the share of the multilateral debt of Asia

Table IV.1. **Annual rate of increase of external debt stocks by maturity and income group**

Country	1982-87	1987-92	1990-91	1991-92
Total developing countries				
Total debt	8.7	2.8	4.0	3.3
Long-term debt	10.7	1.4	3.6	1.1
Short-term debt	1.9	7.9	5.6	11.3
Low-income countries				
Total debt	13.2	5.6	6.7	5.9
Long-term debt	14.8	5.1	5.8	5.5
Short-term debt	7.0	10.0	12.3	9.8
Low middle-income countries				
Total debt	9.1	2.5	3.2	0.0
Long-term debt	10.3	1.6	2.9	−0.3
Short-term debt	2.6	7.2	5.2	0.0
Upper middle-income countries				
Total debt	5.6	0.2	2.2	3.7
Long-term debt	7.8	−2.2	1.8	−1.9
Short-term debt	0.1	5.3	3.0	16.0

and Central and South America has also risen in absolute and relative terms. In the case of the latter region, the share of multilateral debt in its total debt stock almost doubled in ten years.

Multilateral debt is the major component of the debt of Sub-Saharan African countries.

The fall in bank debt can be partly explained by commercial debt reduction operations, especially under the Brady Plan. However, the most important factor was probably the fall in new bank loans to all regions, with the exception of Asia, during the second half of the 1980s. In Central and South America, long-term bank and bond debt also fell in absolute terms from 1987.

Changes in the degree of concessionality of debt

Since 1984, a growing proportion of long-term debt, including multilateral debt, has been on concessional terms (in 1991, 26 per cent for total long-term debt and over 32 per cent for multilateral debt). In principle, the higher the income level of the borrower country, the lower the degree of concessionality. The least-developed countries thus receive the most concessional terms.

The least-developed countries have benefited most from the growing concessionality of debt-creating flows.

However, some of the countries classified as "high-income countries" in 1992 – principally Israel, Lebanon and especially Iraq – receive a large proportion of loans on concessional terms. Iraq borrowed heavily from the former Soviet Union; at end-1992, over half of its long-term debt was concessional. There are also wide regional disparities: at end-1991, about 60 per cent of the long-term debt of South Asia (including India and Pakistan) was concessional, compared with less than 13 per cent for Central and South America.

C. Debt service of developing countries

Trends in debt service payments

Actual debt service payments fell gradually from 1989 to an estimated $150 billion in 1992. Lower international interest rates, a higher degree of concessionality on some loans, and debt and debt service reduction operations, were the main reasons for the fall in the debt service (measured in current prices and exchange rates). In addition to these factors, the decline in debt service also reflected the inability of some countries to meet their commitments (as witnessed by the accumulation of arrears).

Composition of LLDC debt

The composition of the debt of the least-developed countries (LLDCs) is very atypical and could be problematical in the context of future debt restructuring. ODA-related debt and official or guaranteed export credits granted by OECD countries have already been substantially restructured or cancelled.

LLDC debt is currently characterised by a relatively high proportion of multilateral and non-OECD Member country debt (respectively 38.6 and 28.3 per cent of their external debt stocks at end-1992). The two main components of this debt are not included in multilateral restructurings: by definition, multilateral debt cannot be renegotiated, and some bilateral creditors (including the former Soviet Union, China and the Arab countries) do not participate in the Paris Club negotiations. Gambia and Cambodia illustrate this trend. Non-OECD debt represents the bulk of Cambodia's debt (80.8 per cent at end-1991), whereas multilateral debt is the major component of Gambia's debt (66.4 per cent at end-1991).

In contrast, the long-term private debt of the LLDCs as a whole is increasingly marginal, though not the service on it (respectively 1.8 and 8.7 per cent at end-1992). However, this category of debt represents a relatively large share of the external debt of some individual LLDCs. For example, at end-1991 Gambia's bank debt represented 8.7 per cent of its external debt stock, but principal and interest payments on it accounted for 44 per cent of its total debt service.

There is still scope for debt or debt service reductions, either through the Paris Club for official debt, or the IDA Debt Reduction Facility for buy-backs of bank debt at a discount. It is unlikely, however, that they would be sufficient to ease the difficulties being experienced by some LLDCs in generating enough foreign exchange to service their external debt, given the size of their multilateral debt and debts to official creditors who do not participate in the Paris Club negotiations.

Chart IV.3. Composition of the debt and debt service of the least-developed countries in 1991 (in percentage)

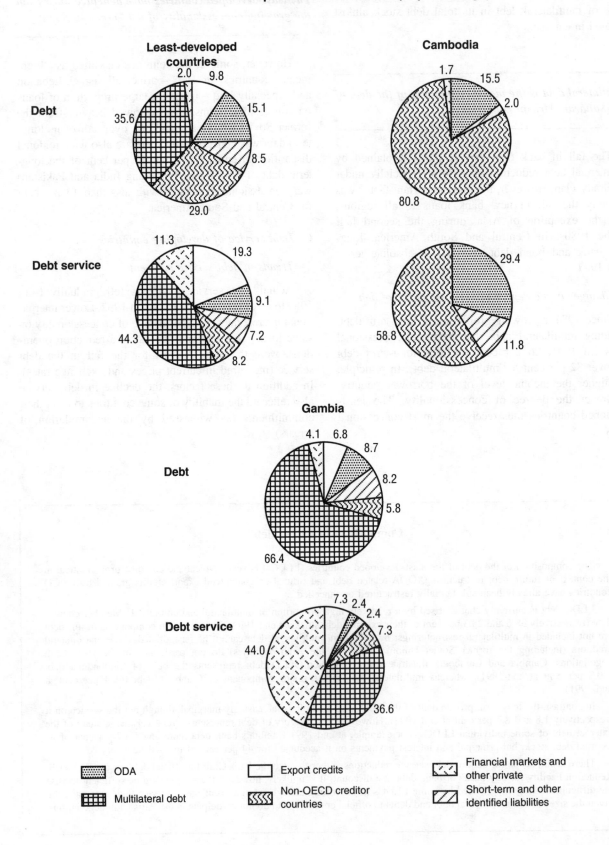

Table IV.2. **Share of long-term concessional debt by income group and region, 1982-1992**

In percentage

Country	1982	1991
Least-developed countries	36.9	55.6
Other low-income countries	34.4	33.7
Low middle-income countries	32.3	31.8
Upper middle-income countries	4.9	6.6
of which: high-income countries	12.9	25.0
Sub-Saharan Africa	20.3	32.4
Latin America	11.6	12.9
South Asia	62.6	59.8
Total developing countries	21.3	26.2

The fall in debt service payments varied between groups of countries. From 1988, the debt service of the least-developed countries, and especially that of the upper middle-income countries, fell in absolute terms, mainly because of official debt restructuring for the former group and bank debt restructuring for the latter group. The debt service of the low middle-income countries started to fall only after 1990. Sub-Saharan Africa and Central and South America were the regions most affected by this reduction.

Structure of debt service payments

Reflecting changes in the nature of developing country debt, the composition of debt service payments underwent three major developments over the past ten years:

- A significant and gradual increase in service payments on multilateral debt. The share of multilateral debt service in total long-term debt service rose from 8 per cent in 1982 to nearly 28 per cent in 1992. As Chart IV.4 shows, the increase was particularly marked in Central and South America and Sub-Saharan Africa.
- A parallel reduction in debt service payments, especially by Central and South American countries, to banks and other creditors.
- A decline in service payments on export credits, especially by Sub-Saharan African and Asian countries.

D. The financial situation of indebted countries

The external debt of the developing countries is no longer growing rapidly; as Chart IV.5 shows, their actual debt service fell in recent years.

Since 1987, the rate of growth of their income (GDP) has been higher, on average, than that of their debt stock. This may indicate that the solvency of the developing countries in aggregate has improved, and that their exter-

nal indebtedness is more sustainable in the long-term. The financial terms of their debt stock have also evolved favourably and the ability of many countries to pay their debt service has improved (see Chart IV.6). However, this view needs to be qualified in light of the accumulation of arrears. Also, the growth of short-term debt and non-renegotiable multilateral debt continues to be disquieting.

Debt service payments have been falling since 1989, but the financial situation of many developing countries remains fragile.

The weight of external debt, and disparities according to origin of claims

The weight of external debt, measured in terms of the ratio of debt service to total debt stock, fell sharply over the past decade for all categories of claims. However, the ratio still varies widely according to countries' income levels and the origin of claims. If this ratio is taken as an indicator of the debt burden, export credits and bank and bond debt are seen to be the most expensive. The ratio is low for ODA-related debt and bilateral loans granted by non-OECD countries. It is relatively high for multilateral debt, although again it varies markedly according to the income level of the country.

Ability to meet debt service payments

Export earnings are making it easier for many countries to meet debt service payments than in the past. The ambitious adjustment programmes they have implemented have enabled them to increase export volume. Despite the fall in most commodity prices, strong export

Chart IV.4. **Composition of LDC actual service payments by category and by region (in percentage)**

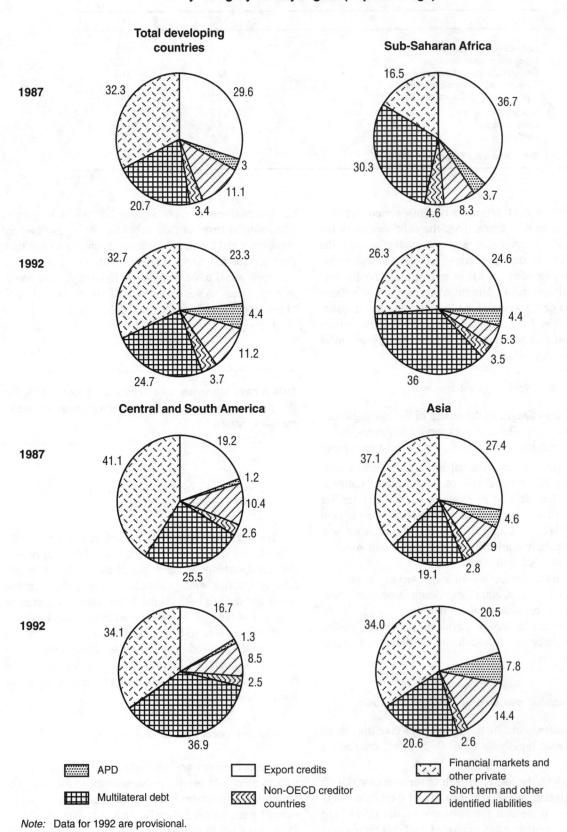

Total developing countries

1987

32.3, 29.6, 3, 11.1, 3.4, 20.7

Sub-Saharan Africa

1987

16.5, 36.7, 3.7, 8.3, 4.6, 30.3

1992

32.7, 23.3, 4.4, 11.2, 3.7, 24.7

1992

26.3, 24.6, 4.4, 5.3, 3.5, 36

Central and South America

1987

19.2, 1.2, 10.4, 2.6, 25.5, 41.1

Asia

1987

37.1, 27.4, 4.6, 9, 2.8, 19.1

1992

16.7, 1.3, 8.5, 2.5, 36.9, 34.1

1992

34.0, 20.5, 7.8, 14.4, 2.6, 20.6

Legend:
- ▦ APD
- ▯ Export credits
- ◪ Financial markets and other private
- ▦ Multilateral debt
- ◩ Non-OECD creditor countries
- ◩ Short term and other identified liabilities

Note: Data for 1992 are provisional.

Chart IV.5. Trends in LDC debt and actual debt service 1982-92, in $ billion

Debt stock

Debt service

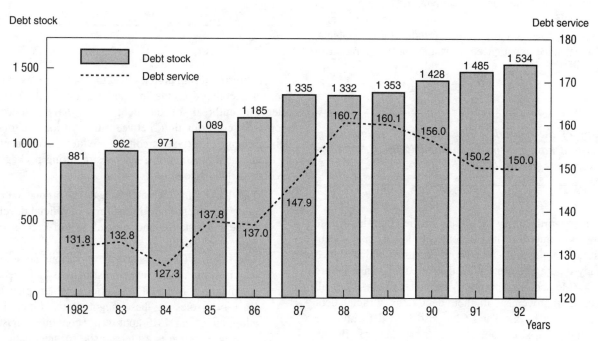

Debt stock

Debt service

Note: Data for 1992 are provisional.

Chart IV.6. Changes in debt ratios, 1982-91 (debt service/value of exports) by income groups

Debt ratio 1991

Debt ratio 1991

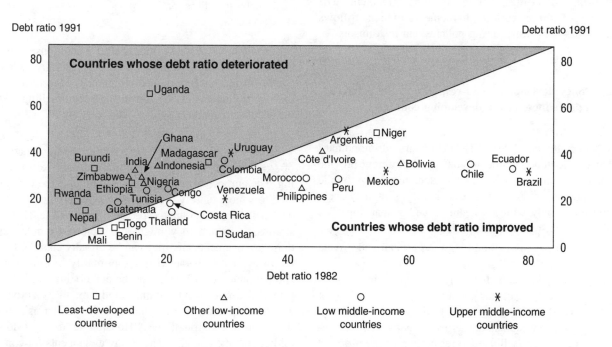

Debt ratio 1982

□	△	○	*
Least-developed countries	Other low-income countries	Low middle-income countries	Upper middle-income countries

Note: Debt service in this instance denotes actual service of long-term and IMF debt, and interest payments on short-term liabilities.

performance and a lower debt service have resulted in an improvement in this indicator of the financial situation of a number of developing countries. The most striking examples are Chile, Mexico, Bolivia, the Philippines and Venezuela. However, other countries, including some least-developed countries (*e.g.* Burundi, Ethiopia, Ghana, Uganda) have experienced a disquieting deterioration in this ratio.

Many of the countries whose financial situation has improved have benefited considerably from debt reorganisation agreements.

It is worth noting that many of the countries whose debt ratio improved had benefited following major debt restructuring agreements. Those countries which signed Brady-type agreements with their creditor banks before 1991 (Mexico, Philippines, Venezuela, Costa Rica) all saw an improvement in their debt ratio. Official debt restructuring by the Paris Club also helped to improve the financial situation of countries such as Benin, Bolivia, Niger and the Philippines. For countries such as Brazil and Peru, however, the improvement indicated by Chart IV.6 is misleading, as the accumulation of arrears distorts the evaluation of their financial situation (since actual debt service was much less than what it should have been). These arrears are now being cleared thanks to bank and/or offical debt restructuring agreements. The scope of these various agreements which follows describes debt restructuring policies and instruments.

2. Policy developments in response to the external indebtedness of the developing countries

Since the late 1980s, LDC debt restructuring policies have undergone significant changes. They now provide for reduction in debt stocks and debt service by public and private creditors, whereas in they past they were concerned only with rescheduling and refinancing. The aims of debt restructuring packages are to:

- improve co-operation between official and private creditors;
- clarify the scope for debt management by the governments of debtor countries;
- start funds flowing again to the LDCs in order to revive investment and growth; restructuring agreements can facilitate the restoration of investor and lender confidence.

Debt reorganisation policies now include the reduction, and not just the rescheduling, of debt stocks and debt service.

Debt restructuring policies, and the measures taken to prevent a collapse of the international financial system after the outbreak of the debt crisis, have required increased co-ordination between the various actors: debtor countries, private creditors, creditor governments and multilateral institutions. Debt restructuring packages involve various actors:

- The Paris Club, which reschedules official debt, *i.e.* government loans in the form of official development assistance and official export credits or guaranteed credits;
- The London Club, consisting of various advisory banking committees, which restructures bank debt;
- International financial institutions, which play at least two roles in these negotiations. First, the adoption of an IMF-approved economic adjustment programme is a prerequisite for negotiations with the Paris and London Clubs. Second, for bank debt renegotiations, international financial institutions have often had to provide funds to debtor countries, either to facilitate the operation, to provide guarantees for loans to replace old ones, or to allow the recipient country to buy back part of its debt at a discount.

In addition to these multilateral operations, some OECD countries have forgiven debt bilaterally. Also, creditor banks have carried out voluntary restructuring of their portfolios, mainly by converting debt or selling it in the secondary market.

Another major development has been the introduction of ''menus'' of options for multilateral debt restructuring. The purpose of such options is to involve the various creditors more closely in negotiations by helping them to deal with any constraints, especially fiscal and legal constraints, to which they might be subject. Complex as these arrangements are, they can be broadly classified on the basis of the characteristics – primarily income level and the nature of the debt – of the debtors involved. The principal arrangements of this kind are: the ''Toronto terms'', subsequently the ''enhanced Toronto terms'' (for the poorest countries); the ''Houston terms'' for low middle-income countries and Brady agreements for commercial debt.

A. Policies implemented by developing countries

A.1. Economic policies and performance of developing countries

At the beginning of the 1990s, there were signs of a revival in growth in many developing countries after a decade of poor performance. The IMF estimated that the overall rate of real GDP growth in the developing countries in 1992 was over 6 per cent. This can be attributed for the most part to the stabilization measures and structural reforms undertaken by these countries. However, there are still wide disparities between countries:

- The Asian continent is still at the forefront, mainly on account of its strong foreign trade performance;
- In Central and South America, sounder policies, especially in the monetary and financial area, have enabled the most heavily-indebted countries to regain access to international capital markets. The most striking examples are Mexico and, more recently, Argentina, Chile and Venezuela. The situation and prospects for Brazil are less certain;
- African countries are still in a critical situation. In some countries, economic reforms have not lived up to expectations in terms of renewed growth and investment. A steady deterioration in the terms-of-trade and adverse climatic conditions are partly responsible for the persistence of poor economic performance. In some cases, structural adjustment measures may have had a negative impact, at least in the short term, on government revenue, making external debt management still more difficult.

After a decade of poor results, the outlook for growth is more optimistic, except for Africa.

A.2. External debt restructuring and economic policies of the developing countries

The adoption of appropriate economic policies is often set as a prerequisite for debt restructuring by private and public creditors. Debt restructuring aims to restore the financial viability of the debtor country and to consolidate ajustment efforts. By removing some of the uncertainty about the country's ability to meet its commitments, it helps to restore domestic and foreign investor confidence, chiefly by making monetary and fiscal policy more predictable, and to permit a revival of investment and growth.

Mexico's economic success is, for example, not solely due to the major debt restructuring agreement negotiated with the banks. The way was prepared by its efforts to reduce fiscal imbalances and to bring inflation under control, and its sweeping liberalisation of trade and the tax system. The reform of the financial system also helped to mobilise domestic saving more effectively and to allocate resources more efficiently. Private investors' confidence in the ambitious reform programme encouraged flight capital to return and attracted new foreign direct investment, making it easier for Mexico to borrow on international capital markets.

B. Official debt: principles of restructuring agreements and their evolution

B.1. Multilateral initiatives: the Paris Club

The principles which underpin Paris Club official debt renegotiation agreements have evolved considerably in response to the scale of the developing countries' indebtedness. Initially, the Paris Club was an exceptional arrangement whereby repayment of principal and interest was postponed pending a country's return to financial health. But the frequent, if not systematic, recourse by some countries to the Paris Club since the onset of the debt crisis called into question this approach and, by the same token, the principles which underpin renegotiations. The payments difficulties of some debtor countries can no longer be put down to a transitory liquidity crisis. Their repeated requests for debt restructuring point more to a problem of solvency. The rescheduling or refinancing of their debt at market rates are no longer appropriate solutions. As a result, the principles of debt renegotiation have undergone considerable change, the two most important of which are:

- partial debt cancellation for the poorest countries, rather than only rescheduling or refinancing;
- a gradual treatment of debt stocks, instead of only loans falling due in the near future.

The number of agreements and the amounts rescheduled in the Paris Club have grown considerably. Since 1988, partial debt forgiveness for the poorest countries has been included in Paris Club agreements.

Multilateral initiatives for the poorest countries

Following the Toronto Summit (June 1988), the debts of the poorest countries were renegotiated for the first time by the Paris Club according to a menu of options comprising debt or debt service reductions. These were the so-called "Toronto terms". The grant element can amount to 33 per cent of the value of the debt (principal and interest) during a relatively short period – the so-called consolidation period (which in principle is the same as that in the adjustment programme which the debtor has concluded with IMF). Often, the renegotiated maturities represented only a fraction of the total debt stock. The long-term impact of such agreements was important only if the country benefited from a succession of them, each granting relief on a small part of the debt – usually the part falling due within a 12-18 month period.

Recognising this limitation of the Toronto terms, in September 1990 John Major, then Chancellor of the Exchequer, put forward new principles for renegotiating the official debt of the poorest countries in the Paris Club – the so-called "Trinidad terms". These were:

– that all eligible debt (*i.e.* that contracted prior to the cut-off date set by the Paris Club) be re-examined, and not just the maturities falling due within the consolidation period;
– that the degree of concessionality be increased, with two-thirds of eligible debt being cancelled, the remainder to be rescheduled over a longer period (25 years, including a five-year grace period).

These proposals were not accepted by all the participants. Nonetheless, in December 1991 the Paris Club introduced new principles for restructuring the official debt of the poorest countries, which were modelled on the Trinidad terms. These "enhanced Toronto terms", which are still in force, are more favourable than the Toronto terms but do not go as far as the Trinidad proposals, namely:

– The debt relief is at most equivalent to 50 per cent of the outstanding payments (principal and interest) on the consolidated debt;
– The restructuring does not apply to all the eligible debt (*i.e.* to that contracted before the cut-off date in the first agreement). However, when the debtor country has concluded a multi-annual adjustment agreement with the IMF, the consolidation period can be spread over several years (usually three). Also, official creditors have the option of re-examining the stock of eligible debt (*i.e.* debt contracted prior to the cut-off date in the first Paris Club agreement) in the future. Some agreements include

a "goodwill clause" whereby creditors undertake to grant further debt relief after three or four years if the debtor country has met its commitments to the Paris Club and the IMF, and if it has obtained comparable debt relief from other creditors (banks and bilateral creditors which are not members of the Paris Club).

The Paris Club now aims to provide sufficient debt relief to ensure that a country no longer has to have systematic recourse to the Club. Thus, its support is extended to include debt forgiveness for the poorest countries instead of only liquidity contributions in the form of refinancing or rescheduling.

Multilateral initiatives for other developing countries

In comparison to the poorer developing countries, the bilateral debt of middle-income countries *vis-à-vis* the Paris Club is smaller. However, the low middle-income countries (LMICs) have a larger share of debt (ODA and official export credits and guarantees) with Paris Club creditors than the upper middle-income countries (UMICs) – respectively about 21 and 12 per cent of their external debt in 1992. But these figures mask large differences within LMICs. For example, Cameroon's bilateral debt vis-à-vis Paris Club creditors represented more than 50 per cent of its external debt stock in 1991.

Debt forgiveness is not offered to middle-income countries, despite the fact that their financial situation is often critical.

Middle-income countries do not benefit from debt forgiveness within the Paris Club (with two exceptions – Egypt and Poland, examined in 1991 – but which did not set a precedent). Nonetheless, creditor governments did agree (Houston, September 1990) to extend the LMICs' repayment period to 20 years for ODA loans and to 15 years for other official credits (previously 10 years).

The application of the Houston terms also opened up the possibility of converting part of the debt into local currency-denominated funds for the financing of development projects – in the area of environmental protection, for example. All ODA loans are convertible, but official and guaranteed export credits only partially so (usually 10 per cent). However, the scope for debt conversion is still limited and, given that these measures have been implemented only recently, it is difficult to assess their impact.

Limitations of Paris Club agreements

For some developing countries, the benefits of a Paris Club agreement are limited:

- Official debt refinancing or rescheduling cannot be a lasting solution for middle-income countries. They provide only temporary help in restoring financial viability, and the uncertainty surrounding the long-term can undermine private investors' confidence. This makes any revival in investment and growth more difficult;
- Some countries are heavily-indebted to official creditors who do not take part in the Paris Club negotiations – the former Soviet Union, the Arab countries and China. This is the case of a number of LLDCs, such as Zambia, Mali, Angola, Mozambique and Ethiopia. A Paris Club agreement, even on very concessional terms, has therefore only a limited impact on such a country's financial situation as it affects only a relatively small share of its external debt;
- Paris Club reschedulings also have only a limited impact on the financial situation of countries that borrowed heavily from banks in the past (for example, Niger, Côte d'Ivoire and Nigeria). Added to this, it is extremely difficult and costly for low-income countries to conclude negotiations with creditor banks.

The agreed minutes of the Paris Club meetings contain a clause which stipulates that when a country signs an agreement with its official creditors, it must try to obtain a comparable agreement with its other creditors. This is to ensure that the debt relief granted by one creditor does not benefit another, rather than the country being given the relief. Although fair in principle, this clause can hinder negotiations in the Paris Club. It is not always easy to apply it, especially to the poorest countries with relatively little bargaining power. The IDA Debt Reduction Facility set up in 1990 by the World Bank helps to overcome this difficulty for the poorest countries with bank debts, by allowing them to buy back all or part of their commercial debt at a high discount. The problem of countries that are heavily in debt to creditors that do not participate in the Paris Club negotiations has still not been resolved.

Main Paris Club agreements in 1992

In 1992, a record amount of debt was rescheduled by the Paris Club – over $19 billion (13.2 per cent of which was for Argentina and Brazil). The enhanced Toronto terms were applied to 10 countries, including 8 in Sub-Saharan Africa; debt worth more than $2.8 billion was restructured under these terms. The grant element awarded under the Toronto terms remained below 50 per cent because some creditors availed themselves of the non-concessional option. The proposal to the United States Congress in May 1993 concerning the possibility of partial debt cancellations for the poorest African countries should, if adopted, increase the grant element in these agreements. In response to the acute debt problems of some countries, the participating creditors have shown more flexibility than in the past, agreeing to reschedule debt contracted after the cut-off date (despite the rule concerning the fixed cut-off date).

B.2. Bilateral initiatives

Some donors have cancelled large amounts of debt outside the Paris Club. In fact, these bilateral debt cancellations have been larger than those granted by the Paris Club to the poorest countries.

Over the period 1982-91, DAC countries actually cancelled over $10.5 billion of ODA-related debt, export credits and guaranteed debt owed by the developing countries. Bilateral debt relief represented a larger proportion of this amount than multilateral relief (by the Paris Club to the poorest countries under the Toronto terms and subsequently the enhanced Toronto terms). Most of the bilateral cancellations were for countries in Sub-Saharan Africa.

Bilateral debt forgiveness has expanded considerably since the beginning of the 1990s.

Most of the cancellations took place in 1990 and 1991 – about $8.5 billion, 80 per cent of which were provided by France, Germany, and the United States. Other countries such as Denmark, Sweden and the United Kingdom also forgave relatively large amounts of debt, but spread more evenly throughout the 1980s.

Debt cancellations by DAC countries, 1982-91

in $ million

Years	1982	1983	1984	1985	1986	1987	1988	1989	1990	1991
Amount	83	157	118	289	312	200	300	629	4313	4167

Source: DAC Statistics.
Note: These data exclude the cancellation of Egypt's military debt in 1991.

Paris Club: Principles of Operation and Recent Developments

The Paris Club is an *ad hoc* arrangement by creditor governments, mainly those of OECD countries. It examines, on a case-by-case basis, requests from countries that have difficulty in servicing long-term loans from official bodies, or officially-guaranteed loans. It was set up in 1956 to find a solution to the liquidity problems of Argentina. To date, 205 rescheduling agreements have been concluded for the developing countries, for a total amount of over $155 billion. Since the debt crisis, the number of Paris Club meetings has increased sharply. Between 1983 and 1992, it negotiated 161 agreements, compared with 25 over the period 1973-82. This indicates that many countries have been finding it increasingly difficult to cope with the level of their external debt. The evolution of the principles which underpin the renegotiations reflect changes in the way debt problems are perceived – instead of dealing with temporary liquidity crises the Paris Club agreements now seek to address underlying problems of solvency.

Principles and evolution of the Paris Club

1. *Rescheduled debt*

1.a *A wider variety of debt.* The first Paris Club rescheduling agreements covered only guaranteed commercial debt at market rates. Subsequent agreements also included inter-governmental loans, then interest, and sometimes amounts carried over from previous reschedulings, and arrears.

1.b *Fixed cut-off date.* Eligible debt is debt contracted prior to a cut-off date fixed at the first rescheduling. The purpose of having a fixed cut-off date is to ensure that the supply of finance is not curbed after a debt restructuring; new loans are not affected. There have been very few derogations from this principle, but with some notable exceptions since 1991.

1.c *Consolidated and rescheduled debt.* The Paris Club never renegotiates the total debt stock but only part of the outstanding short- and medium-term maturities, known as the "consolidated debt". In principle, only part of the consolidated debt may be rescheduled.

However, the percentage rescheduled has risen steeply, reaching 100 per cent since 1988.

1.d *Lengthening of the consolidation period.* This is partly linked to the provision of IMF multi-annual loans. Its purpose is to allow the debtor country to avoid having successive recourse to the Club, thereby permitting a relative reduction in the number of agreements per year.

1.e *Treatment of consolidated debt versus treatment of the total debt stock.* Under the enhanced Toronto terms the Paris Club members can also re-examine the total debt stock of the poorest (IDA-only) countries under the goodwill clause. A limited possibility of debt conversion was recently introduced for the poorest and middle-income countries.

2. *Rescheduling conditions*

2.a *Concessionality.* ODA debt claims are no longer rescheduled at market rates but on concessional terms in accordance with ODA conditions of eligibility since 1987. In December 1991, the rescheduling period for such debt was extended to 30 years, including a 12-year grace period.

2.b *Emergence of option "menus".* These make debt management more flexible for creditors, and can guarantee the poorest debtors the possibility of relief on their official commercial or officially-guaranteed credits (grant element increased to 50 per cent by the enhanced Toronto terms).

2.c *Lengthening of maturities for rescheduled loans.* The Houston agreeement for LMICs extended the payback period for ODA loans to 20 years, including a 10-year grace period (previously 10 years, of which a 5-6-year grace period). At the same time, the enhanced Toronto terms increased the repayment period to 23 years, irrespective of the option chosen by the creditor (except for the non-concessional option, which consists in rescheduling debt at market rates with a 25-year maturity and a 14-year grace period).

Cancellations of ODA-related debt by DAC countries, 1990-1991

in $ million

	1990	1991
Total	2 779	4 138
of which:		
Canada	575	0
France	244	633
Germany	1 460	437
Japan	122	160
Netherlands	105	163
United States	174	2 536

Source: DAC Statistics.

Besides being bilateral, this debt relief differs from that granted by the Paris Club in two other respects:

- it also applies to countries that are not eligible for debt relief from the Paris Club;
- prior agreement between the debtor country and the IMF is not necessarily required.

The initiative announced by France at the Libreville Summit in 1992 is an example of such relief. A debt conversion fund for development was set up for Cameroon, Congo, Gabon and Côte d'Ivoire, countries which hitherto had been excluded from debt cancellations. Eligibility is not conditional on the conclusion of a prior

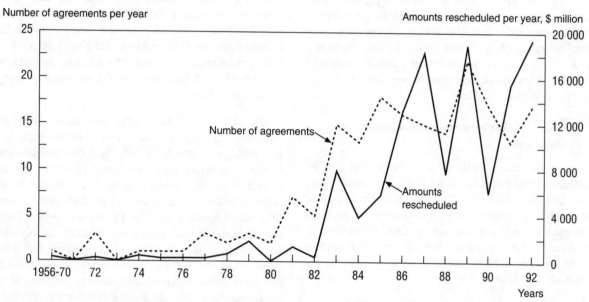

Chart IV.7 **Number of Paris Club agreements,
and amounts of developing country debt rescheduled,
1956-92**

Number of agreements per year

Amounts rescheduled per year, $ million

Number of agreements

Amounts
rescheduled

Source: Secretariat estimates.
Note: On account of its exceptional nature, the agreement signed with Egypt in 1991 is not included.

Chart IV.8 **Features of Paris Club agreements: percentage of consolidated debt, of agreements
which consolidate arrears, and of agreements which consolidate previously rescheduled debt**

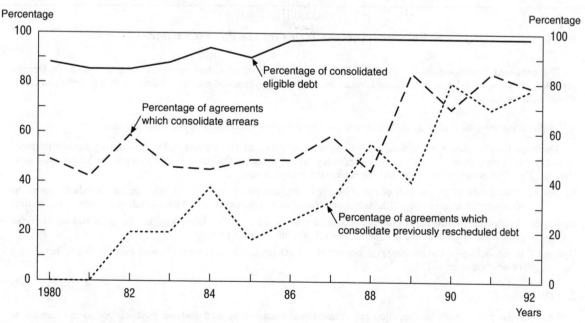

Percentage

Percentage

Percentage of consolidated
eligible debt

Percentage of agreements
which consolidate arrears

Percentage of agreements which
consolidate previously rescheduled debt

Source: Secretariat estimates.
Note: On account of its exceptional nature, the agreement signed with Egypt in 1991 is not included.

agreement with the IMF. The fund is designed to promote high priority development projects (basic productive activities, local development and social projects, environmental protection). It aims to correct the short-term negative impact that structural adjustment programmes can have on social development, the environment and productive investment. In return for the total or partial financing of an eligible project by the beneficiary country, France undertakes to cancel a certain amount of ODA debt. Conditional debt cancellation rather than debt conversion is thus involved.

C. Commercial debt restructuring: principles and developments

As in the case of official debt, bank debt can be restructured multilaterally (under Brady-type agreements or the *IDA Debt Reduction Facility*), or by the creditors. The multilateral approach aims to overcome the problem of burden-sharing which arises in debt restructurings. Co-ordination helps to ensure that the debt relief granted by one creditor does not benefit, *de facto*, another by increasing the value of that debt.

Multilateral bank debt restructuring

Since 1989 the agreements negotiated by banks and debtor countries under the Brady initiative included options for debt and debt service reduction. This served to take account of the fall in the value of debt on the secondary market. The time when agreements provided solely for the rescheduling or refinancing of bank debt is thus at an end. Initially, these debt and debt service reduction agreements did not apply to the poorest countries, but were applied for the first time in 1991 to low-income countries (Mozambique and Niger), which found that a solution to their commercial debt problem was found in the IDA facility set up for that purpose, as well as through bilateral grants.

In 1990, major Brady-type agreements were concluded by severely-indebted countries (Costa Rica, Mexico, Philippines and Venezuela) and commercial banks. Fewer agreements were concluded in 1991, and they related to smaller amounts; only Uruguay and Nigeria reached Brady-type agreements with their creditor banks. In 1992, Argentina and the Philippines signed Brady-type agreements with their creditor banks. In July 1992, an agreement in principle was negotiated for Brazil, which provides for the restructuring of an estimated $44 billion of commercial debt. Reform policies and better economic performance in a number of developing countries facilitated such agreements. Good trade results also enabled them to pay part of their interest arrears and to finance the rescheduling of their commercial debt.

The Enhanced Toronto Terms for the Poorest Countries

The enhanced Toronto terms for the Paris Club renegotiations of IDA-only countries came into force in December 1991. They distinguish between official commercial credits or government-guaranteed debt on the one hand and ODA-related debt on the other.

1. *Official commercial credits or credits guaranteed by governments or their appropriate institutions*

There are three options for restructuring the payments of principal and interest falling due during the consolidation period (which varies from 12 to 35 months depending on the agreement). The first two comprise a 50 per cent grant element. The third is not concessional but the repayment period is longer.

Option A: Cancellation of 50 per cent of the principal falling due during the consolidation period. Rescheduling of the remainder at market rates with repayment spread over a period of 23 years, including a 6-year grace period;

Option B: Rescheduling of the entire consolidated amount at a reduced rate of interest so that the grant element is 50 per cent, with repayment spread over 23 years, but with no grace period;

Option C: Rescheduling of the consolidated amount at market rates, with repayment spread over 25 years, including a 14-year grace period.

2. *ODA-related debt*

ODA-related debt cannot be cancelled but concessional rates are applied and the payback period is extended to 30 years, including a 12-year grace period.

Multilateral and bilateral grants now permit the poorest countries to buy back some or all of their debt at a discount.

The implementation of the *IDA Debt Reduction Facility* also made possible significant reductions in the debt of the poorest countries. After Niger and Mozambique in 1991, Bolivia and Guyana reached an agreement in principle in 1992 on the buy-back at a discount of their commercial debt, to be financed by the IDA facility and bilateral grants. A similar agreement was concluded for Uganda in 1993, and negotiations are now under way for many other countries. In 1992 the conditions attached to the facility were relaxed to further its use:

– the debtor country can use part of the funds to pay for the legal and/or financial consultants required to prepare the agreement;
– short-term debt can also be bought back.

The high discounts granted by banks under this type of agreement may possibly encourage bilateral creditors in the Paris Club to examine debt stock in a few years time, on the principle of comparable treatment of creditors.

Voluntary debt conversions by banks

There were fewer of these operations in 1991-1992 than in previous years, mainly because of the upturn in the secondary debt market and the slower pace of privatisations. They involved Central and South American bank debt, with a major privatisation in Argentina accounting for a large proportion of the total amount of debt conversion in 1992. There were also large debt-for-nature swaps, notably in Bolivia, Brazil and Panama.

D. The role of international financial institutions and multilateral debt

As the earlier analysis of the composition of debt shows, the amount and share of multilateral debt rose steeply over the past decade. The reasons for this were:

– the major involvement of international financial institutions in restructuring official and bank debt;
– the urgent need for financing to restructure indebted economies, at a time when a number of creditors were holding back because of the accumulation of arrears.

The World Bank's IDA Debt Reduction Facility for Buying Back the Debt of the Poorest Countries

Bank debt is only a small component of the total debt of most of the poorest developing countries (about 5 per cent of the provisional figures for 1992). However, payments on bank debt can represent a large part of the debt service of some countries. For example, the long-term bank debt of Niger, the first country to benefit from the IDA facility, represented 7.8 per cent of the country's total external debt before the agreement (end-1990). On the other hand, its payments on this debt amounted to more than 47 per cent of its external debt service.

To find a solution to this problem, the World Bank set up a debt reduction fund in 1989 for the poorest countries, which receive only IDA loans, to be used for buying back all or part of the bank debt of these countries. The minimum discount was set at 70 per cent of the face value of the debt. The debt reduction facility was endowed with a capital of $100 million. The allocation per eligible country was fixed at $10 million, with possible recourse to bilateral grants to make up the difference between the allocation and the amount needed to finance the operation.

Amounts and conditions on which bank debt is restructured by the IDA Debt Reduction Facility

Country	Year	Buy-back amount ($ million)	Buy-back price (% of face value)	Cost ($ million)
Niger	1991	107	18.0	19.3
Mozambique	1991	124	10.0	13.4
Guyana	1992	69	14.0	10.0
Uganda	1993	153	12.0	18.4
Bolivia[1]	1993	170	16.0	27

Source: Secretariat estimates.

1. The agreement comprises three options: *a)* buy-back of debt at a discount; *b)* debt-for-bond swaps; *c)* debt to be swapped for development funds available to non-governmental organisations.

The international financial institutions have played an important role in financing structural adjustment and in the implementation of debt restructuring operations.

Funding for debt restructuring operations

In principle, international financial institutions never renegotiate their own loans. Nonetheless, they do have a role in debt rescheduling operations, by contributing financially to adjustment programmes which precede debt rescheduling and by providing financial advisory services.

In the past, a few debtor countries such as Peru and Zambia have accumulated arrears to the IMF and World Bank. When this happens, a new agreement with the IMF and, in consequence, the possibility of a debt rescheduling with the Paris and London Clubs, are ruled out. At the same time, the debtor country is denied access to new multilateral funds. To find a way out of this impasse, bilateral donors have provided new short-term funds to allow debtor countries to regularise their situation with the international financial institutions, which have then disbursed new loans. The short-term funds supplied by the bilateral donors thus enable the debtor country to regain access to multilateral loans, making it eligible to apply for the Paris and London Clubs to have its official and bank debt rescheduled.

When the contributions of these institutions are in the form of loans, the debtor country's multilateral debt increases accordingly:

- To obtain a rescheduling of its external debt by the Paris or London Clubs, a debtor country must first adopt an IMF-approved adjustment programme which is tied to a standby arrangement, or the provision of a Structural Adjustment Facility (SAF) or an Enhanced Structural Adjustment Facility (ESAF).
- The IMF and the World Bank also provide funds for Brady-type agreements. Debtor countries can use these funds to buy back all or part of their bank debt at a discount, or to finance a guarantee fund for bonds that are swapped for old claims. These guarantees become a debt of the beneficiary country to the international financial institutions. Bank debt is thus replaced partly by new multilateral credits.
- A Debt Reduction Fund of $100 million was set up by the IBRD in 1989 for low-income countries (those which receive only IDA loans). These funds ($10 million per country) are grants and therefore do not increase the beneficiary's debts to international financial institutions.

Contributions in addition to official and bank debt reschedulings

The financial difficulties encountered by many developing countries since the beginning of the 1980s have resulted in an accumulation of arrears to public and private creditors. In consequence, lenders became reluctant to make new loans, with the result that during the ten years following the onset of the debt crisis, countries which previously had borrowed essentially on the international financial market had to turn to multilateral institutions. They, in turn, only provided funds on condition that the countries first adopted adjustment programmes, which explains the growing involvement of multilateral institutions in lending to these countries.

Summary and prospects

The persistence of financial difficulties in the developing countries after the onset of the debt crisis has resulted in considerable progress being made in debt restructuring. From 1988, Paris Club restructuring for the poorest countries included partial debt cancellations. Although the Paris Club still does not forgive debts for other countries, it has extended the pay-back periods for rescheduled loans. Bilateral donors have also cancelled large volumes of debt outside multilateral negotiations. New bank debt restructuring packages which permit debt and debt service reduction have also been put in place. Very recently, multilateral and bilateral grants have enabled some of the poorest countries to buy back all or part of their bank debt. Brady-type agreements have been very successful in some middle-income countries.

Trends in debt and debt service have been evolving in a positive manner and significant progress has been achieved in the terms and amounts of debt restructured. However, the situation of many countries still gives cause for concern.

Debt restructuring has consolidated the adjustment efforts made by some developing countries. It has also enabled a few countries to gain renewed access to funds. This said, however, it seems to have been insufficient for some low-income and low middle-income countries, as attested by their mounting arrears, which in turn also limit their access to new funds. In addition, the continu-

External Debt of the Former Soviet Union (FSU)

The external debt of the FSU has more than doubled since Perestroïka was launched in 1985. In June 1992, it had reached more than $70 billion. At the same time, the country's financial situation and credibility have deteriorated sharply, as arrears to banks and official export agencies have grown sharply.

This has been accompanied by major changes in the composition of its debt:

- Up to 1990, there was a steep increase in non-guaranteed bank loans, brought to a halt by the accumulation of arrears, which resulted in changes in banking practices. Only guaranteed bank loans increased after 1990.
- The share of officially-guaranteed commercial credits fell sharply from 1983, but picked up again from 1991. After having represented more than half of the external debt stock, their share fell to about 19 per cent in 1988, but rose again to 34 per cent in June 1992.

In June 1992, the Bank for International Settlements estimated that over one-third of the FSU's bank loans would mature by mid-1994. To these large repayments has to be added the servicing of guaranteed non-bank export credits. Following the signature of various agreements between Russia and most of the republics of the FSU, Russia undertook to honour all the payments due on the external debt of the FSU in exchange for the right to the foreign assets of the FSU (the so-called zero option or equivalent agreements).

As its economic situation deteriorated in 1992 (falling production and export earnings, and a surging budget deficit), Russia had to negotiate with the members of the Paris Club. An agreement was concluded in April 1993 whereby a large part of its official or guaranteed export credits ($15 billion) would be rescheduled over 10 years, with a 6-month moratorium.

Given the efforts made by the OECD countries to reschedule official credits in the Paris Club or to provide new funds to support the transition process, the question of burden-sharing is very much to the fore. In accordance with the principle of comparable treatment of creditors, the Paris Club expects the banking community to grant Russia debt relief comparable to that granted by governments. The banks have received practically no repayments for more than a year, have already set aside large provisions for their loans to Russia and have granted extensions for the payment of debt service. Nevertheless, some banks have already expressed reservations about rescheduling Russia's debt on terms comparable to those granted by the Paris Club.

Chart IV.9 **Changes in the external debt of the former Soviet Union 1983-June 1992, in $ million**

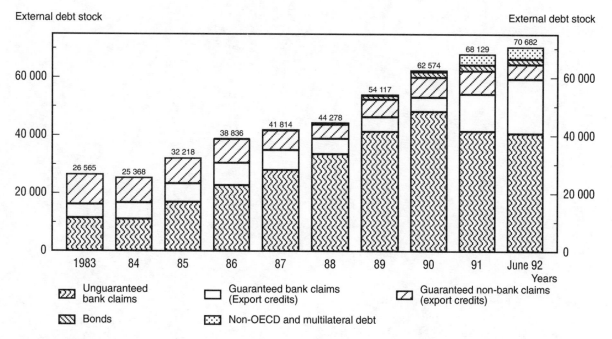

Note: Data for 1992 are provisional.

61

ing growth of non-renegotiable multilateral debt could rapidly become a problem.

The burden-sharing of debt restructuring is a question which arises with increasing frequency. Debt restructuring very often involves a transfer between the various actors – recipient countries, donor countries, creditor banks and multilateral institutions. The debt relief granted by one creditor may ultimately enable the recipient country to meet its commitments to other creditors. Greater co-operation between the various creditors (banks, bilateral donors which may or may not participate in the Paris Club negotiations, multilateral institutions) is desirable. Such co-operation is a prerequisite both for the future development of debt restructuring and to ensure that restructuring benefits the indebted countries first and foremost.

The financial difficulties of the former Soviet Union (FSU) and the other Central and Eastern European countries (CEECs) could also influence the future of debt restructuring for the developing countries:

– In the past, the former Soviet Union made large financial transfers to some developing countries. These gross flows have fallen and will continue to do so, and may even dry up given the economic situation of the former Soviet Union. Some developing countries have large outstanding debts to the former Soviet Union and the CEECs. The possibility of restructuring these debts, and the mechanisms that would be required, are questions that still have to be addressed;

– The former Soviet Union itself needs finance on a large scale; it is also finding it increasingly difficult to honour its commitments. OECD countries recently increased their financial support to the countries of the former Soviet bloc to facilitate their transition to a market economy. There is some concern that this support, either in the form of new resources or debt restructuring, could reduce the resources available for the developing countries.

Chapter V

External Indebtedness Tables

List of Tables V.1 to V.17

Table V.1

**Total disbursed debt of developing countries at year-end 1984-92
by source and terms of lending**

$ billion

	1984	1985	1986	1987	1988	1989	1990	1991	1992
Long-term debt									
I. OECD Countries and capital markets	547	598	637	698	684	685	683	705	710
A. ODA	60	74	90	112	113	115	127	136	141
B. Total export credits	136	158	174	198	171	181	194	202	191
Official export credits	61	72	80	95	89	95	97	104	..
Guaranteed supplier credits	30	32	30	30	23	22	23	22	..
Guaranteed bank credits	45	54	64	73	59	64	75	77	..
C. Financial markets	339	353	360	373	383	372	344	349	360
Banks	310	314	316	324	331	313	280	275	..
Bonds	29	39	44	48	52	59	64	75	..
D. Other private	12	13	13	15	16	17	18	18	18
II. Multilateral	118	146	178	216	210	218	245	262	272
of which: Concessional	37	42	49	58	62	67	76	85	..
Non-concessional	81	104	129	157	149	150	168	177	..
memo: total IMF	34	38	40	41	34	32	32	33	32
III. Non-OECD creditor countries	107	116	128	153	161	168	167	165	164
Sub-total: Long-term debt	**772**	**860**	**943**	**1067**	**1056**	**1071**	**1094**	**1133**	**1146**
of which: Concessional	143	165	192	237	248	258	281	301	..
Non-concessional	630	695	751	829	808	812	813	832	..
Short-term debt									
Banks	154	175	182	197	199	204	237	251	286
Export credits	25	31	38	45	47	51	64	67	68
Sub-total: Short-term debt	**179**	**206**	**220**	**242**	**246**	**255**	**301**	**318**	**354**
Other identified liabilities	20	22	21	27	30	27	33	34	34
Total external debt	**971**	**1089**	**1185**	**1335**	**1332**	**1353**	**1428**	**1485**	**1534**

Table V.2

**Total annual debt service of developing countries during 1984-92
by source and terms of lending**

$ billion

	1984	1985	1986	1987	1988	1989	1990	1991	1992
Long-term debt service payments									
I. OECD Countries and capital markets	88.8	98.8	93.2	95.9	103.3	101.3	93.2	90.4	90.6
A. ODA	3.1	3.1	4.0	4.4	5.8	5.7	6.3	6.2	6.6
B. Export credits	33.6	40.7	41.9	43.8	37.0	40.2	35.6	33.7	35.0
C. Financial markets	50.4	53.5	45.8	46.3	59.0	53.7	48.9	47.0	45.5
D. Other private	1.8	1.4	1.6	1.4	1.5	1.7	2.4	3.5	3.5
II. Multilateral	13.0	16.5	23.4	30.3	32.0	30.0	34.7	36.0	37.1
of which: Concessional	1.2	1.5	2.1	2.3	2.4	2.3	2.4	2.4	..
memo: total IMF	4.9	6.7	9.6	12.2	10.7	10.0	10.4	8.8	10.8
III. Non-OECD creditor countries	4.0	5.2	4.7	5.0	4.9	5.4	6.3	5.8	5.5
Sub-total: Long-term debt service	**105.9**	**120.7**	**121.6**	**131.5**	**140.7**	**137.4**	**134.3**	**132.3**	**133.2**
of which: Concessional	4.6	5.2	7.0	7.7	9.0	8.7	10.1	9.8	..
Amortization, long-term debt	51.9	65.8	70.4	80.2	79.7	79.4	80.4	82.6	88.2
Interest, long-term debt	54.1	54.9	51.2	51.3	61.0	58.0	53.9	49.6	45.0
Interest, short-term debt	21.4	17.1	15.3	16.3	20.0	22.7	21.7	17.9	16.8
Total debt service	**127.3**	**137.8**	**137.0**	**147.9**	**160.7**	**160.1**	**156.0**	**150.2**	**150.0**

Table V.3

**Total disbursed debt of low-income developing countries at year-end 1984-92
by source and terms of lending**

$ billion

	1984	1985	1986	1987	1988	1989	1990	1991	1992
Long-term debt									
I. OECD Countries and capital markets	124	146	171	209	212	220	232	241	249
A. ODA	38	47	58	73	75	77	85	90	92
B. Total export credits	44	53	63	72	63	70	66	71	71
Official export credits	22	27	35	42	41	45	41	45	..
Guaranteed supplier credits	10	10	10	9	8	9	7	7	..
Guaranteed bank credits	13	16	19	21	15	16	18	19	..
C. Financial markets	38	42	47	60	69	68	75	73	79
Banks	35	37	40	51	60	58	63	60	..
Bonds	3	4	7	9	10	10	11	13	..
D. Other private	3	4	4	4	5	6	6	7	7
II. Multilateral	57	69	81	99	101	109	123	137	152
of which: Concessional	30	35	40	48	52	58	66	75	..
Non-concessional	27	34	41	50	49	51	56	62	..
memo: total IMF	15	16	17	17	14	13	12	14	15
III. Non-OECD creditor countries	38	41	46	54	57	60	62	63	63
Sub-total: Long-term debt	**219**	**255**	**298**	**362**	**371**	**389**	**416**	**440**	**464**
of which: Concessional	71	85	101	126	133	141	161	175	..
Non-concessional	148	170	197	236	238	249	255	265	..
Short-term debt									
Banks	30	36	37	39	41	37	50	58	66
Export credits	9	11	14	17	17	19	23	24	24
Sub-total: Short-term debt	**39**	**47**	**51**	**56**	**58**	**56**	**73**	**82**	**90**
Other identified liabilities	8	8	6	8	10	6	7	7	6
Total external debt	**266**	**310**	**355**	**426**	**438**	**452**	**496**	**529**	**560**

Table V.4

**Total annual debt service of low-income developing countries during 1984-92
by source and terms of lending**

$ billion

	1984	1985	1986	1987	1988	1989	1990	1991	1992
Long-term debt service payments									
I. OECD Countries and capital markets	16.6	20.8	19.2	20.3	25.7	26.6	27.4	25.8	25.1
A. ODA	1.8	1.8	2.2	2.5	3.5	3.3	3.7	3.5	3.3
B. Export credits	7.9	10.7	10.9	11.7	10.4	11.3	10.8	9.9	9.5
C. Financial markets	6.4	7.7	5.2	5.2	11.2	11.6	12.2	11.3	11.2
D. Other private	0.5	0.6	0.8	0.8	0.7	0.5	0.8	1.1	1.1
II. Multilateral	4.7	5.9	8.3	10.1	10.5	10.3	12.4	12.7	12.4
of which: Concessional	0.7	0.9	1.5	1.6	1.7	1.6	1.7	1.7	..
memo: total IMF	2.3	3.1	4.0	4.6	4.2	3.9	4.2	3.2	3.7
III. Non-OECD creditor countries	1.6	1.9	1.6	1.7	1.8	1.6	1.6	1.4	1.4
Sub-total: Long-term debt service	**22.8**	**28.7**	**29.1**	**32.1**	**38.0**	**38.6**	**41.5**	**39.9**	**38.9**
of which: Concessional	2.5	2.8	3.7	4.2	5.2	4.9	5.5	5.3	..
Amortization, long-term debt	12.6	17.1	17.5	19.5	22.2	21.2	24.1	23.6	22.1
Interest, long-term debt	10.2	11.6	11.7	12.7	15.8	17.4	17.4	16.3	16.8
Interest, short-term debt	4.7	4.0	3.5	3.7	4.5	4.7	4.6	4.0	3.7
Total debt service	**27.5**	**32.7**	**32.7**	**35.8**	**42.5**	**43.4**	**46.0**	**43.9**	**42.6**

Table V.5

**Total disbursed debt of least developed countries at year-end 1984-92
by source and terms of lending**

$ billion

	1984	1985	1986	1987	1988	1989	1990	1991	1992
Long-term debt									
I. OECD Countries and capital markets	19	22	26	31	31	31	33	31	30
A. ODA	8	10	12	16	17	17	18	18	17
B. Total export credits	8	10	11	12	11	11	12	11	11
Official export credits	5	6	7	9	8	9	9	9	..
Guaranteed supplier credits	2	2	2	2	2	1	1	1	..
Guaranteed bank credits	2	2	2	2	1	1	1	1	..
C. Financial markets	3	3	3	3	3	3	3	2	2
Banks	3	3	3	3	3	3	3	2	..
Bonds	0	0	0	0	0	0	0	0	..
D. Other private	0	0	0	0	0	0	0	0	0
II. Multilateral	17	20	24	29	31	33	38	41	46
of which: Concessional	11	14	16	21	23	26	31	35	..
Non-concessional	6	6	7	8	8	7	7	6	..
memo: total IMF	5	5	5	6	6	5	5	5	5
III. Non-OECD creditor countries	19	21	24	29	32	33	33	34	34
Sub-total: Long-term debt	**55**	**63**	**74**	**90**	**94**	**97**	**104**	**106**	**109**
of which: Concessional	23	28	34	44	49	52	58	63	..
Non-concessional	32	36	40	46	45	45	45	43	..
Short-term debt									
Banks	3	4	4	4	4	4	5	4	4
Export credits	1	2	3	4	4	4	5	5	6
Sub-total: Short-term debt	**5**	**6**	**7**	**8**	**8**	**8**	**10**	**9**	**10**
Other identified liabilities	1	1	2	2	3	1	1	0	0
Total external debt	**61**	**70**	**82**	**101**	**105**	**106**	**114**	**116**	**120**

Table V.6

**Total annual debt service of least developed countries during 1984-92
by source and terms of lending**

$ billion

	1984	1985	1986	1987	1988	1989	1990	1991	1992
Long-term debt service payments									
I. OECD Countries and capital markets	1.8	1.9	2.1	1.9	2.4	2.6	2.5	1.7	1.7
A. ODA	0.3	0.3	0.4	0.4	0.5	0.5	0.5	0.4	0.4
B. Export credits	1.0	1.1	1.3	1.2	1.1	1.2	1.4	0.8	0.9
C. Financial markets	0.5	0.5	0.4	0.3	0.7	0.9	0.7	0.5	0.4
D. Other private	0.0	0.0	0.0	0.0	0.0	0.0	0.0	0.0	0.0
II. Multilateral	1.3	1.4	2.1	1.9	1.7	1.9	1.8	1.9	2.2
of which: Concessional	0.3	0.4	0.6	0.6	0.6	0.6	0.6	0.6	..
memo: total IMF	0.8	0.8	1.3	1.0	0.8	1.1	0.8	0.6	0.8
III. Non-OECD creditor countries	0.5	0.5	0.7	0.6	0.7	0.7	0.5	0.4	0.4
Sub-total: Long-term debt service	**3.6**	**3.7**	**4.9**	**4.4**	**4.8**	**5.2**	**4.8**	**4.0**	**4.3**
of which: Concessional	0.6	0.7	1.1	1.1	1.3	1.3	1.2	1.1	..
Amortization, long-term debt	2.0	2.2	2.9	2.6	2.9	3.2	2.9	2.3	2.7
Interest, long-term debt	1.6	1.6	2.0	1.9	1.9	2.0	1.9	1.7	1.6
Interest, short-term debt	0.5	0.4	0.4	0.4	0.6	0.5	0.4	0.3	0.3
Total debt service	**4.1**	**4.2**	**5.3**	**4.9**	**5.4**	**5.8**	**5.3**	**4.3**	**4.6**

Table V.7

**Total disbursed debt of lower middle-income developing countries at year-end 1984-92
by source and terms of lending**

$ billion

	1984	1985	1986	1987	1988	1989	1990	1991	1992
Long-term debt									
I. OECD Countries and capital markets	117	133	140	154	149	151	161	170	167
A. ODA	14	17	21	26	26	26	30	33	35
B. Total export credits	32	40	44	51	44	45	54	56	53
Official export credits	13	16	18	21	19	19	21	22	..
Guaranteed supplier credits	8	9	8	8	7	6	9	8	..
Guaranteed bank credits	11	15	19	23	18	19	24	25	..
C. Financial markets	70	74	73	75	78	78	76	80	78
Banks	65	66	65	65	66	64	60	63	..
Bonds	5	8	9	10	12	14	16	17	..
D. Other private	2	2	2	2	2	2	1	1	1
II. Multilateral	28	36	44	54	51	51	56	58	56
of which: Concessional	5	6	7	7	7	7	8	8	..
Non-concessional	23	30	38	47	44	44	48	50	..
memo: total IMF	7	8	8	8	6	6	5	5	4
III. Non-OECD creditor countries	59	65	70	84	88	90	91	88	89
Sub-total: Long-term debt	**204**	**233**	**254**	**292**	**289**	**293**	**308**	**317**	**312**
of which: Concessional	57	62	70	85	88	90	96	101	..
Non-concessional	148	171	185	207	201	202	212	216	..
Short-term debt									
Banks	23	26	30	32	29	31	40	43	43
Export credits	6	8	9	11	12	13	18	18	18
Sub-total: Short-term debt	**28**	**34**	**39**	**43**	**41**	**44**	**58**	**61**	**61**
Other identified liabilities	2	3	3	3	3	3	3	5	5
Total external debt	**235**	**270**	**296**	**338**	**333**	**339**	**370**	**382**	**378**

Table V.8

**Total annual debt service of lower middle-income developing countries during 1984-92
by source and terms of lending**

$ billion

	1984	1985	1986	1987	1988	1989	1990	1991	1992
Long-term debt service payments									
I. OECD Countries and capital markets	20.3	24.8	22.1	21.4	25.8	27.5	29.7	26.9	26.0
A. ODA	0.8	0.8	1.0	1.1	1.4	1.5	1.8	1.9	2.0
B. Export credits	9.3	10.3	10.4	10.5	10.0	11.1	11.8	11.2	11.0
C. Financial markets	10.0	13.6	10.5	9.7	14.2	14.6	15.8	13.6	12.8
D. Other private	0.2	0.1	0.1	0.1	0.2	0.3	0.2	0.2	0.2
II. Multilateral	3.8	5.0	6.8	8.1	8.8	8.5	9.3	9.9	10.2
of which: Concessional	0.3	0.4	0.4	0.5	0.5	0.5	0.5	0.5	..
memo: total IMF	1.3	1.8	2.4	2.6	2.2	2.0	1.9	1.3	1.5
III. Non-OECD creditor countries	1.7	2.3	2.3	2.5	2.5	3.1	4.1	2.8	2.9
Sub-total: Long-term debt service	**25.8**	**32.1**	**31.2**	**32.0**	**37.1**	**39.1**	**43.1**	**39.6**	**39.1**
of which: Concessional	1.3	1.5	2.0	2.3	2.4	2.4	3.4	2.9	..
Amortization, long-term debt	13.7	19.3	18.5	18.5	23.7	25.2	28.6	26.4	26.0
Interest, long-term debt	12.1	12.8	12.7	13.5	13.5	13.9	14.5	13.2	13.1
Interest, short-term debt	3.7	2.6	2.5	2.6	3.1	3.4	3.6	3.1	2.6
Total debt service	**29.4**	**34.7**	**33.7**	**34.6**	**40.3**	**42.4**	**46.7**	**42.7**	**41.7**

Table V.9

**Total disbursed debt of total African countries at year-end 1984-92
by source and terms of lending**

$ billion

	1984	1985	1986	1987	1988	1989	1990	1991	1992
Long-term debt									
I. OECD Countries and capital markets	85	100	110	127	126	130	129	130	123
A. ODA	15	18	23	28	29	32	34	36	37
B. Total export credits	44	54	65	74	62	67	63	65	59
Official export credits	22	27	34	41	39	43	38	40	..
Guaranteed supplier credits	8	9	8	7	7	6	6	5	..
Guaranteed bank credits	14	18	23	26	16	18	19	20	..
C. Financial markets	24	24	19	21	31	26	26	22	22
Banks	23	23	17	20	29	25	24	21	..
Bonds	1	1	1	1	2	2	2	2	..
D. Other private	2	3	3	3	4	5	5	6	5
II. Multilateral	26	32	39	49	49	52	58	63	68
of which: Concessional	12	14	16	21	22	25	28	32	..
Non-concessional	14	18	23	28	27	27	30	31	..
memo: total IMF	7	8	8	9	8	8	8	9	8
III. Non-OECD creditor countries	30	32	35	39	42	45	44	42	41
Sub-total: Long-term debt	**141**	**164**	**183**	**215**	**217**	**227**	**232**	**235**	**232**
of which: Concessional	29	34	41	51	54	59	65	71	..
Non-concessional	112	130	143	165	163	168	166	164	..
Short-term debt									
Banks	16	18	24	24	21	23	24	22	23
Export credits	6	8	11	15	16	19	23	23	24
Sub-total: Short-term debt	**22**	**26**	**34**	**39**	**37**	**41**	**46**	**45**	**47**
Other identified liabilities	2	2	2	4	4	3	3	3	3
Total external debt	**165**	**192**	**220**	**258**	**258**	**272**	**281**	**283**	**282**

Table V.10

**Total annual debt service of total African countries during 1984-92
by source and terms of lending**

$ billion

	1984	1985	1986	1987	1988	1989	1990	1991	1992
Long-term debt service payments									
I. OECD Countries and capital markets	16.0	17.6	16.3	12.6	17.5	19.4	21.0	18.6	17.2
A. ODA	0.6	0.7	0.8	0.8	1.2	1.1	1.4	1.0	1.1
B. Export credits	9.2	11.6	11.0	9.1	8.9	10.2	11.0	10.0	9.8
C. Financial markets	5.8	4.7	3.7	1.9	6.8	7.7	7.9	6.6	5.4
D. Other private	0.4	0.6	0.8	0.8	0.7	0.4	0.7	1.0	0.9
II. Multilateral	2.6	3.2	4.6	5.1	5.5	5.5	6.0	6.5	7.3
of which: Concessional	0.3	0.5	0.7	0.7	0.7	0.7	0.7	0.7	..
memo: total IMF	1.2	1.5	2.2	2.0	1.9	2.0	1.7	1.4	2.0
III. Non-OECD creditor countries	1.1	1.5	1.0	1.0	1.1	1.3	1.2	1.8	1.8
Sub-total: Long-term debt service	**19.7**	**22.4**	**21.9**	**18.6**	**24.1**	**26.2**	**28.2**	**26.9**	**26.3**
of which: Concessional	1.0	1.1	1.5	1.5	1.9	1.9	2.2	2.3	..
Amortization, long-term debt	12.8	14.3	13.5	10.6	14.4	15.0	18.7	17.2	17.2
Interest, long-term debt	6.9	8.1	8.4	8.1	9.7	11.3	9.5	9.7	9.1
Interest, short-term debt	2.4	1.9	1.9	2.2	2.5	2.7	2.4	1.7	1.3
Total debt service	**22.1**	**24.3**	**23.8**	**20.9**	**26.6**	**28.9**	**30.6**	**28.7**	**27.6**

Table V.11

**Total disbursed debt of Sub-Saharan African countries at year-end 1984-92
by source and terms of lending**

$ billion

	1984	1985	1986	1987	1988	1989	1990	1991	1992
Long-term debt									
I. OECD Countries and capital markets	40	46	54	67	66	71	73	73	67
A.	7	9	11	15	15	17	18	18	18
B.	17	21	30	36	29	35	36	38	35
	7	9	17	21	20	25	27	28	..
	3	3	3	3	3	3	3	3	..
	7	9	11	11	6	6	7	7	..
C.	14	13	10	13	17	15	13	10	9
	13	13	9	13	17	14	13	10	..
	0	0	1	1	0	0	0	0	..
D.	2	3	3	3	4	5	5	6	5
II. Mul...	19	23	28	36	36	38	44	47	51
of w...	9	11	13	17	19	21	26	29	..
	10	13	15	19	17	16	18	18	..
	6	7	7	8	7	6	7	7	6
III. Non-	16	17	20	23	24	26	28	28	27
Sub-total:	**75**	**87**	**103**	**126**	**126**	**135**	**144**	**147**	**145**
of which	16	19	24	32	34	38	44	48	..
	59	67	79	94	92	97	100	100	..
Short-term									
Banks	6	7	11	11	10	10	12	11	11
Export c...	3	4	6	9	9	11	13	13	12
Sub-total:	**9**	**12**	**17**	**20**	**19**	**21**	**25**	**24**	**23**
Other iden...	1	1	1	1	1	1	1	1	1
Total exte...	**84**	**99**	**121**	**147**	**146**	**157**	**170**	**172**	**169**

Table V.12

**Total annual debt service of Sub-Saharan African countries during 1984-92
by source and terms of lending**

$ billion

	1984	1985	1986	1987	1988	1989	1990	1991	1992
Long-term debt service payments									
I. OECD Countries and capital markets	6.9	8.4	7.5	6.2	7.6	7.4	8.5	7.1	6.3
A. ODA	0.3	0.3	0.4	0.4	0.6	0.6	0.7	0.5	0.5
B. Export credits	3.2	4.5	4.6	4.0	3.0	3.4	3.9	3.1	2.8
C. Financial markets	2.9	3.0	1.7	1.0	3.4	2.9	3.2	2.5	2.0
D. Other private	0.4	0.6	0.8	0.8	0.6	0.4	0.7	1.0	1.0
II. Multilateral	1.8	2.2	3.2	3.3	3.6	3.7	3.6	3.8	4.1
of which: Concessional	0.3	0.3	0.5	0.5	0.6	0.6	0.5	0.6	..
memo: total IMF	1.0	1.2	1.7	1.5	1.5	1.6	1.2	0.8	1.3
III. Non-OECD creditor countries	0.6	0.9	0.6	0.5	0.5	0.5	0.5	0.4	0.4
Sub-total: Long-term debt service	**9.3**	**11.4**	**11.2**	**10.0**	**11.8**	**11.5**	**12.5**	**11.2**	**10.8**
of which: Concessional	0.6	0.7	0.9	1.0	1.2	1.1	1.2	1.0	..
Amortization, long-term debt	5.7	7.5	7.0	6.0	6.6	5.7	7.4	6.2	6.2
Interest, long-term debt	3.7	4.0	4.2	4.0	5.2	5.8	5.1	5.0	4.6
Interest, short-term debt	1.0	0.8	0.8	1.0	1.1	1.0	0.9	0.7	0.6
Total debt service	**10.3**	**12.2**	**12.0**	**10.9**	**12.9**	**12.6**	**13.5**	**11.9**	**11.4**

Table V.13

**Total disbursed debt of Central and South American countries at year-end 1984-92
by source and terms of lending**

$ billion

	1984	1985	1986	1987	1988	1989	1990	1991	1992
Long-term debt									
I. OECD Countries and capital markets	265	267	280	289	280	269	246	240	241
A. ODA	8	10	12	13	13	13	15	14	13
B. Total export credits	31	35	38	46	45	47	55	59	59
Official export credits	13	16	17	24	26	28	33	35	..
Guaranteed supplier credits	6	6	6	5	5	5	5	4	..
Guaranteed bank credits	12	13	16	16	13	14	16	19	..
C. Financial markets	217	214	222	221	212	199	167	157	160
Banks	201	195	204	203	194	176	142	130	..
Bonds	16	18	18	18	19	23	25	27	..
D. Other private	8	8	8	9	9	9	9	9	9
II. Multilateral	35	45	57	70	67	68	79	80	79
of which: Concessional	5	5	5	6	6	6	7	7	..
Non-concessional	30	40	51	64	61	62	72	73	..
memo: total IMF	12	15	16	18	16	16	18	17	15
III. Non-OECD creditor countries	29	29	30	36	36	36	36	37	37
Sub-total: Long-term debt	**329**	**342**	**368**	**395**	**383**	**373**	**360**	**357**	**357**
of which: Concessional	31	33	36	42	43	44	46	46	..
Non-concessional	298	309	331	353	339	329	314	311	..
Short-term debt									
Banks	53	61	58	60	59	60	63	68	75
Export credits	4	6	8	11	12	12	16	17	17
Sub-total: Short-term debt	**57**	**67**	**67**	**71**	**71**	**72**	**79**	**85**	**92**
Other identified liabilities	3	3	3	4	4	4	5	5	5
Total external debt	**389**	**412**	**438**	**469**	**458**	**449**	**444**	**446**	**454**

Table V.14

**Total annual debt service of Central and South American countries during 1984-92
by source and terms of lending**

$ billion

	1984	1985	1986	1987	1988	1989	1990	1991	1992
Long-term debt service payments									
I. OECD Countries and capital markets	35.3	33.8	30.6	26.5	35.5	28.7	24.2	27.4	24.6
A. ODA	0.3	0.4	0.6	0.5	0.5	0.6	0.6	0.7	0.6
B. Export credits	6.2	7.0	9.0	8.3	7.3	7.9	8.0	8.0	7.9
C. Financial markets	27.7	25.8	20.4	17.1	27.0	19.3	14.5	17.0	14.3
D. Other private	1.1	0.6	0.6	0.5	0.7	1.0	1.1	1.8	1.8
II. Multilateral	4.0	5.0	8.3	11.0	11.4	11.6	14.0	15.6	17.4
of which: Concessional	0.3	0.3	0.3	0.3	0.3	0.3	0.4	0.5	..
memo: total IMF	0.9	1.4	3.1	4.5	4.0	4.3	5.1	4.9	5.2
III. Non-OECD creditor countries	1.2	1.3	1.3	1.1	1.0	1.0	1.5	1.2	1.2
Sub-total: Long-term debt service	**40.6**	**40.3**	**40.2**	**38.5**	**47.9**	**41.3**	**39.7**	**44.2**	**43.2**
of which: Concessional	0.7	0.8	1.2	1.1	1.0	1.0	1.5	1.2	..
Amortization, long-term debt	12.5	13.4	17.9	17.6	20.3	19.5	20.1	27.1	28.1
Interest, long-term debt	28.1	26.8	22.3	20.9	27.6	21.8	19.6	17.1	15.1
Interest, short-term debt	6.6	5.1	4.5	4.4	5.3	5.9	4.7	4.3	4.0
Total debt service	**47.2**	**45.4**	**44.8**	**43.0**	**53.2**	**47.2**	**44.4**	**48.5**	**47.2**

Table V.15

Total disbursed debt of total Asian countries at year-end 1984-92
by source and terms of lending

$ billion

	1984	1985	1986	1987	1988	1989	1990	1991	1992
Long-term debt									
I. OECD Countries and capital markets	124	147	163	185	182	185	203	227	237
A. ODA	29	37	46	58	59	59	65	71	75
B. Total export credits	32	35	35	36	29	31	37	39	40
Official export credits	11	13	13	13	12	13	14	17	..
Guaranteed supplier credits	10	11	9	8	5	6	6	6	..
Guaranteed bank credits	10	11	13	15	11	12	17	16	..
C. Financial markets	62	73	81	89	92	93	99	114	119
Banks	54	59	60	65	67	68	72	83	..
Bonds	8	15	21	25	25	25	26	31	..
D. Other private	2	2	2	2	3	3	3	3	3
II. Multilateral	43	51	60	68	68	72	81	92	99
of which: Concessional	18	21	23	27	29	31	36	42	..
Non-concessional	25	30	36	41	39	40	45	50	..
memo: total IMF	11	12	12	11	8	7	5	7	8
III. Non-OECD creditor countries	31	35	38	48	52	53	54	55	56
Sub-total: Long-term debt	**199**	**233**	**261**	**302**	**302**	**310**	**338**	**374**	**392**
of which: Concessional	69	82	95	119	124	128	141	153	..
Non-concessional	129	151	166	184	178	182	197	221	..
Short-term debt									
Banks	43	51	53	63	67	65	87	103	108
Export credits	7	8	9	9	10	9	10	10	10
Sub-total: Short-term debt	**51**	**59**	**62**	**72**	**77**	**74**	**97**	**113**	**118**
Other identified liabilities	8	8	6	6	8	5	6	6	6
Total external debt	**257**	**300**	**329**	**381**	**387**	**390**	**442**	**493**	**516**

Table V.16

Total annual debt service of total Asian countries during 1984-92
by source and terms of lending

$ billion

	1984	1985	1986	1987	1988	1989	1990	1991	1992
Long-term debt service payments									
I. OECD Countries and capital markets	19.9	29.4	27.6	37.7	30.3	32.1	30.2	28.1	30.3
A. ODA	1.7	1.6	2.0	2.5	3.3	3.2	3.2	3.6	3.8
B. Export credits	7.9	11.3	10.5	14.9	10.0	11.3	9.4	9.2	10.0
C. Financial markets	10.2	16.3	14.9	20.1	16.8	17.3	17.1	14.7	16.0
D. Other private	0.2	0.2	0.2	0.1	0.2	0.3	0.5	0.6	0.5
II. Multilateral	4.2	5.7	7.3	10.4	10.3	8.9	10.2	9.7	10.0
of which: Concessional	0.4	0.6	0.9	1.1	1.0	1.0	1.1	0.9	..
memo: total IMF	1.9	2.8	3.1	4.5	3.5	2.7	3.1	2.3	2.6
III. Non-OECD creditor countries	0.9	1.1	1.3	1.5	1.2	1.3	1.6	1.3	1.3
Sub-total: Long-term debt service	**25.1**	**36.2**	**36.2**	**49.6**	**41.9**	**42.3**	**42.0**	**39.1**	**41.6**
of which: Concessional	2.2	2.5	3.3	4.1	4.7	4.5	5.0	5.0	..
Amortization, long-term debt	13.3	23.8	24.1	35.8	28.1	27.1	26.7	24.7	26.2
Interest, long-term debt	11.8	12.4	12.1	13.8	13.8	15.2	15.4	14.4	15.4
Interest, short-term debt	6.3	5.1	4.5	5.0	6.4	7.3	7.5	6.6	7.0
Total debt service	**31.4**	**41.3**	**40.8**	**54.5**	**48.3**	**49.6**	**49.5**	**45.7**	**48.6**

Table V.17. **Multilateral official debt reorganisation for developing countries**

Debtor country and date of agreement	Consolidation period	Estimated amount[a] rescheduled ($ million)	Maturity (years)[b]
Angola			
July 1989	July 1989-September 1990	445	10
Argentina			
June 1956	1955-June 1956	500	9
October 1962	1963-1964	270	8
June 1965	1965	274	5
January 1985	1985	2 200	10
May 1987	May 1986-June 1988	1 400	10
December 1989	January 1990-March 1991	2 400	10
September 1991	October 1991-July 1992	1 700	10
July 1992	July 1992-April 1995	2 700	16
Benin			
June 1989	June 1989-June 1990	193	Menu
December 1991	January 1992-August 1993	152	Menu*
June 1993	August 1993-December 1993	25	Menu*
Bolivia			
June 1986	July 1986-June 1987	450	10
November 1988	October 1988-December 1989	300	9
March 1990	1990-1991	276	Menu
January 1992	18 months	65	Menu*
Brazil			
May 1961	June 1961-1965	300	5½
July 1964	1964-1965	270	5
November 1983	August 1983-December 1984	3 400	8½
January 1987	January 1987-June 1987	3 800	6
July 1988	August 1988-March 1990	5 000	10
February 1992	January 1992-August 1993	10 500	14
Burkina Faso			
March 1991	March 1991-May 1992	71	Menu
May 1993	April 1993-December 1993	36	Menu*
Cambodia			
January 1972	1972	2	8
October 1972	1973	2	10
Cameroon			
May 1989	April 1989-March 1990	535	10
January 1992	January 1992-October 1992	960	15
Central Afr. Republic			
June 1981	1981	50	9
July 1983	1983	19	10
November 1985	July 1985-December 1986	14	10
December 1988	1989-June 1990	(8)	Menu
June 1990	1990	4	Menu
Chile			
February 1965	1965-1966	90	5-6
April 1972	November 1971-1972	258	8
March 1974	1973-1974	460	8½
May 1975	1975	230	9
July 1985	July 1985-1986	170	7
April 1987	Mid-April 1987-1988	150	7
Congo			
July 1986	August 1986-March 1988	750	10
September 1990	September 1990-May 1992	1 052	15

a) Including in several cases, arrears accumulated prior to the consolidation period.
b) Data relate to consolidation of export credits.
* Improved Toronto terms.

Table V.17. **Multilateral official debt reorganisation for developing countries** *(Cont'd)*

Debtor country and date of agreement	Consolidation period	Estimated amount[a] rescheduled ($ million)	Maturity (years)[b]
Costa Rica			
January 1983	July 1982-December 1983	115	9
April 1985	1985	190	10
May 1989	April 1989-May 1990	182	10
July 1991	July 1991-March 1992	125	10
June 1993		58	
Côte d'Ivoire			
May 1984	December 1983-1984	(300)	9
June 1985	1985	230	9
June 1986	1986-1988	500	9
December 1987	January 1988-April 1989	560	10
December 1989	1990-April 1991	880	14
November 1991	October 1991-September 1992	930	15
Cuba			
February 1983	September 1982-December 1983	415	8½
July 1984	1984	250	9
July 1985	1985	150	10
July 1986	1986	..	10
Dominican Republic			
May 1985	1985-March 1986	290	10
November 1991	October 1991-April 1993	780	15
Ecuador			
July 1983	June 1983-March 1984	195	8
April 1985	1985-1987	400	8
January 1988	January 1988-February 1989	310	10
October 1989	November 1989-December 1990	394	10
January 1992	January 1992-December 1992	339	15
Egypt			
May 1987	Mid-May 1987-November 1988	8 500	10
May 1991	Debt Reduction Agreement	28 164	n.a
El Salvador			
September 1990	September 1990-September 1991	143	15
Ethiopia			
December 1992	December 1992-January 1996	441	Menu*
Gabon			
June 1978	Not available	105	..
January 1987	October 1986-December 1987	390	10
March 1988	1988	280	10
September 1989	September 1989-December 1990	545	10
October 1991	October 1991-January 1993	490	10
Gambia			
September 1986	October 1986-September 1987	25	10
Ghana			
December 1966	June 1966-1968	170	10
October 1968	1969-June 1972	100	9
July 1970	July 1970-June 1972	(18)	10
March 1970	February 1972 onwards	190	29
Guatemala			
March 1993		440	

a) Including in several cases, arrears accumulated prior to the consolidation period.
b) Data relate to consolidation of export credits.
* Improved Toronto terms.

Table V.17. **Multilateral official debt reorganisation for developing countries** (Cont'd)

Debtor country and date of agreement	Consolidation period	Estimated amount[a] rescheduled ($ million)	Maturity (years)[b]
Guinea			
April 1986	January 1986-February 1987	190	10
April 1989	1989	155	Menu
November 1992	Arrears up to December 1992	203	Menu*
Guinea Bissau			
October 1987	July 1987-1988	22	20
October 1989	October 1989-December 1990	21	Menu
Guinea (Equatorial)			
July 1985	1985-June 1986	38	10
November 1992		203	
Guyana			
May 1989	1989-February 1990	195	20
September 1990	September 1990-July 1993	123	Menu
May 1993	August 1993-December 1993	39	Menu*
Honduras			
September 1990	September 1990-July 1991	280	15
October 1992	September 1992-July 1995	180	Menu*
India			
March 1968	April 1968-March 1971	(100)	25-30
June 1971	April 1971-March 1972	100	25-30
February 1973	April 1972-March 1974	340	25-30
October 1974	April 1974-March 1975	194	25-30
June 1975	April 1975-March 1976	228	25-30
May 1976	April 1976-March 1977	200	25-30
July 1977	April 1977-March 1978	110	25-30
Indonesia			
December 1966	July 1966-1967	310	10
October 1967	1968	110	10
October 1968	1969	180	10
April 1970	1970-1983	2 090	30
Jamaica			
July 1984	1984-March 1985	120	9
July 1985	April 1985-March 1986	68	10
March 1987	1987-March 1988	126	10
October 1988	June 1988-November 1989	(160)	10
April 1990	December 1989-May 1991	160	10
July 1991	June 1991-July 1992	97	15
January 1993	October 1992-September 1995	291	16
Jordan			
July 1989	July 1989-December 1990	590	10
February 1992	January 1992-June 1993	771	15
Liberia			
December 1980	July 1980-December 1981	20	9
December 1981	January 1982-June 1983	30	9
December 1983	July 1983-June 1984	10	9
December 1984	July 1984-June 1985	18	10
Madagascar			
April 1981	January 1981-June 1982	240	9
July 1982	July 1982-June 1983	107	9
March 1984	July 1983-1984	340	11
May 1985	1985-March 1986	280	11
October 1986	April 1986-December 1987	110	10
October 1988	April 1988-December 1989	180	Menu
July 1990	June 1990-June 1991	130	Menu

a) Including in several cases, arrears accumulated prior to the consolidation period.
b) Data relate to consolidation of export credits.
* Improved Toronto terms.

Table V.17. **Multilateral official debt reorganisation for developing countries** *(Cont'd)*

Debtor country and date of agreement	Consolidation period	Estimated amount[a] rescheduled ($ million)	Maturity (years)[b]
Malawi			
September 1982	July 1982-June 1983	25	8
October 1983	July 1983-June 1984	20	8
April 1988	April 1988-May 1989	30	20
Mali			
October 1988	July 1988-October 1989	30	Menu
November 1989	November 1989-December 1991	21	Menu
October 1992	October 1992-September 1995	20	Menu*
Mauritania			
April 1985	1985-March 1986	70	9
May 1986	April 1986-March 1987	30	9
June 1987	April 1987-May 1988	80	15
June 1989	June 1989-May 1990	52	Menu
January 1993	January 1993-December 1994	218	Menu*
Mexico			
June 1983	July 1983-December 1983	1 620	6
September 1986	September 1986-March 1988	1 850	9
May 1989	June 1989-May 1992	2 400	10
Morocco			
October 1983	September 1983-December 1984	1 200	8
September 1985	September 1985-February 1987	1 100	9
March 1987	March 1987-June 1988	950	10
October 1988	July 1988-December 1989	1 050	10
September 1990	September 1990-March 1991	1 390	15
February 1992	February 1992-January 1993	1 250	15
Mozambique			
October 1984	July 1984-June 1985	400	11
June 1987	June 1987-December 1988	570	20
June 1990	July 1990-December 1992	707	Menu
March 1993	March 1993-March 1995	440	
Nicaragua			
December 1991	January 1992-March 1993	722	Menu*
Niger			
November 1983	October 1983-September 1984	30	9
November 1984	October 1984-September 1985	30	10
November 1985	December 1985-December 1986	35	10
November 1986	December 1986-December 1987	39	10
April 1988	December 1987-December 1988	40	20
December 1988	January 1989-December 1990	40	Menu
September 1990	September 1990-December 1992	116	Menu
Nigeria			
December 1986	October 1986-December 1987	7 000	10
March 1989	1989-April 1990	6 000	10
January 1991	January 1991-March 1992	3 400	15
Pakistan			
May 1972	May 1971-June 1973	236	4
July 1973	July 1973-June 1974	107	4
June 1974	July 1974-June 1978	650	25-30
January 1981	January 1981-July 1982	232	(25-30)

a) Including in several cases, arrears accumulated prior to the consolidation period.
b) Data relate to consolidation of export credits.
* Improved Toronto terms.

Debtor country and date of agreement	Consolidation period	Estimated amount[a] rescheduled ($ million)	Maturity (years)[b]
Panama			
September 1985	September 1985-December 1986	20	8
November 1990	November 1990-March 1992	185	10
Peru			
September 1968	July 1968-1969	120	4
November 1969	1970-1971	(100)	5
November 1978	1979-1980	520	$6^1/_2$-$7^1/_2$
July 1983	May 1983-April 1984	500	8
June 1984	May 1984-July 1985	900	9
September 1991	October 1991-January 1993	5 900	15
May 1993	January 1993-March 1996	1 884	16
Philippines			
December 1984	1985-June 1986	850	10
January 1987	1987-June 1988	870	10
May 1989	June 1989-June 1991	1 900	10
June 1991	18 months	1 062	15
Senegal			
October 1981	July 1981-June 1982	75	9
November 1982	July 1982-June 1983	80	9
December 1983	July 1983-June 1984	78	9
January 1985	1985-June 1986	110	9
November 1986	July 1986-October 1987	90	10
November 1987	November 1987-October 1988	70	16
January 1989	November 1988-December 1989	170	Menu
February 1990	January 1990-July 1991	107	Menu
June 1991	July 1991-July 1992	150	Menu
Sierra Leone			
September 1977	July 1976-June 1978	29	11
February 1980	July 1979-December 1981	20	$7^1/_4$-$9^3/_4$
February 1984	January 1984-January 1985	80	$10^1/_2$
November 1986	July 1986-Mid-November 1987	85	10
November 1992	November 1992-February 1994	164	Menu*
Somalia			
March 1985	January 1985-January 1986	140	10
July 1987	January 1987-January 1988	65	20
Sudan			
November 1979	October 1979-June 1981	475	7-10
March 1982	July 1981-December 1982	105	10
February 1983	January 1983-January 1984	540	16
May 1984	January 1984-January 1985	280	16
Tanzania			
September 1986	October 1986-September 1987	1 200	10
December 1988	January 1989-June 1989	300	Menu
March 1990	January 1990-January 1991	199	Menu
January 1992	January 1992-July 1994	691	Menu*
Togo			
June 1979	January 1979-January 1980	220	10
February 1981	January 1981-January 1982	232	9
April 1983	January 1983-January 1984	150	10
June 1984	January 1984-April 1985	(70)	10
June 1985	May 1985-April 1986	31	11
March 1988	1988-Mid-April 1989	24	16
June 1989	mid-April 1989-June 1990	76	Menu

a) Including in several cases, arrears accumulated prior to the consolidation period.

b) Data relate to consolidation of export credits.

* Improved Toronto terms.

Table V.17. **Multilateral official debt reorganisation for developing countries** *(Cont'd)*

Debtor country and date of agreement	Consolidation period	Estimated amount[a] rescheduled ($ million)	Maturity (years)[b]
July 1990	July 1990-June 1991	92	Menu
June 1992	July 1992-June 1993	52	Menu*
Trinidad & Tobago			
January 1989	January 1989-February 1990	180	10
April 1990	March 1990-March 1991	110	10
Turkey			
May 1959	August 1958-1963	440	12
March 1965	1965-1967	220	6-12
May 1978	January 1977-June 1979	1 300	6-8
July 1979	May 1978-June 1980	1 200	7-8
July 1980	July 1980-June 1983	3 000	8-10
Uganda			
November 1981	July 1981-June 1982	50	8-10
December 1982	July 1982-June 1983	20	10
June 1987	July 1987-June 1988	70	15
January 1989	January 1989-June 1990	100	Menu
June 1992	January 1992-November 1992	39	Menu*

a) Including in several cases, arrears accumulated prior to the consolidation period.
b) Data relate to consolidation of export credits.
* Improved Toronto terms.

Chapter VI

Technical Notes

This chapter reviews current definitions and technical issues regarding the external financial situation of developing countries.

1. Resource flows

The data used in Chapters II and III are in terms of *net* resource flows, used in the Survey to describe net disbursements.

Three categories of net resource flows to developing countries are identified:

- official development finance;
- officially-supported export credits;
- private flows.

In the case of the first two categories, governments in the originating countries are the donors, creditors or guarantors. In the third category, private entities are the donors or creditors.

Official development finance (ODF) comprises flows from official bilateral and multilateral institutions whose main objective is the promotion of the economic and social welfare of developing countries. Bilateral donors encompass, in this publication, the Members of the OECD's Development Assistance Committee (the "DAC donors"), other OECD non-DAC countries, and the countries of Central and Eastern Europe. Luxembourg became a Member of the DAC in 1992 and its ODF position is recorded retrospectively as a DAC donor for the period 1984-92 in the tables in Chapter III.

ODF consists of:

i) Official development assistance (ODA) transactions. Each ODA transaction conveys a grant element of at least 25 per cent. The average grant element of ODA in recent years has been around 90 per cent with that for ODA loans approaching 60 per cent. (For a discussion of financial concessionality and the grant element concept, see the 1984 and 1986 *Development Co-operation Reviews*).

ii) Other less concessional or non-concessional flows. These consist mainly of lending at, or close to, market rates by bilateral sources and multilateral development banks (MDBs), including the World Bank and the Asian, African and Inter-American Development Banks. A smaller portion consists of other transactions such as the net acquisition by the official sector of securities issued by developing countries at market terms. Certain refinancing loans which do not qualify as ODA are also included.

Export credits comprise both officially-financed export credits and officially-guaranteed private export credits (including bank-financed credits).

Private flows consist mainly of direct investment, bank lending, bond lending and private export credits which are not officially guaranteed. The category "other private" groups a heterogeneous set of "private" transactions, including private suppliers' credits as well as transactions in securities and other non-bank financial transactions. Private grants from non-governmental organisations are also included as a separate category of private flows. Changes in reported interest arrears are included in export credit and bank lending as appropriate.

The definition of these three categories differs from the dual presentation of "official" and "private" flows in publications of other international institutions. By identifying export credits which are elsewhere reported as "private" flows, but which in fact are guaranteed by creditor governments, the use of creditor sources makes it possible to distinguish private credits which are officially guaranteed in creditor countries from other private lending. There are major differences between the two types. In the case of non-payment, guaranteed "export credit" loans become the obligations of creditor governments so that the lender carries no major exposure risk.

Throughout this Survey "bank lending" or "bank loans" thus refer only to bank lending which is *not* officially guaranteed in creditor countries. The net flow of bank loans in this Survey is derived primarily from data on changes in outstanding claims, after adjustment for valuation effects. The external claims are those of banks in OECD countries and banks (including affiliates of banks in the OECD reporting area) located in major financial centres.

For a number of developing countries, net flows from banks on a cash-flow basis are not properly reflected by such adjusted changes in outstanding claims. A number of transactions other than repayment of principal, in particular in Central and South America, has accounted for significant declines in outstanding creditor reported claims in recent years, *e.g.* write-offs, debt conversions, sales to non-reporting institutions etc. Other transactions partially reflected in changes in outstanding claims include debt buy-backs, changes in interest arrears or special covenants of the new agreements under the Brady Strategy. In this Survey, estimates of aggregate bank flows, on a cash-flow basis, to continents and income groups include conservative adjustments for these items.

After adjustment to achieve the same geographical and definitional coverage, the figures, which include both long- and short-term lending, are broadly consistent with other published sources.

Other features of the financial reporting in this Survey which deserve special note are as follows:

- *Total net resource flows* are total flows *to* developing countries disbursed *from* multilateral and bilateral sources. Contributions *to* multilateral institutions from bilateral sources are, of course, not taken into consideration in this context, but are reflected in the constant price section of Table III.1
- Total net resource flows to developing countries, as recorded in the tables in Chapter III, are essentially from OECD countries; ODF also includes flows originating in the countries of Central and Eastern Europe and international bank lending is from OECD and other international finance centres.
- The change in end-year outstanding amounts of arrears and short-term finance as reported in OECD creditor sources is included.
- All flow figures are expressed in US dollars at the current prices and average exchange rates of the year concerned but references are made to trends on the basis of constant prices and exchange rates.
- *1992 data* are preliminary, based on partial returns as of June 1993.
- Some of the data available from donor sources do not provide a comprehensive distribution of flows by recipient countries. *Unallocated amounts* by developing country region and income group are not only significant, but also have been growing over recent years.

- Annex 2 provides details of the developing-country income groups used in the tables in Chapters III and V. As countries move from one income group to another, the statistics for each group are adjusted retrospectively for the 1984-92 period.

2. External debt

The agreed international definition of external debt and a full description of the methodology used in compiling the data shown in this survey are contained in a joint report by OECD, BIS, IMF and the World Bank: *External Debt: Definition, Statistical Coverage and Methodology* published by the OECD, Paris 1988.

In all tables in Chapter V, ''multilateral debt'' and ''total debt'' include the use of IMF credit, both non-concessional and concessional.

3. Financial statistics: measurement issues

The large divergences between statistical series of flows or indebtedness published by different reporting institutions are more apparent than real. Progress has been achieved in bringing transparency to the definitions and methodology of the main sources of debt stock data. Regarding flows of financial resources, a detailed reconciliation of the aggregates published by the OECD, World Bank and IMF has been undertaken by the three organisations. (See the May 1991 World Economic Outlook of the IMF).

The main factors accounting for the apparent discrepancies in resource flow aggregates include:

- different geographical coverage;
- different statistical treatment of certain transactions;
- differences in presentation of final aggregates.

Differences in *geographical coverage* can be significant, *e.g.* the World Bank's and IMF's figures include (and the OECD figures in this publication exclude) Poland, Hungary and Romania while the OECD figures include and the Bank and Fund figures generally exclude data for over 50 developing countries and territories (the DAC list of developing countries appears in Annex 2).

Main differences in *statistical treatment* relate to a number of categories of transaction listed below (and for which OECD coverage generally is more comprehensive than that of other sources):

i) official grants (including technical co-operation) and private grants from non-governmental organisations;

ii) short-term finance and build-up in arrears of interest payments;

iii) foreign direct investment (FDI), in particular FDI to developing countries through offshore centres;

iv) portfolio investment, including in new emerging securities markets in LDCs;

v) debt restructuring, debt forgiveness, write-offs, debt conversions etc., entailing in several cases a number of notional entries with different treatment in creditor and debtor sources, and/or different date of recording;

vi) other factors such as valuation effects.

Also worth noting, the OECD presentation of flows comprises *three* major categories, with different underlying motivations: official development finance, export credits (official or officially-guaranteed private credits), and private flows other than export credits. Other sources usually contain only *two* categories: official/public (including official export credits), and private (including private export credits even when they are officially guaranteed).

Finally, confusion can also exist between two *different measures*:

i) on the one hand, net flows reflecting financial statements (based on debtor or creditor sources as the case may be), which trace transactions only on the *liabilities* side of the capital account of LDCs' balance-of-payments (*i.e.* net inflow minus repayment on previous loan inflow), and:

ii) net flow measured on *both* the assets and liabilities sides of the capital account, *i.e.* including also movements in external reserves and other assets, consisting essentially of direct investment, export credit and bank lending *by* developing countries. In this case, the net capital account or even the current balance, are often used as a proxy of net inflow.

Where asset transactions are very large, in particular for major capital-exporting countries, the difference between the two concepts is of great importance. But asset transactions can also be quite important for the IMF-defined group of ''net debtor countries''. In sum, the above distinction helps understand why in some cases net resource flows to LDCs can be much higher than the net capital account of LDCs and even higher than their current account deficit.

4. Comparison of two OECD publications

The *Geographical Distribution of Financial Resources Report* (referred to here as the Report) concentrates on data on long-term resource flows from individual donors to individual developing countries, but only shows certain aggregates. The *Financing and External Debt Survey* (the Survey) contains aggregate data of resource flows to recipient income groups and continents. The main differences between the two are as follows:

ODF statistics in the Survey tables come from the same data base as the Report, but the Survey Tables include estimates by the Secretariat to allocate some ''unallocated'' amounts.

Export credit statistics in the Survey tables consist of:

i) DAC countries' long-term export credits, which also come from the same data base, but which aggregate official and private export credits (these two categories are split in the Report, although a memo item for the combined total is given);

ii) short-term DAC export credits; and

iii) other countries' export credits, which are not included in the Report.

Data on private flows in the Survey tables are on an altogether different basis from the Report. They exclude private export credits, which are incorporated under export credits; these are shown under ''private'' in the Report. The Survey includes and the Report excludes, grants by non-Governmental Organisations and a number of other transactions. It allows for short-term flows and interest arrears, excluded from the Report. Its approach to the transactions of the bank sector and portfolio investment is also different: the data in the Report which are part of the ''Total Receipts'' refer essentially to long-term transactions by banks resident in DAC Member countries only and also include various portfolio transactions other than bank loans (*e.g.*, securities) carried out by both banks and non-banks. The Survey is based on the OECD/BIS data bank, which not only covers short-term bank flows but also bank loans from countries and territories outside the DAC reporting area, including, as regards financial (offshore) centres, loans by subsidiaries of banks resident in DAC Member countries. Bank transactions which are not included in the ''Total Receipts'' of the Report do figure, however, in a memo item in the Report showing ''changes in banks'' claims.

Table VI.1. **Valuation effects on long-term indebtedness**

Per cent

	1985	1987	1988	1989	1990	1991	1992
Total LDCs:							
Debt	+ 5	+ 7	–3	–1	+5	0	–2
Debt service	+ 2	+ 8	+3	–3	+5	0	0
LICs:							
Debt	+ 5	+ 9	–4	–2	+6	0.5	–3
Debt service	+ 2	+10	+3	–4	+5	0	0
Total LDC ODA debt	+14	+16	–4	–3	+7	+2	–3
Total LDC export credit debt	+10	+13	–5	–1	+8	0	–7

5. Valuation effects

Highlights of recent valuation effects are provided below in respect of long-term indebtedness:

6. Sources of statistical data in this survey

Resource flow data are reported to the OECD by creditor sources (with the exception of data on bond lending which are taken from the World Bank Debtor Reporting System). Flows of official development finance and export credits from the countries of Central and Eastern Europe and from Arab donor countries are Secretariat estimates. For details on the statistical sources used for net ODF and export credit data by country, see: *Geographical Distribution of Financial Flows to Developing Countries, 1988-91*, OECD, Paris 1993. As indicated in Section 1 above, the figures for bank lending since 1983 have been derived by the Secretariat from changes in the figures on the stock of debt prepared jointly by the OECD and BIS.

Data on indebtedness to OECD countries and international capital markets come from OECD creditor sources. From 1983 on, bank-financed guaranteed export credits are separated from other bank lending by collation of the export credit and bank claims data reported respectively to the OECD and the Bank for International Settlements. Full details on the methodology for this are contained in: *External Debt Statistics: the Debt and Other External Liabilities of Developing, Central and Eastern European and Certain Other Countries and Territories, at end-December 1990 and 1991*, OECD, 1992. Data on debt owed to multilateral institutions generally come from the World Bank's DRS.

In the tables in Chapters III and V, slight discrepancies in totals are due to rounding.

Annex 1

**External Indebtedness of Individual Developing Countries and Territories:
Total Disbursed Debt at Year-End and Annual Debt Service During 1984-91**

Note on the Table for Greece: The data include a significant amount (not found in official Greek data on debt) of claims on international shipping companies' headquarters in Greece which, being considered offshore, are not covered in Greek National Accounts and whose loans are serviced by their own receipts and reserves. "Other identified liabilities" refers mainly to foreign exchange deposits by Greek nationals resident abroad in anticipation of their eventual return to Greece, as well as by Greek seamen and recently returned emigrants.

US $ Million

	1984	1985	1986	1987	1988	1989	1990	1991
GROSS DEBT								
Long term								
I. OECD countries and capital markets	155	146	143	146	134	128	128	121
ODA	133	141	142	146	132	126	123	116
Official/off. supported	22	–	–	–	–	–	–	–
Official export credits	22	–	–	–	–	–	–	–
Guaranteed supplier credits	–	–	–	–	–	–	–	–
Guaranteed bank credits	0	–	–	–	–	–	–	–
Financial markets	–	5	1	–	2	2	5	5
Banks	–	5	1	–	2	2	5	5
Bonds	–	–	–	–	–	–	–	–
Other private	–	–	–	–	–	–	–	–
II. Multilateral	109	119	129	139	137	133	131	131
of which: concessional	109	119	129	139	137	133	131	131
non-concessional	–	–	–	–	–	–	–	–
memo: IMF, total	–	–	–	–	–	–	–	–
III. Non-OECD Creditor countries	1790	2004	2463	3741	4863	4759	4788	5018
C.E.E.C.	1688	1902	2364	3644	4767	4665	4695	4925
Arab countries	102	102	99	96	96	94	94	94
Other countries and unspecified	–	–	–	–	–	–	–	–
Subtotal: Long term debt	*2054*	*2270*	*2735*	*4026*	*5134*	*5019*	*5046*	*5269*
of which: concessional	2031	2265	2734	4026	5132	5017	5041	5264
non-concessional	22	5	1	0	2	2	5	5
Short term								
Subtotal: Short term debt	*6*	*5*	*18*	*15*	*21*	*35*	*40*	*35*
Banks	6	5	18	15	20	35	40	34
Export credits	0	0	0	0	1	0	0	1
Other identified liabilities	–	–	–	–	–	–	–	–
Total identified debt	**2060**	**2275**	**2753**	**4041**	**5154**	**5054**	**5086**	**5305**
SERVICE PAYMENTS								
Long term								
I. OECD countries and capital markets	13	27	9	10	10	10	12	9
ODA	10	5	8	10	10	10	11	8
Official/off. supported	3	22	–	–	–	–	0	–
Financial markets	–	–	0	0	–	0	0	0
Other private	–	–	–	–	–	–	–	–
II. Multilateral	1	12	3	12	4	5	5	5
of which: concessional	1	12	3	12	4	5	5	5
memo: IMF, total	–	–	–	–	–	–	–	–
III. Non-OECD creditor countries	28	7	33	28	24	26	96	55
Subtotal: Service payments, long term debt	*42*	*46*	*45*	*49*	*38*	*41*	*112*	*68*
of which: concessional	39	24	45	49	38	41	112	68
Amortization, long term debt	8	26	12	9	10	11	12	11
Interest, long term debt	34	20	33	40	28	30	101	57
Interest, short term debt	1	0	1	1	1	3	3	2
Total service payments	**43**	**47**	**46**	**50**	**39**	**43**	**115**	**70**

US $ Million

	1984	1985	1986	1987	1988	1989	1990	1991
GROSS DEBT								
Long term								
I. OECD countries and capital markets	1	1	16	1	13	10	32	37
ODA	–	–	–	–	–	2	2	2
Official/off. supported	1	1	0	1	13	9	3	13
Official export credits	–	–	–	–	–	–	–	–
Guaranteed supplier credits	1	1	0	–	–	–	–	3
Guaranteed bank credits	–	–	–	1	13	9	3	11
Financial markets	–	–	16	–	–	–	27	21
Banks	–	–	16	–	–	–	27	21
Bonds	–	–	–	–	–	–	–	–
Other private	–	–	–	–	–	–	–	–
II. Multilateral	–	–	–	–	–	–	–	–
of which: concessional	–	–	–	–	–	–	–	–
non-concessional	–	–	–	–	–	–	–	–
memo: IMF, total	–	–	–	–	–	–	–	–
III. Non-OECD Creditor countries	121	118	117	133	131	127	127	127
C.E.E.C.	121	118	117	133	131	127	127	127
Arab countries	–	–	–	–	–	–	–	–
Other countries and unspecified	–	–	–	–	–	–	–	–
Subtotal: Long term debt	*122*	*119*	*134*	*134*	*144*	*137*	*159*	*164*
of which: concessional	121	118	117	133	131	129	129	129
non-concessional	1	1	16	1	13	9	30	35
Short term								
Subtotal: Short term debt	*10*	*93*	*36*	*86*	*103*	*388*	*434*	*367*
Banks	6	85	32	82	100	383	421	352
Export credits	4	8	4	4	3	4	14	15
Other identified liabilities	–	–	–	–	–	–	–	–
Total identified debt	**132**	**213**	**169**	**221**	**247**	**525**	**593**	**530**
SERVICE PAYMENTS								
Long term								
I. OECD countries and capital markets	–	–	1	1	0	5	2	2
ODA	–	–	–	–	–	–	0	0
Official/off. supported	–	–	1	0	0	5	2	0
Financial markets	–	–	–	1	–	–	–	2
Other private	–	–	–	–	–	–	–	–
II. Multilateral	–	–	–	–	–	–	–	–
of which: concessional	–	–	–	–	–	–	–	–
memo: IMF, total	–	–	–	–	–	–	–	–
III. Non-OECD creditor countries	–	–	–	–	–	1	3	10
Subtotal: Service payments, long term debt	*–*	*–*	*1*	*1*	*0*	*7*	*4*	*12*
of which: concessional	–	–	–	–	–	1	3	10
Amortization, long term debt	–	–	1	0	0	3	1	–
Interest, long term debt	–	–	–	1	0	4	3	12
Interest, short term debt	1	4	4	4	8	22	34	24
Total service payments	**1**	**4**	**5**	**5**	**8**	**29**	**39**	**36**

ALGERIA

	1984	1985	1986	1987	1988	1989	1990	1991
GROSS DEBT								
Long term								
I. OECD countries and capital markets	13085	16224	17294	18375	17692	17743	19623	20432
ODA	236	272	303	340	306	292	343	448
Official/off. supported	8739	10343	11857	13229	9755	10216	11090	12076
Official export credits	2678	2844	2681	2762	2391	2207	2340	2524
Guaranteed supplier credits	2671	2757	2460	1824	1350	1418	993	852
Guaranteed bank credits	3389	4742	6716	8644	6014	6590	7757	8699
Financial markets	4056	5581	5117	4793	7623	7229	8187	7906
Banks	3824	4901	4339	3970	6455	5882	6669	6470
Bonds	232	680	777	823	1168	1347	1518	1436
Other private	55	27	17	13	9	5	2	2
II. Multilateral	443	554	926	1221	1414	2269	2867	3828
of which: concessional	13	14	38	61	71	113	205	222
non-concessional	430	540	888	1160	1343	2156	2662	3605
memo: IMF, total	–	–	–	–	–	619	670	995
III. Non-OECD Creditor countries	3761	3997	3950	4574	5051	5509	5904	5900
C.E.E.C.	3400	3817	3742	4284	4234	4383	4451	4403
Arab countries	151	35	21	35	511	716	875	955
Other countries and unspecified	209	145	188	255	306	410	577	542
Subtotal: Long term debt	*17288*	*20775*	*22170*	*24171*	*24158*	*25522*	*28394*	*30159*
of which: concessional	249	286	340	402	377	405	549	671
non-concessional	17039	20488	21829	23769	23782	25117	27845	29489
Short term								
Subtotal: Short term debt	*2030*	*2097*	*3233*	*3677*	*3380*	*4347*	*3560*	*3817*
Banks	943	744	1698	2467	2064	2517	1673	1717
Export credits	1087	1353	1535	1209	1317	1831	1887	2100
Other identified liabilities	–	–	–	–	–	–	–	–
Total identified debt	**19318**	**22871**	**25403**	**27848**	**27539**	**29869**	**31954**	**33976**
SERVICE PAYMENTS								
Long term								
I. OECD countries and capital markets	4346	4345	4538	3478	4890	6405	7849	7283
ODA	19	36	26	33	30	30	32	26
Official/off. supported	2966	3176	2933	2922	2928	3682	3934	4025
Financial markets	1361	1133	1571	515	1923	2688	3879	3231
Other private	–	–	8	8	8	5	4	1
II. Multilateral	143	191	174	271	303	329	496	596
of which: concessional	2	2	4	4	7	6	6	8
memo: IMF, total	–	–	–	–	–	22	62	59
III. Non-OECD creditor countries	245	405	220	170	271	329	436	670
Subtotal: Service payments, long term debt	*4735*	*4942*	*4932*	*3919*	*5464*	*7064*	*8781*	*8549*
of which: concessional	21	38	30	38	37	36	38	34
Amortization, long term debt	3542	3639	3440	2322	4277	5388	7177	6626
Interest, long term debt	1192	1303	1492	1598	1187	1675	1603	1923
Interest, short term debt	247	164	177	235	278	343	323	203
Total service payments	**4982**	**5105**	**5109**	**4154**	**5742**	**7406**	**9104**	**8751**

ANGOLA

US $ Million

	1984	1985	1986	1987	1988	1989	1990	1991
GROSS DEBT								
Long term								
I. OECD countries and capital markets	745	799	899	1172	1270	1461	1443	1537
ODA	45	77	134	200	268	196	214	220
Official/off. supported	600	605	689	892	738	844	992	951
Official export credits	76	132	138	163	145	148	135	131
Guaranteed supplier credits	128	81	60	82	153	167	199	306
Guaranteed bank credits	396	391	491	647	440	528	658	514
Financial markets	100	117	75	80	263	421	238	367
Banks	100	117	75	80	263	421	238	367
Bonds	–	–	–	–	–	–	–	–
Other private	–	–	–	–	–	–	–	–
II. Multilateral	16	20	34	46	50	53	56	88
of which: concessional	16	20	28	5	10	14	20	28
non-concessional	–	–	6	42	40	39	36	60
memo: IMF, total	–	–	–	–	–	–	–	–
III. Non-OECD Creditor countries	1755	1797	1972	2564	3663	4429	5323	5346
C.E.E.C.	1755	1797	1972	2562	2810	3475	4316	4316
Arab countries	–	–	1	2	5	7	7	7
Other countries and unspecified	–	–	–	–	848	947	1000	1022
Subtotal: Long term debt	*2516*	*2616*	*2905*	*3782*	*4982*	*5943*	*6823*	*6972*
of which: concessional	61	97	162	204	278	210	233	248
non-concessional	2455	2519	2743	3578	4704	5733	6590	6724
Short term								
Subtotal: Short term debt	*196*	*456*	*594*	*586*	*644*	*826*	*1172*	*1444*
Banks	134	375	475	339	326	389	654	724
Export credits	62	81	119	247	318	437	518	720
Other identified liabilities	–	–	–	–	–	–	–	–
Total identified debt	**2711**	**3072**	**3499**	**4368**	**5626**	**6770**	**7995**	**8416**
SERVICE PAYMENTS								
Long term								
I. OECD countries and capital markets	236	336	233	254	115	176	256	142
ODA	0	0	0	4	4	5	12	7
Official/off. supported	207	316	210	223	61	130	193	115
Financial markets	29	20	22	27	51	42	52	21
Other private	–	–	–	–	–	–	–	–
II. Multilateral	–	11	2	3	6	6	7	6
of which: concessional	–	11	0	0	0	0	0	0
memo: IMF, total	–	–	–	–	–	–	–	–
III. Non-OECD creditor countries	1	1	1	75	51	96	50	62
Subtotal: Service payments, long term debt	*237*	*348*	*236*	*333*	*173*	*279*	*313*	*211*
of which: concessional	0	11	0	4	4	5	12	7
Amortization, long term debt	183	277	174	230	84	127	172	143
Interest, long term debt	54	71	62	103	89	152	141	68
Interest, short term debt	19	24	32	31	30	40	53	51
Total service payments	**256**	**372**	**267**	**363**	**202**	**319**	**366**	**262**

ARGENTINA

US $ Million

	1984	1985	1986	1987	1988	1989	1990	1991
GROSS DEBT								
Long term								
I. OECD countries and capital markets	34174	37058	37643	43564	42140	47281	42431	40610
ODA	130	151	170	206	266	305	405	536
Official/off. supported	2364	4064	3489	5285	5281	6213	6633	7972
Official export credits	769	2188	1478	3509	3467	4416	4857	5712
Guaranteed supplier credits	637	706	794	940	929	877	780	787
Guaranteed bank credits	958	1170	1217	836	886	920	996	1473
Financial markets	29680	30843	31983	35874	34092	38264	32594	29303
Banks	21944	21069	22256	26083	24966	25469	20550	18569
Bonds	7736	9774	9728	9790	9127	12795	12043	10733
Other private	2000	2000	2000	2200	2500	2500	2800	2800
II. Multilateral	2538	4214	5318	8082	7706	7448	8078	7892
of which: concessional	109	111	111	119	100	82	71	56
non-concessional	2429	4103	5208	7963	7607	7366	8006	7837
memo: IMF, total	1098	2312	2741	3853	3678	3100	3083	2483
III. Non-OECD Creditor countries	457	357	452	521	560	528	575	508
C.E.E.C.	274	299	397	377	321	272	242	242
Arab countries	–	–	–	–	–	–	1	1
Other countries and unspecified	184	58	55	143	239	256	332	265
Subtotal: Long term debt	*37170*	*41629*	*43413*	*52167*	*50406*	*55257*	*51084*	*49011*
of which: concessional	240	263	280	324	366	387	476	591
non-concessional	36930	41366	43133	51843	50041	54870	50608	48419
Short term								
Subtotal: Short term debt	*4414*	*8170*	*9932*	*9517*	*12990*	*7460*	*10451*	*11718*
Banks	3710	7168	8824	8158	11614	6074	9030	10512
Export credits	703	1002	1108	1359	1376	1386	1421	1206
Other identified liabilities	2337	2231	2530	2406	2597	1552	1888	1900
Total identified debt	**43920**	**52030**	**55875**	**64090**	**65993**	**64269**	**63423**	**62628**
SERVICE PAYMENTS								
Long term								
I. OECD countries and capital markets	2056	4772	3907	3553	2188	2338	1549	1947
ODA	7	5	79	4	15	7	22	12
Official/off. supported	320	719	907	552	691	298	545	792
Financial markets	1419	3888	2781	2877	1328	1783	557	697
Other private	310	160	140	120	154	250	425	446
II. Multilateral	385	368	997	1326	1436	1763	1754	2328
of which: concessional	22	20	28	20	20	22	19	25
memo: IMF, total	89	120	582	844	755	992	974	1228
III. Non-OECD creditor countries	62	83	60	87	64	51	62	157
Subtotal: Service payments, long term debt	*2503*	*5223*	*4964*	*4966*	*3688*	*4151*	*3364*	*4432*
of which: concessional	29	25	106	24	35	28	40	37
Amortization, long term debt	528	1077	2331	2153	1905	2232	1702	3043
Interest, long term debt	1975	4145	2633	2813	1783	1919	1662	1389
Interest, short term debt	726	631	725	780	1018	1012	–	721
Total service payments	**3229**	**5854**	**5689**	**5746**	**4706**	**5163**	**3364**	**5153**

BAHAMAS

US $ Million

	1984	1985	1986	1987	1988	1989	1990	1991
GROSS DEBT								
Long term								
I. OECD countries and capital markets	374	399	858	681	496	526	524	671
ODA	3	3	3	4	4	4	5	–
Official/off. supported	71	66	55	60	24	39	49	141
Official export credits	6	5	5	5	3	1	–	53
Guaranteed supplier credits	36	25	19	33	6	0	1	1
Guaranteed bank credits	30	37	31	22	15	38	48	87
Financial markets	300	330	800	617	467	483	470	530
Banks	300	330	800	617	467	483	470	530
Bonds	–	–	–	–	–	–	–	–
Other private	–	–	–	–	–	–	–	–
II. Multilateral	15	16	20	29	31	32	71	71
of which: concessional	0	1	1	3	4	5	6	6
non-concessional	15	16	20	26	27	27	65	65
memo: IMF, total	–	–	–	–	–	–	–	–
III. Non-OECD Creditor countries	2	2	2	2	1	1	1	1
C.E.E.C.	–	–	–	–	–	–	–	–
Arab countries	–	–	–	–	–	–	–	–
Other countries and unspecified	2	2	2	2	1	1	1	2
Subtotal: Long term debt	*391*	*417*	*880*	*711*	*528*	*559*	*596*	*743*
of which: concessional	5	5	5	9	10	10	12	7
non-concessional	386	412	875	702	518	549	584	736
Short term								
Subtotal: Short term debt	*209*	*203*	*516*	*415*	*314*	*322*	*314*	*354*
Banks	200	190	500	400	303	314	300	340
Export credits	9	13	16	15	11	9	14	14
Other identified liabilities	–	–	–	–	–	–	–	–
Total identified debt	**600**	**621**	**1396**	**1125**	**842**	**881**	**910**	**1097**
SERVICE PAYMENTS								
Long term								
I. OECD countries and capital markets	1	96	75	135	70	118	82	58
ODA	1	–	–	0	–	0	0	0
Official/off. supported	40	64	51	77	12	13	16	11
Financial markets	41	33	24	57	59	105	66	46
Other private	–	–	–	–	–	–	–	–
II. Multilateral	3	5	4	4	6	4	5	8
of which: concessional	0	0	0	–	0	0	0	0
memo: IMF, total	–	–	–	–	–	–	–	–
III. Non-OECD creditor countries	0	0	0	0	0	–	0	–
Subtotal: Service payments, long term debt	*84*	*202*	*80*	*139*	*77*	*122*	*87*	*66*
of which: concessional	1	0	0	0	0	0	0	0
Amortization, long term debt	43	57	47	55	17	73	23	24
Interest, long term debt	41	44	33	84	60	49	64	42
Interest, short term debt	33	17	24	32	29	29	26	20
Total service payments	**116**	**219**	**204**	**171**	**106**	**151**	**113**	**86**

US $ Million

	1984	1985	1986	1987	1988	1989	1990	1991
GROSS DEBT								
Long term								
I. OECD countries and capital markets	374	605	789	804	787	731	872	1407
ODA	–	–	–	–	–	–	–	–
Official/off. supported	115	119	281	209	174	131	289	756
Official export credits	–	–	–	–	–	–	–	20
Guaranteed supplier credits	34	48	248	187	159	105	85	61
Guaranteed bank credits	80	71	33	22	15	27	203	675
Financial markets	259	487	508	595	613	599	583	651
Banks	128	150	160	140	149	126	132	203
Bonds	132	337	348	455	465	473	451	448
Other private	–	–	–	–	–	–	–	–
II. Multilateral	29	29	30	31	36	36	35	35
of which: concessional	17	17	18	19	19	19	19	19
non-concessional	12	12	12	12	17	17	17	17
memo: IMF, total	–	–	–	–	–	–	–	–
III. Non-OECD Creditor countries	325	359	401	389	389	376	368	368
C.E.E.C.	–	–	–	–	–	–	–	–
Arab countries	325	359	401	389	389	376	368	368
Other countries and unspecified	–	–	–	–	–	–	–	–
Subtotal: Long term debt	*728*	*993*	*1220*	*1224*	*1212*	*1142*	*1275*	*1810*
of which: concessional	342	376	419	408	408	395	387	387
non-concessional	386	617	801	815	804	747	888	1423
Short term								
Subtotal: Short term debt	*207*	*269*	*255*	*233*	*234*	*349*	*332*	*408*
Banks	167	200	200	180	191	288	250	310
Export credits	40	69	55	53	42	61	82	98
Other identified liabilities	–	–	–	–	–	–	–	–
Total identified debt	**934**	**1262**	**1475**	**1456**	**1446**	**1491**	**1607**	**2218**
SERVICE PAYMENTS								
Long term								
I. OECD countries and capital markets	132	136	176	121	134	139	138	105
ODA	–	–	–	–	–	–	–	–
Official/off. supported	104	111	118	108	107	93	46	61
Financial markets	28	25	58	14	27	47	92	44
Other private	–	–	–	–	–	–	–	–
II. Multilateral	1	3	2	3	1	2	2	3
of which: concessional	1	2	1	2	1	0	1	2
memo: IMF, total	–	–	–	–	–	–	–	–
III. Non-OECD creditor countries	10	24	37	23	8	16	15	35
Subtotal: Service payments, long term debt	*143*	*162*	*215*	*148*	*143*	*157*	*154*	*143*
of which: concessional	11	25	38	26	9	17	16	38
Amortization, long term debt	112	128	128	76	90	77	89	65
Interest, long term debt	31	34	87	72	53	80	65	79
Interest, short term debt	24	19	18	17	19	26	28	22
Total service payments	**166**	**181**	**233**	**165**	**162**	**183**	**182**	**165**

US $ Million

	1984	1985	1986	1987	1988	1989	1990	1991
GROSS DEBT								
Long term								
I. OECD countries and capital markets	2418	2861	3153	3948	4510	3847	4049	3914
ODA	2093	2559	2922	3747	4280	3630	3816	3700
Official/off. supported	113	141	123	143	158	215	233	214
Official export credits	20	14	9	9	9	35	47	58
Guaranteed supplier credits	36	23	28	20	28	14	19	11
Guaranteed bank credits	57	103	86	114	121	166	167	145
Financial markets	212	161	108	57	72	2	–	–
Banks	212	161	108	57	72	2	–	–
Bonds	–	–	–	–	–	–	–	–
Other private	–	–	–	–	–	–	–	–
II. Multilateral	2742	3321	3993	5013	5417	5843	7036	8032
of which: concessional	2372	2894	3491	4414	4829	5376	6725	7886
non-concessional	370	427	503	599	589	467	311	145
memo: IMF, total	462	520	539	841	840	719	626	748
III. Non-OECD Creditor countries	547	542	627	699	652	578	591	555
C.E.E.C.	163	161	199	213	196	165	209	179
Arab countries	228	232	269	323	300	285	272	285
Other countries and unspecified	155	150	159	163	156	128	110	91
Subtotal: Long term debt	*5707*	*6724*	*7773*	*9659*	*10579*	*10268*	*11676*	*12501*
of which: concessional	4464	5453	6413	8161	9109	9006	10541	11587
non-concessional	1243	1271	1360	1498	1470	1262	1135	914
Short term								
Subtotal: Short term debt	*95*	*59*	*172*	*312*	*317*	*388*	*391*	*246*
Banks	74	35	145	280	295	361	341	203
Export credits	21	24	27	32	23	27	50	43
Other identified liabilities	32	50	35	103	135	20	25	23
Total identified debt	**5834**	**6833**	**7980**	**10075**	**11032**	**10676**	**12091**	**12770**
SERVICE PAYMENTS								
Long term								
I. OECD countries and capital markets	127	138	134	128	204	222	204	222
ODA	49	50	84	85	127	109	106	126
Official/off. supported	46	66	33	23	38	67	55	38
Financial markets	32	21	17	20	40	47	43	58
Other private	–	–	–	–	–	–	–	–
II. Multilateral	157	178	262	300	220	251	355	284
of which: concessional	38	65	86	99	107	98	102	108
memo: IMF, total	105	124	186	207	139	167	246	162
III. Non-OECD creditor countries	52	71	65	81	87	89	109	94
Subtotal: Service payments, long term debt	*336*	*387*	*461*	*508*	*511*	*563*	*669*	*600*
of which: concessional	87	115	170	185	234	206	208	235
Amortization, long term debt	189	243	304	328	310	373	479	431
Interest, long term debt	147	145	157	180	201	189	190	169
Interest, short term debt	13	9	10	20	34	38	33	21
Total service payments	**348**	**396**	**471**	**529**	**544**	**600**	**702**	**621**

BARBADOS

US $ Million

	1984	1985	1986	1987	1988	1989	1990	1991
GROSS DEBT								
Long term								
I. OECD countries and capital markets	166	207	260	298	359	366	436	427
ODA	29	26	27	28	30	29	29	28
Official/off. supported	90	91	89	89	89	75	77	80
Official export credits	33	28	32	30	42	36	37	40
Guaranteed supplier credits	3	3	4	4	3	2	2	7
Guaranteed bank credits	54	60	54	55	44	37	38	33
Financial markets	46	90	143	181	240	262	330	319
Banks	46	65	80	100	117	153	215	250
Bonds	–	25	63	81	123	109	115	69
Other private	–	–	–	–	–	–	–	–
II. Multilateral	139	160	175	180	172	163	178	176
of which: concessional	50	52	53	52	52	51	53	53
non-concessional	89	108	122	128	120	112	125	123
memo: IMF, total	43	48	40	22	10	4	1	–
III. Non-OECD Creditor countries	29	40	37	42	33	23	23	24
C.E.E.C.	–	–	–	–	–	–	–	–
Arab countries	–	–	–	–	–	–	–	–
Other countries and unspecified	29	40	37	42	33	23	23	24
Subtotal: Long term debt	*334*	*407*	*472*	*520*	*564*	*552*	*638*	*627*
of which: concessional	79	78	80	81	82	80	83	81
non-concessional	255	329	391	439	483	472	555	546
Short term								
Subtotal: Short term debt	*50*	*54*	*54*	*77*	*86*	*111*	*118*	*122*
Banks	41	40	40	60	70	92	100	110
Export credits	8	14	14	17	16	20	18	12
Other identified liabilities	–	–	–	–	–	–	–	–
Total identified debt	**384**	**461**	**526**	**596**	**650**	**663**	**756**	**749**
SERVICE PAYMENTS								
Long term								
I. OECD countries and capital markets	20	33	34	47	36	39	60	85
ODA	2	2	1	1	3	2	2	1
Official/off. supported	7	26	19	17	14	18	18	21
Financial markets	11	5	13	29	19	18	40	63
Other private	–	–	–	–	–	–	–	–
II. Multilateral	12	16	33	45	34	23	28	27
of which: concessional	2	2	3	3	4	4	4	4
memo: IMF, total	3	4	17	24	12	–	4	1
III. Non-OECD creditor countries	1	3	3	2	6	13	14	4
Subtotal: Service payments, long term debt	*33*	*51*	*69*	*94*	*76*	*74*	*102*	*117*
of which: concessional	4	5	4	5	7	6	6	6
Amortization, long term debt	15	27	44	66	43	45	68	83
Interest, long term debt	19	24	25	28	34	29	34	33
Interest, short term debt	5	4	4	5	7	9	10	7
Total service payments	**38**	**56**	**72**	**98**	**83**	**83**	**112**	**124**

BELIZE

US $ Million

	1984	1985	1986	1987	1988	1989	1990	1991
GROSS DEBT								
Long term								
I. OECD countries and capital markets	44	57	73	83	88	73	80	101
ODA	19	31	42	51	54	53	62	64
Official/off. supported	18	20	16	18	20	20	17	38
Official export credits	5	10	9	7	9	9	12	21
Guaranteed supplier credits	7	6	4	4	3	7	2	13
Guaranteed bank credits	6	4	3	6	9	3	3	3
Financial markets	7	6	14	14	14	–	–	–
Banks	7	6	14	14	14	–	–	–
Bonds	–	–	–	–	–	–	–	–
Other private	–	–	–	–	–	–	–	–
II. Multilateral	36	47	49	52	49	55	58	61
of which: concessional	23	23	23	24	24	30	32	35
non-concessional	12	23	26	29	25	25	25	25
memo: IMF, total	5	11	12	11	8	3	0	–
III. Non-OECD Creditor countries	3	4	4	3	1	1	2	8
C.E.E.C.	–	–	–	–	–	–	–	–
Arab countries	–	–	–	–	–	–	–	–
Other countries and unspecified	3	4	4	3	1	1	2	8
Subtotal: Long term debt	*83*	*108*	*125*	*138*	*138*	*129*	*140*	*170*
of which: concessional	43	54	65	75	77	83	95	99
non-concessional	41	54	60	63	61	46	45	71
Short term								
Subtotal: Short term debt	*28*	*22*	*37*	*14*	*22*	*81*	*49*	*19*
Banks	27	19	34	9	15	75	42	12
Export credits	1	3	3	5	7	6	7	7
Other identified liabilities	16	12	18	18	18	18	17	16
Total identified debt	**128**	**142**	**181**	**170**	**178**	**228**	**206**	**206**
SERVICE PAYMENTS								
Long term								
I. OECD countries and capital markets	4	7	8	8	11	8	8	11
ODA	0	1	1	1	1	1	2	3
Official/off. supported	3	5	7	4	4	5	3	3
Financial markets	1	1	1	3	6	1	3	5
Other private	–	–	–	–	–	–	–	–
II. Multilateral	2	5	6	6	8	10	9	7
of which: concessional	1	3	3	2	2	3	3	3
memo: IMF, total	0	0	2	3	4	5	3	0
III. Non-OECD creditor countries	0	0	1	1	2	0	1	0
Subtotal: Service payments, long term debt	*6*	*12*	*15*	*15*	*21*	*18*	*17*	*18*
of which: concessional	1	4	3	3	3	4	5	6
Amortization, long term debt	2	8	10	10	16	11	12	13
Interest, long term debt	4	4	5	5	5	7	5	5
Interest, short term debt	5	3	3	3	3	6	7	3
Total service payments	**10**	**15**	**18**	**18**	**24**	**25**	**24**	**21**

US $ Million

	1984	1985	1986	1987	1988	1989	1990	1991
GROSS DEBT								
Long term								
I. OECD countries and capital markets	275	292	304	310	359	344	403	251
ODA	24	40	63	91	94	140	171	172
Official/off. supported	153	182	166	138	182	173	223	71
Official export credits	16	20	11	12	10	59	117	71
Guaranteed supplier credits	17	19	16	16	149	105	103	–
Guaranteed bank credits	119	144	139	110	23	9	4	–
Financial markets	99	69	75	81	83	32	10	9
Banks	99	69	75	81	83	32	10	9
Bonds	–	–	–	–	–	–	–	–
Other private	–	–	–	–	–	–	–	–
II. Multilateral	202	240	297	366	381	441	562	635
of which: concessional	178	213	264	326	342	404	523	598
non-concessional	24	27	32	40	39	38	39	38
memo: IMF, total	11	11	10	8	4	10	9	22
III. Non-OECD Creditor countries	40	41	46	54	101	327	335	339
C.E.E.C.	7	8	9	11	55	50	51	57
Arab countries	7	10	13	15	15	20	20	18
Other countries and unspecified	26	23	25	28	31	258	265	264
Subtotal: Long term debt	*517*	*573*	*647*	*730*	*840*	*1113*	*1301*	*1226*
of which: concessional	202	253	327	417	436	543	694	770
non-concessional	316	320	320	313	405	570	607	456
Short term								
Subtotal: Short term debt	*111*	*212*	*314*	*386*	*126*	*159*	*181*	*178*
Banks	34	55	60	76	18	33	26	14
Export credits	77	157	254	310	108	126	155	164
Other identified liabilities	–	–	–	–	–	–	–	–
Total identified debt	**628**	**785**	**961**	**1116**	**967**	**1272**	**1482**	**1404**
SERVICE PAYMENTS								
Long term								
I. OECD countries and capital markets	38	19	30	20	14	19	11	15
ODA	1	1	2	3	5	9	4	4
Official/off. supported	26	7	14	12	3	2	5	8
Financial markets	11	11	14	6	7	8	3	4
Other private	–	–	–	–	–	–	–	–
II. Multilateral	7	12	15	14	14	13	33	22
of which: concessional	4	6	9	9	9	7	15	12
memo: IMF, total	1	1	3	3	3	2	2	0
III. Non-OECD creditor countries	0	1	1	1	0	–	0	3
Subtotal: Service payments, long term debt	*45*	*32*	*46*	*35*	*28*	*32*	*44*	*40*
of which: concessional	5	7	11	12	14	16	19	16
Amortization, long term debt	22	14	23	14	12	16	22	18
Interest, long term debt	23	18	22	21	16	16	23	22
Interest, short term debt	8	7	7	8	7	5	3	1
Total service payments	**53**	**38**	**53**	**43**	**36**	**36**	**48**	**42**

BERMUDA

US $ Million

	1984	1985	1986	1987	1988	1989	1990	1991
GROSS DEBT								
Long term								
I. OECD countries and capital markets	328	284	333	363	298	339	445	796
ODA	–	–	–	–	–	–	46	40
Official/off. supported	248	219	178	158	97	87	74	228
Official export credits	112	89	75	58	7	17	27	3
Guaranteed supplier credits	108	96	61	45	45	40	32	24
Guaranteed bank credits	28	34	42	55	46	30	15	201
Financial markets	80	65	155	205	201	252	325	529
Banks	40	45	50	100	96	147	220	180
Bonds	40	20	105	105	105	105	105	349
Other private	–	–	–	–	–	–	–	–
II. Multilateral	–	–	–	–	–	–	–	–
of which: concessional	–	–	–	–	–	–	–	–
non-concessional	–	–	–	–	–	–	–	–
memo: IMF, total	–	–	–	–	–	–	–	–
III. Non-OECD Creditor countries	0	0	0	0	0	0	0	0
C.E.E.C.	–	–	–	–	–	–	–	–
Arab countries	0	0	0	0	0	0	0	0
Other countries and unspecified	–	–	–	–	–	–	–	–
Subtotal: Long term debt	*328*	*284*	*333*	*364*	*298*	*339*	*445*	*796*
of which: concessional	0	0	0	0	0	0	46	40
non-concessional	328	284	333	363	298	339	399	757
Short term								
Subtotal: Short term debt	*207*	*227*	*247*	*310*	*298*	*450*	*679*	*566*
Banks	200	220	240	300	288	440	670	560
Export credits	7	7	7	10	10	10	9	6
Other identified liabilities	–	–	–	–	–	–	–	–
Total identified debt	**535**	**511**	**580**	**674**	**596**	**789**	**1124**	**1362**
SERVICE PAYMENTS								
Long term								
I. OECD countries and capital markets	106	108	96	66	97	75	45	69
ODA	–	–	–	–	–	–	0	8
Official/off. supported	98	100	82	54	77	56	21	21
Financial markets	8	8	14	13	20	19	24	40
Other private	–	–	–	–	–	–	–	–
II. Multilateral	–	0	–	–	–	–	–	–
of which: concessional	–	0	–	–	–	–	–	–
memo: IMF, total	–	–	–	–	–	–	–	–
III. Non-OECD creditor countries	0	0	0	0	0	0	0	–
Subtotal: Service payments, long term debt	*106*	*108*	*96*	*66*	*97*	*75*	*45*	*69*
of which: concessional	0	0	0	0	0	0	0	8
Amortization, long term debt	84	77	70	39	71	46	18	36
Interest, long term debt	22	31	26	27	26	29	27	33
Interest, short term debt	22	18	16	19	24	34	47	37
Total service payments	**129**	**126**	**112**	**85**	**121**	**109**	**92**	**106**

BOLIVIA

US $ Million

	1984	1985	1986	1987	1988	1989	1990	1991
GROSS DEBT								
Long term								
I. OECD countries and capital markets	1944	2286	2277	2243	1834	1746	1967	1693
ODA	491	583	597	741	870	814	1028	735
Official/off. supported	185	205	419	560	521	584	680	721
Official export credits	46	61	308	391	427	481	573	606
Guaranteed supplier credits	84	83	53	61	41	44	43	65
Guaranteed bank credits	56	60	58	108	53	59	64	50
Financial markets	1268	1498	1261	942	443	348	259	237
Banks	1230	1461	1224	906	408	313	224	202
Bonds	39	38	37	36	35	35	35	35
Other private	–	–	–	–	–	–	–	–
II. Multilateral	712	784	1034	1290	1488	1692	1849	1955
of which: concessional	368	409	510	576	711	906	1044	1144
non-concessional	344	375	524	714	777	786	806	811
memo: IMF, total	96	82	192	186	197	252	257	245
III. Non-OECD Creditor countries	1045	1016	1087	1243	1086	351	224	180
C.E.E.C.	23	24	23	25	12	23	22	22
Arab countries	–	–	–	–	–	–	–	–
Other countries and unspecified	1022	992	1064	1217	1074	328	203	158
Subtotal: Long term debt	*3701*	*4085*	*4398*	*4776*	*4408*	*3789*	*4041*	*3827*
of which: concessional	858	992	1107	1318	1581	1720	2072	1878
non-concessional	2842	3094	3291	3459	2827	2069	1969	1949
Short term								
Subtotal: Short term debt	*278*	*442*	*735*	*669*	*599*	*419*	*313*	*269*
Banks	229	345	569	551	464	343	197	173
Export credits	49	97	166	118	135	76	116	96
Other identified liabilities	46	54	54	31	37	6	6	6
Total identified debt	**4025**	**4581**	**5187**	**5476**	**5044**	**4214**	**4360**	**4102**
SERVICE PAYMENTS								
Long term								
I. OECD countries and capital markets	146	93	69	94	260	177	95	141
ODA	20	27	18	48	13	28	47	83
Official/off. supported	40	43	37	44	37	47	30	29
Financial markets	86	22	13	3	211	102	17	29
Other private	–	–	–	–	–	–	–	–
II. Multilateral	87	84	157	156	199	202	244	216
of which: concessional	9	14	19	23	26	25	30	30
memo: IMF, total	31	29	43	43	67	24	58	60
III. Non-OECD creditor countries	154	98	27	20	28	27	72	35
Subtotal: Service payments, long term debt	*387*	*275*	*253*	*269*	*488*	*405*	*411*	*392*
of which: concessional	29	41	37	70	39	53	77	113
Amortization, long term debt	137	143	150	159	183	172	255	254
Interest, long term debt	250	132	102	110	304	234	155	138
Interest, short term debt	30	28	35	42	41	35	20	12
Total service payments	**417**	**303**	**288**	**311**	**529**	**441**	**431**	**404**

US $ Million

	1984	1985	1986	1987	1988	1989	1990	1991
GROSS DEBT								
Long term								
I. OECD countries and capital markets	158	187	271	314	317	187	199	183
ODA	45	46	46	49	66	73	79	80
Official/off. supported	102	135	225	264	251	114	120	104
Official export credits	80	104	180	227	207	71	73	67
Guaranteed supplier credits	5	3	9	4	13	11	10	3
Guaranteed bank credits	18	27	36	33	31	32	36	33
Financial markets	11	7	1	1	–	–	–	–
Banks	10	6	–	–	–	–	–	–
Bonds	1	1	1	1	–	–	–	–
Other private	–	–	–	–	–	–	–	–
II. Multilateral	146	213	259	341	327	349	363	399
of which: concessional	47	53	54	67	70	96	114	150
non-concessional	99	160	205	274	257	253	248	249
memo: IMF, total	–	–	–	–	–	–	–	–
III. Non-OECD Creditor countries	24	30	29	30	29	26	23	21
C.E.E.C.	–	–	–	–	–	–	–	–
Arab countries	24	28	26	26	26	23	21	19
Other countries and unspecified	–	2	3	3	3	2	2	2
Subtotal: Long term debt	*328*	*430*	*559*	*685*	*673*	*562*	*584*	*604*
of which: concessional	92	99	99	117	135	169	193	230
non-concessional	236	332	460	569	537	393	391	374
Short term								
Subtotal: Short term debt	*13*	*18*	*11*	*16*	*17*	*12*	*17*	*28*
Banks	10	16	8	10	6	5	5	13
Export credits	3	2	3	6	11	7	12	15
Other identified liabilities	4	2	4	11	12	10	13	10
Total identified debt	**345**	**451**	**574**	**712**	**702**	**584**	**614**	**642**
SERVICE PAYMENTS								
Long term								
I. OECD countries and capital markets	24	23	18	26	42	25	45	27
ODA	2	2	3	3	5	4	5	5
Official/off. supported	11	9	15	22	33	18	36	17
Financial markets	10	12	0	0	4	3	5	5
Other private	–	–	–	–	–	–	–	–
II. Multilateral	14	20	32	49	48	45	60	59
of which: concessional	2	3	3	3	4	4	5	6
memo: IMF, total	–	–	–	–	–	–	–	–
III. Non-OECD creditor countries	1	2	2	3	5	3	3	3
Subtotal: Service payments, long term debt	*38*	*45*	*52*	*77*	*95*	*73*	*108*	*88*
of which: concessional	4	5	6	7	9	8	10	11
Amortization, long term debt	25	27	20	37	57	39	71	57
Interest, long term debt	14	18	32	39	37	34	37	32
Interest, short term debt	4	2	1	1	2	2	2	2
Total service payments	**42**	**47**	**53**	**78**	**97**	**75**	**110**	**90**

BRASIL

US $ Million

	1984	1985	1986	1987	1988	1989	1990	1991
GROSS DEBT								
Long term								
I. OECD countries and capital markets	84138	83274	83231	83064	84500	77529	73786	70669
ODA	1567	1784	2222	2428	2083	1927	1994	1871
Official/off. supported	11887	11490	12829	15187	14005	15803	18288	15926
Official export credits	5330	5404	5762	8639	9655	10420	12566	11957
Guaranteed supplier credits	2001	1743	1865	1252	1003	1351	1042	978
Guaranteed bank credits	4557	4342	5203	5295	3347	4033	4679	2990
Financial markets	68284	67507	65699	62840	65854	57241	50866	50233
Banks	66586	65690	63911	61324	64308	55058	48526	48701
Bonds	1698	1816	1787	1516	1546	2183	2339	1532
Other private	2400	2494	2481	2610	2558	2558	2639	2639
II. Multilateral	9807	11978	14528	16287	14746	13511	13208	12312
of which: concessional	156	171	200	198	165	137	116	98
non-concessional	9651	11806	14328	16090	14582	13374	13092	12214
memo: IMF, total	4185	4619	4501	3976	3333	2423	1821	1237
III. Non-OECD Creditor countries	1051	810	700	566	248	239	247	333
C.E.E.C.	161	138	145	176	207	198	192	175
Arab countries	291	232	173	110	24	23	18	37
Other countries and unspecified	598	439	382	280	17	17	37	122
Subtotal: Long term debt	*94995*	*96061*	*98460*	*99918*	*99494*	*91279*	*87242*	*83314*
of which: concessional	1722	1955	2423	2625	2248	2063	2110	1969
non-concessional	93273	94106	96037	97292	97246	89216	85132	81345
Short term								
Subtotal: Short term debt	*7177*	*8241*	*14603*	*17391*	*11767*	*15294*	*18364*	*14237*
Banks	5779	6871	11886	14305	8216	11902	13426	9007
Export credits	1398	1370	2716	3086	3551	3393	4938	5230
Other identified liabilities	–	–	–	–	–	–	–	–
Total identified debt	**102172**	**104302**	**113063**	**117308**	**111261**	**106573**	**105606**	**97551**
SERVICE PAYMENTS								
Long term								
I. OECD countries and capital markets	12069	8414	7895	4837	11774	7158	3459	5126
ODA	29	125	157	132	76	84	85	92
Official/off. supported	1746	988	2045	2351	1711	1728	1245	1314
Financial markets	10053	7110	5506	2189	9793	5079	1940	3229
Other private	240	192	186	165	193	267	190	491
II. Multilateral	1095	1487	2500	3435	3311	2981	3489	3169
of which: concessional	35	34	46	46	42	41	41	30
memo: IMF, total	204	403	979	1455	1180	1069	996	717
III. Non-OECD creditor countries	137	106	67	110	53	40	65	54
Subtotal: Service payments, long term debt	*13300*	*10007*	*10462*	*8382*	*15137*	*10178*	*7014*	*8349*
of which: concessional	65	158	204	178	118	124	125	123
Amortization, long term debt	2557	2264	3321	4094	3816	5127	4545	4425
Interest, long term debt	10744	7743	7141	4288	11322	5051	2469	3923
Interest, short term debt	742	567	687	960	968	983	1119	715
Total service payments	**14042**	**10575**	**11149**	**9342**	**16105**	**11161**	**8133**	**9064**

US $ Million

	1984	1985	1986	1987	1988	1989	1990	1991
GROSS DEBT								
Long term								
I. OECD countries and capital markets	112	147	175	239	253	284	346	345
ODA	49	71	100	156	166	202	248	264
Official/off. supported	41	55	59	69	74	71	90	75
Official export credits	31	39	44	53	47	49	57	57
Guaranteed supplier credits	2	4	4	6	21	11	17	7
Guaranteed bank credits	7	12	11	10	6	11	17	11
Financial markets	22	20	16	15	13	11	8	6
Banks	22	20	16	15	13	11	8	6
Bonds	–	–	–	–	–	–	–	–
Other private	–	–	–	–	–	–	–	–
II. Multilateral	255	308	390	447	465	499	565	618
of which: concessional	237	284	352	392	405	432	484	538
non-concessional	18	25	38	55	61	67	81	79
memo: IMF, total	11	10	8	6	3	1	0	9
III. Non-OECD Creditor countries	32	46	45	61	70	72	74	92
C.E.E.C.	–	–	–	–	6	6	7	7
Arab countries	17	24	27	33	37	35	43	53
Other countries and unspecified	16	22	18	28	27	30	24	32
Subtotal: Long term debt	*399*	*502*	*610*	*747*	*788*	*854*	*985*	*1054*
of which: concessional	285	355	452	547	571	634	732	803
non-concessional	113	146	158	200	217	220	252	252
Short term								
Subtotal: Short term debt	*32*	*45*	*58*	*76*	*65*	*62*	*130*	*59*
Banks	6	11	10	16	7	8	5	5
Export credits	26	35	49	60	58	54	125	54
Other identified liabilities	23	29	25	33	33	37	39	30
Total identified debt	**453**	**576**	**693**	**855**	**887**	**953**	**1154**	**1143**
SERVICE PAYMENTS								
Long term								
I. OECD countries and capital markets	12	15	9	9	13	23	6	14
ODA	1	2	2	4	5	13	0	5
Official/off. supported	8	11	5	3	6	5	4	6
Financial markets	2	2	2	2	3	5	2	3
Other private	–	–	–	–	–	–	–	–
II. Multilateral	9	8	15	17	25	23	21	37
of which: concessional	7	5	11	13	20	14	15	18
memo: IMF, total	1	2	3	3	3	2	1	–
III. Non-OECD creditor countries	0	4	4	3	1	2	1	2
Subtotal: Service payments, long term debt	*21*	*27*	*28*	*29*	*39*	*48*	*28*	*53*
of which: concessional	8	7	13	17	24	27	16	23
Amortization, long term debt	11	17	17	16	23	31	16	29
Interest, long term debt	10	10	11	13	16	17	12	24
Interest, short term debt	6	5	5	6	8	8	8	5
Total service payments	**27**	**32**	**33**	**35**	**46**	**56**	**36**	**58**

US $ Million

	1984	1985	1986	1987	1988	1989	1990	1991
GROSS DEBT								
Long term								
I. OECD countries and capital markets	59	100	112	155	144	161	190	193
ODA	29	57	81	123	124	144	171	182
Official/off. supported	13	11	22	28	14	11	12	10
Official export credits	2	2	2	3	3	3	3	3
Guaranteed supplier credits	4	2	–	4	9	4	5	3
Guaranteed bank credits	7	7	19	21	2	4	4	4
Financial markets	18	32	10	4	6	6	7	1
Banks	18	32	10	4	6	6	7	1
Bonds	–	–	–	–	–	–	–	–
Other private	–	–	–	–	–	–	–	–
II. Multilateral	209	258	354	489	550	607	703	790
of which: concessional	185	226	314	438	499	558	654	745
non-concessional	24	32	40	51	51	49	49	44
memo: IMF, total	16	15	22	21	33	40	43	49
III. Non-OECD Creditor countries	84	88	87	111	109	103	100	91
C.E.E.C.	26	25	24	24	24	23	24	20
Arab countries	25	31	36	51	51	52	50	47
Other countries and unspecified	33	32	27	35	35	27	25	24
Subtotal: Long term debt	*352*	*446*	*554*	*755*	*804*	*871*	*993*	*1074*
of which: concessional	214	283	395	561	623	702	825	927
non-concessional	138	163	159	194	181	169	168	146
Short term								
Subtotal: Short term debt	*12*	*26*	*23*	*37*	*21*	*21*	*31*	*31*
Banks	4	8	10	12	9	8	22	22
Export credits	8	17	13	25	13	14	9	9
Other identified liabilities	4	4	7	4	3	2	2	2
Total identified debt	**368**	**476**	**584**	**796**	**828**	**894**	**1025**	**1107**
SERVICE PAYMENTS								
Long term								
I. OECD countries and capital markets	6	9	15	13	20	19	22	14
ODA	1	1	2	3	7	7	8	3
Official/off. supported	3	2	8	9	4	5	3	3
Financial markets	2	5	5	1	9	8	11	8
Other private	–	–	–	–	–	–	–	–
II. Multilateral	14	12	15	21	19	20	21	22
of which: concessional	6	9	9	12	12	13	12	13
memo: IMF, total	7	3	4	5	4	3	1	0
III. Non-OECD creditor countries	4	3	6	7	10	9	10	13
Subtotal: Service payments, long term debt	*24*	*24*	*35*	*41*	*49*	*48*	*53*	*50*
of which: concessional	7	10	11	15	18	19	20	17
Amortization, long term debt	15	15	22	27	31	31	37	33
Interest, long term debt	9	9	13	14	18	17	16	17
Interest, short term debt	2	2	2	2	3	2	2	2
Total service payments	**26**	**26**	**37**	**44**	**51**	**50**	**55**	**51**

CAMBODIA

US $ Million

	1984	1985	1986	1987	1988	1989	1990	1991
GROSS DEBT								
Long term								
I. OECD countries and capital markets	231	236	241	249	244	245	251	248
ODA	230	236	241	249	244	245	249	248
Official/off. supported	–	–	0	1	–	–	–	–
Official export credits	–	–	0	1	–	–	–	–
Guaranteed supplier credits	–	–	–	–	–	–	–	–
Guaranteed bank credits	–	–	–	–	–	–	–	–
Financial markets	1	–	0	0	–	–	2	–
Banks	1	–	0	0	–	–	2	–
Bonds	–	–	–	–	–	–	–	–
Other private	–	–	–	–	–	–	–	–
II. Multilateral	16	17	19	22	21	24	25	26
of which: concessional	0	0	0	0	0	4	4	4
non-concessional	15	17	19	22	21	20	22	22
memo: IMF, total	12	14	15	18	17	16	18	18
III. Non-OECD Creditor countries	477	456	447	689	870	1137	1240	1290
C.E.E.C.	477	456	447	689	870	1137	1240	1290
Arab countries	–	–	–	–	–	–	–	–
Other countries and unspecified	–	–	–	–	–	–	–	–
Subtotal: Long term debt	*724*	*709*	*708*	*961*	*1136*	*1406*	*1516*	*1564*
of which: concessional	708	692	689	938	1115	1385	1492	1542
non-concessional	16	17	19	22	21	20	24	22
Short term								
Subtotal: Short term debt	*4*	*6*	*7*	*14*	*13*	*18*	*33*	*32*
Banks	–	–	0	6	6	10	25	24
Export credits	4	6	7	8	7	8	8	8
Other identified liabilities	–	–	–	–	–	–	–	–
Total identified debt	**729**	**715**	**715**	**975**	**1149**	**1423**	**1550**	**1596**
SERVICE PAYMENTS								
Long term								
I. OECD countries and capital markets	0	1	5	0	1	0	6	5
ODA	0	0	5	0	0	0	5	5
Official/off. supported	–	–	–	–	0	–	1	–
Financial markets	0	1	–	0	0	–	–	0
Other private	–	–	–	–	–	–	–	–
II. Multilateral	1	7	1	1	1	0	2	0
of which: concessional	–	6	–	0	–	0	0	0
memo: IMF, total	1	1	1	1	1	–	1	–
III. Non-OECD creditor countries	–	6	8	9	10	10	23	10
Subtotal: Service payments, long term debt	*1*	*14*	*14*	*11*	*12*	*11*	*30*	*15*
of which: concessional	0	12	13	9	11	11	27	15
Amortization, long term debt	0	1	0	0	0	0	1	–
Interest, long term debt	1	13	14	11	12	11	29	15
Interest, short term debt	0	0	0	0	0	1	1	1
Total service payments	**1**	**14**	**14**	**11**	**13**	**12**	**31**	**17**

CAMEROON

	1984	1985	1986	1987	1988	1989	1990	1991
GROSS DEBT								
Long term								
I. OECD countries and capital markets	1619	2002	1955	2584	2504	2899	3313	3422
ODA	406	496	648	838	868	1043	1155	1273
Official/off. supported	874	1073	1279	1478	986	1248	1544	1626
Official export credits	263	328	361	461	403	584	716	708
Guaranteed supplier credits	101	225	157	200	86	192	260	257
Guaranteed bank credits	509	520	761	817	497	471	568	660
Financial markets	340	434	29	268	649	609	614	523
Banks	340	434	29	268	649	609	614	523
Bonds	–	–	–	–	–	–	–	–
Other private	–	–	–	–	–	–	–	–
II. Multilateral	594	718	895	1112	1149	1226	1412	1542
of which: concessional	343	354	373	389	369	370	375	369
non-concessional	251	364	522	723	780	856	1037	1173
memo: IMF, total	30	27	22	16	100	113	121	121
III. Non-OECD Creditor countries	132	126	117	119	113	104	99	94
C.E.E.C.	4	3	2	–	–	1	1	1
Arab countries	73	75	74	77	73	72	69	66
Other countries and unspecified	55	48	41	41	40	32	29	28
Subtotal: Long term debt	*2345*	*2847*	*2967*	*3815*	*3765*	*4230*	*4824*	*5058*
of which: concessional	748	850	1021	1227	1237	1413	1530	1642
non-concessional	1596	1997	1946	2588	2528	2817	3294	3416
Short term								
Subtotal: Short term debt	*419*	*517*	*847*	*804*	*908*	*824*	*1246*	*1243*
Banks	189	200	533	454	479	327	587	596
Export credits	230	318	313	350	429	496	659	647
Other identified liabilities	–	–	–	–	–	–	–	–
Total identified debt	**2764**	**3364**	**3813**	**4619**	**4673**	**5053**	**6070**	**6301**
SERVICE PAYMENTS								
Long term								
I. OECD countries and capital markets	315	558	639	372	550	323	414	337
ODA	18	27	19	31	34	21	45	25
Official/off. supported	259	462	533	333	101	113	183	143
Financial markets	37	69	87	8	415	189	186	169
Other private	–	–	–	–	–	–	–	–
II. Multilateral	50	60	82	108	123	119	152	204
of which: concessional	13	15	19	20	20	16	17	18
memo: IMF, total	3	6	8	9	9	5	13	22
III. Non-OECD creditor countries	8	9	9	10	4	0	3	3
Subtotal: Service payments, long term debt	*373*	*627*	*730*	*489*	*677*	*443*	*568*	*545*
of which: concessional	31	42	38	51	55	37	62	43
Amortization, long term debt	234	484	556	333	511	264	353	297
Interest, long term debt	138	143	174	156	166	178	215	248
Interest, short term debt	33	34	41	50	55	54	53	45
Total service payments	**406**	**661**	**772**	**540**	**732**	**497**	**621**	**589**

CAPE VERDE

US $ Million

	1984	1985	1986	1987	1988	1989	1990	1991
GROSS DEBT								
Long term								
I. OECD countries and capital markets	11	12	17	22	17	19	12	17
ODA	0	4	6	8	7	7	8	7
Official/off. supported	11	9	11	14	10	10	2	8
Official export credits	6	4	7	3	–	0	–	–
Guaranteed supplier credits	0	0	0	–	0	0	–	–
Guaranteed bank credits	4	4	4	11	9	10	2	8
Financial markets	–	–	0	1	–	2	2	2
Banks	–	–	0	1	–	2	2	2
Bonds	–	–	–	–	–	–	–	–
Other private	–	–	–	–	–	–	–	–
II. Multilateral	41	55	64	74	76	82	91	91
of which: concessional	30	42	49	58	62	69	78	80
non-concessional	11	13	15	16	14	13	13	11
memo: IMF, total	–	–	–	–	–	–	–	–
III. Non-OECD Creditor countries	35	39	39	40	32	34	36	36
C.E.E.C.	5	6	7	8	9	13	16	17
Arab countries	1	3	4	5	6	5	5	5
Other countries and unspecified	29	29	28	27	18	15	15	14
Subtotal: Long term debt	*87*	*106*	*120*	*136*	*125*	*135*	*139*	*145*
of which: concessional	31	45	55	65	69	76	86	87
non-concessional	56	61	65	71	56	59	53	58
Short term								
Subtotal: Short term debt	*0*	*2*	*6*	*10*	*2*	*2*	*4*	*5*
Banks	–	–	–	4	0	–	1	2
Export credits	0	2	6	6	2	2	3	3
Other identified liabilities	–	–	–	–	–	–	–	–
Total identified debt	**87**	**108**	**126**	**146**	**128**	**136**	**143**	**150**
SERVICE PAYMENTS								
Long term								
I. OECD countries and capital markets	2	1	1	1	1	1	2	2
ODA	0	–	0	0	0	0	0	0
Official/off. supported	2	1	1	0	1	1	2	1
Financial markets	–	–	–	0	0	0	0	0
Other private	–	–	–	–	–	–	–	–
II. Multilateral	2	2	1	4	4	3	3	4
of which: concessional	1	1	1	2	2	1	1	1
memo: IMF, total	–	–	–	–	–	–	–	–
III. Non-OECD creditor countries	3	3	3	3	1	1	1	1
Subtotal: Service payments, long term debt	*8*	*6*	*5*	*8*	*7*	*5*	*6*	*6*
of which: concessional	1	1	1	2	2	2	2	1
Amortization, long term debt	5	3	3	4	3	3	5	4
Interest, long term debt	3	3	2	4	4	2	2	2
Interest, short term debt	0	0	0	0	0	0	0	0
Total service payments	**8**	**6**	**6**	**8**	**7**	**5**	**6**	**6**

US $ Million

	1984	1985	1986	1987	1988	1989	1990	1991
GROSS DEBT								
Long term								
I. OECD countries and capital markets	92	135	167	237	214	224	258	252
ODA	39	67	96	158	155	173	203	202
Official/off. supported	50	65	68	71	49	42	46	41
Official export credits	42	56	60	61	40	35	38	30
Guaranteed supplier credits	4	4	6	9	8	7	8	11
Guaranteed bank credits	4	4	2	1	0	0	0	0
Financial markets	3	4	2	8	10	9	9	9
Banks	3	4	2	8	10	9	9	9
Bonds	–	–	–	–	–	–	–	–
Other private	–	–	–	–	–	–	–	–
II. Multilateral	122	160	219	300	337	371	502	551
of which: concessional	94	124	168	239	286	334	471	523
non-concessional	28	36	51	62	51	37	31	28
memo: IMF, total	35	39	42	52	50	35	37	33
III. Non-OECD Creditor countries	42	42	52	60	68	61	67	113
C.E.E.C.	4	4	4	4	4	4	3	3
Arab countries	9	9	9	14	24	21	22	28
Other countries and unspecified	29	29	39	42	40	37	41	82
Subtotal: Long term debt	*256*	*337*	*438*	*597*	*619*	*656*	*827*	*915*
of which: concessional	134	191	265	397	442	507	674	724
non-concessional	122	147	173	200	177	149	153	191
Short term								
Subtotal: Short term debt	*13*	*16*	*11*	*25*	*32*	*45*	*45*	*53*
Banks	5	3	9	5	16	26	27	35
Export credits	8	13	2	20	16	19	18	18
Other identified liabilities	–	–	–	–	–	–	–	–
Total identified debt	**269**	**353**	**449**	**622**	**651**	**701**	**872**	**968**
SERVICE PAYMENTS								
Long term								
I. OECD countries and capital markets	24	10	12	9	10	14	12	7
ODA	16	5	6	2	5	7	0	4
Official/off. supported	8	5	6	6	2	2	9	2
Financial markets	0	0	0	0	3	5	2	1
Other private	–	–	–	–	–	–	–	–
II. Multilateral	11	16	15	13	18	23	19	13
of which: concessional	2	3	5	6	6	6	6	6
memo: IMF, total	10	14	11	9	13	15	11	4
III. Non-OECD creditor countries	2	3	2	2	0	0	3	0
Subtotal: Service payments, long term debt	*37*	*28*	*30*	*23*	*29*	*38*	*34*	*20*
of which: concessional	18	8	11	8	11	13	6	10
Amortization, long term debt	27	19	19	12	16	26	22	9
Interest, long term debt	10	10	11	12	12	12	12	11
Interest, short term debt	1	1	1	1	2	3	3	3
Total service payments	**38**	**29**	**31**	**24**	**31**	**41**	**38**	**22**

CHAD

US $ Million

	1984	1985	1986	1987	1988	1989	1990	1991
GROSS DEBT								
Long term								
I. OECD countries and capital markets	22	21	27	63	78	89	131	160
ODA	5	11	20	51	65	83	115	130
Official/off. supported	15	7	7	11	12	5	15	30
Official export credits	1	2	2	2	2	2	8	8
Guaranteed supplier credits	13	5	3	7	9	2	7	7
Guaranteed bank credits	–	–	3	2	1	1	0	15
Financial markets	3	3	–	0	–	–	–	–
Banks	3	3	–	0	–	–	–	–
Bonds	–	–	–	–	–	–	–	–
Other private	–	–	–	–	–	–	–	–
II. Multilateral	90	100	120	159	190	254	348	419
of which: concessional	85	92	112	146	179	248	341	412
non-concessional	4	9	9	13	11	7	7	7
memo: IMF, total	8	12	11	20	17	24	30	31
III. Non-OECD Creditor countries	35	29	32	34	41	39	35	49
C.E.E.C.	–	–	–	–	3	3	3	3
Arab countries	32	26	26	27	26	23	18	21
Other countries and unspecified	2	3	6	7	11	14	15	25
Subtotal: Long term debt	*147*	*151*	*179*	*257*	*308*	*382*	*514*	*627*
of which: concessional	90	103	131	198	245	331	457	542
non-concessional	57	48	48	59	64	51	58	86
Short term								
Subtotal: Short term debt	*17*	*23*	*34*	*48*	*50*	*48*	*50*	*42*
Banks	1	2	2	6	14	15	19	13
Export credits	16	21	32	42	36	34	31	29
Other identified liabilities	–	–	–	–	–	–	–	–
Total identified debt	**163**	**174**	**214**	**305**	**358**	**430**	**564**	**669**
SERVICE PAYMENTS								
Long term								
I. OECD countries and capital markets	6	5	1	1	2	3	6	4
ODA	4	0	0	1	2	2	4	2
Official/off. supported	0	0	0	1	1	0	2	1
Financial markets	2	5	0	–	0	1	0	1
Other private	–	–	–	–	–	–	–	–
II. Multilateral	5	7	7	5	6	9	9	6
of which: concessional	2	3	5	4	4	4	4	5
memo: IMF, total	4	5	3	2	3	5	4	0
III. Non-OECD creditor countries	2	2	–	–	–	–	0	0
Subtotal: Service payments, long term debt	*12*	*14*	*8*	*6*	*8*	*12*	*15*	*10*
of which: concessional	6	3	5	5	5	6	8	8
Amortization, long term debt	11	12	5	4	4	8	10	5
Interest, long term debt	1	2	2	2	4	4	4	6
Interest, short term debt	0	0	0	1	1	2	2	1
Total service payments	**13**	**15**	**8**	**7**	**10**	**14**	**17**	**12**

CHILE

US $ Million

	1984	1985	1986	1987	1988	1989	1990	1991
GROSS DEBT								
Long term								
I. OECD countries and capital markets	15902	15996	15664	14602	12155	9994	9350	9415
ODA	490	490	537	465	464	433	399	348
Official/off. supported	517	799	795	1006	1145	1209	1507	1696
Official export credits	43	36	111	169	420	460	680	794
Guaranteed supplier credits	146	378	294	273	276	290	302	389
Guaranteed bank credits	328	385	391	564	450	460	526	513
Financial markets	14874	14694	14325	13131	10546	8352	7444	7371
Banks	14694	14495	14208	12996	10489	8309	7405	7051
Bonds	180	199	116	134	57	43	39	320
Other private	20	14	7	–	–	–	–	–
II. Multilateral	1696	2620	3625	4683	4713	4821	5299	5271
of which: concessional	99	105	115	129	114	105	100	90
non-concessional	1597	2515	3509	4554	4599	4716	5199	5181
memo: IMF, total	779	1088	1331	1465	1322	1270	1156	958
III. Non-OECD Creditor countries	220	140	106	84	68	58	50	39
C.E.E.C.	0	–	–	–	–	–	–	–
Arab countries	0	0	0	0	–	–	–	–
Other countries and unspecified	220	139	106	84	68	58	50	39
Subtotal: Long term debt	*17818*	*18756*	*19394*	*19369*	*16936*	*14872*	*14699*	*14725*
of which: concessional	589	595	652	594	578	538	499	438
non-concessional	17229	18161	18742	18775	16358	14335	14200	14287
Short term								
Subtotal: Short term debt	*3222*	*4186*	*4335*	*3098*	*1793*	*1670*	*1530*	*848*
Banks	3123	4006	4172	2861	1478	1322	1159	435
Export credits	99	180	164	237	315	348	371	413
Other identified liabilities	–	–	–	–	–	–	–	–
Total identified debt	**21039**	**22942**	**23729**	**22468**	**18729**	**16543**	**16229**	**15573**
SERVICE PAYMENTS								
Long term								
I. OECD countries and capital markets	1975	1773	1464	1409	1702	1658	1309	1259
ODA	40	22	62	49	38	45	42	85
Official/off. supported	189	314	267	255	262	264	325	343
Financial markets	1746	1437	1121	1091	1402	1349	942	830
Other private	–	–	14	14	–	–	–	–
II. Multilateral	139	192	488	771	726	797	902	935
of which: concessional	13	8	9	10	13	12	15	15
memo: IMF, total	46	64	265	457	360	303	326	294
III. Non-OECD creditor countries	78	59	44	36	27	25	18	14
Subtotal: Service payments, long term debt	*2192*	*2025*	*1997*	*2216*	*2455*	*2480*	*2229*	*2208*
of which: concessional	53	30	71	59	51	57	56	100
Amortization, long term debt	545	428	615	707	901	1003	931	1112
Interest, long term debt	1647	1597	1382	1509	1554	1477	1298	1096
Interest, short term debt	404	302	288	256	194	155	130	67
Total service payments	**2596**	**2327**	**2285**	**2472**	**2649**	**2635**	**2360**	**2275**

CHINA

US $ Million

	1984	1985	1986	1987	1988	1989	1990	1991
GROSS DEBT								
Long term								
I. OECD countries and capital markets	5947	8671	14399	22613	27326	31729	38888	42909
ODA	1136	1946	2956	4383	4871	5522	6839	7749
Official/off. supported	3427	3753	4072	3734	3707	5510	6581	8115
Official export credits	1311	1944	2532	2281	2498	2922	3378	4255
Guaranteed supplier credits	1567	1192	935	822	578	1486	1133	1441
Guaranteed bank credits	549	617	605	630	631	1102	2070	2419
Financial markets	1383	2972	7371	14497	18747	20697	25468	27045
Banks	1283	1788	4623	10106	13618	15520	20102	21838
Bonds	100	1184	2748	4390	5129	5177	5366	5207
Other private	–	–	–	–	–	–	–	–
II. Multilateral	574	1323	2882	4008	4766	5669	6545	7482
of which: concessional	501	808	1169	1718	2114	2488	3128	3681
non-concessional	73	515	1713	2290	2651	3181	3417	3801
memo: IMF, total	303	340	1072	1155	1013	908	469	–
III. Non-OECD Creditor countries	101	225	275	277	287	306	284	259
C.E.E.C.	–	7	28	35	40	85	88	85
Arab countries	57	100	99	121	166	160	149	140
Other countries and unspecified	44	118	148	121	81	62	47	34
Subtotal: Long term debt	*6622*	*10219*	*17556*	*26898*	*32378*	*37704*	*45717*	*50650*
of which: concessional	1637	2755	4125	6101	6986	8010	9967	11430
non-concessional	4984	7465	13431	20797	25392	29694	35750	39220
Short term								
Subtotal: Short term debt	*6028*	*10337*	*8883*	*8516*	*11908*	*7537*	*9899*	*16595*
Banks	2785	7250	5705	5873	9182	5709	8453	14634
Export credits	3243	3086	3179	2643	2726	1828	1446	1961
Other identified liabilities	–	–	–	–	–	–	–	–
Total identified debt	**12649**	**20556**	**26439**	**35414**	**44286**	**45242**	**55616**	**67245**
SERVICE PAYMENTS								
Long term								
I. OECD countries and capital markets	875	1540	1330	2871	3219	3799	4701	3995
ODA	41	57	81	111	179	185	242	284
Official/off. supported	683	1057	811	2145	1420	1618	1723	1343
Financial markets	151	426	439	615	1620	1996	2736	2368
Other private	–	–	–	–	–	–	–	–
II. Multilateral	11	32	116	355	318	389	1001	879
of which: concessional	5	6	47	97	102	96	106	72
memo: IMF, total	2	2	38	131	134	147	555	475
III. Non-OECD creditor countries	4	10	33	60	65	41	43	44
Subtotal: Service payments, long term debt	*889*	*1582*	*1479*	*3287*	*3602*	*4229*	*5745*	*4917*
of which: concessional	46	64	128	208	281	280	349	356
Amortization, long term debt	556	1268	1008	2366	2222	2274	3559	2543
Interest, long term debt	333	314	472	921	1380	1955	2186	2374
Interest, short term debt	525	671	653	600	817	875	724	795
Total service payments	**1414**	**2253**	**2133**	**3887**	**4419**	**5104**	**6468**	**5712**

US $ Million

	1984	1985	1986	1987	1988	1989	1990	1991
GROSS DEBT								
Long term								
I. OECD countries and capital markets	6529	7337	8808	8896	9222	9094	9000	8868
ODA	826	855	867	913	863	821	830	825
Official/off. supported	1384	2047	2912	3166	3130	2928	3377	3160
Official export credits	745	1055	1423	1642	1738	1619	1641	1553
Guaranteed supplier credits	146	175	244	369	333	372	359	344
Guaranteed bank credits	494	817	1244	1155	1058	936	1377	1262
Financial markets	4318	4436	5029	4575	5027	5195	4693	4784
Banks	4301	4420	4983	4469	4923	4918	4418	4426
Bonds	17	16	46	106	104	277	275	359
Other private	–	–	–	242	203	151	99	99
II. Multilateral	2333	3408	4561	5773	5612	5651	6103	6161
of which: concessional	272	281	299	298	282	276	264	244
non-concessional	2062	3127	4262	5475	5330	5375	5839	5917
memo: IMF, total	–	–	–	–	–	–	–	–
III. Non-OECD Creditor countries	155	166	185	195	232	327	379	360
C.E.E.C.	14	13	13	15	15	15	15	15
Arab countries	–	–	–	–	–	–	–	–
Other countries and unspecified	141	152	171	180	217	312	364	345
Subtotal: Long term debt	*9017*	*10912*	*13553*	*14864*	*15066*	*15073*	*15482*	*15389*
of which: concessional	1098	1136	1167	1211	1145	1097	1094	1069
non-concessional	7919	9776	12387	13653	13921	13975	14388	14320
Short term								
Subtotal: Short term debt	*2434*	*1480*	*824*	*1603*	*1619*	*1275*	*1518*	*1383*
Banks	2326	1329	505	1018	1085	753	988	893
Export credits	107	151	319	586	533	522	530	489
Other identified liabilities	–	–	–	–	–	–	–	–
Total identified debt	**11450**	**12392**	**14377**	**16468**	**16685**	**16348**	**17000**	**16771**
SERVICE PAYMENTS								
Long term								
I. OECD countries and capital markets	961	1128	1346	1683	1995	2582	2405	2178
ODA	51	49	58	68	62	77	62	64
Official/off. supported	390	530	688	732	706	899	874	823
Financial markets	519	548	600	883	1149	1502	1401	1232
Other private	–	–	–	–	78	104	67	59
II. Multilateral	342	424	625	794	892	873	1003	1093
of which: concessional	34	29	30	26	25	23	29	28
memo: IMF, total	–	–	–	–	–	–	–	–
III. Non-OECD creditor countries	20	35	34	53	52	66	75	102
Subtotal: Service payments, long term debt	*1323*	*1587*	*2006*	*2531*	*2939*	*3522*	*3483*	*3374*
of which: concessional	85	78	88	95	87	101	91	92
Amortization, long term debt	685	749	1140	1336	1726	2194	2208	2238
Interest, long term debt	638	837	865	1195	1213	1328	1275	1135
Interest, short term debt	310	159	77	72	105	106	95	72
Total service payments	**1633**	**1746**	**2083**	**2603**	**3044**	**3628**	**3578**	**3446**

COMOROS

US $ Million

	1984	1985	1986	1987	1988	1989	1990	1991
GROSS DEBT								
Long term								
I. OECD countries and capital markets	7	15	19	29	33	41	47	46
ODA	6	12	17	28	30	38	44	43
Official/off. supported	1	1	1	1	1	1	1	1
Official export credits	1	1	1	1	1	1	1	1
Guaranteed supplier credits	–	–	–	–	–	–	–	–
Guaranteed bank credits	0	0	–	–	–	–	–	–
Financial markets	1	2	0	–	2	2	2	2
Banks	1	2	0	–	2	2	2	2
Bonds	–	–	–	–	–	–	–	–
Other private	–	–	–	–	–	–	–	–
II. Multilateral	51	69	92	109	107	107	120	116
of which: concessional	47	63	80	95	94	94	107	103
non-concessional	4	7	12	14	13	13	14	14
memo: IMF, total	–	–	–	–	–	–	–	1
III. Non-OECD Creditor countries	43	48	48	51	51	49	48	41
C.E.E.C.	–	–	–	–	–	–	–	–
Arab countries	38	43	44	46	45	44	44	37
Other countries and unspecified	5	5	5	5	6	4	4	4
Subtotal: Long term debt	102	132	159	188	191	197	216	203
of which: concessional	53	74	98	123	124	132	150	146
non-concessional	49	58	61	66	67	65	65	58
Short term								
Subtotal: Short term debt	3	4	5	10	3	3	1	1
Banks	1	2	3	5	1	2	–	–
Export credits	2	2	2	5	2	1	1	1
Other identified liabilities	–	–	–	–	–	–	–	–
Total identified debt	**105**	**135**	**164**	**199**	**194**	**201**	**216**	**204**
SERVICE PAYMENTS								
Long term								
I. OECD countries and capital markets	0	1	2	0	0	1	2	2
ODA	0	0	0	0	0	1	2	1
Official/off. supported	0	0	0	0	0	0	1	1
Financial markets	0	0	1	0	–	0	0	0
Other private	–	–	–	–	–	–	–	–
II. Multilateral	1	1	1	0	0	0	0	2
of which: concessional	1	1	1	0	0	0	0	2
memo: IMF, total	–	–	–	–	–	–	–	–
III. Non-OECD creditor countries	1	0	1	0	–	–	–	–
Subtotal: Service payments, long term debt	3	2	3	1	1	1	3	3
of which: concessional	1	1	1	1	1	1	2	3
Amortization, long term debt	1	1	2	0	0	0	1	1
Interest, long term debt	2	2	1	1	1	1	1	3
Interest, short term debt	0	0	0	1	1	0	0	0
Total service payments	**3**	**2**	**3**	**2**	**1**	**2**	**3**	**3**

US $ Million

	1984	1985	1986	1987	1988	1989	1990	1991
GROSS DEBT								
Long term								
I. OECD countries and capital markets	1057	1508	1844	2312	2186	2073	1875	2001
ODA	92	128	213	362	345	375	527	593
Official/off. supported	582	776	1351	1713	1265	1125	1306	1242
Official export credits	53	87	383	691	657	670	914	989
Guaranteed supplier credits	61	104	140	123	112	91	72	44
Guaranteed bank credits	468	585	828	900	496	365	320	209
Financial markets	382	604	279	236	576	573	41	165
Banks	382	604	279	236	576	573	41	165
Bonds	–	–	–	–	–	–	–	–
Other private	–	–	–	–	–	–	–	–
II. Multilateral	203	254	412	521	572	549	581	578
of which: concessional	100	115	142	157	150	155	168	171
non-concessional	104	139	270	363	422	394	413	407
memo: IMF, total	11	10	19	19	15	11	11	6
III. Non-OECD Creditor countries	494	543	543	628	611	639	724	753
C.E.E.C.	217	243	274	320	293	336	409	424
Arab countries	103	102	85	87	93	91	84	85
Other countries and unspecified	174	198	184	221	225	212	230	244
Subtotal: Long term debt	*1754*	*2305*	*2799*	*3460*	*3370*	*3262*	*3179*	*3331*
of which: concessional	192	243	356	519	495	530	695	764
non-concessional	1562	2062	2443	2941	2875	2732	2484	2567
Short term								
Subtotal: Short term debt	*231*	*480*	*695*	*717*	*806*	*1037*	*1257*	*933*
Banks	173	366	614	610	557	661	681	701
Export credits	58	114	80	107	249	376	576	232
Other identified liabilities	–	–	–	–	–	–	–	–
Total identified debt	**1985**	**2785**	**3494**	**4177**	**4176**	**4299**	**4436**	**4264**
SERVICE PAYMENTS								
Long term								
I. OECD countries and capital markets	315	318	399	413	375	303	430	352
ODA	5	7	6	11	10	8	12	13
Official/off. supported	252	274	306	363	88	117	228	147
Financial markets	58	37	87	40	278	179	190	192
Other private	–	–	–	–	–	–	–	–
II. Multilateral	12	23	43	37	44	57	68	13
of which: concessional	3	5	5	4	5	4	4	0
memo: IMF, total	1	2	3	4	4	4	8	6
III. Non-OECD creditor countries	39	36	8	1	0	1	1	6
Subtotal: Service payments, long term debt	*366*	*377*	*450*	*452*	*419*	*361*	*500*	*371*
of which: concessional	9	13	11	15	15	12	16	14
Amortization, long term debt	256	259	302	317	284	186	329	282
Interest, long term debt	110	119	148	135	135	175	170	89
Interest, short term debt	22	26	37	46	51	59	60	45
Total service payments	**388**	**404**	**487**	**498**	**470**	**420**	**560**	**415**

COSTA RICA

US $ Million

	1984	1985	1986	1987	1988	1989	1990	1991
GROSS DEBT								
Long term								
I. OECD countries and capital markets	1750	2016	2032	1962	1277	1507	1967	2058
ODA	389	495	574	633	633	652	719	796
Official/off. supported	182	247	256	283	284	326	309	399
Official export credits	99	147	178	201	208	265	256	346
Guaranteed supplier credits	43	47	24	23	31	15	20	25
Guaranteed bank credits	40	53	54	58	44	45	34	27
Financial markets	1178	1274	1202	1046	360	529	939	863
Banks	967	1053	995	881	295	474	330	263
Bonds	211	221	207	165	65	55	609	599
Other private	–	–	–	–	–	–	–	–
II. Multilateral	715	936	1097	1228	1119	1108	1152	1272
of which: concessional	204	227	235	238	246	243	246	237
non-concessional	511	709	862	990	873	866	906	1035
memo: IMF, total	156	189	172	132	71	35	11	83
III. Non-OECD Creditor countries	403	406	270	275	362	359	393	501
C.E.E.C.	0	–	–	–	–	–	–	–
Arab countries	–	–	–	–	–	–	–	–
Other countries and unspecified	403	406	270	275	362	359	393	501
Subtotal: Long term debt	*2868*	*3358*	*3399*	*3465*	*2757*	*2974*	*3512*	*3831*
of which: concessional	593	722	809	872	879	895	965	1033
non-concessional	2275	2637	2590	2593	1878	2080	2547	2798
Short term								
Subtotal: Short term debt	*312*	*387*	*406*	*507*	*996*	*652*	*528*	*492*
Banks	272	340	361	434	915	573	434	417
Export credits	40	47	45	74	81	79	93	75
Other identified liabilities	–	–	–	–	–	–	–	–
Total identified debt	**3179**	**3745**	**3805**	**3972**	**3753**	**3626**	**4040**	**4323**
SERVICE PAYMENTS								
Long term								
I. OECD countries and capital markets	237	259	126	64	81	83	584	112
ODA	9	5	18	16	17	23	26	20
Official/off. supported	60	54	47	30	40	42	37	31
Financial markets	168	201	61	18	23	18	521	61
Other private	–	–	–	–	–	–	–	–
II. Multilateral	92	117	159	197	203	194	185	191
of which: concessional	10	13	17	11	15	12	15	16
memo: IMF, total	39	36	51	74	62	39	29	12
III. Non-OECD creditor countries	63	69	132	7	36	41	28	38
Subtotal: Service payments, long term debt	*392*	*445*	*418*	*268*	*320*	*318*	*797*	*341*
of which: concessional	19	18	35	27	33	36	41	36
Amortization, long term debt	141	177	254	143	172	174	312	179
Interest, long term debt	251	268	164	125	148	144	486	162
Interest, short term debt	40	27	26	30	33	50	26	28
Total service payments	**432**	**472**	**444**	**298**	**353**	**368**	**823**	**369**

COTE D'IVOIRE

US $ Million

	1984	1985	1986	1987	1988	1989	1990	1991
GROSS DEBT								
Long term								
I. OECD countries and capital markets	5514	7070	7598	8528	8664	9574	10444	10981
ODA	277	403	529	782	860	1021	1351	1602
Official/off. supported	1238	1459	1928	2366	2145	2320	2737	2755
Official export credits	541	884	1238	1778	1894	2071	2404	2417
Guaranteed supplier credits	184	93	213	96	89	62	77	60
Guaranteed bank credits	512	482	477	491	161	187	257	277
Financial markets	1645	2049	2221	2035	1923	1344	931	688
Banks	1642	2046	2217	2032	1921	1343	931	688
Bonds	3	4	4	2	2	1	–	–
Other private	2355	3159	2920	3346	3735	4889	5425	5935
II. Multilateral	1612	1875	2212	2858	2652	2532	3206	3330
of which: concessional	163	183	202	236	208	204	322	307
non-concessional	1449	1692	2010	2622	2444	2328	2885	3022
memo: IMF, total	637	665	659	604	509	370	431	371
III. Non-OECD Creditor countries	28	30	22	17	17	17	6	6
C.E.E.C.	–	–	–	–	–	–	–	–
Arab countries	–	–	–	–	–	–	–	–
Other countries and unspecified	28	30	22	17	17	17	6	6
Subtotal: Long term debt	*7154*	*8976*	*9833*	*11404*	*11332*	*12123*	*13657*	*14316*
of which: concessional	440	586	730	1018	1068	1225	1673	1909
non-concessional	6715	8389	9102	10386	10265	10898	11984	12407
Short term								
Subtotal: Short term debt	*667*	*671*	*1027*	*1507*	*1695*	*2489*	*2773*	*2587*
Banks	511	395	710	1114	1257	1852	2046	1827
Export credits	156	276	317	393	437	637	727	760
Other identified liabilities	111	200	271	386	328	282	280	200
Total identified debt	**7933**	**9847**	**11130**	**13297**	**13355**	**14894**	**16710**	**17103**
SERVICE PAYMENTS								
Long term								
I. OECD countries and capital markets	817	1123	1744	1625	1371	1187	1612	1911
ODA	13	19	25	18	58	30	82	73
Official/off. supported	172	175	511	557	206	201	236	256
Financial markets	216	337	460	283	465	552	552	567
Other private	416	592	749	767	642	404	741	1015
II. Multilateral	215	310	369	425	548	477	493	526
of which: concessional	12	11	16	23	20	10	16	5
memo: IMF, total	89	163	189	193	228	200	155	137
III. Non-OECD creditor countries	5	12	9	6	0	0	12	–
Subtotal: Service payments, long term debt	*1036*	*1446*	*2122*	*2056*	*1919*	*1664*	*2117*	*2438*
of which: concessional	25	30	41	41	77	40	98	78
Amortization, long term debt	476	850	1444	1553	1304	903	1574	1647
Interest, long term debt	561	596	678	502	615	761	543	791
Interest, short term debt	88	64	69	103	131	103	17	–
Total service payments	**1124**	**1510**	**2191**	**2158**	**2050**	**1767**	**2135**	**2438**

CUBA

US $ Million

	1984	1985	1986	1987	1988	1989	1990	1991
GROSS DEBT								
Long term								
I. OECD countries and capital markets	823	1076	1099	1360	1177	1019	1887	1731
ODA	29	34	38	46	42	46	62	61
Official/off. supported	522	681	647	829	463	419	378	453
Official export credits	146	182	156	195	164	167	173	215
Guaranteed supplier credits	132	123	102	140	66	53	24	93
Guaranteed bank credits	244	376	389	494	233	199	181	146
Financial markets	272	361	414	484	671	554	1447	1216
Banks	272	361	414	484	671	554	1447	1216
Bonds	–	–	–	–	–	–	–	–
Other private	–	–	–	–	–	–	–	–
II. Multilateral	16	18	20	24	24	23	24	24
of which: concessional	5	6	7	10	10	9	10	10
non-concessional	11	12	13	14	14	14	14	14
memo: IMF, total	–	–	–	–	–	–	–	–
III. Non-OECD Creditor countries	17785	18339	19143	23154	24252	24424	24470	25000
C.E.E.C.	17785	18339	19143	23154	24252	24424	24470	25000
Arab countries	–	–	–	–	–	–	–	–
Other countries and unspecified	–	–	–	–	–	–	–	–
Subtotal: Long term debt	*18624*	*19433*	*20262*	*24538*	*25453*	*25466*	*26381*	*26755*
of which: concessional	17819	18379	19188	23210	24304	24478	24541	25071
non-concessional	804	1054	1074	1328	1149	987	1839	1684
Short term								
Subtotal: Short term debt	*849*	*1249*	*2171*	*2367*	*2120*	*2220*	*3294*	*3367*
Banks	628	881	1712	1737	1312	1313	2070	2100
Export credits	221	368	459	630	808	907	1224	1267
Other identified liabilities	–	–	–	–	–	–	–	–
Total identified debt	**19473**	**20682**	**22433**	**26905**	**27573**	**27686**	**29675**	**30122**
SERVICE PAYMENTS								
Long term								
I. OECD countries and capital markets	320	307	278	248	122	212	623	229
ODA	1	2	1	0	1	0	0	1
Official/off. supported	245	229	211	175	36	35	471	30
Financial markets	74	77	66	72	85	176	151	198
Other private	–	–	–	–	–	–	–	–
II. Multilateral	–	5	0	3	1	2	1	1
of which: concessional	–	5	0	2	1	1	0	0
memo: IMF, total	–	–	–	–	–	–	–	–
III. Non-OECD creditor countries	80	101	212	220	140	140	488	30
Subtotal: Service payments, long term debt	*400*	*413*	*490*	*470*	*263*	*354*	*1113*	*260*
of which: concessional	81	107	214	222	141	141	489	31
Amortization, long term debt	254	221	277	246	46	116	540	117
Interest, long term debt	146	192	213	224	216	237	572	143
Interest, short term debt	80	76	105	135	135	128	148	131
Total service payments	**480**	**489**	**595**	**605**	**398**	**482**	**1261**	**391**

CYPRUS

US $ Million

	1984	1985	1986	1987	1988	1989	1990	1991
GROSS DEBT								
Long term								
I. OECD countries and capital markets	537	710	870	1118	1184	1388	1945	2218
ODA	29	37	45	55	48	47	50	46
Official/off. supported	111	192	208	272	238	310	416	369
Official export credits	13	17	18	19	15	13	11	7
Guaranteed supplier credits	11	15	8	55	57	38	47	37
Guaranteed bank credits	87	160	183	198	166	260	357	325
Financial markets	397	481	617	790	898	1030	1479	1804
Banks	397	481	617	790	898	1030	1329	1654
Bonds	–	–	–	–	–	–	150	150
Other private	–	–	–	–	–	–	–	–
II. Multilateral	271	409	592	871	803	825	897	884
of which: concessional	12	18	85	216	225	295	341	338
non-concessional	259	391	507	656	578	530	556	546
memo: IMF, total	3	–	–	–	–	–	–	–
III. Non-OECD Creditor countries	37	40	39	38	34	30	31	39
C.E.E.C.	1	–	–	–	–	1	1	0
Arab countries	7	11	11	17	22	25	30	39
Other countries and unspecified	29	29	27	21	12	4	–	–
Subtotal: Long term debt	*845*	*1159*	*1501*	*2027*	*2021*	*2243*	*2872*	*3141*
of which: concessional	41	55	130	271	273	342	391	384
non-concessional	804	1104	1371	1756	1748	1901	2481	2758
Short term								
Subtotal: Short term debt	*295*	*419*	*515*	*644*	*869*	*958*	*1406*	*1111*
Banks	257	357	451	580	803	890	1297	1021
Export credits	38	62	64	64	66	68	109	91
Other identified liabilities	274	353	431	1067	1176	865	2145	2570
Total identified debt	**1414**	**1931**	**2448**	**3738**	**4066**	**4066**	**6423**	**6823**
SERVICE PAYMENTS								
Long term								
I. OECD countries and capital markets	111	149	189	286	210	368	268	275
ODA	4	2	3	6	4	4	5	5
Official/off. supported	33	61	66	72	58	87	96	95
Financial markets	74	86	121	208	147	277	168	175
Other private	–	–	–	–	–	–	–	–
II. Multilateral	29	36	54	74	112	151	104	117
of which: concessional	0	0	2	6	11	15	19	19
memo: IMF, total	3	3	–	–	–	–	–	–
III. Non-OECD creditor countries	3	5	6	11	13	13	6	6
Subtotal: Service payments, long term debt	*143*	*191*	*249*	*370*	*334*	*532*	*379*	*397*
of which: concessional	4	3	4	12	15	19	23	24
Amortization, long term debt	76	113	157	252	190	371	196	213
Interest, long term debt	67	78	91	118	144	161	183	185
Interest, short term debt	55	55	58	91	150	173	222	216
Total service payments	**199**	**245**	**307**	**461**	**484**	**705**	**602**	**613**

DJIBOUTI

US $ Million

	1984	1985	1986	1987	1988	1989	1990	1991
GROSS DEBT								
Long term								
I. OECD countries and capital markets	70	135	77	138	100	41	52	47
ODA	15	12	13	70	64	7	22	25
Official/off. supported	24	33	64	68	23	21	20	18
Official export credits	2	3	4	5	3	3	3	3
Guaranteed supplier credits	14	5	0	0	–	–	–	0
Guaranteed bank credits	8	24	60	63	20	17	17	15
Financial markets	31	90	–	–	13	14	10	4
Banks	31	90	–	–	13	14	10	4
Bonds	–	–	–	–	–	–	–	–
Other private	–	–	–	–	–	–	–	–
II. Multilateral	23	39	54	75	80	79	90	105
of which: concessional	23	39	54	75	80	79	90	105
non-concessional	–	–	–	–	–	–	–	–
memo: IMF, total	–	–	–	–	–	–	–	–
III. Non-OECD Creditor countries	24	34	40	48	51	48	45	46
C.E.E.C.	–	–	–	–	–	–	–	–
Arab countries	15	28	34	42	45	44	41	42
Other countries and unspecified	9	6	5	5	5	4	4	4
Subtotal: Long term debt	*117*	*208*	*170*	*261*	*230*	*169*	*187*	*198*
of which: concessional	38	51	66	145	143	86	112	130
non-concessional	79	156	104	116	87	82	75	68
Short term								
Subtotal: Short term debt	*24*	*30*	*54*	*12*	*26*	*48*	*25*	*25*
Banks	18	21	47	4	18	41	18	18
Export credits	6	9	7	8	8	7	7	7
Other identified liabilities	68	68	61	56	61	41	32	30
Total identified debt	**208**	**305**	**285**	**329**	**318**	**258**	**244**	**253**
SERVICE PAYMENTS								
Long term								
I. OECD countries and capital markets	15	31	55	47	41	27	32	6
ODA	2	12	4	1	2	0	3	0
Official/off. supported	10	3	14	14	6	5	6	0
Financial markets	3	16	37	32	34	21	23	6
Other private	–	–	–	–	–	–	–	–
II. Multilateral	1	1	3	5	6	5	5	5
of which: concessional	1	1	3	5	6	5	5	5
memo: IMF, total	–	–	–	–	–	–	–	–
III. Non-OECD creditor countries	1	0	1	4	4	5	5	5
Subtotal: Service payments, long term debt	*17*	*33*	*58*	*55*	*51*	*37*	*42*	*16*
of which: concessional	2	13	7	6	7	6	8	5
Amortization, long term debt	12	27	43	48	44	31	35	12
Interest, long term debt	5	6	15	8	7	6	6	4
Interest, short term debt	5	8	7	6	6	8	6	3
Total service payments	**22**	**40**	**66**	**62**	**57**	**45**	**48**	**19**

DOMINICAN REPUBLIC

US $ Million

	1984	1985	1986	1987	1988	1989	1990	1991
GROSS DEBT								
Long term								
I. OECD countries and capital markets	2115	1926	2144	2108	1912	1956	1779	1734
ODA	461	518	706	639	592	614	603	609
Official/off. supported	204	658	657	717	679	599	620	605
Official export credits	82	466	473	476	487	484	484	484
Guaranteed supplier credits	8	14	15	49	41	27	49	40
Guaranteed bank credits	114	178	169	192	150	88	87	80
Financial markets	1380	680	711	681	572	673	486	451
Banks	1380	680	711	681	572	673	486	451
Bonds	–	–	–	–	–	–	–	–
Other private	70	70	70	70	70	70	70	70
II. Multilateral	666	861	953	1035	962	904	935	974
of which: concessional	309	352	377	399	409	424	443	434
non-concessional	358	508	576	636	553	480	491	540
memo: IMF, total	221	297	304	284	218	123	72	89
III. Non-OECD Creditor countries	339	345	383	473	478	467	460	438
C.E.E.C.	–	–	–	–	–	–	–	–
Arab countries	–	–	–	–	–	–	–	–
Other countries and unspecified	339	345	383	473	478	467	460	438
Subtotal: Long term debt	*3120*	*3131*	*3480*	*3616*	*3352*	*3327*	*3173*	*3146*
of which: concessional	770	870	1083	1039	1000	1038	1047	1043
non-concessional	2351	2261	2397	2578	2352	2290	2127	2103
Short term								
Subtotal: Short term debt	*365*	*231*	*130*	*119*	*315*	*311*	*446*	*442*
Banks	285	120	59	8	93	46	113	46
Export credits	80	111	71	111	222	265	333	396
Other identified liabilities	–	–	–	–	–	–	–	–
Total identified debt	**3485**	**3363**	**3610**	**3735**	**3667**	**3638**	**3619**	**3589**
SERVICE PAYMENTS								
Long term								
I. OECD countries and capital markets	191	214	229	138	168	91	31	55
ODA	14	15	32	17	27	21	16	21
Official/off. supported	32	77	108	43	63	39	13	13
Financial markets	127	116	84	73	73	25	–	16
Other private	18	6	5	4	5	7	2	5
II. Multilateral	53	82	118	137	134	175	136	165
of which: concessional	6	8	10	9	16	12	11	29
memo: IMF, total	28	51	68	84	68	103	67	52
III. Non-OECD creditor countries	50	56	61	60	61	53	62	44
Subtotal: Service payments, long term debt	*295*	*351*	*408*	*335*	*363*	*319*	*230*	*264*
of which: concessional	19	23	42	26	43	33	28	50
Amortization, long term debt	113	128	194	170	166	201	154	166
Interest, long term debt	182	223	214	165	198	119	76	97
Interest, short term debt	30	18	8	4	6	9	–	–
Total service payments	**325**	**369**	**416**	**339**	**369**	**328**	**230**	**264**

ECUADOR

US $ Million

	1984	1985	1986	1987	1988	1989	1990	1991
GROSS DEBT								
Long term								
I. OECD countries and capital markets	5828	6145	6812	6882	6429	6684	7019	6841
ODA	180	232	251	359	398	397	449	528
Official/off. supported	1107	1206	1188	1297	1409	1626	1867	1836
Official export credits	608	674	625	698	782	1007	1182	1142
Guaranteed supplier credits	200	212	197	232	280	157	163	114
Guaranteed bank credits	299	319	366	366	347	462	521	579
Financial markets	4541	4707	5373	5227	4622	4661	4703	4477
Banks	4539	4707	5373	5227	4622	4661	4703	4477
Bonds	2	0	–	–	–	–	–	–
Other private	–	. –	–	–	–	–	–	–
II. Multilateral	891	1183	1719	2338	2347	2290	2392	2432
of which: concessional	231	288	341	388	412	435	451	504
non-concessional	660	895	1378	1951	1935	1855	1941	1928
memo: IMF, total	238	360	486	490	405	325	265	182
III. Non-OECD Creditor countries	311	291	330	457	574	696	718	732
C.E.E.C.	12	11	11	9	9	29	27	32
Arab countries	–	–	–	–	–	–	–	–
Other countries and unspecified	299	280	319	448	565	667	692	700
Subtotal: Long term debt	*7031*	*7619*	*8861*	*9678*	*9350*	*9669*	*10129*	*10005*
of which: concessional	412	520	592	747	810	831	900	1032
non-concessional	6619	7099	8269	8931	8541	8838	9229	8973
Short term								
Subtotal: Short term debt	*1613*	*1769*	*1498*	*1645*	*2149*	*2294*	*2043*	*2221*
Banks	1551	1605	1248	1337	1876	2005	1803	1910
Export credits	62	164	250	308	273	290	240	311
Other identified liabilities	–	–	–	–	–	–	–	–
Total identified debt	**8643**	**9388**	**10359**	**11323**	**11500**	**11964**	**12173**	**12227**
SERVICE PAYMENTS								
Long term								
I. OECD countries and capital markets	682	666	503	176	463	349	468	485
ODA	9	12	19	11	16	32	29	11
Official/off. supported	128	202	155	126	145	269	213	308
Financial markets	544	453	330	39	302	49	225	165
Other private	–	–	–	–	–	–	–	–
II. Multilateral	94	128	177	355	467	427	449	477
of which: concessional	7	8	9	11	13	15	16	20
memo: IMF, total	15	21	36	152	170	119	145	155
III. Non-OECD creditor countries	40	56	39	28	48	115	139	120
Subtotal: Service payments, long term debt	*816*	*850*	*718*	*558*	*977*	*891*	*1055*	*1081*
of which: concessional	16	20	28	21	28	47	45	32
Amortization, long term debt	194	259	165	269	658	542	621	622
Interest, long term debt	622	591	553	290	320	350	434	459
Interest, short term debt	205	135	106	100	137	179	153	114
Total service payments	**1021**	**985**	**824**	**658**	**1114**	**1071**	**1208**	**1195**

US $ Million

	1984	1985	1986	1987	1988	1989	1990	1991
GROSS DEBT								
Long term								
I. OECD countries and capital markets	21686	25418	25917	27816	28475	26753	20525	20549
ODA	6009	6869	7803	9113	9495	9749	10630	11673
Official/off. supported	13025	16342	16761	17889	16699	15116	7408	7225
Official export credits	10182	12683	11432	12468	12843	11096	4017	4256
Guaranteed supplier credits	1218	1336	2389	1788	1664	1636	1330	981
Guaranteed bank credits	1625	2323	2940	3633	2193	2384	2061	1988
Financial markets	2651	2207	1352	815	2281	1888	2487	1651
Banks	2602	2148	1299	763	2229	1887	2487	1651
Bonds	49	59	53	52	52	1	–	–
Other private	–	–	–	–	–	–	–	–
II. Multilateral	3662	4070	4496	5560	5363	5428	3862	3491
of which: concessional	2570	2634	2665	2875	2814	2850	1438	1404
non-concessional	1092	1436	1831	2685	2549	2578	2424	2088
memo: IMF, total	206	184	144	262	190	161	125	127
III. Non-OECD Creditor countries	5085	5148	5257	5725	6341	6708	3822	3709
C.E.E.C.	2193	2241	2307	2738	3112	2897	2899	2903
Arab countries	2561	2584	2610	2627	2575	3205	273	258
Other countries and unspecified	331	323	340	360	654	607	651	548
Subtotal: Long term debt	*30433*	*34636*	*35669*	*39101*	*40179*	*38889*	*28209*	*27749*
of which: concessional	8579	9504	10468	11987	12309	12599	12068	13077
non-concessional	21853	25132	25201	27114	27869	26290	16141	14673
Short term								
Subtotal: Short term debt	*6979*	*7117*	*8526*	*9347*	*8525*	*9702*	*11367*	*11514*
Banks	6500	6621	7268	6554	5899	6029	6059	5900
Export credits	479	496	1257	2793	2626	3673	5308	5614
Other identified liabilities	922	1066	1274	1837	1980	1656	1427	1163
Total identified debt	**38333**	**42819**	**45469**	**50285**	**50684**	**50248**	**41004**	**40426**
SERVICE PAYMENTS								
Long term								
I. OECD countries and capital markets	2950	2974	2519	1493	3064	3386	2488	1997
ODA	203	215	245	156	379	307	426	187
Official/off. supported	1666	2441	2108	1230	2029	1848	1771	1566
Financial markets	1082	317	166	107	655	1231	291	245
Other private	–	–	–	–	–	–	–	–
II. Multilateral	165	233	322	386	450	396	550	686
of which: concessional	42	56	68	75	72	57	90	129
memo: IMF, total	23	47	61	71	69	37	62	91
III. Non-OECD creditor countries	163	113	81	128	161	168	109	85
Subtotal: Service payments, long term debt	*3279*	*3319*	*2922*	*2007*	*3674*	*3950*	*3147*	*2768*
of which: concessional	245	271	313	231	451	364	516	316
Amortization, long term debt	2083	1523	1208	677	1742	1797	1762	1771
Interest, long term debt	1196	1797	1714	1330	1933	2154	1384	997
Interest, short term debt	768	653	596	637	701	765	697	486
Total service payments	**4047**	**3972**	**3518**	**2644**	**4375**	**4715**	**3843**	**3255**

EL SALVADOR

US $ Million

	1984	1985	1986	1987	1988	1989	1990	1991
GROSS DEBT								
Long term								
I. OECD countries and capital markets	796	853	764	850	889	942	1041	1051
ODA	406	500	548	607	679	701	757	809
Official/off. supported	158	184	176	163	137	130	139	180
Official export credits	89	102	109	105	84	71	89	71
Guaranteed supplier credits	9	10	9	10	5	5	3	3
Guaranteed bank credits	60	72	58	49	48	55	47	107
Financial markets	232	169	40	80	72	111	145	61
Banks	203	150	30	80	72	111	145	61
Bonds	29	19	10	–	–	–	–	–
Other private	–	–	–	–	–	–	–	–
II. Multilateral	644	720	732	758	739	783	788	851
of which: concessional	321	349	362	364	367	424	436	466
non-concessional	323	371	370	394	372	359	351	386
memo: IMF, total	125	111	62	22	11	5	0	–
III. Non-OECD Creditor countries	251	234	161	154	144	97	68	61
C.E.E.C.	–	–	–	–	–	–	–	–
Arab countries	–	–	–	–	–	–	–	–
Other countries and unspecified	251	234	161	154	144	97	68	61
Subtotal: Long term debt	*1691*	*1807*	*1658*	*1762*	*1772*	*1821*	*1897*	*1963*
of which: concessional	727	849	910	972	1046	1125	1194	1275
non-concessional	965	958	748	790	725	697	703	688
Short term								
Subtotal: Short term debt	*114*	*95*	*342*	*349*	*275*	*268*	*254*	*163*
Banks	97	71	292	264	161	193	182	115
Export credits	17	24	49	85	113	75	72	49
Other identified liabilities	–	–	–	–	–	–	–	–
Total identified debt	**1805**	**1902**	**1999**	**2111**	**2046**	**2089**	**2150**	**2127**
SERVICE PAYMENTS								
Long term								
I. OECD countries and capital markets	112	133	106	95	90	78	85	177
ODA	10	13	16	22	15	22	16	17
Official/off. supported	22	49	44	48	35	47	48	101
Financial markets	80	71	46	25	40	9	21	59
Other private	–	–	–	–	–	–	–	–
II. Multilateral	50	86	129	119	77	69	111	92
of which: concessional	7	10	16	18	20	16	29	22
memo: IMF, total	14	34	64	48	11	5	5	0
III. Non-OECD creditor countries	56	60	51	37	40	35	47	31
Subtotal: Service payments, long term debt	*218*	*279*	*286*	*251*	*207*	*181*	*244*	*299*
of which: concessional	17	23	32	40	35	37	45	39
Amortization, long term debt	130	181	194	165	135	111	144	212
Interest, long term debt	88	98	92	86	72	71	100	87
Interest, short term debt	11	8	15	24	25	24	21	12
Total service payments	**229**	**288**	**301**	**275**	**232**	**205**	**265**	**311**

US $ Million

	1984	1985	1986	1987	1988	1989	1990	1991
GROSS DEBT								
Long term								
I. OECD countries and capital markets	27	40	52	63	64	62	71	86
ODA	–	–	0	8	17	24	31	33
Official/off. supported	23	38	51	53	33	28	40	53
Official export credits	12	32	47	52	22	19	30	28
Guaranteed supplier credits	8	4	–	–	10	9	10	10
Guaranteed bank credits	3	2	4	1	0	0	–	15
Financial markets	4	2	1	1	15	10	–	–
Banks	4	2	1	1	15	10	–	–
Bonds	–	–	–	–	–	–	–	–
Other private	–	–	–	–	–	–	–	–
II. Multilateral	22	27	33	50	61	68	72	86
of which: concessional	8	13	19	35	46	57	63	78
non-concessional	14	14	13	15	15	11	10	9
memo: IMF, total	13	13	11	12	14	9	6	13
III. Non-OECD Creditor countries	28	32	41	45	40	38	39	39
C.E.E.C.	4	4	5	5	–	4	4	4
Arab countries	–	–	–	–	–	–	–	1
Other countries and unspecified	24	27	37	40	40	35	35	35
Subtotal: Long term debt	*78*	*99*	*126*	*158*	*165*	*168*	*182*	*211*
of which: concessional	8	13	20	44	64	81	94	111
non-concessional	69	85	107	114	102	87	89	101
Short term								
Subtotal: Short term debt	*2*	*17*	*23*	*15*	*16*	*19*	*37*	*19*
Banks	2	1	13	2	2	2	16	12
Export credits	0	16	10	13	14	17	21	7
Other identified liabilities	–	–	–	–	–	–	–	–
Total identified debt	**80**	**115**	**149**	**173**	**181**	**187**	**219**	**231**
SERVICE PAYMENTS								
Long term								
I. OECD countries and capital markets	2	3	3	3	2	3	1	1
ODA	–	–	–	0	0	0	0	1
Official/off. supported	1	2	3	3	2	2	–	–
Financial markets	0	0	0	0	0	1	1	–
Other private	–	–	–	–	–	–	–	–
II. Multilateral	7	9	4	4	3	6	5	3
of which: concessional	0	0	2	2	2	1	2	1
memo: IMF, total	7	8	4	2	2	6	4	1
III. Non-OECD creditor countries	–	–	0	1	0	–	–	–
Subtotal: Service payments, long term debt	*9*	*12*	*8*	*8*	*6*	*9*	*6*	*3*
of which: concessional	0	0	2	2	2	2	3	1
Amortization, long term debt	7	8	4	3	3	5	4	2
Interest, long term debt	2	4	4	5	4	4	2	1
Interest, short term debt	1	0	1	1	0	0	1	1
Total service payments	**10**	**12**	**9**	**8**	**6**	**9**	**7**	**4**

ETHIOPIA

US $ Million

	1984	1985	1986	1987	1988	1989	1990	1991
GROSS DEBT								
Long term								
I. OECD countries and capital markets	462	539	589	717	712	658	744	847
ODA	187	223	263	323	317	367	419	466
Official/off. supported	268	304	317	385	358	242	272	267
Official export credits	26	37	28	26	19	12	9	16
Guaranteed supplier credits	88	100	117	172	197	121	142	141
Guaranteed bank credits	154	167	172	187	142	108	121	111
Financial markets	–	–	–	–	30	45	50	111
Banks	–	–	–	–	30	45	50	111
Bonds	–	–	–	–	–	–	–	–
Other private	7	12	10	9	7	4	2	2
II. Multilateral	601	672	773	931	990	1072	1239	1550
of which: concessional	486	575	647	803	882	972	1151	1454
non-concessional	115	98	126	128	108	100	88	95
memo: IMF, total	98	71	84	76	55	30	6	–
III. Non-OECD Creditor countries	2291	2846	3472	4666	5176	5072	5188	5187
C.E.E.C.	2002	2534	3152	4331	4841	4741	4859	4859
Arab countries	244	253	253	251	249	247	247	247
Other countries and unspecified	45	59	68	84	86	84	82	81
Subtotal: Long term debt	*3354*	*4057*	*4835*	*6315*	*6878*	*6803*	*7171*	*7584*
of which: concessional	673	797	910	1126	1199	1339	1570	1920
non-concessional	2681	3259	3924	5189	5679	5464	5601	5664
Short term								
Subtotal: Short term debt	*63*	*79*	*75*	*71*	*73*	*83*	*158*	*199*
Banks	47	53	27	29	11	8	91	114
Export credits	16	26	48	42	62	74	67	85
Other identified liabilities	45	44	43	44	48	49	59	51
Total identified debt	**3462**	**4180**	**4953**	**6430**	**6999**	**6934**	**7388**	**7834**
SERVICE PAYMENTS								
Long term								
I. OECD countries and capital markets	64	75	92	106	127	162	149	91
ODA	11	11	10	13	16	28	16	5
Official/off. supported	53	51	64	83	104	111	90	80
Financial markets	0	12	12	0	2	18	41	6
Other private	–	–	6	9	5	5	2	–
II. Multilateral	51	59	65	53	52	60	56	47
of which: concessional	12	17	23	26	28	24	20	25
memo: IMF, total	36	42	42	25	21	27	27	6
III. Non-OECD creditor countries	17	23	41	44	74	53	11	3
Subtotal: Service payments, long term debt	*131*	*157*	*198*	*203*	*253*	*275*	*216*	*141*
of which: concessional	23	28	33	39	44	51	36	29
Amortization, long term debt	97	116	152	139	178	201	163	105
Interest, long term debt	34	41	47	64	75	75	52	37
Interest, short term debt	10	9	7	7	8	10	13	12
Total service payments	**141**	**165**	**206**	**210**	**261**	**285**	**229**	**154**

FIJI

	1984	1985	1986	1987	1988	1989	1990	1991
GROSS DEBT								
Long term								
I. OECD countries and capital markets	237	245	227	216	199	187	155	104
ODA	17	5	4	3	2	25	4	4
Official/off. supported	70	80	75	88	81	58	63	44
Official export credits	54	52	52	70	50	43	46	36
Guaranteed supplier credits	13	24	20	15	28	13	10	4
Guaranteed bank credits	3	4	3	3	3	2	6	5
Financial markets	149	161	148	125	116	105	88	56
Banks	149	161	148	125	116	105	88	56
Bonds	0	0	0	0	–	–	–	–
Other private	–	–	–	–	–	–	–	–
II. Multilateral	144	158	173	201	200	188	195	192
of which: concessional	16	19	23	27	23	22	23	24
non-concessional	128	139	150	174	177	166	172	168
memo: IMF, total	13	15	8	7	4	1	–	–
III. Non-OECD Creditor countries	19	15	14	19	21	19	19	4
C.E.E.C.	–	–	–	–	–	–	–	–
Arab countries	–	–	–	–	–	–	–	–
Other countries and unspecified	19	15	14	19	21	19	19	4
Subtotal: Long term debt	*399*	*419*	*414*	*435*	*419*	*394*	*369*	*300*
of which: concessional	33	24	27	29	24	46	27	28
non-concessional	366	395	388	406	395	348	342	271
Short term								
Subtotal: Short term debt	*40*	*27*	*87*	*33*	*32*	*129*	*30*	*24*
Banks	36	22	81	28	28	40	20	19
Export credits	4	5	6	5	4	89	10	5
Other identified liabilities	–	–	–	–	8	14	13	23
Total identified debt	**439**	**446**	**501**	**468**	**460**	**537**	**412**	**347**
SERVICE PAYMENTS								
Long term								
I. OECD countries and capital markets	42	39	33	39	37	57	51	44
ODA	2	2	0	2	2	2	2	2
Official/off. supported	14	16	13	15	13	15	12	16
Financial markets	26	21	20	22	21	40	38	26
Other private	–	–	–	–	–	–	–	–
II. Multilateral	17	26	32	29	32	32	50	35
of which: concessional	1	1	2	2	2	2	3	3
memo: IMF, total	1	6	9	3	3	3	1	–
III. Non-OECD creditor countries	3	3	2	3	2	2	2	18
Subtotal: Service payments, long term debt	*62*	*67*	*67*	*70*	*71*	*91*	*103*	*97*
of which: concessional	4	3	2	4	4	4	4	4
Amortization, long term debt	27	35	38	39	38	61	73	71
Interest, long term debt	35	32	29	31	33	30	30	25
Interest, short term debt	5	3	4	4	3	8	8	3
Total service payments	**67**	**70**	**71**	**74**	**74**	**99**	**111**	**99**

GABON

US $ Million

	1984	1985	1986	1987	1988	1989	1990	1991
GROSS DEBT								
Long term								
I. OECD countries and capital markets	983	1191	1535	1895	2060	2092	2347	2266
ODA	61	91	135	202	225	306	447	502
Official/off. supported	758	966	1400	1653	1450	1251	1421	1464
Official export credits	98	135	173	473	676	725	887	949
Guaranteed supplier credits	201	265	295	164	169	120	167	154
Guaranteed bank credits	460	566	932	1016	605	407	367	360
Financial markets	163	134	–	40	385	535	478	300
Banks	163	134	–	40	385	535	478	300
Bonds	0	–	–	–	–	–	–	–
Other private	–	–	–	–	–	–	–	–
II. Multilateral	65	95	159	227	298	373	459	471
of which: concessional	18	24	29	36	31	30	32	29
non-concessional	47	72	130	190	267	344	427	442
memo: IMF, total	–	–	34	60	133	135	140	121
III. Non-OECD Creditor countries	45	37	49	63	56	57	62	65
C.E.E.C.	0	0	0	–	–	–	–	–
Arab countries	17	12	25	30	27	26	29	32
Other countries and unspecified	27	25	24	33	30	32	33.	33
Subtotal: Long term debt	*1093*	*1323*	*1743*	*2185*	*2414*	*2523*	*2867*	*2801*
of which: concessional	79	115	164	238	256	336	479	531
non-concessional	1014	1209	1579	1947	2158	2187	2389	2270
Short term								
Subtotal: Short term debt	*255*	*359*	*521*	*598*	*686*	*894*	*1099*	*1108*
Banks	165	237	410	423	467	537	580	418
Export credits	90	122	111	175	219	357	519	690
Other identified liabilities	–	–	–	–	–	–	–	–
Total identified debt	**1347**	**1682**	**2263**	**2783**	**3100**	**3416**	**3967**	**3909**
SERVICE PAYMENTS								
Long term								
I. OECD countries and capital markets	337	321	179	76	112	173	211	169
ODA	5	6	3	9	11	5	6	8
Official/off. supported	304	297	174	56	84	93	143	114
Financial markets	29	19	1	12	17	75	61	46
Other private	–	–	–	–	–	–	–	–
II. Multilateral	10	9	15	22	30	35	61	73
of which: concessional	2	1	2	2	3	3	3	3
memo: IMF, total	2	–	–	2	4	9	27	36
III. Non-OECD creditor countries	23	18	5	4	5	4	2	1
Subtotal: Service payments, long term debt	*370*	*348*	*200*	*102*	*147*	*212*	*274*	*242*
of which: concessional	7	7	5	11	13	8	10	11
Amortization, long term debt	298	260	106	41	55	82	114	114
Interest, long term debt	72	88	93	60	92	130	160	128
Interest, short term debt	26	25	30	35	43	54	56	38
Total service payments	**396**	**373**	**229**	**137**	**190**	**266**	**330**	**280**

GAMBIA

	1984	1985	1986	1987	1988	1989	1990	1991
GROSS DEBT								
Long term								
I. OECD countries and capital markets	58	55	57	71	69	73	77	81
ODA	14	17	25	33	28	32	36	36
Official/off. supported	22	24	20	24	22	22	16	28
Official export credits	1	1	7	10	9	10	4	7
Guaranteed supplier credits	12	15	8	10	9	10	11	9
Guaranteed bank credits	8	8	5	5	4	2	–	12
Financial markets	21	13	12	14	19	19	25	17
Banks	21	13	12	14	19	19	25	17
Bonds	–	–	–	–	–	–	–	–
Other private	1	1	–	–	–	–	–	–
II. Multilateral	104	118	147	197	196	218	252	274
of which: concessional	67	77	109	154	161	188	226	256
non-concessional	37	41	37	43	35	30	26	18
memo: IMF, total	33	33	30	38	35	38	45	44
III. Non-OECD Creditor countries	40	40	39	40	39	36	25	24
C.E.E.C.	–	–	–	–	–	–	–	–
Arab countries	29	31	30	32	31	30	20	19
Other countries and unspecified	11	9	8	8	8	6	5	5
Subtotal: Long term debt	202	214	242	308	304	327	355	379
of which: concessional	81	94	134	187	189	219	262	292
non-concessional	121	120	108	121	115	108	92	87
Short term								
Subtotal: Short term debt	43	26	44	48	61	26	32	34
Banks	38	19	21	20	25	7	12	19
Export credits	5	7	23	28	36	19	20	15
Other identified liabilities	–	–	–	–	–	–	–	–
Total identified debt	**245**	**240**	**286**	**356**	**365**	**352**	**386**	**413**
SERVICE PAYMENTS								
Long term								
I. OECD countries and capital markets	3	5	3	16	9	8	34	22
ODA	1	1	1	3	3	3	4	1
Official/off. supported	0	2	1	3	3	1	7	3
Financial markets	2	2	1	10	3	4	24	18
Other private	–	–	0	–	–	–	–	–
II. Multilateral	7	6	27	19	15	14	16	15
of which: concessional	2	2	4	8	6	6	7	5
memo: IMF, total	5	5	21	10	8	7	7	7
III. Non-OECD creditor countries	2	–	1	1	1	1	14	3
Subtotal: Service payments, long term debt	12	11	32	35	24	22	65	40
of which: concessional	3	2	5	12	9	9	11	7
Amortization, long term debt	6	5	22	28	16	14	51	32
Interest, long term debt	6	6	10	8	9	8	13	8
Interest, short term debt	3	3	2	2	2	2	1	1
Total service payments	**15**	**13**	**33**	**37**	**26**	**24**	**66**	**41**

US $ Million

	1984	1985	1986	1987	1988	1989	1990	1991
GROSS DEBT								
Long term								
I. OECD countries and capital markets	842	925	807	999	951	1007	867	778
ODA	452	516	574	713	712	796	617	518
Official/off. supported	96	123	165	209	225	211	249	238
Official export credits	12	19	27	38	18	24	31	48
Guaranteed supplier credits	36	32	22	19	76	35	47	42
Guaranteed bank credits	47	72	116	152	131	151	171	148
Financial markets	294	286	68	77	14	–	–	21
Banks	294	286	68	77	14	–	–	21
Bonds	–	–	–	–	–	–	–	–
Other private	–	–	–	–	–	–	–	–
II. Multilateral	917	1239	1580	1994	2067	2207	2573	2849
of which: concessional	331	436	646	981	1268	1589	1994	2349
non-concessional	586	804	934	1013	799	618	579	500
memo: IMF, total	515	701	786	867	762	737	745	834
III. Non-OECD Creditor countries	144	160	141	129	122	116	110	114
C.E.E.C.	46	41	37	34	41	36	32	30
Arab countries	62	59	52	52	36	37	37	43
Other countries and unspecified	36	60	52	44	46	44	41	41
Subtotal: Long term debt	*1903*	*2324*	*2528*	*3123*	*3140*	*3331*	*3549*	*3740*
of which: concessional	782	952	1220	1694	1981	2385	2611	2867
non-concessional	1121	1372	1308	1429	1160	946	938	873
Short term								
Subtotal: Short term debt	*182*	*182*	*318*	*321*	*355*	*226*	*382*	*467*
Banks	129	113	209	201	247	96	197	289
Export credits	53	69	109	120	108	130	185	177
Other identified liabilities	4	3	4	4	13	17	33	70
Total identified debt	**2089**	**2509**	**2850**	**3447**	**3508**	**3574**	**3965**	**4277**
SERVICE PAYMENTS								
Long term								
I. OECD countries and capital markets	80	93	122	91	157	149	145	114
ODA	23	27	24	33	37	26	29	19
Official/off. supported	23	24	38	51	13	43	105	57
Financial markets	34	42	60	7	106	80	11	37
Other private	–	–	–	–	–	–	–	–
II. Multilateral	51	76	122	284	377	283	214	185
of which: concessional	11	19	26	32	31	30	32	36
memo: IMF, total	27	47	85	238	324	226	153	107
III. Non-OECD creditor countries	27	23	33	25	26	19	18	12
Subtotal: Service payments, long term debt	*157*	*192*	*277*	*401*	*561*	*450*	*377*	*311*
of which: concessional	34	45	50	65	68	56	61	55
Amortization, long term debt	75	94	163	291	448	342	282	217
Interest, long term debt	82	98	114	110	113	109	95	95
Interest, short term debt	16	12	13	17	21	19	19	22
Total service payments	**173**	**204**	**290**	**417**	**582**	**470**	**396**	**333**

GIBRALTAR

US $ Million

	1984	1985	1986	1987	1988	1989	1990	1991
GROSS DEBT								
Long term								
I. OECD countries and capital markets	57	85	67	80	155	408	640	866
ODA	2	2	2	2	2	1	1	1
Official/off. supported	14	9	6	4	2	0	0	7
Official export credits	–	–	–	0	–	–	–	7
Guaranteed supplier credits	2	1	1	3	0	0	0	0
Guaranteed bank credits	13	8	5	0	2	–	–	–
Financial markets	40	74	60	75	151	407	639	858
Banks	40	74	60	75	151	407	639	858
Bonds	–	–	–	–	–	–	–	–
Other private	–		–		–		–	–
II. Multilateral	–	–	–	–	–	–	–	–
of which: concessional	–	–	–	–	–	–	–	–
non-concessional	–	–	–	–	–	–	–	–
memo: IMF, total	–	–	–	–	–	–	–	–
III. Non-OECD Creditor countries	–	–	–	–	–	–	–	–
C.E.E.C.	–	–	–	–	–	–	–	–
Arab countries	–	–	–	–	–	–	–	–
Other countries and unspecified	–	–	–	–	–	–	–	–
Subtotal: Long term debt	*57*	*85*	*67*	*80*	*155*	*408*	*640*	*866*
of which: concessional	2	2	2	2	2	1	1	1
non-concessional	55	84	66	78	153	407	639	865
Short term								
Subtotal: Short term debt	*58*	*61*	*129*	*239*	*467*	*744*	*1316*	*1905*
Banks	54	56	122	232	460	734	1307	1784
Export credits	4	6	7	7	7	10	9	121
Other identified liabilities	–	–	–	–	–	–	–	–
Total identified debt	**115**	**147**	**196**	**320**	**622**	**1152**	**1957**	**2771**
SERVICE PAYMENTS								
Long term								
I. OECD countries and capital markets	19	18	20	17	15	20	64	97
ODA	0	0	0	0	0	0	0	0
Official/off. supported	9	6	5	4	6	2	–	11
Financial markets	10	12	15	12	8	18	64	85
Other private	–	–	–	–	–	–	–	–
II. Multilateral	–	–	–	–	–	–	–	–
of which: concessional	–	–	–	–	–	–	–	–
memo: IMF, total	–	–	–	–	–	–	–	–
III. Non-OECD creditor countries	–	–	–	–	–	–	–	–
Subtotal: Service payments, long term debt	*19*	*18*	*20*	*17*	*15*	*20*	*64*	*97*
of which: concessional	0	0	0	0	0	0	0	0
Amortization, long term debt	13	13	14	11	7	6	27	51
Interest, long term debt	6	5	6	6	7	14	37	46
Interest, short term debt	8	5	6	13	28	55	86	97
Total service payments	**27**	**23**	**26**	**30**	**43**	**75**	**149**	**193**

GREECE

US $ Million

	1984	1985	1986	1987	1988	1989	1990	1991
GROSS DEBT								
Long term								
I. OECD countries and capital markets	10670	12577	12541	13918	13579	15158	16170	19101
ODA	162	174	168	177	167	148	149	137
Official/off. supported	1728	1818	1945	2190	2058	2171	2433	2879
Official export credits	637	670	721	1025	1445	1735	2018	1837
Guaranteed supplier credits	310	275	226	216	172	143	97	247
Guaranteed bank credits	781	873	998	948	441	293	317	795
Financial markets	8780	10585	10427	11551	11354	12839	13588	16084
Banks	8421	9400	9228	9793	9283	9726	9279	9121
Bonds	360	1185	1200	1758	2071	3113	4309	6963
Other private	–	–	–	–	–	–	–	–
II. Multilateral	1197	1812	3300	5245	4968	4968	4952	5407
of which: concessional	21	58	355	515	641	641	641	596
non-concessional	1176	1754	2945	4730	4327	4327	4311	4811
memo: IMF, total	–	–	–	–	–	–	–	–
III. Non-OECD Creditor countries	127	147	181	162	72	57	57	57
C.E.E.C.	–	–	–	–	10	7	7	–
Arab countries	127	147	181	161	57	50	50	50
Other countries and unspecified	–	–	–	1	5	–	–	–
Subtotal: Long term debt	11994	14536	16022	19324	18618	20183	21179	24565
of which: concessional	310	379	704	854	880	846	847	790
non-concessional	11684	14157	15318	18471	17738	19337	20332	23775
Short term								
Subtotal: Short term debt	3403	4526	4222	4282	4758	5344	6050	5887
Banks	3165	4128	3778	3808	4249	4705	5369	5216
Export credits	238	398	444	474	509	640	681	671
Other identified liabilities	5395	6362	7666	9565	10139	11853	14211	13860
Total identified debt	**20792**	**25425**	**27910**	**33171**	**33516**	**37380**	**41440**	**44312**
SERVICE PAYMENTS								
Long term								
I. OECD countries and capital markets	1820	1934	2009	3065	2358	2313	2534	2814
ODA	16	15	9	20	13	15	14	13
Official/off. supported	552	648	637	661	436	391	418	811
Financial markets	1253	1272	1364	2384	1909	1907	2102	1990
Other private	–	–	–	–	–	–	–	–
II. Multilateral	158	198	339	451	545	427	395	350
of which: concessional	1	3	12	29	30	26	13	13
memo: IMF, total	–	–	–	–	–	–	–	–
III. Non-OECD creditor countries	36	65	105	99	134	1	1	1
Subtotal: Service payments, long term debt	2014	2197	2453	3615	3037	2741	2930	3165
of which: concessional	53	82	125	148	177	42	28	27
Amortization, long term debt	916	1111	1342	2390	1594	1145	1323	1672
Interest, long term debt	1098	1086	1111	1225	1443	1595	1607	1494
Interest, short term debt	909	806	773	886	1147	1439	1548	1196
Total service payments	**2924**	**3003**	**3226**	**4501**	**4184**	**4180**	**4477**	**4361**

GUATEMALA

US $ Million

	1984	1985	1986	1987	1988	1989	1990	1991
GROSS DEBT								
Long term								
I. OECD countries and capital markets	1962	1999	1986	1877	1228	1290	1080	1024
ODA	159	185	197	249	308	327	364	400
Official/off. supported	131	264	244	199	161	142	181	158
Official export credits	39	38	36	22	12	6	22	1
Guaranteed supplier credits	8	32	21	4	18	18	19	15
Guaranteed bank credits	84	194	188	173	131	117	140	143
Financial markets	1673	1550	1544	1429	759	821	535	466
Banks	1205	1068	1072	980	530	621	343	290
Bonds	468	482	472	450	229	200	192	176
Other private	–	–	–	–	–	–	–	–
II. Multilateral	701	820	891	950	980	980	1056	1030
of which: concessional	243	253	270	276	294	316	330	346
non-concessional	458	567	621	674	686	663	726	684
memo: IMF, total	150	116	70	59	88	73	67	64
III. Non-OECD Creditor countries	281	278	294	287	276	244	223	199
C.E.E.C.	–	–	–	–	–	–	–	–
Arab countries	–	–	–	–	–	–	–	–
Other countries and unspecified	281	278	294	287	276	244	223	199
Subtotal: Long term debt	*2944*	*3097*	*3170*	*3114*	*2484*	*2513*	*2359*	*2253*
of which: concessional	401	438	467	525	602	644	694	746
non-concessional	2543	2659	2703	2589	1882	1870	1665	1507
Short term								
Subtotal: Short term debt	*319*	*368*	*331*	*423*	*547*	*542*	*600*	*717*
Banks	293	253	189	245	291	309	244	343
Export credits	26	115	143	178	256	232	356	374
Other identified liabilities	–	–	–	–	–	–	–	–
Total identified debt	**3263**	**3464**	**3502**	**3537**	**3031**	**3055**	**2959**	**2970**
SERVICE PAYMENTS								
Long term								
I. OECD countries and capital markets	319	397	374	349	366	201	183	75
ODA	6	7	7	4	9	11	11	13
Official/off. supported	47	95	111	50	23	17	61	35
Financial markets	266	296	257	295	334	173	112	26
Other private	–	–	–	–	–	–	–	–
II. Multilateral	66	119	144	141	150	133	79	175
of which: concessional	8	8	10	14	16	16	10	22
memo: IMF, total	10	60	65	25	32	20	19	8
III. Non-OECD creditor countries	37	56	43	28	52	50	41	34
Subtotal: Service payments, long term debt	*423*	*572*	*561*	*518*	*568*	*385*	*303*	*284*
of which: concessional	14	15	17	18	24	27	20	35
Amortization, long term debt	233	353	347	285	377	243	157	165
Interest, long term debt	190	220	214	233	191	141	146	119
Interest, short term debt	37	25	18	18	27	34	30	24
Total service payments	**460**	**598**	**580**	**536**	**595**	**419**	**333**	**308**

US $ Million

	1984	1985	1986	1987	1988	1989	1990	1991
GROSS DEBT								
Long term								
I. OECD countries and capital markets	282	366	446	564	576	709	732	750
ODA	132	165	227	319	382	459	528	567
Official/off. supported	132	170	184	194	142	198	173	155
Official export credits	21	45	102	96	72	167	134	131
Guaranteed supplier credits	94	115	64	81	61	21	25	7
Guaranteed bank credits	18	10	19	17	9	11	14	16
Financial markets	17	32	35	51	52	52	31	28
Banks	17	32	35	51	52	52	31	28
Bonds	–	–	–	–	–	–	–	–
Other private	–	–	–	–	–	–	–	–
II. Multilateral	255	300	398	499	536	628	734	855
of which: concessional	168	201	273	354	408	523	646	786
non-concessional	86	99	125	145	128	106	88	69
memo: IMF, total	40	42	52	54	61	61	51	55
III. Non-OECD Creditor countries	562	609	710	744	848	782	899	916
C.E.E.C.	308	338	422	433	480	477	549	581
Arab countries	93	97	106	114	125	88	94	93
Other countries and unspecified	161	174	182	196	243	217	256	242
Subtotal: Long term debt	*1099*	*1275*	*1554*	*1807*	*1960*	*2119*	*2365*	*2521*
of which: concessional	301	366	500	673	790	981	1174	1353
non-concessional	798	909	1054	1134	1170	1138	1191	1168
Short term								
Subtotal: Short term debt	*109*	*166*	*200*	*240*	*240*	*237*	*307*	*285*
Banks	50	77	77	82	80	81	121	96
Export credits	59	89	123	158	160	156	186	189
Other identified liabilities	–	–	–	–	–	–	–	–
Total identified debt	**1207**	**1441**	**1754**	**2048**	**2200**	**2356**	**2672**	**2806**
SERVICE PAYMENTS								
Long term								
I. OECD countries and capital markets	31	21	17	44	81	56	79	29
ODA	4	6	4	12	10	11	12	12
Official/off. supported	25	12	11	24	10	12	40	4
Financial markets	2	4	2	8	61	33	28	13
Other private	–	–	–	–	–	–	–	–
II. Multilateral	18	18	38	42	40	46	49	41
of which: concessional	5	8	11	12	15	13	11	11
memo: IMF, total	3	4	14	16	8	11	16	10
III. Non-OECD creditor countries	70	37	27	70	46	47	73	67
Subtotal: Service payments, long term debt	*119*	*76*	*82*	*156*	*166*	*148*	*201*	*137*
of which: concessional	9	14	15	24	25	25	22	22
Amortization, long term debt	96	56	57	120	134	102	159	100
Interest, long term debt	24	20	25	36	32	47	42	38
Interest, short term debt	6	6	6	6	8	9	10	8
Total service payments	**125**	**82**	**87**	**162**	**174**	**157**	**212**	**145**

US $ Million

	1984	1985	1986	1987	1988	1989	1990	1991
GROSS DEBT								
Long term								
I. OECD countries and capital markets	47	64	69	82	59	66	85	70
ODA	6	1	1	1	1	1	1	1
Official/off. supported	6	18	39	62	37	47	58	50
Official export credits	2	4	33	47	21	20	32	5
Guaranteed supplier credits	0	6	6	–	1	5	2	0
Guaranteed bank credits	4	8	0	14	16	23	23	45
Financial markets	35	45	29	19	21	18	26	19
Banks	35	45	29	19	21	18	26	19
Bonds	–	–	–	–	–	–	–	–
Other private	–	–	–	–	–	–	–	–
II. Multilateral	75	103	125	174	183	209	257	279
of which: concessional	63	87	107	154	167	194	242	265
non-concessional	11	16	18	19	17	14	14	15
memo: IMF, total	4	3	2	5	3	5	5	5
III. Non-OECD Creditor countries	162	183	193	212	181	178	187	188
C.E.E.C.	87	88	94	107	106	103	112	112
Arab countries	22	26	27	30	37	37	37	38
Other countries and unspecified	53	69	72	74	38	38	37	37
Subtotal: Long term debt	*284*	*349*	*387*	*467*	*424*	*453*	*528*	*537*
of which: concessional	69	87	108	155	167	195	243	266
non-concessional	215	262	279	312	257	257	285	271
Short term								
Subtotal: Short term debt	*15*	*32*	*21*	*18*	*24*	*32*	*71*	*60*
Banks	12	23	–	2	–	9	20	8
Export credits	3	9	21	16	24	23	51	52
Other identified liabilities	–	–	–	–	–	–	–	–
Total identified debt	**299**	**381**	**408**	**486**	**448**	**485**	**599**	**597**
SERVICE PAYMENTS								
Long term								
I. OECD countries and capital markets	5	11	6	5	6	5	2	7
ODA	0	6	1	0	1	0	0	0
Official/off. supported	1	2	2	3	2	1	0	5
Financial markets	4	3	3	2	3	4	2	2
Other private	–	–	–	–	–	–	–	–
II. Multilateral	1	2	2	5	5	7	4	4
of which: concessional	0	0	1	2	1	4	2	2
memo: IMF, total	1	1	1	1	1	1	0	–
III. Non-OECD creditor countries	2	2	2	4	2	2	0	–
Subtotal: Service payments, long term debt	*8*	*15*	*10*	*14*	*13*	*14*	*7*	*11*
of which: concessional	0	7	1	2	2	4	2	2
Amortization, long term debt	4	10	4	4	5	7	1	4
Interest, long term debt	4	5	6	10	8	6	5	7
Interest, short term debt	1	2	1	0	0	1	1	1
Total service payments	**9**	**17**	**11**	**14**	**13**	**14**	**8**	**12**

GUYANA

US $ Million

	1984	1985	1986	1987	1988	1989	1990	1991
GROSS DEBT								
Long term								
I. OECD countries and capital markets	305	306	273	307	344	395	681	425
ODA	137	137	139	158	163	164	303	92
Official/off. supported	34	60	45	45	64	135	306	266
Official export credits	16	17	17	20	19	106	283	238
Guaranteed supplier credits	3	4	16	14	42	29	23	15
Guaranteed bank credits	15	39	12	12	3	0	0	13
Financial markets	93	68	52	70	83	62	42	36
Banks	88	62	46	62	76	56	35	29
Bonds	5	6	6	7	7	6	8	7
Other private	42	42	37	35	34	33	30	30
II. Multilateral	309	356	409	476	467	479	584	637
of which: concessional	155	175	191	207	205	211	361	403
non-concessional	154	181	218	269	262	267	223	234
memo: IMF, total	82	91	100	116	110	106	113	149
III. Non-OECD Creditor countries	142	179	227	234	226	555	581	565
C.E.E.C.	16	22	43	41	5	19	19	19
Arab countries	8	8	28	29	29	28	28	29
Other countries and unspecified	119	149	156	164	192	508	534	518
Subtotal: Long term debt	*757*	*841*	*910*	*1017*	*1037*	*1428*	*1847*	*1627*
of which: concessional	292	312	330	364	368	375	665	495
non-concessional	465	530	580	653	669	1053	1182	1131
Short term								
Subtotal: Short term debt	*76*	*85*	*97*	*114*	*72*	*72*	*145*	*113*
Banks	60	56	66	75	36	31	101	64
Export credits	16	29	31	38	36	41	44	49
Other identified liabilities	15	15	19	14	12	5	7	–
Total identified debt	**847**	**941**	**1026**	**1145**	**1121**	**1505**	**1998**	**1740**
SERVICE PAYMENTS								
Long term								
I. OECD countries and capital markets	18	14	18	16	13	32	72	25
ODA	0	0	1	1	1	4	38	9
Official/off. supported	9	5	3	4	4	19	25	8
Financial markets	9	8	4	4	7	8	5	5
Other private	–	–	10	7	1	0	4	2
II. Multilateral	21	13	12	9	10	19	250	45
of which: concessional	4	2	3	2	3	8	32	13
memo: IMF, total	11	4	1	0	0	6	146	8
III. Non-OECD creditor countries	4	4	5	5	2	1	4	4
Subtotal: Service payments, long term debt	*42*	*31*	*35*	*30*	*25*	*51*	*326*	*74*
of which: concessional	4	2	5	4	4	13	69	23
Amortization, long term debt	13	10	13	11	9	20	207	36
Interest, long term debt	29	21	22	19	17	31	119	38
Interest, short term debt	8	6	5	6	6	4	6	5
Total service payments	**50**	**38**	**41**	**36**	**31**	**55**	**333**	**79**

HAITI

US $ Million

	1984	1985	1986	1987	1988	1989	1990	1991
GROSS DEBT								
Long term								
I. OECD countries and capital markets	258	284	250	263	298	264	279	186
ODA	117	139	134	153	188	169	190	112
Official/off. supported	26	30	44	42	44	30	32	15
Official export credits	16	15	13	12	9	8	16	6
Guaranteed supplier credits	6	4	4	2	4	1	1	1
Guaranteed bank credits	4	11	27	28	30	21	15	8
Financial markets	65	65	22	19	17	15	7	9
Banks	65	65	22	19	17	15	7	9
Bonds	–	–	–	–	–	–	–	–
Other private	50	50	50	50	50	50	50	50
II. Multilateral	368	401	421	500	479	487	522	555
of which: concessional	284	319	355	441	447	460	498	534
non-concessional	84	82	67	59	32	28	24	21
memo: IMF, total	101	96	79	80	47	40	36	34
III. Non-OECD Creditor countries	10	7	7	4	4	3	3	2
C.E.E.C.	–	–	–	–	–	–	–	–
Arab countries	–	–	–	–	–	–	–	–
Other countries and unspecified	10	7	7	4	4	3	3	2
Subtotal: Long term debt	*636*	*692*	*678*	*767*	*781*	*754*	*803*	*743*
of which: concessional	401	458	488	593	635	628	688	645
non-concessional	235	234	189	174	146	126	115	98
Short term								
Subtotal: Short term debt	*89*	*92*	*91*	*141*	*136*	*158*	*116*	*107*
Banks	76	70	30	69	60	80	31	14
Export credits	13	22	61	72	76	78	85	93
Other identified liabilities	–	–	–	–	–	–	–	–
Total identified debt	**725**	**784**	**769**	**908**	**917**	**912**	**920**	**851**
SERVICE PAYMENTS								
Long term								
I. OECD countries and capital markets	23	17	15	10	11	12	6	6
ODA	2	1	3	2	3	1	4	4
Official/off. supported	6	5	2	4	2	4	1	2
Financial markets	9	7	7	2	3	2	1	1
Other private	5	4	4	3	4	5	–	–
II. Multilateral	11	23	35	41	38	32	22	15
of which: concessional	5	7	10	12	13	12	11	11
memo: IMF, total	8	19	29	34	30	23	12	5
III. Non-OECD creditor countries	3	2	2	3	1	1	0	0
Subtotal: Service payments, long term debt	*36*	*43*	*52*	*54*	*50*	*45*	*29*	*22*
of which: concessional	7	9	12	14	15	14	15	15
Amortization, long term debt	12	19	29	38	34	29	16	9
Interest, long term debt	24	23	22	16	17	17	13	13
Interest, short term debt	10	7	4	4	6	7	5	2
Total service payments	**46**	**49**	**56**	**59**	**56**	**52**	**34**	**24**

HONDURAS

US $ Million

	1984	1985	1986	1987	1988	1989	1990	1991
GROSS DEBT								
Long term								
I. OECD countries and capital markets	988	1065	1421	1379	1451	1511	1817	1126
ODA	332	411	471	569	643	699	822	439
Official/off. supported	215	240	263	320	328	231	269	211
Official export credits	83	88	80	93	91	79	66	99
Guaranteed supplier credits	68	55	77	115	144	65	105	36
Guaranteed bank credits	65	98	105	112	93	87	98	76
Financial markets	440	414	687	489	480	581	726	475
Banks	440	414	687	489	480	581	726	475
Bonds	–	–	–	–	–	–	–	–
Other private	–	–	–	–	–	–	–	–
II. Multilateral	996	1190	1302	1425	1398	1512	1611	1619
of which: concessional	439	478	491	489	504	515	543	558
non-concessional	557	712	811	936	894	997	1068	1061
memo: IMF, total	150	147	110	77	37	35	32	34
III. Non-OECD Creditor countries	164	201	170	222	219	184	184	177
C.E.E.C.	–	–	–	–	–	–	–	–
Arab countries	–	–	–	–	–	–	–	–
Other countries and unspecified	164	201	170	222	219	184	184	177
Subtotal: Long term debt	*2148*	*2456*	*2893*	*3026*	*3067*	*3208*	*3612*	*2922*
of which: concessional	772	889	962	1058	1147	1214	1365	998
non-concessional	1376	1567	1932	1968	1921	1994	2247	1924
Short term								
Subtotal: Short term debt	*181*	*243*	*185*	*474*	*408*	*326*	*323*	*302*
Banks	161	166	85	336	353	256	198	186
Export credits	20	77	100	138	55	70	125	116
Other identified liabilities	115	118	121	129	97	80	198	29
Total identified debt	**2444**	**2817**	**3199**	**3629**	**3572**	**3614**	**4133**	**3253**
SERVICE PAYMENTS								
Long term								
I. OECD countries and capital markets	130	101	103	165	147	93	164	156
ODA	11	7	12	11	22	13	21	21
Official/off. supported	45	52	53	66	34	34	81	78
Financial markets	74	42	39	89	91	47	62	57
Other private	–	–	–	–	–	–	–	–
II. Multilateral	67	106	168	154	191	43	322	193
of which: concessional	12	16	19	17	27	13	38	31
memo: IMF, total	13	30	62	52	41	4	41	5
III. Non-OECD creditor countries	13	24	25	48	67	40	21	33
Subtotal: Service payments, long term debt	*211*	*231*	*297*	*367*	*405*	*176*	*508*	*382*
of which: concessional	23	23	31	28	48	26	60	52
Amortization, long term debt	91	101	158	218	225	80	264	195
Interest, long term debt	120	131	139	149	180	97	243	188
Interest, short term debt	28	26	21	29	41	37	31	19
Total service payments	**239**	**257**	**318**	**396**	**446**	**213**	**539**	**402**

US $ Million

	1984	1985	1986	1987	1988	1989	1990	1991
GROSS DEBT								
Long term								
I. OECD countries and capital markets	3855	5117	7576	7964	7382	7341	6781	7174
ODA	1	0	0	0	0	0	0	0
Official/off. supported	2621	2532	2377	2618	1772	2122	2205	2111
Official export credits	69	46	34	70	66	47	35	44
Guaranteed supplier credits	890	665	528	528	374	482	295	264
Guaranteed bank credits	1663	1820	1815	2020	1332	1593	1875	1804
Financial markets	1133	2484	5099	5146	5359	4969	4276	4762
Banks	800	1300	1600	1728	1814	1410	1809	2129
Bonds	333	1184	3499	3418	3545	3559	2467	2633
Other private	100	100	100	200	250	250	300	300
II. Multilateral	52	45	40	–	–	–	–	–
of which: concessional	–	–	–	–	–	–	–	–
non-concessional	52	45	40	–	–	–	–	–
memo: IMF, total	–	–	–	–	–	–	–	–
III. Non-OECD Creditor countries	7	7	6	7	7	8	8	8
C.E.E.C.	7	7	6	7	7	8	8	–
Arab countries	–	–	–	–	–	–	–	–
Other countries and unspecified	–	–	–	–	–	–	–	–
Subtotal: Long term debt	*3913*	*5168*	*7623*	*7971*	*7389*	*7348*	*6788*	*7181*
of which: concessional	*7*	*7*	*7*	*8*	*8*	*8*	*8*	*8*
non-concessional	*3906*	*5161*	*7616*	*7964*	*7382*	*7340*	*6780*	*7173*
Short term								
Subtotal: Short term debt	*3011*	*3386*	*4161*	*4098*	*4475*	*4787*	*5778*	*6274*
Banks	2691	3100	3800	3620	3801	4222	5200	5690
Export credits	321	286	361	478	674	566	578	584
Other identified liabilities	–	–	–	–	–	–	–	–
Total identified debt	**6925**	**8555**	**11784**	**12069**	**11864**	**12136**	**12566**	**13455**
SERVICE PAYMENTS								
Long term								
I. OECD countries and capital markets	905	859	1174	992	1102	2069	1283	1100
ODA	1	0	0	0	0	0	0	3
Official/off. supported	596	664	689	759	749	1462	466	480
Financial markets	243	176	468	227	339	582	775	566
Other private	65	18	17	6	14	25	43	51
II. Multilateral	10	11	11	39	–	–	–	–
of which: concessional	–	–	–	–	–	–	–	–
memo: IMF, total	–	–	–	–	–	–	–	–
III. Non-OECD creditor countries	–	–	–	–	–	0	0	9
Subtotal: Service payments, long term debt	*915*	*870*	*1185*	*1031*	*1102*	*2069*	*1283*	*1108*
of which: concessional	*1*	*0*	*0*	*0*	*0*	*0*	*0*	*11*
Amortization, long term debt	603	565	872	600	658	1108	755	645
Interest, long term debt	312	305	313	431	444	960	528	463
Interest, short term debt	317	262	256	282	338	412	435	359
Total service payments	**1232**	**1132**	**1441**	**1314**	**1440**	**2481**	**1718**	**1467**

INDIA

US $ Million

	1984	1985	1986	1987	1988	1989	1990	1991
GROSS DEBT								
Long term								
I. OECD countries and capital markets	10366	13648	17141	22678	24167	25320	26986	30154
ODA	6726	8255	9808	11853	11495	11636	12699	13964
Official/off. supported	1390	1591	2213	2539	2798	3070	4438	4549
Official export credits	228	424	488	450	615	827	993	1395
Guaranteed supplier credits	664	621	604	233	168	177	233	297
Guaranteed bank credits	498	546	1120	1855	2014	2066	3211	2857
Financial markets	2251	3801	5120	8287	9875	10614	9850	11641
Banks	1766	2953	3796	6464	7572	7988	6527	6959
Bonds	485	849	1324	1823	2303	2626	3322	4682
Other private	–	–	–	–	–	–	–	–
II. Multilateral	14913	17226	19030	20611	20634	21557	22927	27962
of which: concessional	9486	10745	11474	12482	12727	13145	13844	15264
non-concessional	5426	6482	7556	8128	7907	8411	9083	12698
memo: IMF, total	4456	4832	4768	4023	2573	1892	1143	3471
III. Non-OECD Creditor countries	4197	4803	5479	7424	8221	7900	7812	8183
C.E.E.C.	2900	3374	4129	6246	7300	7086	7114	7673
Arab countries	397	430	447	430	287	286	287	256
Other countries and unspecified	900	1000	902	748	634	529	410	254
Subtotal: Long term debt	*29476*	*35678*	*41650*	*50714*	*53022*	*54777*	*57725*	*66299*
of which: concessional	16212	19000	21282	24335	24222	24781	26543	29228
non-concessional	13264	16678	20368	26378	28800	29996	31182	37071
Short term								
Subtotal: Short term debt	*2490*	*3527*	*3301*	*3297*	*3751*	*3945*	*4780*	*3740*
Banks	1867	2670	2303	2375	2720	2587	3641	2465
Export credits	623	857	999	922	1032	1358	1139	1275
Other identified liabilities	470	623	826	1268	1566	1641	1926	1718
Total identified debt	**32436**	**39828**	**45777**	**55279**	**58339**	**60363**	**64431**	**71757**
SERVICE PAYMENTS								
Long term								
I. OECD countries and capital markets	1044	1649	2117	2061	2429	2297	2518	2408
ODA	443	420	410	587	676	681	714	697
Official/off. supported	409	740	795	834	942	861	748	946
Financial markets	193	489	912	640	811	755	1057	764
Other private	–	–	–	–	–	–	–	–
II. Multilateral	878	1068	1595	2366	2422	2370	2344	2208
of which: concessional	140	211	313	343	366	364	405	306
memo: IMF, total	507	625	965	1378	1444	1264	997	704
III. Non-OECD creditor countries	173	268	309	278	336	264	199	268
Subtotal: Service payments, long term debt	*2095*	*2986*	*4022*	*4704*	*5187*	*4931*	*5061*	*4884*
of which: concessional	583	631	723	930	1042	1045	1119	1003
Amortization, long term debt	994	1795	2676	3099	3273	2804	2954	2845
Interest, long term debt	1101	1191	1345	1606	1914	2126	2106	2038
Interest, short term debt	286	291	281	300	395	490	510	368
Total service payments	**2382**	**3277**	**4303**	**5004**	**5582**	**5421**	**5570**	**5251**

US $ Million

	1984	1985	1986	1987	1988	1989	1990	1991
GROSS DEBT								
Long term								
I. OECD countries and capital markets	20893	23366	25939	31313	30144	32004	36267	39305
ODA	6165	7749	9514	12329	12449	12779	13960	15734
Official/off. supported	6228	7091	6938	8764	6937	7054	7679	8645
Official export credits	1372	1571	1495	2559	2607	2843	3559	4588
Guaranteed supplier credits	2656	2847	2109	2034	1653	1620	1320	1121
Guaranteed bank credits	2200	2674	3334	4171	2678	2592	2799	2935
Financial markets	8406	8410	9350	10062	10626	12043	14495	14793
Banks	7614	7601	8205	8889	9632	11229	13062	12933
Bonds	791	809	1146	1173	995	814	1433	1860
Other private	95	115	137	159	132	128	133	133
II. Multilateral	4311	5352	7024	10346	11346	12495	14746	16037
of which: concessional	925	973	1004	1069	1168	1286	1573	1778
non-concessional	3386	4379	6020	9277	10178	11210	13174	14259
memo: IMF, total	413	46	51	716	623	608	494	165
III. Non-OECD Creditor countries	1129	1136	1123	1142	1177	1091	1020	930
C.E.E.C.	661	678	696	723	685	617	616	567
Arab countries	77	103	115	135	160	161	162	145
Other countries and unspecified	390	355	312	284	332	313	243	219
Subtotal: Long term debt	*26333*	*29854*	*34086*	*42801*	*42667*	*45590*	*52034*	*56272*
of which: concessional	7090	8722	10517	13398	13617	14065	15533	17512
non-concessional	19243	21132	23569	29403	29050	31526	36501	38760
Short term								
Subtotal: Short term debt	*5338*	*5926*	*6453*	*7401*	*8428*	*8352*	*15838*	*20292*
Banks	4477	5001	5251	6194	7339	7206	13685	18150
Export credits	862	925	1202	1206	1089	1146	2153	2142
Other identified liabilities	36	35	25	33	32	100	159	322
Total identified debt	**31707**	**35815**	**40564**	**50235**	**51127**	**54043**	**68031**	**76886**
SERVICE PAYMENTS								
Long term								
I. OECD countries and capital markets	3170	4406	3778	4763	6259	6226	6420	7150
ODA	378	392	466	632	801	772	812	906
Official/off. supported	1714	1928	2205	2872	2135	1799	1998	1887
Financial markets	1078	2086	1092	1241	3304	3637	3599	4338
Other private	–	–	15	19	19	18	12	19
II. Multilateral	417	895	789	1053	1362	1436	1881	2224
of which: concessional	18	19	23	24	27	34	52	69
memo: IMF, total	33	405	4	22	92	51	216	348
III. Non-OECD creditor countries	147	182	143	195	128	124	201	120
Subtotal: Service payments, long term debt	*3734*	*5483*	*4710*	*6012*	*7748*	*7786*	*8502*	*9494*
of which: concessional	396	412	489	655	829	806	864	975
Amortization, long term debt	1836	3540	2824	3790	5233	5032	5441	6428
Interest, long term debt	1898	1943	1886	2221	2515	2753	3062	3066
Interest, short term debt	551	462	417	470	621	747	1001	1090
Total service payments	**4285**	**5944**	**5128**	**6482**	**8369**	**8533**	**9504**	**10585**

US $ Million

	1984	1985	1986	1987	1988	1989	1990	1991
GROSS DEBT								
Long term								
I. OECD countries and capital markets	2080	1713	893	1273	1243	1608	3556	4792
ODA	180	209	242	287	206	185	122	84
Official/off. supported	1493	1178	497	985	967	1336	2950	4242
Official export credits	160	153	146	166	157	135	–	–
Guaranteed supplier credits	1094	889	310	663	669	1026	2729	3509
Guaranteed bank credits	239	136	41	157	141	175	220	733
Financial markets	407	326	154	–	70	87	485	465
Banks	407	326	154	–	70	87	485	465
Bonds	–	–	–	–	–	–	–	–
Other private	–	–	–	–	–	–	–	–
II. Multilateral	267	240	210	317	202	143	116	76
of which: concessional	–	–	–	18	11	7	3	2
non-concessional	267	240	210	299	191	136	112	74
memo: IMF, total	–	–	–	–	–	–	–	–
III. Non-OECD Creditor countries	100	60	30	–	0	16	2	0
C.E.E.C.	100	60	30	–	–	16	2	0
Arab countries	–	–	–	–	–	–	–	–
Other countries and unspecified	–	–	–	–	0	0	0	0
Subtotal: Long term debt	*2447*	*2013*	*1133*	*1589*	*1446*	*1767*	*3674*	*4868*
of which: concessional	180	209	242	305	217	192	125	86
non-concessional	2268	1804	890	1284	1229	1575	3549	4782
Short term								
Subtotal: Short term debt	*2328*	*3243*	*2968*	*3413*	*3253*	*4177*	*7273*	*9218*
Banks	722	1367	1203	1265	1420	2024	2911	5140
Export credits	1606	1876	1765	2148	1833	2153	4362	4078
Other identified liabilities	–	–	–	–	–	–	–	–
Total identified debt	**4775**	**5256**	**4101**	**5002**	**4699**	**5944**	**10947**	**14085**
SERVICE PAYMENTS								
Long term								
I. OECD countries and capital markets	1582	1066	791	849	838	128	630	301
ODA	21	19	10	12	9	2	101	45
Official/off. supported	1199	633	707	784	808	117	520	218
Financial markets	362	414	73	53	21	8	9	37
Other private	–	–	–	–	–	–	–	–
II. Multilateral	76	73	82	99	105	74	77	48
of which: concessional	–	–	6	7	6	6	4	2
memo: IMF, total	–	–	–	–	–	–	–	–
III. Non-OECD creditor countries	9	50	32	31	9	3	15	1
Subtotal: Service payments, long term debt	*1667*	*1189*	*904*	*979*	*952*	*205*	*722*	*350*
of which: concessional	21	19	16	19	15	8	105	47
Amortization, long term debt	1461	1057	664	861	900	86	559	301
Interest, long term debt	206	132	240	118	52	119	162	49
Interest, short term debt	295	201	185	190	227	286	424	447
Total service payments	**1963**	**1390**	**1089**	**1169**	**1179**	**491**	**1146**	**797**

US $ Million

	1984	1985	1986	1987	1988	1989	1990	1991
GROSS DEBT								
Long term								
I. OECD countries and capital markets	3952	5594	6834	8769	8082	9410	7421	5633
ODA	149	191	255	408	388	324	320	343
Official/off. supported	2781	5185	5716	8143	5546	6182	4909	2918
Official export credits	94	68	4	57	58	42	26	22
Guaranteed supplier credits	1036	1738	2000	2551	1194	1331	1097	821
Guaranteed bank credits	1651	3379	3712	5534	4295	4810	3785	2075
Financial markets	1021	218	863	218	2148	2904	2192	2372
Banks	1021	218	863	218	2148	2904	2192	2372
Bonds	–	–	–	–	–	–	–	–
Other private	–	–	–	–	–	–	–	–
II. Multilateral	312	313	374	368	356	362	368	368
of which: concessional	9	13	21	23	20	26	38	38
non-concessional	302	299	352	345	336	336	329	329
memo: IMF, total	–	–	–	–	–	–	–	–
III. Non-OECD Creditor countries	2274	2603	4187	5460	6457	6493	6513	6953
C.E.E.C.	2000	2300	3884	5157	6154	6190	6210	6650
Arab countries	274	303	303	303	303	303	303	303
Other countries and unspecified	–	–	–	–	–	–	–	1
Subtotal: Long term debt	*6538*	*8510*	*11394*	*14597*	*14895*	*16265*	*14301*	*12954*
of which: concessional	2433	2807	4463	5891	6864	6842	6871	7334
non-concessional	4105	5703	6931	8706	8030	9423	7430	5619
Short term								
Subtotal: Short term debt	*2512*	*4329*	*5606*	*5810*	*5214*	*6512*	*8544*	*8235*
Banks	1315	2010	3429	3958	3415	4306	5187	3173
Export credits	1197	2319	2177	1852	1799	2206	3357	5062
Other identified liabilities	–	–	–	–	–	–	–	–
Total identified debt	**9050**	**12839**	**17000**	**20407**	**20109**	**22777**	**22846**	**21189**
SERVICE PAYMENTS								
Long term								
I. OECD countries and capital markets	1105	1693	3212	2440	1568	3153	781	358
ODA	13	14	12	8	27	31	48	–
Official/off. supported	1090	1677	2832	2301	1432	2478	461	358
Financial markets	1	2	368	131	109	644	272	–
Other private	–	–	–	–	–	–	–	–
II. Multilateral	10	83	41	33	181	28	31	24
of which: concessional	0	2	1	2	3	1	1	1
memo: IMF, total	–	–	–	–	–	–	–	–
III. Non-OECD creditor countries	9	90	55	25	26	26	68	21
Subtotal: Service payments, long term debt	*1124*	*1867*	*3309*	*2498*	*1774*	*3207*	*880*	*403*
of which: concessional	23	107	68	35	56	58	116	22
Amortization, long term debt	965	1499	2524	1940	1235	2502	601	0
Interest, long term debt	159	367	785	559	539	705	279	402
Interest, short term debt	243	277	317	376	403	445	468	220
Total service payments	**1368**	**2143**	**3625**	**2874**	**2177**	**3652**	**1347**	**623**

US $ Million

	1984	1985	1986	1987	1988	1989	1990	1991
GROSS DEBT								
Long term								
I. OECD countries and capital markets	19444	19695	19444	19685	18870	17837	17387	18424
ODA	2152	2348	2592	2836	2648	2651	2832	3036
Official/off. supported	10089	10186	10741	10823	10151	9446	9868	9789
Official export credits	8880	8800	9087	9273	4502	3481	3243	3000
Guaranteed supplier credits	181	280	455	359	345	260	231	342
Guaranteed bank credits	1028	1106	1198	1191	5304	5706	6395	6448
Financial markets	7204	7161	6112	6026	6071	5740	4687	5599
Banks	4391	4855	4318	4663	5000	5008	4173	4126
Bonds	2812	2306	1795	1363	1071	731	514	1473
Other private	–	–	–	–	–	–	–	–
II. Multilateral	81	83	84	85	68	69	80	80
of which: concessional	2	–	–	–	–	2	2	2
non-concessional	79	83	84	85	68	68	78	78
memo: IMF, total	–	–	–	–	–	–	–	–
III. Non-OECD Creditor countries	–	–	–	–	–	–	–	–
C.E.E.C.	–	–	–	–	–	–	–	–
Arab countries	–	–	–	–	–	–	–	–
Other countries and unspecified	–	–	–	–	–	–	–	–
Subtotal: Long term debt	*19525*	*19778*	*19528*	*19770*	·*18938*	*17907*	*17467*	*18504*
of which: concessional	2154	2348	2592	2836	2648	2653	2834	3037
non-concessional	17371	17430	16937	16934	16290	15254	14633	15467
Short term								
Subtotal: Short term debt	*4234*	*4568*	*4062*	*3427*	*2813*	*2222*	*2652*	*2382*
Banks	4145	4329	3716	3039	2457	1891	2164	1859
Export credits	89	239	347	388	357	331	488	524
Other identified liabilities	–	–	–	–	–	–	–	–
Total identified debt	**23759**	**24345**	**23591**	**23197**	**21751**	**20129**	**20119**	**20886**
SERVICE PAYMENTS								
Long term								
I. OECD countries and capital markets	3079	2914	3147	3072	3787	3679	2811	2397
ODA	111	115	113	176	192	170	221	223
Official/off. supported	1411	1461	1498	1741	2053	2140	1361	1383
Financial markets	1556	1338	1535	1155	1543	1369	1228	790
Other private	–	–	–	–	–	–	–	–
II. Multilateral	20	22	23	22	47	58	20	16
of which: concessional	2	2	–	–	–	–	0	0
memo: IMF, total	–	–	–	–	–	–	–	–
III. Non-OECD creditor countries	–	–	–	–	–	–	–	–
Subtotal: Service payments, long term debt	*3099*	*2935*	*3170*	*3095*	*3835*	*3737*	*2831*	*2413*
of which: concessional	114	118	113	176	192	170	222	223
Amortization, long term debt	1515	1226	1517	1332	1860	2371	1533	1208
Interest, long term debt	1584	1710	1653	1762	1974	1366	1298	1204
Interest, short term debt	475	361	293	258	250	226	202	150
Total service payments	**3575**	**3296**	**3463**	**3353**	**4084**	**3964**	**3033**	**2562**

JAMAICA

	1984	1985	1986	1987	1988	1989	1990	1991
GROSS DEBT								
Long term								
I. OECD countries and capital markets	1575	2094	2121	2059	2097	2414	2531	2348
ODA	695	821	990	1075	1141	1267	1454	1319
Official/off. supported	397	500	432	497	541	551	641	588
Official export credits	128	178	182	190	210	248	326	377
Guaranteed supplier credits	41	86	82	144	165	133	157	71
Guaranteed bank credits	228	236	168	164	167	170	158	140
Financial markets	460	755	686	476	405	587	433	439
Banks	459	755	686	476	405	587	433	439
Bonds	0	0	–	–	–	–	–	–
Other private	24	17	14	11	10	8	3	3
II. Multilateral	1183	1441	1582	1837	1576	1485	1533	1584
of which: concessional	145	150	168	192	193	197	202	200
non-concessional	1037	1291	1414	1645	1383	1288	1330	1384
memo: IMF, total	629	693	678	679	483	383	357	391
III. Non-OECD Creditor countries	510	510	434	406	365	325	337	318
C.E.E.C.	–	–	–	–	–	–	–	–
Arab countries	94	88	75	67	47	40	22	13
Other countries and unspecified	416	422	360	339	318	285	315	304
Subtotal: Long term debt	*3268*	*4044*	*4138*	*4302*	*4038*	*4224*	*4400*	*4250*
of which: concessional	840	972	1158	1267	1334	1464	1657	1519
non-concessional	2428	3073	2980	3036	2703	2760	2743	2731
Short term								
Subtotal: Short term debt	*249*	*252*	*233*	*295*	*375*	*464*	*414*	*209*
Banks	212	221	170	203	255	358	284	117
Export credits	37	31	63	92	120	106	129	91
Other identified liabilities	42	50	62	85	104	86	91	115
Total identified debt	**3559**	**4347**	**4433**	**4682**	**4517**	**4774**	**4905**	**4574**
SERVICE PAYMENTS								
Long term								
I. OECD countries and capital markets	124	183	292	224	239	243	284	266
ODA	23	25	22	21	57	51	30	53
Official/off. supported	51	101	128	114	98	134	147	139
Financial markets	50	57	136	84	81	55	103	74
Other private	–	–	7	5	3	3	4	1
II. Multilateral	188	190	278	433	421	366	333	333
of which: concessional	9	9	11	11	12	11	15	14
memo: IMF, total	121	117	174	288	261	205	145	111
III. Non-OECD creditor countries	51	100	107	70	86	51	54	153
Subtotal: Service payments, long term debt	*363*	*474*	*678*	*727*	*746*	*660*	*671*	*753*
of which: concessional	33	34	33	32	69	62	45	67
Amortization, long term debt	153	264	412	448	485	427	430	527
Interest, long term debt	210	209	266	280	261	234	242	226
Interest, short term debt	30	23	18	20	30	42	40	21
Total service payments	**393**	**496**	**696**	**747**	**776**	**703**	**711**	**774**

US $ Million

	1984	1985	1986	1987	1988	1989	1990	1991
GROSS DEBT								
Long term								
I. OECD countries and capital markets	1740	1981	2074	2482	2890	3168	3730	3827
ODA	507	615	754	914	862	879	1148	1653
Official/off. supported	797	973	910	1004	1128	1336	1637	1501
Official export credits	528	510	486	421	184	229	311	325
Guaranteed supplier credits	201	258	210	178	134	130	95	74
Guaranteed bank credits	68	205	215	405	809	977	1232	1102
Financial markets	436	392	410	564	900	953	945	673
Banks	436	392	410	564	662	695	688	521
Bonds	–	–	–	–	238	258	258	152
Other private	–	–	–	–	–	–	–	–
II. Multilateral	305	482	630	836	818	956	1117	1092
of which: concessional	166	171	178	208	231	306	321	316
non-concessional	139	310	452	628	586	650	796	776
memo: IMF, total	–	63	70	81	48	96	94	95
III. Non-OECD Creditor countries	824	974	1065	1212	1189	1131	1173	1160
C.E.E.C.	242	334	432	540	584	578	632	627
Arab countries	560	621	617	613	557	506	495	485
Other countries and unspecified	21	20	17	60	47	47	46	48
Subtotal: Long term debt	*2869*	*3436*	*3769*	*4530*	*4896*	*5255*	*6020*	*6078*
of which: concessional	674	787	932	1122	1094	1186	1468	1968
non-concessional	2195	2650	2837	3408	3802	4069	4552	4110
Short term								
Subtotal: Short term debt	*740*	*705*	*1047*	*1468*	*1332*	*1267*	*1357*	*1265*
Banks	521	523	948	1267	1180	1058	1029	853
Export credits	219	182	99	201	151	209	328	411
Other identified liabilities	684	800	888	914	886	618	582	1197
Total identified debt	**4293**	**4942**	**5705**	**6912**	**7114**	**7140**	**7959**	**8540**
SERVICE PAYMENTS								
Long term								
I. OECD countries and capital markets	295	505	316	375	640	363	376	244
ODA	24	26	25	39	51	31	67	60
Official/off. supported	223	434	257	300	212	205	192	94
Financial markets	47	45	34	36	376	126	117	90
Other private	–	–	–	–	–	–	–	–
II. Multilateral	29	48	64	104	153	160	164	160
of which: concessional	10	13	11	14	17	16	22	24
memo: IMF, total	–	3	5	5	33	41	18	8
III. Non-OECD creditor countries	51	71	76	91	121	65	55	65
Subtotal: Service payments, long term debt	*375*	*624*	*456*	*569*	*913*	*588*	*595*	*468*
of which: concessional	35	40	37	53	68	47	89	85
Amortization, long term debt	196	398	261	353	617	325	308	226
Interest, long term debt	179	226	194	216	297	263	287	242
Interest, short term debt	139	120	117	148	182	178	144	115
Total service payments	**514**	**743**	**573**	**717**	**1095**	**766**	**739**	**583**

KENYA

US $ Million

	1984	1985	1986	1987	1988	1989	1990	1991
GROSS DEBT								
Long term								
I. OECD countries and capital markets	1732	1929	2164	2538	2586	2878	2793	2908
ODA	662	818	1028	1307	1368	1528	1242	1314
Official/off. supported	531	617	680	827	763	873	958	1329
Official export credits	222	242	237	254	211	206	203	223
Guaranteed supplier credits	72	78	75	95	80	140	147	252
Guaranteed bank credits	237	297	368	479	472	527	608	854
Financial markets	538	494	456	404	456	478	592	265
Banks	538	494	456	404	456	478	592	265
Bonds	–	–	–	–	–	–	–	–
Other private	–	–	–	–	–	–	–	–
II. Multilateral	1523	1872	2098	2372	2383	2608	3020	3125
of which: concessional	526	592	671	779	920	1272	1782	2025
non-concessional	997	1280	1427	1593	1463	1336	1238	1100
memo: IMF, total	420	522	460	401	455	415	482	493
III. Non-OECD Creditor countries	194	202	174	157	131	116	112	101
C.E.E.C.	–	–	–	–	–	–	–	–
Arab countries	42	71	61	63	93	82	75	65
Other countries and unspecified	152	131	113	93	38	34	37	36
Subtotal: Long term debt	*3448*	*4003*	*4436*	*5066*	*5101*	*5603*	*5925*	*6134*
of which: concessional	1189	1409	1699	2086	2287	2800	3024	3338
non-concessional	2260	2594	2737	2980	2813	2803	2901	2796
Short term								
Subtotal: Short term debt	*386*	*440*	*660*	*795*	*724*	*729*	*895*	*792*
Banks	226	206	426	545	495	503	655	492
Export credits	160	235	235	250	229	226	240	300
Other identified liabilities	50	50	52	10	55	59	55	50
Total identified debt	**3884**	**4494**	**5148**	**5871**	**5880**	**6390**	**6876**	**6976**
SERVICE PAYMENTS								
Long term								
I. OECD countries and capital markets	283	370	347	270	330	363	352	363
ODA	24	29	30	41	67	52	85	46
Official/off. supported	151	188	183	178	156	245	156	190
Financial markets	108	153	133	51	107	67	111	127
Other private	–	–	–	–	–	–	–	–
II. Multilateral	190	227	295	332	333	355	364	292
of which: concessional	17	23	27	30	34	31	40	48
memo: IMF, total	99	117	156	153	129	163	130	58
III. Non-OECD creditor countries	25	39	38	7	9	16	18	17
Subtotal: Service payments, long term debt	*498*	*636*	*680*	*609*	*672*	*734*	*734*	*671*
of which: concessional	41	52	57	71	101	83	125	94
Amortization, long term debt	296	418	450	359	430	449	474	389
Interest, long term debt	202	218	230	250	242	285	260	282
Interest, short term debt	45	36	39	50	61	69	69	49
Total service payments	**544**	**672**	**719**	**659**	**733**	**803**	**803**	**720**

US $ Million

	1984	1985	1986	1987	1988	1989	1990	1991
GROSS DEBT								
Long term								
I. OECD countries and capital markets	312	360	376	371	286	187	182	180
ODA	–	–	–	7	6	–	–	0
Official/off. supported	30	44	52	19	6	4	–	–
Official export credits	–	–	–	–	6	4	–	–
Guaranteed supplier credits	–	–	13	–	–	–	–	–
Guaranteed bank credits	30	44	39	19	–	–	–	–
Financial markets	282	316	324	345	274	183	182	180
Banks	282	316	324	345	274	183	182	180
Bonds	–	–	–	–	–	–	–	–
Other private	–	–	–	–	–	–	–	–
II. Multilateral	–	–	–	–	–	–	–	–
of which: concessional	–	–	–	–	–	–	–	–
non-concessional	–	–	–	–	–	–	–	–
memo: IMF, total	–	–	–	–	–	–	–	–
III. Non-OECD Creditor countries	2560	2595	2666	3210	3150	3529	3589	3589
C.E.E.C.	2560	2595	2666	3210	3150	3529	3589	3589
Arab countries	–	–	–	–	–	–	–	–
Other countries and unspecified	–	–	–	–	–	–	–	–
Subtotal: Long term debt	*2872*	*2954*	*3041*	*3581*	*3437*	*3716*	*3771*	*3770*
of which: concessional	2560	2595	2666	3217	3157	3529	3589	3590
non-concessional	312	360	376	364	280	187	182	180
Short term								
Subtotal: Short term debt	*388*	*618*	*602*	*651*	*643*	*739*	*978*	*688*
Banks	166	326	196	259	215	331	451	314
Export credits	222	292	406	392	428	408	527	374
Other identified liabilities	–	–	–	–	–	–	–	–
Total identified debt	**3260**	**3572**	**3643**	**4232**	**4080**	**4456**	**4749**	**4458**
SERVICE PAYMENTS								
Long term								
I. OECD countries and capital markets	52	31	48	62	67	89	200	49
ODA	–	0	–	–	–	0	0	0
Official/off. supported	24	6	9	17	9	14	162	9
Financial markets	28	26	39	45	57	75	38	40
Other private	–	–	–	–	–	–	–	–
II. Multilateral	–	5	–	–	–	–	–	–
of which: concessional	–	5	–	–	–	–	–	–
memo: IMF, total	–	–	–	–	–	–	–	–
III. Non-OECD creditor countries	–	34	4	42	2	2	71	100
Subtotal: Service payments, long term debt	*52*	*70*	*52*	*104*	*69*	*92*	*271*	*149*
of which: concessional	–	39	4	42	2	3	71	100
Amortization, long term debt	19	33	19	74	30	54	175	27
Interest, long term debt	33	37	33	30	39	37	96	122
Interest, short term debt	19	20	19	17	19	25	33	24
Total service payments	**71**	**91**	**70**	**121**	**88**	**116**	**304**	**173**

US $ Million

	1984	1985	1986	1987	1988	1989	1990	1991
GROSS DEBT								
Long term								
I. OECD countries and capital markets	25529	31028	29311	24504	20804	19315	19661	25947
ODA	2478	2867	3260	3809	3535	3232	2816	2973
Official/off. supported	6580	6835	6465	4954	3864	3546	4538	2758
Official export credits	3585	3723	3503	1861	1488	1318	1172	971
Guaranteed supplier credits	1066	1117	971	1078	833	741	613	590
Guaranteed bank credits	1928	1995	1992	2015	1544	1487	2754	1197
Financial markets	16472	21326	19586	15742	13405	12536	12306	20216
Banks	15312	18392	15627	10916	9095	8614	8178	13337
Bonds	1159	2934	3959	4826	4309	3923	4128	6879
Other private	–	–	–	–	–	–	–	–
II. Multilateral	5385	6099	6862	6406	4571	3851	3794	3588
of which: concessional	184	185	188	194	184	173	168	159
non-concessional	5201	5914	6674	6212	4387	3678	3626	3429
memo: IMF, total	1567	1508	1549	525	–	–	–	–
III. Non-OECD Creditor countries	64	54	52	51	45	47	50	47
C.E.E.C.	–	–	–	–	–	–	–	–
Arab countries	60	53	52	51	45	47	50	47
Other countries and unspecified	4	1	–	–	–	–	–	–
Subtotal: Long term debt	*30978*	*37181*	*36224*	*30962*	*25421*	*23212*	*23504*	*29583*
of which: concessional	2661	3052	3448	4003	3720	3405	2984	3132
non-concessional	28317	34128	32776	26959	21701	19807	20520	26451
Short term								
Subtotal: Short term debt	*17181*	*18190*	*17545*	*16940*	*17952*	*18975*	*22953*	*24842*
Banks	16261	17253	16278	15643	15503	16940	20714	23733
Export credits	920	937	1267	1296	2449	2035	2239	1110
Other identified liabilities	556	795	576	495	403	297	296	267
Total identified debt	**48715**	**56165**	**54345**	**48396**	**43776**	**42485**	**46753**	**54692**
SERVICE PAYMENTS								
Long term								
I. OECD countries and capital markets	5004	7526	8760	15188	6701	6332	4921	3494
ODA	221	184	232	329	377	356	256	271
Official/off. supported	1571	3111	2101	3532	1879	1891	1611	1331
Financial markets	3212	4231	6427	11327	4445	4085	3054	1892
Other private	–	–	–	–	–	–	–	–
II. Multilateral	954	1188	1363	2754	2417	1173	954	770
of which: concessional	10	10	10	11	13	12	13	14
memo: IMF, total	401	517	403	1287	557	–	–	–
III. Non-OECD creditor countries	52	13	11	13	9	6	9	12
Subtotal: Service payments, long term debt	*6010*	*8726*	*10134*	*17956*	*9127*	*7511*	*5885*	*4276*
of which: concessional	230	194	242	341	389	368	270	284
Amortization, long term debt	3353	6064	7471	15348	7207	5849	4413	3102
Interest, long term debt	2656	2662	2662	2608	1920	1662	1471	1174
Interest, short term debt	1886	1506	1262	1227	1432	1693	1763	1446
Total service payments	**7896**	**10232**	**11395**	**19182**	**10558**	**9204**	**7648**	**5722**

US $ Million

	1984	1985	1986	1987	1988	1989	1990	1991
GROSS DEBT								
Long term								
I. OECD countries and capital markets	850	717	726	522	507	591	539	792
ODA	–	–	–	–	–	–	–	–
Official/off. supported	349	325	490	362	155	155	62	44
Official export credits	–	–	–	–	–	–	–	–
Guaranteed supplier credits	254	262	289	214	106	114	42	26
Guaranteed bank credits	95	63	202	148	49	40	20	18
Financial markets	501	393	236	160	353	437	477	748
Banks	361	253	116	120	313	397	437	698
Bonds	140	140	120	40	40	40	40	50
Other private	–	–	–	–	–	–	–	–
II. Multilateral	–	–	–	–	–	–	–	–
of which: concessional	–	–	–	–	–	–	–	–
non-concessional	–	–	–	–	–	–	–	–
memo: IMF, total	–	–	–	–	–	–	–	–
III. Non-OECD Creditor countries	0	0	0	0	0	0	0	0
C.E.E.C.	0	0	0	0	0	0	0	–
Arab countries	–	–	–	–	–	–	–	–
Other countries and unspecified	–	–	–	–	–	–	–	–
Subtotal: Long term debt	*850*	*717*	*727*	*522*	*508*	*591*	*539*	*792*
of which: concessional	*0*	*0*	*0*	*0*	*0*	*0*	*0*	*0*
non-concessional	*850*	*717*	*726*	*522*	*507*	*591*	*539*	*792*
Short term								
Subtotal: Short term debt	*8373*	*8321*	*7685*	*7455*	*8832*	*10327*	*10486*	*6090*
Banks	8185	8081	7449	7254	8636	10199	10373	5981
Export credits	188	240	236	202	196	128	113	109
Other identified liabilities	–	–	–	–	–	–	–	–
Total identified debt	**9223**	**9039**	**8411**	**7978**	**9340**	**10919**	**11025**	**6882**
SERVICE PAYMENTS								
Long term								
I. OECD countries and capital markets	998	1048	776	924	627	464	257	74
ODA	–	–	–	1	–	–	–	–
Official/off. supported	789	887	722	830	613	430	213	36
Financial markets	210	161	54	94	14	34	45	38
Other private	–	–	–	–	–	–	–	–
II. Multilateral	–	–	–	–	–	–	–	–
of which: concessional	–	–	–	–	–	–	–	–
memo: IMF, total	–	–	–	–	–	–	–	–
III. Non-OECD creditor countries	–	–	–	–	–	0	0	–
Subtotal: Service payments, long term debt	*998*	*1048*	*776*	*924*	*627*	*464*	*257*	*74*
of which: concessional	*–*	*–*	*–*	*1*	*–*	*0*	*0*	*–*
Amortization, long term debt	948	978	729	903	609	417	212	38
Interest, long term debt	50	70	47	21	18	47	46	36
Interest, short term debt	937	684	544	522	651	862	863	495
Total service payments	**1935**	**1732**	**1320**	**1446**	**1278**	**1326**	**1120**	**569**

US $ Million

	1984	1985	1986	1987	1988	1989	1990	1991
GROSS DEBT								
Long term								
I. OECD countries and capital markets	47	58	66	79	69	65	69	68
ODA	44	55	66	79	69	65	69	68
Official/off. supported	3	3	–	–	–	–	–	–
Official export credits	–	–	–	–	–	–	–	–
Guaranteed supplier credits	2	0	–	–	–	–	–	–
Guaranteed bank credits	1	3	–	–	–	–	–	–
Financial markets	0	–	–	–	–	–	–	–
Banks	0	–	–	–	–	–	–	–
Bonds	–	–	–	–	–	–	–	–
Other private	–	–	–	–	–	–	–	–
II. Multilateral	66	75	93	105	119	188	270	319
of which: concessional	66	75	93	105	119	188	270	319
non-concessional	0	–	–	0	0	–	–	–
memo: IMF, total	11	10	9	6	3	8	8	21
III. Non-OECD Creditor countries	926	937	1023	1206	1291	1248	1279	1281
C.E.E.C.	903	908	992	1175	1259	1216	1247	1247
Arab countries	–	–	–	–	–	–	–	–
Other countries and unspecified	23	30	31	31	32	32	32	34
Subtotal: Long term debt	*1040*	*1070*	*1182*	*1390*	*1479*	*1501*	*1618*	*1669*
of which: concessional	110	129	159	184	188	253	339	387
non-concessional	929	941	1023	1206	1291	1248	1279	1281
Short term								
Subtotal: Short term debt	*29*	*72*	*7*	*12*	*7*	*6*	*5*	*12*
Banks	26	68	1	5	4	4	2	9
Export credits	3	4	6	7	3	2	3	3
Other identified liabilities	–	–	–	–	–	–	–	–
Total identified debt	**1069**	**1142**	**1189**	**1402**	**1486**	**1508**	**1623**	**1680**
SERVICE PAYMENTS								
Long term								
I. OECD countries and capital markets	4	4	3	4	5	11	4	3
ODA	2	2	2	4	5	4	4	3
Official/off. supported	2	2	0	–	0	8	1	–
Financial markets	0	0	–	–	–	–	–	–
Other private	–	–	–	–	–	–	–	–
II. Multilateral	2	4	5	6	6	5	5	5
of which: concessional	2	4	5	6	6	5	5	5
memo: IMF, total	1	2	3	3	3	2	1	0
III. Non-OECD creditor countries	2	3	2	2	2	–	–	–
Subtotal: Service payments, long term debt	*8*	*11*	*10*	*12*	*13*	*17*	*10*	*8*
of which: concessional	4	6	8	10	11	9	9	8
Amortization, long term debt	7	9	8	10	11	14	7	5
Interest, long term debt	1	1	2	2	2	2	3	3
Interest, short term debt	2	4	2	0	0	0	0	0
Total service payments	**10**	**14**	**12**	**12**	**14**	**17**	**10**	**8**

LEBANON

US $ Million

	1984	1985	1986	1987	1988	1989	1990	1991
GROSS DEBT								
Long term								
I. OECD countries and capital markets	368	402	316	350	344	363	306	249
ODA	30	33	37	42	51	58	60	60
Official/off. supported	262	294	199	183	158	162	91	69
Official export credits	116	125	103	82	62	34	13	7
Guaranteed supplier credits	49	48	7	10	10	29	19	9
Guaranteed bank credits	97	121	89	92	86	100	60	52
Financial markets	75	75	80	124	135	143	155	120
Banks	75	75	80	124	135	143	155	120
Bonds	–	–	–	–	–	–	–	–
Other private	–	–	–	–	–	–	–	–
II. Multilateral	80	92	99	108	89	83	84	79
of which: concessional	37	40	39	40	36	34	38	40
non-concessional	43	52	60	68	53	50	45	38
memo: IMF, total	–	–	–	–	–	–	–	–
III. Non-OECD Creditor countries	29	34	59	62	67	62	75	75
C.E.E.C.	–	–	–	4	12	15	36	43
Arab countries	29	34	34	34	30	26	23	20
Other countries and unspecified	–	–	25	25	25	21	17	13
Subtotal: Long term debt	*477*	*528*	*474*	*520*	*500*	*508*	*465*	*402*
of which: concessional	68	73	76	82	87	92	98	101
non-concessional	409	454	398	438	413	417	367	302
Short term								
Subtotal: Short term debt	*455*	*464*	*452*	*541*	*593*	*636*	*808*	*813*
Banks	422	425	420	500	544	574	625	500
Export credits	33	39	32	41	50	62	183	313
Other identified liabilities	–	–	–	–	–	–	381	594
Total identified debt	**932**	**992**	**925**	**1061**	**1093**	**1144**	**1654**	**1809**
SERVICE PAYMENTS								
Long term								
I. OECD countries and capital markets	186	189	61	60	73	83	75	67
ODA	5	4	2	3	4	0	1	4
Official/off. supported	100	92	54	50	34	38	35	15
Financial markets	81	93	5	8	35	45	38	48
Other private	–	–	–	–	–	–	–	–
II. Multilateral	15	15	19	16	23	14	20	15
of which: concessional	6	6	7	8	8	7	5	6
memo: IMF, total	–	–	–	–	–	–	–	–
III. Non-OECD creditor countries	2	4	5	7	7	12	16	20
Subtotal: Service payments, long term debt	*203*	*209*	*85*	*82*	*102*	*109*	*111*	*102*
of which: concessional	11	10	9	10	12	7	6	9
Amortization, long term debt	171	175	40	52	68	73	68	72
Interest, long term debt	32	34	45	30	35	36	43	30
Interest, short term debt	49	37	30	33	43	52	67	64
Total service payments	**252**	**246**	**115**	**115**	**146**	**161**	**177**	**166**

LESOTHO

	1984	1985	1986	1987	1988	1989	1990	1991
GROSS DEBT								
Long term								
I. OECD countries and capital markets	11	17	20	28	46	49	63	82
ODA	2	3	1	3	4	7	20	29
Official/off. supported	8	14	18	21	41	38	43	53
Official export credits	3	3	10	7	11	9	8	12
Guaranteed supplier credits	3	8	7	9	17	11	8	12
Guaranteed bank credits	2	3	1	6	14	18	28	30
Financial markets	0	–	–	4	1	4	–	–
Banks	0	–	–	4	1	4	–	–
Bonds	–	–	–	–	–	–	–	–
Other private	–	–	–	–	–	–	–	–
II. Multilateral	107	145	168	207	222	258	307	343
of which: concessional	100	123	145	178	193	228	273	313
non-concessional	8	21	23	29	28	29	34	30
memo: IMF, total	4	4	3	2	5	10	15	15
III. Non-OECD Creditor countries	16	12	10	19	14	12	21	30
C.E.E.C.	–	–	–	–	–	–	–	–
Arab countries	6	9	8	8	7	7	7	8
Other countries and unspecified	10	3	1	10	7	5	14	22
Subtotal: Long term debt	*134*	*173*	*197*	*254*	*282*	*319*	*391*	*455*
of which: concessional	102	126	146	180	197	235	293	342
non-concessional	32	47	51	74	85	84	98	114
Short term								
Subtotal: Short term debt	*1*	*0*	*5*	*13*	*9*	*9*	*79*	*43*
Banks	–	–	4	12	8	9	9	42
Export credits	1	0	1	1	1	0	70	1
Other identified liabilities	1	1	1	3	3	4	1	3
Total identified debt	**135**	**174**	**203**	**270**	**294**	**333**	**471**	**502**
SERVICE PAYMENTS								
Long term								
I. OECD countries and capital markets	9	7	3	4	7	12	12	12
ODA	0	0	0	0	0	0	0	0
Official/off. supported	9	6	3	4	4	11	9	11
Financial markets	0	1	–	–	3	1	3	1
Other private	–	–	–	–	–	–	–	–
II. Multilateral	3	7	9	10	11	11	12	13
of which: concessional	2	4	5	6	6	6	6	5
memo: IMF, total	0	1	1	1	1	1	2	0
III. Non-OECD creditor countries	13	8	2	2	7	2	2	5
Subtotal: Service payments, long term debt	*25*	*22*	*14*	*15*	*24*	*25*	*25*	*30*
of which: concessional	3	4	5	6	6	6	6	5
Amortization, long term debt	21	18	10	9	18	17	17	19
Interest, long term debt	4	5	4	6	6	8	8	11
Interest, short term debt	0	0	0	1	1	1	4	4
Total service payments	**25**	**22**	**15**	**16**	**26**	**26**	**29**	**34**

LIBERIA

US $ Million

	1984	1985	1986	1987	1988	1989	1990	1991
GROSS DEBT								
Long term								
I. OECD countries and capital markets	626	670	779	880	807	698	776	748
ODA	245	280	340	390	369	362	384	383
Official/off. supported	181	190	239	350	288	185	212	185
Official export credits	145	159	212	318	256	132	151	117
Guaranteed supplier credits	12	11	7	16	10	32	30	14
Guaranteed bank credits	24	21	20	15	21	21	31	53
Financial markets	200	200	200	141	150	151	180	180
Banks	200	200	200	141	150	151	180	180
Bonds	–	–	–	–	–	–	–	–
Other private	–	–	–	–	–	–	–	–
II. Multilateral	460	551	635	754	727	709	762	756
of which: concessional	123	150	175	210	206	203	214	205
non-concessional	337	402	460	544	521	506	548	551
memo: IMF, total	233	253	282	327	309	299	322	324
III. Non-OECD Creditor countries	59	63	64	64	78	79	79	79
C.E.E.C.	–	–	–	–	15	15	15	15
Arab countries	27	27	27	27	27	27	27	27
Other countries and unspecified	32	36	37	37	37	37	37	37
Subtotal: Long term debt	*1145*	*1284*	*1478*	*1698*	*1612*	*1486*	*1617*	*1583*
of which: concessional	368	429	515	600	575	566	598	588
non-concessional	776	855	962	1098	1037	921	1018	995
Short term								
Subtotal: Short term debt	*142*	*116*	*113*	*125*	*130*	*129*	*156*	*151*
Banks	120	100	100	110	117	118	145	140
Export credits	22	16	13	15	13	11	11	11
Other identified liabilities	–	–	–	–	–	–	–	–
Total identified debt	**1287**	**1400**	**1591**	**1823**	**1742**	**1616**	**1773**	**1734**
SERVICE PAYMENTS								
Long term								
I. OECD countries and capital markets	46	42	50	66	55	38	56	56
ODA	10	8	8	7	10	12	5	4
Official/off. supported	16	16	28	44	33	12	38	39
Financial markets	20	18	14	15	12	14	14	13
Other private	–	–	–	–	–	–	–	–
II. Multilateral	57	35	23	3	3	3	1	1
of which: concessional	4	2	2	0	0	3	0	1
memo: IMF, total	40	18	0	0	2	3	1	1
III. Non-OECD creditor countries	4	–	–	–	–	–	–	–
Subtotal: Service payments, long term debt	*106*	*77*	*72*	*69*	*58*	*41*	*58*	*57*
of which: concessional	14	9	10	7	11	15	5	5
Amortization, long term debt	48	28	28	35	27	16	27	24
Interest, long term debt	58	48	44	35	31	25	31	32
Interest, short term debt	15	10	7	8	10	11	11	9
Total service payments	**121**	**87**	**80**	**77**	**68**	**52**	**69**	**65**

LIBYA

	1984	1985	1986	1987	1988	1989	1990	1991
GROSS DEBT								
Long term								
I. OECD countries and capital markets	794	1064	279	275	40	23	21	210
ODA	–	–	6	7	–	–	–	–
Official/off. supported	471	683	256	267	40	23	21	165
Official export credits	–	–	12	–	–	–	–	–
Guaranteed supplier credits	465	676	239	241	25	8	4	141
Guaranteed bank credits	6	7	5	27	15	15	17	23
Financial markets	323	382	16	–	–	–	–	46
Banks	323	382	16	–	–	–	–	46
Bonds	–	–	–	–	–	–	–	–
Other private	–	–	–	–	–	–	–	–
II. Multilateral	–	31	29	64	64	64	64	64
of which: concessional	–	–	–	–	–	–	–	–
non-concessional	–	31	29	64	64	64	64	64
memo: IMF, total	–	–	–	–	–	–	–	–
III. Non-OECD Creditor countries	1496	1550	1529	1846	2303	2756	2756	2756
C.E.E.C.	1496	1550	1529	1846	2303	2756	2756	2756
Arab countries	–	–	–	–	–	–	–	–
Other countries and unspecified	–	–	–	–	–	–	–	–
Subtotal: Long term debt	*2290*	*2645*	*1837*	*2184*	*2407*	*2843*	*2841*	*3030*
of which: concessional	1496	1550	1535	1853	2303	2756	2756	2756
non-concessional	794	1096	302	331	104	87	85	274
Short term								
Subtotal: Short term debt	*1772*	*2113*	*1765*	*2271*	*3015*	*2798*	*2098*	*1597*
Banks	1162	1078	892	654	1492	1909	1462	1251
Export credits	610	1036	873	1617	1524	889	636	346
Other identified liabilities	–	–	–	–	–	–	–	–
Total identified debt	**4062**	**4759**	**3602**	**4455**	**5422**	**5641**	**4938**	**4627**
SERVICE PAYMENTS								
Long term								
I. OECD countries and capital markets	769	608	518	247	215	113	398	70
ODA	–	–	–	–	–	–	–	–
Official/off. supported	723	565	484	241	213	113	398	70
Financial markets	46	43	34	7	2	–	–	1
Other private	–	–	–	–	–	–	–	–
II. Multilateral	–	4	14	2	17	4	4	4
of which: concessional	–	2	–	–	–	–	–	–
memo: IMF, total	–	–	–	–	–	–	–	–
III. Non-OECD creditor countries	–	–	–	–	–	115	55	600
Subtotal: Service payments, long term debt	*769*	*612*	*532*	*249*	*231*	*232*	*458*	*675*
of which: concessional	–	2	–	–	–	115	55	600
Amortization, long term debt	727	567	501	243	229	112	397	470
Interest, long term debt	43	45	31	6	3	120	60	204
Interest, short term debt	195	154	121	118	183	231	174	91
Total service payments	**964**	**765**	**653**	**368**	**414**	**463**	**631**	**765**

MACAO

US $ Million

	1984	1985	1986	1987	1988	1989	1990	1991
GROSS DEBT								
Long term								
I. OECD countries and capital markets	78	98	86	181	191	251	149	92
ODA	–	–	–	–	–	–	–	–
Official/off. supported	7	10	2	14	12	4	2	0
Official export credits	2	7	–	7	5	4	2	–
Guaranteed supplier credits	5	3	2	0	0	–	–	0
Guaranteed bank credits	0	–	–	7	7	–	–	–
Financial markets	71	87	84	167	179	247	147	92
Banks	71	87	84	167	179	247	147	92
Bonds	–	–	–	–	–	–	–	–
Other private	–	–	–	–	–	–	–	–
II. Multilateral	–	–	–	–	–	–	–	–
of which: concessional	–	–	–	–	–	–	–	–
non-concessional	–	–	–	–	–	–	–	–
memo: IMF, total	–	–	–	–	–	–	–	–
III. Non-OECD Creditor countries	–	–	–	–	–	–	–	–
C.E.E.C.	–	–	–	–	–	–	–	–
Arab countries	–	–	–	–	–	–	–	–
Other countries and unspecified	–	–	–	–	–	–	–	–
Subtotal: Long term debt	*78*	*98*	*86*	*181*	*191*	*251*	*149*	*92*
of which: concessional	–	–	–	–	–	–	–	–
non-concessional	78	98	86	181	191	251	149	92
Short term								
Subtotal: Short term debt	*720*	*796*	*892*	*1351*	*1240*	*1266*	*1415*	*1696*
Banks	720	796	891	1350	1238	1261	1411	1688
Export credits	0	0	1	1	2	5	4	8
Other identified liabilities	–	–	–	–	–	–	–	–
Total identified debt	**798**	**894**	**978**	**1532**	**1431**	**1516**	**1564**	**1788**
SERVICE PAYMENTS								
Long term								
I. OECD countries and capital markets	14	14	9	12	19	24	29	13
ODA	–	–	–	–	–	–	–	–
Official/off. supported	2	2	2	4	4	2	1	1
Financial markets	12	12	7	8	15	23	28	12
Other private	–	–	–	–	–	–	–	–
II. Multilateral	–	–	–	–	–	–	–	–
of which: concessional	–	–	–	–	–	–	–	–
memo: IMF, total	–	–	–	–	–	–	–	–
III. Non-OECD creditor countries	–	–	–	–	–	–	–	–
Subtotal: Service payments, long term debt	*14*	*14*	*9*	*12*	*19*	*24*	*29*	*13*
of which: concessional	–	–	–	–	–	–	–	–
Amortization, long term debt	7	7	3	5	4	7	7	2
Interest, long term debt	8	7	7	7	15	17	23	11
Interest, short term debt	78	62	57	77	104	113	111	93
Total service payments	**92**	**76**	**67**	**89**	**122**	**137**	**140**	**106**

MADAGASCAR

	1984	1985	1986	1987	1988	1989	1990	1991
GROSS DEBT								
Long term								
I. OECD countries and capital markets	746	937	1065	1347	1358	1299	1208	1182
ODA	234	337	482	683	700	730	600	568
Official/off. supported	404	485	469	564	561	529	571	579
Official export credits	202	298	344	417	379	391	396	465
Guaranteed supplier credits	83	68	42	75	141	87	73	72
Guaranteed bank credits	119	120	83	73	42	51	102	42
Financial markets	108	114	114	100	97	40	36	34
Banks	108	114	114	100	97	40	36	34
Bonds	–	–	–	–	–	–	–	–
Other private	–	–	–	–	–	–	–	–
II. Multilateral	558	662	837	1085	1122	1192	1387	1560
of which: concessional	385	469	601	805	875	999	1230	1440
non-concessional	173	193	236	280	247	194	157	120
memo: IMF, total	171	184	203	238	190	165	144	127
III. Non-OECD Creditor countries	445	439	515	584	563	583	592	591
C.E.E.C.	191	193	268	327	333	329	343	344
Arab countries	212	208	213	224	197	192	193	193
Other countries and unspecified	42	38	34	33	34	62	56	54
Subtotal: Long term debt	*1749*	*2038*	*2417*	*3017*	*3044*	*3074*	*3186*	*3333*
of which: concessional	618	806	1083	1488	1575	1728	1830	2009
non-concessional	1130	1232	1334	1529	1469	1345	1357	1324
Short term								
Subtotal: Short term debt	*102*	*113*	*230*	*231*	*258*	*288*	*356*	*313*
Banks	63	62	80	43	41	65	85	56
Export credits	39	51	150	188	217	223	271	257
Other identified liabilities	–	–	–	–	–	–	–	–
Total identified debt	**1851**	**2151**	**2647**	**3248**	**3302**	**3362**	**3542**	**3646**
SERVICE PAYMENTS								
Long term								
I. OECD countries and capital markets	48	77	117	114	120	143	108	83
ODA	10	10	22	23	13	32	12	16
Official/off. supported	27	56	85	80	64	65	83	45
Financial markets	11	12	10	12	43	45	13	22
Other private	–	–	–	–	–	–	–	–
II. Multilateral	48	58	83	79	93	99	99	82
of which: concessional	9	10	18	24	28	23	27	25
memo: IMF, total	38	49	67	54	59	65	61	40
III. Non-OECD creditor countries	3	2	4	9	9	8	6	3
Subtotal: Service payments, long term debt	*99*	*138*	*205*	*203*	*222*	*250*	*214*	*168*
of which: concessional	19	19	40	47	41	55	39	42
Amortization, long term debt	43	71	113	95	112	136	146	96
Interest, long term debt	56	66	91	108	110	114	68	72
Interest, short term debt	13	7	6	5	5	6	7	5
Total service payments	**111**	**145**	**211**	**208**	**226**	**256**	**221**	**173**

MALAWI

US $ Million

	1984	1985	1986	1987	1988	1989	1990	1991
GROSS DEBT								
Long term								
I. OECD countries and capital markets	279	267	258	337	332	307	317	320
ODA	119	113	137	186	203	199	215	223
Official/off. supported	62	87	81	96	76	68	66	66
Official export credits	41	65	53	82	53	36	27	33
Guaranteed supplier credits	8	10	8	10	12	10	16	7
Guaranteed bank credits	13	12	20	4	11	23	23	27
Financial markets	98	67	40	54	52	39	36	31
Banks	98	67	40	54	52	39	36	31
Bonds	–	–	–	–	–	–	–	–
Other private	–	–	–	–	–	–	–	–
II. Multilateral	550	651	773	926	953	1015	1191	1306
of which: concessional	358	418	527	662	720	821	1013	1157
non-concessional	192	233	246	264	233	193	179	149
memo: IMF, total	125	146	133	117	106	100	115	115
III. Non-OECD Creditor countries	40	30	28	28	21	20	17	12
C.E.E.C.	–	–	–	–	–	–	–	–
Arab countries	–	–	–	–	–	–	–	–
Other countries and unspecified	40	30	28	28	21	20	17	12
Subtotal: Long term debt	*868*	*947*	*1060*	*1292*	*1305*	*1341*	*1525*	*1638*
of which: concessional	476	530	664	849	923	1021	1228	1380
non-concessional	392	417	396	443	381	321	297	258
Short term								
Subtotal: Short term debt	*46*	*83*	*76*	*42*	*49*	*43*	*48*	*34*
Banks	30	58	53	26	26	19	15	12
Export credits	16	25	23	16	23	24	33	22
Other identified liabilities	6	7	7	9	9	10	12	9
Total identified debt	**921**	**1037**	**1143**	**1343**	**1363**	**1394**	**1586**	**1680**
SERVICE PAYMENTS								
Long term								
I. OECD countries and capital markets	53	64	61	35	33	53	47	36
ODA	5	9	6	8	10	12	15	10
Official/off. supported	26	16	21	20	18	36	28	22
Financial markets	23	39	34	7	5	6	5	4
Other private	–	–	–	–	–	–	–	–
II. Multilateral	48	44	65	72	71	67	62	64
of which: concessional	7	8	11	12	14	12	13	16
memo: IMF, total	31	29	38	44	38	33	25	25
III. Non-OECD creditor countries	6	6	7	5	2	3	3	5
Subtotal: Service payments, long term debt	*108*	*114*	*134*	*112*	*106*	*123*	*112*	*104*
of which: concessional	12	18	16	20	24	24	27	26
Amortization, long term debt	69	77	95	74	66	82	75	70
Interest, long term debt	39	37	39	38	41	41	38	34
Interest, short term debt	7	5	6	4	4	5	4	3
Total service payments	**114**	**120**	**139**	**116**	**110**	**128**	**117**	**107**

US $ Million

	1984	1985	1986	1987	1988	1989	1990	1991
GROSS DEBT								
Long term								
I. OECD countries and capital markets	15184	16691	17032	18057	15780	14407	14175	16496
ODA	722	1081	1345	1994	2007	1793	2252	2538
Official/off. supported	896	2355	2673	2496	1177	979	1121	1384
Official export credits	199	440	460	546	481	236	243	226
Guaranteed supplier credits	282	1113	1231	846	236	227	391	549
Guaranteed bank credits	415	802	982	1104	460	516	486	609
Financial markets	13566	13255	13014	13567	12596	11636	10802	12574
Banks	10424	7892	7185	7045	6323	5555	4380	5893
Bonds	3143	5363	5829	6522	6273	6081	6423	6681
Other private	–	–	–	–	–	–	–	–
II. Multilateral	1297	1312	1344	1576	1471	1461	1812	1944
of which: concessional	71	70	65	57	38	27	19	17
non-concessional	1227	1242	1279	1519	1434	1435	1794	1927
memo: IMF, total	258	118	–	–	–	–	–	–
III. Non-OECD Creditor countries	209	276	272	218	238	146	122	112
C.E.E.C.	–	–	–	–	–	–	–	–
Arab countries	70	87	93	97	90	82	77	71
Other countries and unspecified	139	189	179	121	148	63	45	41
Subtotal: Long term debt	*16690*	*18280*	*18648*	*19851*	*17489*	*16015*	*16110*	*18552*
of which: concessional	792	1151	1410	2051	2045	1819	2271	2555
non-concessional	15898	17129	17238	17800	15444	14195	13839	15997
Short term								
Subtotal: Short term debt	*484*	*2685*	*2712*	*2345*	*1666*	*1690*	*2947*	*2028*
Banks	388	2579	2604	2199	1527	1531	2726	1833
Export credits	96	107	108	146	139	158	221	195
Other identified liabilities	242	296	260	189	223	327	330	406
Total identified debt	**17416**	**21261**	**21620**	**22385**	**19379**	**18031**	**19386**	**20986**
SERVICE PAYMENTS								
Long term								
I. OECD countries and capital markets	1834	4986	2718	3222	3508	3180	2604	2069
ODA	58	63	73	106	195	180	183	227
Official/off. supported	438	541	536	547	401	637	335	416
Financial markets	1338	4382	2110	2569	2912	2364	2086	1426
Other private	–	–	–	–	–	–	–	–
II. Multilateral	229	354	372	265	301	299	361	364
of which: concessional	18	19	24	24	19	12	14	6
memo: IMF, total	74	175	130	–	–	–	–	–
III. Non-OECD creditor countries	18	26	40	63	39	104	36	25
Subtotal: Service payments, long term debt	*2081*	*5365*	*3130*	*3550*	*3849*	*3584*	*3001*	*2457*
of which: concessional	76	82	97	130	214	192	197	233
Amortization, long term debt	626	3794	1891	2242	2908	2696	2187	1827
Interest, long term debt	1455	1571	1239	1307	941	888	813	630
Interest, short term debt	184	152	202	190	177	176	219	171
Total service payments	**2265**	**5517**	**3332**	**3740**	**4026**	**3760**	**3220**	**2628**

MALI

US $ Million

	1984	1985	1986	1987	1988	1989	1990	1991
GROSS DEBT								
Long term								
I. OECD countries and capital markets	151	298	380	496	473	579	711	743
ODA	112	255	334	437	426	544	685	710
Official/off. supported	32	33	45	47	33	27	23	31
Official export credits	8	9	9	10	9	9	11	18
Guaranteed supplier credits	22	14	16	21	12	2	1	0
Guaranteed bank credits	3	9	20	16	12	16	11	13
Financial markets	7	9	–	11	15	8	2	2
Banks	7	9	–	11	15	8	2	2
Bonds	–	–	–	–	–	–	–	–
Other private	–	1	1	1	–	1	1	1
II. Multilateral	428	498	603	718	769	816	939	1049
of which: concessional	357	409	508	631	698	761	892	1011
non-concessional	71	90	95	87	71	55	47	37
memo: IMF, total	83	98	99	85	74	55	69	60
III. Non-OECD Creditor countries	497	577	650	741	813	780	847	841
C.E.E.C.	234	270	313	368	444	429	472	472
Arab countries	144	167	194	206	207	211	225	226
Other countries and unspecified	120	141	143	167	162	140	150	142
Subtotal: Long term debt	*1076*	*1374*	*1633*	*1956*	*2055*	*2175*	*2497*	*2633*
of which: concessional	469	664	842	1068	1124	1305	1578	1721
non-concessional	608	710	791	888	931	870	920	911
Short term								
Subtotal: Short term debt	*64*	*85*	*90*	*92*	*82*	*90*	*79*	*75*
Banks	36	27	23	25	21	22	21	20
Export credits	28	58	67	67	61	68	58	55
Other identified liabilities	13	15	18	30	38	34	40	30
Total identified debt	**1153**	**1474**	**1741**	**2078**	**2175**	**2299**	**2617**	**2738**
SERVICE PAYMENTS								
Long term								
I. OECD countries and capital markets	6	8	11	12	20	26	17	17
ODA	1	4	6	8	2	11	3	13
Official/off. supported	5	3	5	4	1	3	4	4
Financial markets	1	1	1	–	14	12	10	0
Other private	–	–	–	–	2	0	–	0
II. Multilateral	15	29	41	41	56	48	47	23
of which: concessional	9	17	17	13	30	22	23	9
memo: IMF, total	9	14	28	33	29	27	22	13
III. Non-OECD creditor countries	4	12	8	10	14	11	9	0
Subtotal: Service payments, long term debt	*26*	*49*	*60*	*64*	*90*	*86*	*73*	*40*
of which: concessional	9	21	22	21	32	34	26	22
Amortization, long term debt	14	30	38	40	63	54	47	18
Interest, long term debt	11	19	22	23	27	32	26	23
Interest, short term debt	5	7	6	7	9	9	8	5
Total service payments	**31**	**56**	**66**	**71**	**99**	**95**	**81**	**45**

MALTA

US $ Million

	1984	1985	1986	1987	1988	1989	1990	1991
GROSS DEBT								
Long term								
I. OECD countries and capital markets	51	60	60	130	126	189	228	406
ODA	38	46	46	58	51	48	49	46
Official/off. supported	7	14	7	18	9	4	4	49
Official export credits	0	1	1	1	0	0	1	22
Guaranteed supplier credits	2	5	4	17	8	3	2	3
Guaranteed bank credits	4	8	2	0	1	1	1	24
Financial markets	6	1	6	53	67	137	174	311
Banks	6	1	6	53	67	137	174	311
Bonds	–	–	–	–	–	–	–	–
Other private	–	–	–	–	–	–	–	–
II. Multilateral	5	6	7	8	6	7	23	43
of which: concessional	5	6	7	8	6	6	7	8
non-concessional	–	–	–	–	–	1	16	35
memo: IMF, total	–	–	–	–	–	–	–	–
III. Non-OECD Creditor countries	76	51	49	47	43	38	43	42
C.E.E.C.	–	–	–	–	–	–	–	–
Arab countries	31	34	38	35	31	27	30	30
Other countries and unspecified	45	17	11	12	12	10	12	12
Subtotal: Long term debt	*132*	*117*	*115*	*185*	*176*	*234*	*293*	*491*
of which: concessional	43	52	53	66	57	54	56	54
non-concessional	89	65	62	118	119	180	237	437
Short term								
Subtotal: Short term debt	*87*	*105*	*127*	*182*	*285*	*327*	*442*	*552*
Banks	66	72	96	149	246	287	385	499
Export credits	21	34	31	33	39	40	57	53
Other identified liabilities	20	59	81	132	80	110	201	259
Total identified debt	**240**	**281**	**324**	**499**	**541**	**671**	**936**	**1302**
SERVICE PAYMENTS								
Long term								
I. OECD countries and capital markets	9	8	19	19	19	23	24	37
ODA	1	1	3	4	4	7	3	4
Official/off. supported	6	6	10	15	5	3	2	9
Financial markets	1	1	6	1	10	12	19	25
Other private	–	–	–	–	–	–	–	–
II. Multilateral	1	0	1	1	1	1	0	2
of which: concessional	1	0	1	1	1	1	0	0
memo: IMF, total	–	–	–	–	–	–	–	–
III. Non-OECD creditor countries	6	6	10	6	5	5	4	6
Subtotal: Service payments, long term debt	*15*	*15*	*30*	*25*	*24*	*29*	*29*	*45*
of which: concessional	2	2	4	4	5	8	4	4
Amortization, long term debt	13	13	27	22	16	19	14	28
Interest, long term debt	2	2	2	4	8	10	15	17
Interest, short term debt	10	11	13	18	27	36	45	43
Total service payments	**25**	**26**	**42**	**43**	**52**	**65**	**73**	**88**

MAURITANIA

US $ Million

	1984	1985	1986	1987	1988	1989	1990	1991
GROSS DEBT								
Long term								
I. OECD countries and capital markets	164	234	294	332	331	273	272	280
ODA	46	70	109	140	138	149	123	126
Official/off. supported	99	130	169	179	169	109	132	132
Official export credits	21	37	64	85	97	95	118	97
Guaranteed supplier credits	59	67	68	52	53	4	3	27
Guaranteed bank credits	20	27	37	43	19	10	11	8
Financial markets	19	34	17	13	24	15	17	22
Banks	19	34	17	13	24	15	17	22
Bonds	–	–	–	–	–	–	–	–
Other private	–	–	–	–	–	–	–	–
II. Multilateral	358	386	466	601	597	608	656	669
of which: concessional	214	237	277	368	403	445	530	574
non-concessional	144	150	188	233	194	163	126	96
memo: IMF, total	47	46	56	79	71	69	70	57
III. Non-OECD Creditor countries	670	741	844	903	902	861	883	885
C.E.E.C.	10	10	10	12	11	12	12	12
Arab countries	575	645	694	752	741	719	742	746
Other countries and unspecified	85	86	140	140	149	130	129	127
Subtotal: Long term debt	*1192*	*1361*	*1604*	*1836*	*1830*	*1742*	*1811*	*1834*
of which: concessional	260	307	386	508	541	595	654	700
non-concessional	932	1054	1218	1328	1289	1148	1157	1135
Short term								
Subtotal: Short term debt	*223*	*167*	*199*	*124*	*168*	*165*	*204*	*157*
Banks	188	122	150	59	108	93	129	78
Export credits	35	44	49	66	60	72	75	79
Other identified liabilities	–	–	–	–	–	–	–	–
Total identified debt	**1415**	**1528**	**1803**	**1961**	**1998**	**1908**	**2015**	**1991**
SERVICE PAYMENTS								
Long term								
I. OECD countries and capital markets	16	10	17	10	47	45	34	28
ODA	1	2	3	3	9	9	7	5
Official/off. supported	13	6	11	6	10	8	12	12
Financial markets	2	2	3	1	29	28	15	11
Other private	–	–	–	–	–	–	–	–
II. Multilateral	35	63	49	61	88	59	89	58
of which: concessional	8	15	16	24	26	21	23	19
memo: IMF, total	16	20	19	15	13	15	19	15
III. Non-OECD creditor countries	12	28	32	37	28	27	13	7
Subtotal: Service payments, long term debt	*63*	*101*	*98*	*108*	*163*	*130*	*136*	*92*
of which: concessional	9	16	18	27	34	30	30	24
Amortization, long term debt	32	69	59	73	116	86	98	58
Interest, long term debt	31	31	39	35	47	44	37	34
Interest, short term debt	21	14	11	10	9	12	13	8
Total service payments	**84**	**115**	**109**	**118**	**173**	**143**	**148**	**101**

MAURITIUS

US $ Million

	1984	1985	1986	1987	1988	1989	1990	1991
GROSS DEBT								
Long term								
I. OECD countries and capital markets	201	207	234	321	310	365	559	630
ODA	62	77	107	150	161	183	249	280
Official/off. supported	30	38	43	74	84	90	151	163
Official export credits	18	21	24	36	39	53	91	101
Guaranteed supplier credits	3	2	3	3	4	4	4	4
Guaranteed bank credits	9	15	16	36	40	33	56	59
Financial markets	109	92	84	96	65	92	159	186
Banks	109	92	84	96	65	92	159	186
Bonds	–	–	–	–	–	–	–	–
Other private	–	–	–	–	–	–	–	–
II. Multilateral	298	352	386	435	401	346	323	300
of which: concessional	56	57	59	64	66	70	81	83
non-concessional	242	295	327	371	335	277	242	217
memo: IMF, total	161	165	162	152	103	63	22	–
III. Non-OECD Creditor countries	17	26	36	52	54	49	57	53
C.E.E.C.	–	–	–	–	–	–	–	–
Arab countries	6	9	11	15	18	16	17	16
Other countries and unspecified	10	17	25	37	37	33	40	37
Subtotal: Long term debt	*516*	*585*	*656*	*808*	*765*	*760*	*939*	*983*
of which: concessional	118	134	166	214	227	253	329	364
non-concessional	398	450	490	594	538	507	609	619
Short term								
Subtotal: Short term debt	*30*	*55*	*71*	*77*	*48*	*78*	*136*	*201*
Banks	21	35	48	49	17	44	90	159
Export credits	9	20	24	28	31	34	46	42
Other identified liabilities	7	12	–	–	–	–	–	–
Total identified debt	**553**	**652**	**727**	**885**	**813**	**838**	**1074**	**1184**
SERVICE PAYMENTS								
Long term								
I. OECD countries and capital markets	57	43	30	37	102	42	62	85
ODA	5	6	3	10	15	15	21	20
Official/off. supported	9	7	9	11	13	14	16	17
Financial markets	43	30	18	16	73	13	25	48
Other private	–	–	–	–	–	–	–	–
II. Multilateral	65	85	86	80	93	86	90	70
of which: concessional	4	5	5	6	6	5	5	6
memo: IMF, total	50	66	60	45	51	45	49	23
III. Non-OECD creditor countries	2	3	5	6	5	5	5	4
Subtotal: Service payments, long term debt	*124*	*132*	*121*	*123*	*200*	*133*	*157*	*159*
of which: concessional	9	11	8	16	22	20	26	26
Amortization, long term debt	85	92	81	81	146	90	106	111
Interest, long term debt	39	40	39	42	55	43	50	48
Interest, short term debt	4	4	5	5	5	6	8	10
Total service payments	**129**	**136**	**125**	**128**	**205**	**139**	**165**	**169**

US $ Million

	1984	1985	1986	1987	1988	1989	1990	1991
GROSS DEBT								
Long term								
I. OECD countries and capital markets	72451	69325	71424	70066	65750	59704	50798	51913
ODA	206	296	497	648	587	552	629	725
Official/off. supported	6048	6677	7664	9258	10001	9747	13181	17118
Official export credits	2704	2952	3143	4856	5120	5014	6902	8164
Guaranteed supplier credits	381	616	797	385	353	334	780	578
Guaranteed bank credits	2963	3109	3725	4017	4528	4399	5499	8376
Financial markets	64196	60151	61063	57661	52662	46905	34088	31170
Banks	60234	56443	57687	54795	48444	42973	28021	23128
Bonds	3962	3708	3376	2866	4218	3932	6067	8041
Other private	2000	2200	2200	2500	2500	2500	2900	2900
II. Multilateral	6753	8986	12237	15543	15137	15844	20854	22242
of which: concessional	188	150	136	118	100	88	72	59
non-concessional	6565	8836	12101	15425	15037	15756	20782	22183
memo: IMF, total	2360	2969	4060	5163	4805	5091	6551	6766
III. Non-OECD Creditor countries	150	212	180	37	16	15	71	47
C.E.E.C.	11	8	5	3	5	5	3	1
Arab countries	–	65	64	6	6	6	–	–
Other countries and unspecified	139	138	111	28	5	4	68	45
Subtotal: Long term debt	*79354*	*78522*	*83841*	*85646*	*80903*	*75562*	*71722*	*74202*
of which: concessional	394	447	634	765	687	640	700	785
non-concessional	78960	78076	83207	84880	80216	74923	71022	73417
Short term								
Subtotal: Short term debt	*13963*	*15719*	*13778*	*17981*	*18761*	*23312*	*22533*	*31173*
Banks	13194	14662	12642	16672	17735	21983	20509	28318
Export credits	769	1057	1137	1310	1026	1328	2024	2855
Other identified liabilities	–	–	–	–	–	–	–	–
Total identified debt	**93317**	**94241**	**97619**	**103627**	**99664**	**98874**	**94256**	**105375**
SERVICE PAYMENTS								
Long term								
I. OECD countries and capital markets	10997	10707	9070	8023	9801	8910	7360	10883
ODA	15	18	16	38	37	30	24	35
Official/off. supported	1635	1953	2794	2253	2200	2892	2899	3035
Financial markets	8927	8575	6106	5600	7390	5738	4061	7110
Other private	420	160	154	132	175	250	375	703
II. Multilateral	780	1003	1513	2100	2616	2916	3753	3982
of which: concessional	62	50	30	28	25	20	19	20
memo: IMF, total	115	202	413	650	903	1218	1712	1645
III. Non-OECD creditor countries	47	32	33	16	6	2	13	62
Subtotal: Service payments, long term debt	*11824*	*11743*	*10616*	*10138*	*12423*	*11829*	*11126*	*14927*
of which: concessional	77	68	45	66	62	50	43	54
Amortization, long term debt	4066	4516	4726	3686	5734	4951	4750	10128
Interest, long term debt	7759	7226	5890	6452	6689	6877	6375	4799
Interest, short term debt	1655	1200	979	1064	1440	1835	1837	1569
Total service payments	**13479**	**12943**	**11595**	**11203**	**13863**	**13664**	**12963**	**16496**

US $ Million

	1984	1985	1986	1987	1988	1989	1990	1991
GROSS DEBT								
Long term								
I. OECD countries and capital markets	2	4	2	–	–	2	26	44
ODA	–	–	–	–	–	–	–	26
Official/off. supported	0	0	2	–	–	2	2	18
Official export credits	–	–	–	–	–	–	–	–
Guaranteed supplier credits	–	–	–	–	–	–	–	9
Guaranteed bank credits	0	0	2	–	–	2	2	9
Financial markets	2	4	0	–	–	–	24	–
Banks	2	4	0	–	–	–	24	–
Bonds	–	–	–	–	–	–	–	–
Other private	–	–	–	–	–	–	–	–
II. Multilateral	–	–	–	–	–	–	–	16
of which: concessional	–	–	–	–	–	–	–	–
non-concessional	–	–	–	–	–	–	–	16
memo: IMF, total	–	–	–	–	–	–	–	16
III. Non-OECD Creditor countries	8513	9249	10133	12919	13680	14225	14509	14709
C.E.E.C.	8513	9249	10133	12919	13680	14225	14509	14709
Arab countries	–	–	–	–	–	–	–	–
Other countries and unspecified	–	–	–	–	–	–	–	–
Subtotal: Long term debt	*8515*	*9253*	*10135*	*12919*	*13680*	*14227*	*14535*	*14769*
of which: concessional	8513	9249	10133	12919	13680	14225	14509	14735
non-concessional	2	4	2	–	–	2	26	34
Short term								
Subtotal: Short term debt	*2*	*1*	*8*	*0*	*11*	*4*	*64*	*23*
Banks	–	–	8	–	11	2	61	21
Export credits	2	1	0	0	0	2	3	2
Other identified liabilities	–	–	–	–	–	–	–	–
Total identified debt	**8516**	**9254**	**10143**	**12919**	**13691**	**14231**	**14599**	**14792**
SERVICE PAYMENTS								
Long term								
I. OECD countries and capital markets	0	0	0	0	–	–	0	2
ODA	–	–	–	–	–	–	–	–
Official/off. supported	–	0	–	–	–	–	0	–
Financial markets	0	0	0	0	–	–	–	2
Other private	–	–	–	–	–	–	–	–
II. Multilateral	–	–	–	–	–	–	–	–
of which: concessional	–	–	–	–	–	–	–	–
memo: IMF, total	–	–	–	–	–	–	–	–
III. Non-OECD creditor countries	152	92	160	140	130	130	284	147
Subtotal: Service payments, long term debt	*152*	*92*	*160*	*140*	*130*	*130*	*285*	*149*
of which: concessional	152	92	160	140	130	130	284	147
Amortization, long term debt	10	0	28	–	–	–	0	–
Interest, long term debt	142	92	132	140	130	130	284	149
Interest, short term debt	0	0	0	0	0	1	3	3
Total service payments	**152**	**92**	**161**	**140**	**130**	**131**	**288**	**151**

MOROCCO

US $ Million

	1984	1985	1986	1987	1988	1989	1990	1991
GROSS DEBT								
Long term								
I. OECD countries and capital markets	6504	7789	8638	10034	10243	10482	12312	12494
ODA	1121	1535	2017	2345	2459	2615	3209	3516
Official/off. supported	2921	3698	4410	5573	4622	5787	7103	7087
Official export credits	1447	2089	2594	3596	3496	4199	5121	5283
Guaranteed supplier credits	286	232	216	155	171	104	76	83
Guaranteed bank credits	1188	1378	1600	1822	956	1485	1907	1721
Financial markets	2462	2557	2211	2116	3161	2080	2000	1891
Banks	2397	2509	2179	2092	3149	2073	1993	1885
Bonds	66	48	32	24	12	7	7	7
Other private	–	–	–	–	–	–	–	–
II. Multilateral	2434	3210	3825	4712	4559	4760	5236	5585
of which: concessional	394	456	472	492	453	441	390	474
non-concessional	2040	2754	3353	4220	4106	4319	4847	5111
memo: IMF, total	1085	1274	1094	1119	956	850	750	574
III. Non-OECD Creditor countries	3013	3148	3213	3245	3622	3725	3747	1170
C.E.E.C.	17	14	11	9	12	12	54	121
Arab countries	2969	3107	3176	3210	3583	3687	3667	1023
Other countries and unspecified	27	27	26	26	26	26	26	26
Subtotal: Long term debt	*11952*	*14147*	*15676*	*17992*	*18424*	*18967*	*21296*	*19249*
of which: concessional	1516	1991	2489	2837	2913	3056	3599	3990
non-concessional	10436	12156	13187	15155	15511	15911	17697	15259
Short term								
Subtotal: Short term debt	*1787*	*2053*	*2737*	*2729*	*1894*	*2700*	*2985*	*3054*
Banks	1591	1675	2140	2042	892	1527	1341	1397
Export credits	196	378	597	687	1003	1173	1644	1657
Other identified liabilities	23	–	–	–	–	–	–	–
Total identified debt	**13762**	**16200**	**18413**	**20721**	**20318**	**21668**	**24281**	**22304**
SERVICE PAYMENTS								
Long term								
I. OECD countries and capital markets	548	697	753	674	1034	1348	942	1449
ODA	43	51	85	73	51	97	89	146
Official/off. supported	210	415	497	397	487	706	568	859
Financial markets	295	230	171	204	495	545	285	444
Other private	–	–	–	–	–	–	–	–
II. Multilateral	321	503	782	877	853	878	899	909
of which: concessional	23	42	81	58	55	51	34	35
memo: IMF, total	139	257	442	413	321	330	299	234
III. Non-OECD creditor countries	19	50	31	34	38	57	73	67
Subtotal: Service payments, long term debt	*888*	*1250*	*1566*	*1586*	*1925*	*2284*	*1913*	*2425*
of which: concessional	66	93	167	131	107	148	123	181
Amortization, long term debt	344	582	856	747	845	1133	986	1263
Interest, long term debt	544	669	711	839	1080	1150	927	1162
Interest, short term debt	182	152	149	166	148	152	163	115
Total service payments	**1070**	**1402**	**1715**	**1752**	**2073**	**2436**	**2077**	**2540**

MOZAMBIQUE

US $ Million

	1984	1985	1986	1987	1988	1989	1990	1991
GROSS DEBT								
Long term								
I. OECD countries and capital markets	667	815	1078	1221	1012	1063	947	791
ODA	153	235	339	466	476	545	540	469
Official/off. supported	461	522	550	755	454	505	405	314
Official export credits	109	176	187	357	282	325	175	220
Guaranteed supplier credits	193	194	207	204	25	10	9	14
Guaranteed bank credits	159	152	156	194	148	170	221	80
Financial markets	54	58	189	–	82	14	3	7
Banks	54	58	189	–	82	14	3	7
Bonds	–	–	–	–	–	–	–	–
Other private	–	–	–	–	–	–	–	–
II. Multilateral	88	111	152	257	323	407	539	728
of which: concessional	66	71	103	191	256	332	458	636
non-concessional	22	40	49	66	67	75	81	92
memo: IMF, total	–	–	–	17	41	56	74	118
III. Non-OECD Creditor countries	796	1048	2139	2388	2089	2063	2043	2010
C.E.E.C.	773	1023	1230	1380	1432	1430	1430	1430
Arab countries	23	26	444	454	416	399	382	362
Other countries and unspecified	–	–	465	553	241	234	231	219
Subtotal: Long term debt	*1552*	*1974*	*3369*	*3866*	*3423*	*3533*	*3529*	*3528*
of which: concessional	219	306	443	657	732	877	998	1105
non-concessional	1333	1668	2927	3209	2691	2657	2531	2423
Short term								
Subtotal: Short term debt	*309*	*317*	*291*	*576*	*586*	*708*	*1062*	*964*
Banks	159	170	62	224	207	238	478	437
Export credits	150	147	229	352	379	470	584	527
Other identified liabilities	–	–	–	–	–	–	–	–
Total identified debt	**1861**	**2291**	**3660**	**4441**	**4009**	**4241**	**4590**	**4492**
SERVICE PAYMENTS								
Long term								
I. OECD countries and capital markets	126	132	78	84	86	87	77	73
ODA	1	3	5	7	29	17	24	10
Official/off. supported	111	109	39	63	57	43	45	53
Financial markets	14	20	34	14	–	27	8	10
Other private	–	–	–	–	–	–	–	–
II. Multilateral	4	3	5	8	13	16	15	17
of which: concessional	3	1	1	1	4	6	6	7
memo: IMF, total	–	–	–	0	0	0	0	1
III. Non-OECD creditor countries	3	36	85	4	5	3	–	0
Subtotal: Service payments, long term debt	*132*	*170*	*169*	*96*	*103*	*106*	*92*	*90*
of which: concessional	4	4	6	8	33	24	30	18
Amortization, long term debt	101	129	117	49	49	47	60	51
Interest, long term debt	31	42	51	48	55	59	32	39
Interest, short term debt	18	14	8	10	18	20	30	28
Total service payments	**150**	**184**	**177**	**107**	**121**	**126**	**122**	**118**

US $ Million

	1984	1985	1986	1987	1988	1989	1990	1991
GROSS DEBT								
Long term								
I. OECD countries and capital markets	1351	1785	2374	3125	3194	2833	3135	3184
ODA	1005	1463	2049	2747	2812	2606	2869	3056
Official/off. supported	294	273	253	284	271	152	210	98
Official export credits	55	12	12	14	10	8	8	1
Guaranteed supplier credits	78	88	74	86	139	51	113	40
Guaranteed bank credits	161	174	166	184	122	93	88	58
Financial markets	52	48	72	94	111	75	57	30
Banks	52	48	72	94	111	75	57	30
Bonds	–	–	–	–	–	–	–	–
Other private	–	–	–	–	–	–	–	–
II. Multilateral	741	802	881	935	991	1060	1234	1291
of which: concessional	661	730	836	920	986	1056	1229	1286
non-concessional	80	72	46	15	5	4	6	5
memo: IMF, total	121	108	73	29	8	3	0	–
III. Non-OECD Creditor countries	267	264	265	285	272	301	275	262
C.E.E.C.	166	160	149	140	138	137	135	132
Arab countries	–	–	–	–	–	–	–	–
Other countries and unspecified	101	104	116	145	135	164	141	130
Subtotal: Long term debt	*2359*	*2851*	*3519*	*4344*	*4457*	*4194*	*4645*	*4737*
of which: concessional	1666	2194	2885	3667	3798	3662	4098	4343
non-concessional	693	657	635	677	658	532	547	395
Short term								
Subtotal: Short term debt	*17*	*83*	*55*	*35*	*43*	*105*	*190*	*219*
Banks	9	78	51	32	2	30	56	113
Export credits	8	5	4	3	41	75	134	106
Other identified liabilities	605	740	1133	1346	1603	53	45	45
Total identified debt	**2982**	**3674**	**4708**	**5725**	**6103**	**4353**	**4880**	**5001**
SERVICE PAYMENTS								
Long term								
I. OECD countries and capital markets	135	147	134	123	107	154	42	46
ODA	48	50	62	78	53	28	28	40
Official/off. supported	68	86	68	38	42	64	5	1
Financial markets	19	11	4	7	11	61	10	5
Other private	–	–	–	–	–	–	–	–
II. Multilateral	28	44	65	65	39	27	27	27
of which: concessional	14	20	28	30	29	26	27	26
memo: IMF, total	21	35	51	49	21	6	3	0
III. Non-OECD creditor countries	19	24	27	18	9	51	28	12
Subtotal: Service payments, long term debt	*182*	*215*	*227*	*206*	*155*	*232*	*98*	*86*
of which: concessional	62	70	89	108	82	55	54	66
Amortization, long term debt	109	142	148	125	96	172	51	30
Interest, long term debt	73	72	79	81	59	60	47	55
Interest, short term debt	65	59	68	89	120	76	8	8
Total service payments	**248**	**274**	**295**	**295**	**275**	**309**	**106**	**93**

US $ Million

	1984	1985	1986	1987	1988	1989	1990	1991
GROSS DEBT								
Long term								
I. OECD countries and capital markets	44	81	103	232	321	264	313	374
ODA	30	51	85	124	130	145	193	284
Official/off. supported	2	5	14	80	94	96	101	69
Official export credits	–	–	–	–	–	–	–	–
Guaranteed supplier credits	1	3	9	4	8	1	1	1
Guaranteed bank credits	1	1	5	76	86	95	100	69
Financial markets	12	26	5	28	96	23	20	20
Banks	12	26	5	28	96	23	20	20
Bonds	–	–	–	–	–	–	–	–
Other private	–	–	–	–	–	–	–	–
II. Multilateral	382	477	581	746	870	1060	1312	1564
of which: concessional	374	460	560	710	837	1034	1296	1554
non-concessional	7	17	22	36	33	26	16	11
memo: IMF, total	16	22	24	43	53	52	44	38
III. Non-OECD Creditor countries	25	27	39	45	44	46	46	42
C.E.E.C.	3	4	4	4	3	3	3	3
Arab countries	21	21	25	31	33	35	38	36
Other countries and unspecified	0	2	10	10	8	7	6	4
Subtotal: Long term debt	*450*	*585*	*723*	*1023*	*1235*	*1370*	*1671*	*1980*
of which: concessional	405	510	644	834	967	1179	1488	1838
non-concessional	46	74	79	188	268	191	183	142
Short term								
Subtotal: Short term debt	*24*	*23*	*29*	*13*	*21*	*23*	*8*	*17*
Banks	18	15	22	8	17	18	7	16
Export credits	6	8	7	5	4	5	1	1
Other identified liabilities	16	24	25	26	29	29	31	36
Total identified debt	**491**	**631**	**777**	**1061**	**1285**	**1421**	**1710**	**2033**
SERVICE PAYMENTS								
Long term								
I. OECD countries and capital markets	3	4	9	7	27	59	33	29
ODA	1	1	2	3	4	4	4	5
Official/off. supported	0	2	5	3	19	24	24	14
Financial markets	1	1	2	0	4	31	5	10
Other private	–	–	–	–	–	–	–	–
II. Multilateral	14	15	16	20	22	29	36	29
of which: concessional	7	10	14	17	19	18	21	23
memo: IMF, total	7	7	4	5	5	11	14	6
III. Non-OECD creditor countries	2	2	4	4	4	4	5	8
Subtotal: Service payments, long term debt	*19*	*21*	*29*	*31*	*53*	*92*	*74*	*66*
of which: concessional	9	11	16	20	22	22	25	28
Amortization, long term debt	12	13	17	16	28	56	45	42
Interest, long term debt	7	8	12	14	25	35	29	25
Interest, short term debt	7	4	3	3	4	5	4	3
Total service payments	**26**	**24**	**33**	**34**	**56**	**96**	**78**	**69**

NETHERLANDS ANTILLES

US $ Million

	1984	1985	1986	1987	1988	1989	1990	1991
GROSS DEBT								
Long term								
I. OECD countries and capital markets	588	804	923	1121	879	951	1013	1059
ODA	203	289	385	456	406	429	465	450
Official/off. supported	305	415	428	377	181	98	83	78
Official export credits	29	26	24	4	2	1	–	16
Guaranteed supplier credits	45	47	27	20	21	15	4	1
Guaranteed bank credits	230	342	376	354	158	82	79	61
Financial markets	80	100	110	287	292	425	465	530
Banks	80	100	110	287	292	425	465	530
Bonds	–	–	–	–	–	–	–	–
Other private	–	–	–	–	–	–	–	–
II. Multilateral	11	12	14	15	15	17	18	18
of which: concessional	11	12	14	15	15	17	17	17
non-concessional	–	–	–	0	0	0	1	1
memo: IMF, total	–	–	–	–	–	–	–	–
III. Non-OECD Creditor countries	–	–	–	–	–	–	–	–
C.E.E.C.	–	–	–	–	–	–	–	–
Arab countries	–	–	–	–	–	–	–	–
Other countries and unspecified	–	–	–	–	–	–	–	–
Subtotal: Long term debt	*599*	*816*	*937*	*1136*	*894*	*968*	*1031*	*1077*
of which: concessional	214	302	398	471	421	445	481	467
non-concessional	385	515	538	665	473	523	549	610
Short term								
Subtotal: Short term debt	*167*	*190*	*202*	*219*	*242*	*308*	*327*	*369*
Banks	150	170	180	190	193	281	300	350
Export credits	17	20	22	29	49	27	27	19
Other identified liabilities	–	–	–	–	–	–	–	–
Total identified debt	**766**	**1007**	**1139**	**1355**	**1136**	**1276**	**1357**	**1446**
SERVICE PAYMENTS								
Long term								
I. OECD countries and capital markets	162	145	162	166	120	150	126	86
ODA	11	11	17	22	24	23	22	16
Official/off. supported	135	118	117	132	62	86	51	13
Financial markets	16	16	28	13	35	41	53	57
Other private	–	–	–	–	–	–	–	–
II. Multilateral	0	1	0	1	1	1	1	2
of which: concessional	0	1	0	1	0	0	1	1
memo: IMF, total	–	–	–	–	–	–	–	–
III. Non-OECD creditor countries	–	–	–	–	–	–	–	–
Subtotal: Service payments, long term debt	*162*	*145*	*162*	*167*	*121*	*151*	*127*	*88*
of which: concessional	11	11	17	23	24	24	22	16
Amortization, long term debt	115	93	113	110	66	96	73	42
Interest, long term debt	47	52	49	57	54	55	54	46
Interest, short term debt	17	14	13	14	17	23	26	20
Total service payments	**179**	**160**	**175**	**181**	**138**	**174**	**152**	**108**

NEW CALEDONIA

US $ Million

	1984	1985	1986	1987	1988	1989	1990	1991
GROSS DEBT								
Long term								
I. OECD countries and capital markets	161	226	269	345	288	298	213	260
ODA	86	112	131	178	154	158	181	205
Official/off. supported	74	114	138	167	134	140	32	55
Official export credits	74	114	138	167	134	140	32	55
Guaranteed supplier credits	–	–	–	–	–	–	–	–
Guaranteed bank credits	–	–	–	–	–	–	–	–
Financial markets	–	–	–	–	–	–	–	–
Banks	–	–	–	–	–	–	–	–
Bonds	–	–	–	–	–	–	–	–
Other private	–	–	–	–	–	–	–	–
II. Multilateral	12	13	14	14	14	14	13	13
of which: concessional	4	5	5	6	6	5	5	5
non-concessional	8	8	9	9	9	8	8	8
memo: IMF, total	–	–	–	–	–	–	–	–
III. Non-OECD Creditor countries	–	–	–	–	–	–	–	–
C.E.E.C.	–	–	–	–	–	–	–	–
Arab countries	–	–	–	–	–	–	–	–
Other countries and unspecified	–	–	–	–	–	–	–	–
Subtotal: Long term debt	173	239	283	359	302	312	226	273
of which: concessional	91	117	136	184	160	164	186	210
non-concessional	82	122	147	176	142	148	40	63
Short term								
Subtotal: Short term debt	0	4	4	9	4	5	6	15
Banks	–	2	–	–	1	1	2	10
Export credits	0	2	4	9	3	4	4	5
Other identified liabilities	–	–	–	–	–	–	–	–
Total identified debt	**173**	**243**	**287**	**368**	**306**	**317**	**232**	**288**
SERVICE PAYMENTS								
Long term								
I. OECD countries and capital markets	28	14	18	11	39	32	31	42
ODA	14	9	10	3	16	12	19	17
Official/off. supported	14	5	8	8	23	20	13	25
Financial markets	–	–	–	–	–	0	–	–
Other private	–	–	–	–	–	–	–	–
II. Multilateral	0	0	0	2	2	1	1	1
of which: concessional	0	0	0	1	0	0	0	0
memo: IMF, total	–	–	–	–	–	–	–	–
III. Non-OECD creditor countries	–	–	–	–	–	–	–	–
Subtotal: Service payments, long term debt	28	14	19	13	41	33	33	43
of which: concessional	14	9	11	3	17	12	19	17
Amortization, long term debt	19	6	8	1	23	21	16	37
Interest, long term debt	9	8	10	12	18	13	16	6
Interest, short term debt	0	0	0	0	1	0	0	1
Total service payments	**28**	**14**	**19**	**14**	**42**	**34**	**33**	**44**

US $ Million

	1984	1985	1986	1987	1988	1989	1990	1991
GROSS DEBT								
Long term								
I. OECD countries and capital markets	1875	1995	2011	2079	2090	2096	2104	2506
ODA	335	372	440	497	508	510	553	364
Official/off. supported	168	230	216	268	278	283	296	161
Official export credits	98	135	154	203	196	203	225	117
Guaranteed supplier credits	33	40	29	31	59	60	52	27
Guaranteed bank credits	37	55	33	34	23	20	19	17
Financial markets	1192	1205	1167	1126	1123	1122	1070	1796
Banks	1192	1205	1167	1126	1123	1122	1070	1006
Bonds	–	–	–	–	–	–	–	790
Other private	180	189	189	188	181	181	184	184
II. Multilateral	642	695	745	863	918	928	976	839
of which: concessional	348	360	358	356	356	356	356	307
non-concessional	294	335	387	507	562	572	620	532
memo: IMF, total	9	–	–	–	–	–	–	24
III. Non-OECD Creditor countries	2999	3174	3781	4726	3534	4602	5043	5585
C.E.E.C.	1581	1656	1705	1894	1871	2907	3311	3332
Arab countries	115	115	115	115	115	115	115	115
Other countries and unspecified	1303	1403	1961	2716	1548	1579	1616	2137
Subtotal: Long term debt	*5516*	*5865*	*6538*	*7668*	*6542*	*7626*	*8123*	*8930*
of which: concessional	684	732	798	853	864	866	910	671
non-concessional	4833	5133	5740	6815	5678	6760	7213	8258
Short term								
Subtotal: Short term debt	*380*	*525*	*501*	*543*	*387*	*401*	*963*	*889*
Banks	265	428	376	382	198	204	696	587
Export credits	115	97	125	161	189	197	267	302
Other identified liabilities	–	–	–	–	–	–	–	–
Total identified debt	**5896**	**6390**	**7039**	**8211**	**6929**	**8027**	**9086**	**9818**
SERVICE PAYMENTS								
Long term								
I. OECD countries and capital markets	28	33	23	35	14	18	843	106
ODA	2	3	7	2	1	4	7	15
Official/off. supported	8	16	16	12	10	12	1	2
Financial markets	3	–	–	22	3	2	835	77
Other private	15	14	–	–	–	–	–	13
II. Multilateral	26	15	16	11	8	0	2	348
of which: concessional	6	2	5	5	0	0	0	49
memo: IMF, total	5	10	–	–	–	–	–	0
III. Non-OECD creditor countries	21	20	10	20	11	9	6	37
Subtotal: Service payments, long term debt	*75*	*68*	*49*	*66*	*33*	*28*	*852*	*491*
of which: concessional	8	5	12	7	1	5	7	64
Amortization, long term debt	31	28	16	19	11	12	5	173
Interest, long term debt	44	40	34	47	22	16	847	319
Interest, short term debt	31	34	7	14	25	19	35	39
Total service payments	**106**	**102**	**56**	**80**	**58**	**47**	**886**	**530**

US $ Million

	1984	1985	1986	1987	1988	1989	1990	1991
GROSS DEBT								
Long term								
I. OECD countries and capital markets	554	696	775	856	793	759	746	677
ODA	80	123	159	233	205	230	266	269
Official/off. supported	241	285	329	403	352	282	333	383
Official export credits	144	219	275	365	350	280	326	382
Guaranteed supplier credits	35	11	6	1	–	–	0	–
Guaranteed bank credits	63	55	48	37	2	2	6	1
Financial markets	233	287	286	220	236	247	147	25
Banks	233	287	286	220	236	247	147	25
Bonds	–	–	–	–	–	–	–	–
Other private	–	–	–	–	–	–	–	–
II. Multilateral	286	352	466	599	646	680	787	823
of which: concessional	199	237	323	449	540	594	710	762
non-concessional	87	115	142	150	106	86	77	61
memo: IMF, total	57	78	106	123	95	85	85	73
III. Non-OECD Creditor countries	81	92	95	105	109	106	105	88
C.E.E.C.	–	–	–	–	–	–	–	–
Arab countries	72	72	77	80	83	82	83	68
Other countries and unspecified	9	19	18	24	26	24	21	21
Subtotal: Long term debt	920	1139	1336	1559	1548	1545	1637	1588
of which: concessional	278	360	483	681	745	824	976	1031
non-concessional	642	779	853	878	804	721	662	557
Short term								
Subtotal: Short term debt	127	104	155	87	126	130	156	69
Banks	100	65	110	49	70	66	90	14
Export credits	27	39	45	38	56	64	66	55
Other identified liabilities	70	80	20	103	94	85	90	90
Total identified debt	**1117**	**1323**	**1510**	**1749**	**1768**	**1760**	**1883**	**1747**
SERVICE PAYMENTS								
Long term								
I. OECD countries and capital markets	84	87	110	103	101	101	85	100
ODA	6	8	10	10	7	9	5	6
Official/off. supported	55	57	75	67	35	27	18	23
Financial markets	23	21	25	26	58	64	62	72
Other private	–	–	–	–	–	–	–	–
II. Multilateral	14	19	28	52	61	38	28	23
of which: concessional	5	8	11	13	14	9	8	8
memo: IMF, total	2	6	10	30	38	23	19	14
III. Non-OECD creditor countries	3	4	4	5	5	3	1	1
Subtotal: Service payments, long term debt	101	110	141	159	167	141	114	124
of which: concessional	11	17	21	23	22	19	12	14
Amortization, long term debt	51	62	80	94	102	85	66	84
Interest, long term debt	50	48	61	65	65	56	48	40
Interest, short term debt	20	15	11	12	15	17	17	10
Total service payments	**121**	**124**	**152**	**171**	**182**	**159**	**131**	**135**

US $ Million

	1984	1985	1986	1987	1988	1989	1990	1991
GROSS DEBT								
Long term								
I. OECD countries and capital markets	10314	11160	15207	20520	19934	22946	21842	22099
ODA	260	280	330	398	413	516	546	603
Official/off. supported	3584	5515	11524	13471	10271	14933	14021	15860
Official export credits	288	452	6086	8088	7315	11235	11120	12654
Guaranteed supplier credits	687	1156	665	772	681	1270	783	649
Guaranteed bank credits	2610	3907	4773	4611	2275	2427	2118	2557
Financial markets	6470	5365	3353	6651	9251	7497	7275	5636
Banks	6470	5365	3353	6651	9251	7497	7275	5636
Bonds	–	–	–	–	–	–	–	–
Other private	–	–	–	–	–	–	–	–
II. Multilateral	955	1428	2234	3059	2849	3172	3732	4101
of which: concessional	104	111	118	126	118	111	115	244
non-concessional	851	1317	2116	2933	2731	3061	3617	3856
memo: IMF, total	–	–	–	–	–	–	–	–
III. Non-OECD Creditor countries	1072	843	1232	1506	488	1546	1830	2018
C.E.E.C.	672	843	1144	1419	397	1447	1697	1889
Arab countries	400	–	–	–	–	–	–	–
Other countries and unspecified	–	–	88	88	91	99	133	128
Subtotal: Long term debt	*12341*	*13431*	*18672*	*25085*	*23271*	*27665*	*27404*	*28218*
of which: concessional	364	391	448	525	531	627	661	847
non-concessional	11977	13040	18224	24561	22740	27037	26744	27370
Short term								
Subtotal: Short term debt	*2357*	*3407*	*5892*	*6346*	*5243*	*5530*	*6579*	*6294*
Banks	1336	2256	3855	3171	1969	1421	2233	2057
Export credits	1021	1151	2037	3175	3273	4109	4347	4237
Other identified liabilities	–	–	–	–	–	–	–	–
Total identified debt	**14698**	**16839**	**24564**	**31431**	**28513**	**33195**	**33984**	**34511**
SERVICE PAYMENTS								
Long term								
I. OECD countries and capital markets	2687	3398	1643	1095	2144	2213	2477	1905
ODA	27	25	16	11	10	35	22	15
Official/off. supported	864	1759	1316	946	953	1234	1156	1194
Financial markets	1796	1614	312	138	1181	944	1299	696
Other private	–	–	–	–	–	–	–	–
II. Multilateral	115	131	231	348	447	432	509	646
of which: concessional	8	8	9	10	10	13	18	15
memo: IMF, total	–	–	–	–	–	–	–	–
III. Non-OECD creditor countries	144	487	14	5	14	14	71	33
Subtotal: Service payments, long term debt	*2946*	*4015*	*1888*	*1448*	*2605*	*2660*	*3057*	*2584*
of which: concessional	35	33	25	22	20	48	40	30
Amortization, long term debt	2023	2866	1115	528	637	495	1276	867
Interest, long term debt	923	1150	773	920	1969	2165	1781	1717
Interest, short term debt	283	199	243	269	231	178	174	147
Total service payments	**3229**	**4215**	**2131**	**1717**	**2836**	**2838**	**3231**	**2731**

US $ Million

	1984	1985	1986	1987	1988	1989	1990	1991
GROSS DEBT								
Long term								
I. OECD countries and capital markets	1063	1590	2145	2008	2120	2256	1862	1896
ODA	2	9	31	40	41	44	44	44
Official/off. supported	729	832	912	1014	784	390	401	442
Official export credits	75	61	46	–	–	18	22	88
Guaranteed supplier credits	95	178	112	142	81	58	62	50
Guaranteed bank credits	559	592	754	871	703	314	316	303
Financial markets	332	749	1201	955	1295	1822	1418	1410
Banks	332	749	1201	955	1295	1822	1418	1410
Bonds	–	–	–	–	–	–	–	–
Other private	–	–	–	–	–	–	–	–
II. Multilateral	67	98	126	145	140	136	134	145
of which: concessional	10	20	39	40	51	49	54	59
non-concessional	57	78	87	105	89	87	79	86
memo: IMF, total	–	–	–	–	–	–	–	–
III. Non-OECD Creditor countries	209	619	1100	1138	1104	1062	1052	1049
C.E.E.C.	–	–	–	–	–	–	–	–
Arab countries	209	219	200	188	154	139	129	126
Other countries and unspecified	–	400	900	950	950	923	923	923
Subtotal: Long term debt	*1340*	*2307*	*3370*	*3291*	*3364*	*3453*	*3047*	*3090*
of which: concessional	12	29	70	80	92	93	98	103
non-concessional	1328	2278	3300	3211	3272	3360	2949	2987
Short term								
Subtotal: Short term debt	*511*	*296*	*690*	*654*	*1002*	*921*	*724*	*596*
Banks	421	154	598	577	915	867	640	493
Export credits	89	142	92	77	87	54	84	103
Other identified liabilities	37	29	36	25	64	77	54	18
Total identified debt	**1887**	**2632**	**4096**	**3970**	**4430**	**4452**	**3825**	**3703**
SERVICE PAYMENTS								
Long term								
I. OECD countries and capital markets	206	210	214	363	492	535	751	495
ODA	–	0	0	2	2	2	2	3
Official/off. supported	169	175	142	245	228	291	210	243
Financial markets	37	35	72	116	262	242	538	249
Other private	–	–	–	–	–	–	–	–
II. Multilateral	6	14	20	30	32	31	37	36
of which: concessional	–	1	2	6	7	7	10	10
memo: IMF, total	–	–	–	–	–	–	–	–
III. Non-OECD creditor countries	36	36	40	42	38	50	19	27
Subtotal: Service payments, long term debt	*249*	*260*	*273*	*435*	*563*	*616*	*806*	*558*
of which: concessional	–	1	2	8	9	9	12	13
Amortization, long term debt	142	144	125	226	380	399	595	407
Interest, long term debt	107	116	149	209	183	217	212	151
Interest, short term debt	49	36	36	48	70	93	73	42
Total service payments	**298**	**295**	**309**	**483**	**632**	**709**	**880**	**600**

US $ Million

	1984	1985	1986	1987	1988	1989	1990	1991
GROSS DEBT								
Long term								
I. OECD countries and capital markets	6141	7079	7916	9049	9228	9038	10287	10316
ODA	4621	5198	5931	6815	7101	7072	7492	7693
Official/off. supported	924	1311	1408	1704	1624	1658	2137	2362
Official export credits	655	1017	1158	1328	1244	601	872	880
Guaranteed supplier credits	99	100	68	144	91	107	125	186
Guaranteed bank credits	170	195	182	232	289	949	1140	1296
Financial markets	596	570	577	530	503	308	658	262
Banks	596	570	577	530	503	308	658	262
Bonds	–	–	–	–	–	–	–	–
Other private	–	–	–	–	–	–	–	–
II. Multilateral	3930	4376	4553	5000	5200	6429	7718	9417
of which: concessional	2038	2334	2580	2903	3055	3628	4310	5278
non-concessional	1892	2042	1974	2098	2145	2802	3408	4139
memo: IMF, total	1440	1455	1194	922	557	933	835	1068
III. Non-OECD Creditor countries	1675	1609	1507	1396	1251	1175	1114	1241
C.E.E.C.	390	396	418	409	355	347	373	536
Arab countries	732	721	670	642	625	587	540	509
Other countries and unspecified	553	492	419	346	270	242	202	197
Subtotal: Long term debt	*11746*	*13064*	*13976*	*15445*	*15679*	*16643*	*19120*	*20975*
of which: concessional	6658	7532	8511	9718	10156	10700	11803	12971
non-concessional	5088	5532	5466	5728	5523	5943	7317	8004
Short term								
Subtotal: Short term debt	*671*	*1590*	*2052*	*2311*	*2491*	*2724*	*2589*	*2305*
Banks	622	1501	1919	2176	2369	2611	2438	2132
Export credits	49	89	133	135	122	113	151	173
Other identified liabilities	137	161	195	100	371	387	405	406
Total identified debt	**12554**	**14816**	**16223**	**17857**	**18541**	**19754**	**22114**	**23686**
SERVICE PAYMENTS								
Long term								
I. OECD countries and capital markets	624	727	679	765	894	1584	940	1229
ODA	200	205	232	291	304	411	386	415
Official/off. supported	194	198	312	318	333	1067	461	540
Financial markets	229	324	135	156	258	107	93	274
Other private	–	–	–	–	–	–	–	–
II. Multilateral	331	462	745	774	645	634	774	689
of which: concessional	67	85	147	158	133	118	118	100
memo: IMF, total	194	300	468	501	338	270	220	135
III. Non-OECD creditor countries	186	183	226	206	179	171	169	149
Subtotal: Service payments, long term debt	*1141*	*1371*	*1650*	*1745*	*1719*	*2390*	*1882*	*2068*
of which: concessional	267	290	379	449	437	529	504	516
Amortization, long term debt	691	889	1120	1164	1164	1788	1229	1340
Interest, long term debt	450	482	530	581	555	602	654	728
Interest, short term debt	81	105	135	159	208	267	251	169
Total service payments	**1222**	**1476**	**1785**	**1903**	**1927**	**2657**	**2133**	**2237**

PANANA

US $ Million

	1984	1985	1986	1987	1988	1989	1990	1991
GROSS DEBT								
Long term								
I. OECD countries and capital markets	3095	3340	3800	4529	4355	3969	4308	4185
ODA	183	191	184	188	198	189	190	213
Official/off. supported	123	83	76	69	160	76	78	68
Official export credits	79	40	41	29	87	24	20	33
Guaranteed supplier credits	19	18	10	12	51	33	36	19
Guaranteed bank credits	25	25	25	28	22	20	21	17
Financial markets	2789	3065	3541	4271	3996	3704	4040	3904
Banks	2500	2800	3300	4016	3739	3452	3780	3729
Bonds	289	265	241	254	257	251	260	175
Other private	–	–	–	–	–	–	–	–
II. Multilateral	893	1071	1303	1427	1345	1317	1293	1155
of which: concessional	172	190	205	201	201	201	202	169
non-concessional	721	881	1097	1226	1145	1116	1091	985
memo: IMF, total	271	311	353	346	328	320	272	216
III. Non-OECD Creditor countries	250	233	171	168	286	265	260	257
C.E.E.C.	–	–	–	–	11	12	12	12
Arab countries	2	2	2	2	–	20	20	20
Other countries and unspecified	248	232	169	166	275	233	228	225
Subtotal: Long term debt	*4239*	*4645*	*5274*	*6123*	*5987*	*5551*	*5861*	*5597*
of which: concessional	355	381	389	389	399	390	392	383
non-concessional	3883	4264	4884	5734	5588	5160	5469	5214
Short term								
Subtotal: Short term debt	*535*	*435*	*508*	*635*	*579*	*550*	*604*	*589*
Banks	513	400	480	600	559	520	570	560
Export credits	21	35	28	35	21	30	34	29
Other identified liabilities	–	–	–	–	–	–	–	–
Total identified debt	**4773**	**5080**	**5782**	**6758**	**6566**	**6101**	**6464**	**6186**
SERVICE PAYMENTS								
Long term								
I. OECD countries and capital markets	616	376	327	347	184	132	81	99
ODA	7	7	9	4	0	0	4	4
Official/off. supported	218	82	75	45	19	5	16	39
Financial markets	390	288	243	298	164	126	61	56
Other private	–	–	–	–	–	–	–	–
II. Multilateral	90	133	196	225	8	2	215	228
of which: concessional	10	11	11	12	1	–	9	14
memo: IMF, total	24	52	71	98	0	1	87	69
III. Non-OECD creditor countries	18	29	53	39	3	5	3	7
Subtotal: Service payments, long term debt	*724*	*538*	*576*	*611*	*194*	*139*	*299*	*334*
of which: concessional	18	18	20	17	2	0	13	18
Amortization, long term debt	333	154	204	224	18	7	124	143
Interest, long term debt	391	384	372	387	177	132	175	190
Interest, short term debt	52	40	32	39	48	50	47	35
Total service payments	**776**	**578**	**608**	**650**	**242**	**188**	**346**	**368**

PAPUA NEW GUINEA

US $ Million

	1984	1985	1986	1987	1988	1989	1990	1991
GROSS DEBT								
Long term								
I. OECD countries and capital markets	1564	1670	1360	1436	1460	1572	1517	1458
ODA	39	52	74	118	135	141	181	202
Official/off. supported	536	503	358	348	263	178	201	349
Official export credits	301	278	234	283	250	137	159	217
Guaranteed supplier credits	31	23	18	19	4	1	1	1
Guaranteed bank credits	203	202	106	46	10	40	42	131
Financial markets	989	1116	928	969	1062	1253	1135	907
Banks	944	1036	828	853	986	1218	1098	871
Bonds	45	80	100	116	75	35	37	36
Other private	–	–	–	–	–	–	–	–
II. Multilateral	339	388	427	575	518	550	813	915
of which: concessional	236	263	285	376	294	307	419	458
non-concessional	103	125	141	199	224	243	394	457
memo: IMF, total	34	29	15	12	6	3	61	61
III. Non-OECD Creditor countries	8	6	5	4	2	4	5	15
C.E.E.C.	–	–	–	–	–	–	–	–
Arab countries	2	2	2	2	1	1	1	1
Other countries and unspecified	5	4	3	2	1	2	4	14
Subtotal: Long term debt	*1911*	*2064*	*1792*	*2015*	*1981*	*2126*	*2335*	*2388*
of which: concessional	275	315	359	495	429	448	600	660
non-concessional	1636	1750	1432	1521	1551	1677	1735	1728
Short term								
Subtotal: Short term debt	*145*	*114*	*62*	*107*	*273*	*315*	*190*	*316*
Banks	132	94	36	78	241	279	168	291
Export credits	13	21	26	29	32	36	22	26
Other identified liabilities	47	51	40	62	94	126	100	141
Total identified debt	**2103**	**2229**	**1893**	**2184**	**2347**	**2567**	**2624**	**2846**
SERVICE PAYMENTS								
Long term								
I. OECD countries and capital markets	191	372	447	423	312	392	482	408
ODA	4	9	2	3	6	5	7	8
Official/off. supported	53	63	206	42	55	73	30	27
Financial markets	133	300	240	377	252	314	445	373
Other private	–	–	–	–	–	–	–	–
II. Multilateral	47	25	38	42	69	57	65	76
of which: concessional	4	5	8	16	38	9	25	25
memo: IMF, total	33	9	17	5	5	3	3	6
III. Non-OECD creditor countries	5	2	2	2	2	1	0	5
Subtotal: Service payments, long term debt	*244*	*399*	*488*	*466*	*383*	*450*	*548*	*488*
of which: concessional	9	14	10	19	44	15	33	33
Amortization, long term debt	89	266	342	355	256	323	393	352
Interest, long term debt	155	133	146	111	127	127	155	137
Interest, short term debt	15	15	9	9	21	36	30	22
Total service payments	**259**	**414**	**497**	**476**	**404**	**487**	**578**	**511**

US $ Million

	1984	1985	1986	1987	1988	1989	1990	1991
GROSS DEBT								
Long term								
I. OECD countries and capital markets	641	782	860	882	924	902	855	857
ODA	155	187	229	294	333	306	335	326
Official/off. supported	130	204	270	329	226	289	212	303
Official export credits	47	42	46	66	67	131	86	82
Guaranteed supplier credits	15	3	3	7	12	3	3	3
Guaranteed bank credits	68	160	221	257	147	155	123	218
Financial markets	355	390	360	259	365	307	307	228
Banks	355	390	360	259	365	307	307	228
Bonds	–	–	–	–	–	–	–	–
Other private	–	–	–	–	–	–	–	–
II. Multilateral	416	539	671	830	778	734	734	721
of which: concessional	165	187	204	222	233	234	235	247
non-concessional	251	351	467	609	545	500	499	474
memo: IMF, total	–	–	–	–	–	–	–	–
III. Non-OECD Creditor countries	332	425	450	542	538	448	8	61
C.E.E.C.	–	–	–	–	–	–	–	–
Arab countries	–	–	–	–	–	–	–	–
Other countries and unspecified	332	425	450	542	538	448	8	61
Subtotal: Long term debt	*1390*	*1745*	*1980*	*2255*	*2240*	*2084*	*1597*	*1638*
of which: concessional	320	374	433	515	566	540	571	573
non-concessional	1069	1371	1547	1740	1674	1544	1026	1065
Short term								
Subtotal: Short term debt	*225*	*153*	*180*	*288*	*204*	*310*	*498*	*503*
Banks	217	137	151	252	154	204	309	267
Export credits	8	15	29	36	50	106	188	236
Other identified liabilities	108	95	62	71	83	52	72	90
Total identified debt	**1723**	**1993**	**2223**	**2614**	**2527**	**2446**	**2167**	**2232**
SERVICE PAYMENTS								
Long term								
I. OECD countries and capital markets	102	108	145	116	160	55	91	79
ODA	9	10	10	15	35	11	39	17
Official/off. supported	33	45	49	78	35	17	43	43
Financial markets	60	53	85	23	90	26	10	19
Other private	–	–	–	–	–	–	–	–
II. Multilateral	38	47	67	96	107	106	109	111
of which: concessional	6	8	9	12	11	12	10	13
memo: IMF, total	–	–	–	–	–	–	–	–
III. Non-OECD creditor countries	19	17	35	30	29	4	5	5
Subtotal: Service payments, long term debt	*159*	*171*	*247*	*242*	*295*	*165*	*205*	*195*
of which: concessional	15	18	19	27	46	23	49	30
Amortization, long term debt	84	88	148	133	186	82	126	125
Interest, long term debt	75	83	99	109	109	83	78	70
Interest, short term debt	33	23	16	19	23	23	27	12
Total service payments	**192**	**194**	**263**	**261**	**318**	**188**	**232**	**207**

US $ Million

	1984	1985	1986	1987	1988	1989	1990	1991
GROSS DEBT								
Long term								
I. OECD countries and capital markets	8934	9915	10228	10437	10083	10103	5378	4896
ODA	710	996	1276	1440	1421	1482	1657	2027
Official/off. supported	2498	2889	3126	3488	3368	2729	2788	2173
Official export credits	1184	1768	2015	2282	2235	2172	1767	1682
Guaranteed supplier credits	765	501	372	551	732	223	707	154
Guaranteed bank credits	548	620	738	655	401	333	314	336
Financial markets	4826	5074	4871	4553	4341	4938	926	688
Banks	4825	5074	4870	4552	4340	4937	925	688
Bonds	1	1	1	1	1	1	1	1
Other private	900	955	956	956	954	954	7	7
II. Multilateral	1718	2037	2390	2982	2853	2789	2952	2573
of which: concessional	184	198	207	222	217	220	230	172
non-concessional	1534	1839	2183	2759	2636	2570	2722	2401
memo: IMF, total	675	702	728	845	801	758	755	706
III. Non-OECD Creditor countries	1786	1451	1413	1605	1677	1588	1584	1583
C.E.E.C.	1143	870	844	1020	1007	889	923	971
Arab countries	–	–	–	–	–	–	–	–
Other countries and unspecified	643	581	568	586	670	699	662	612
Subtotal: Long term debt	*12438*	*13403*	*14030*	*15024*	*14613*	*14480*	*9914*	*9052*
of which: concessional	894	1194	1482	1662	1638	1702	1887	2200
non-concessional	11544	12209	12548	13361	12975	12778	8027	6852
Short term								
Subtotal: Short term debt	*2902*	*3248*	*3810*	*4172*	*4307*	*4381*	*4824*	*4890*
Banks	2710	2871	3008	2968	2764	2689	2606	2644
Export credits	192	376	802	1204	1543	1692	2218	2246
Other identified liabilities	–	–	–	–	–	–	–	–
Total identified debt	**15340**	**16651**	**17840**	**19196**	**18920**	**18861**	**14738**	**13942**
SERVICE PAYMENTS								
Long term								
I. OECD countries and capital markets	566	705	425	256	255	299	127	192
ODA	24	16	42	33	26	39	23	34
Official/off. supported	200	327	212	166	152	150	104	71
Financial markets	257	290	104	0	10	15	–	86
Other private	85	72	67	57	67	95	–	1
II. Multilateral	277	256	291	157	66	104	188	730
of which: concessional	15	14	17	10	7	5	5	44
memo: IMF, total	144	97	71	1	1	38	137	73
III. Non-OECD creditor countries	139	270	188	112	117	146	108	112
Subtotal: Service payments, long term debt	*982*	*1231*	*904*	*525*	*438*	*549*	*424*	*1034*
of which: concessional	39	30	59	43	34	44	29	78
Amortization, long term debt	367	568	484	168	134	189	242	625
Interest, long term debt	615	663	419	357	304	359	182	409
Interest, short term debt	322	236	205	76	181	127	11	–
Total service payments	**1303**	**1467**	**1109**	**600**	**620**	**675**	**435**	**1034**

US $ Million

	1984	1985	1986	1987	1988	1989	1990	1991
GROSS DEBT								
Long term								
I. OECD countries and capital markets	11447	13037	16063	17994	16857	15113	15500	15189
ODA	1331	1841	2677	3598	3980	3797	4582	5257
Official/off. supported	3443	3031	3212	3882	3375	3820	3395	4237
Official export credits	1132	1176	1169	2025	1752	2700	2444	3059
Guaranteed supplier credits	917	615	727	506	444	357	342	357
Guaranteed bank credits	1394	1239	1317	1351	1179	763	609	821
Financial markets	6374	7865	9874	10115	9103	7096	7123	5295
Banks	5466	6909	9019	9239	8429	6585	6235	5008
Bonds	908	957	855	876	674	511	888	287
Other private	300	300	300	400	400	400	400	400
II. Multilateral	3713	4647	5453	6279	5870	6161	7187	7659
of which: concessional	317	316	327	844	851	882	1283	1366
non-concessional	3395	4331	5126	5435	5019	5279	5904	6293
memo: IMF, total	885	1168	1266	1260	1093	1177	912	1086
III. Non-OECD Creditor countries	42	66	66	37	31	138	147	146
C.E.E.C.	9	9	8	8	2	8	8	8
Arab countries	6	6	5	5	4	4	4	4
Other countries and unspecified	27	51	52	24	25	126	136	135
Subtotal: Long term debt	*15202*	*17750*	*21582*	*24310*	*22759*	*21412*	*22834*	*22994*
of which: concessional	1648	2157	3004	4442	4831	4679	5864	6623
non-concessional	13554	15593	18579	19869	17928	16733	16969	16371
Short term								
Subtotal: Short term debt	*7398*	*5974*	*4056*	*4146*	*3159*	*2922*	*3142*	*3310*
Banks	6955	5111	3738	3707	2741	2310	2648	2819
Export credits	443	863	318	439	418	612	494	491
Other identified liabilities	5216	4695	1851	1954	2310	1375	1811	1672
Total identified debt	**27816**	**28419**	**27489**	**30410**	**28228**	**25709**	**27787**	**27976**
SERVICE PAYMENTS								
Long term								
I. OECD countries and capital markets	1194	1610	1727	2140	2161	1602	1206	1819
ODA	78	58	191	68	297	108	98	164
Official/off. supported	468	463	718	738	534	542	374	625
Financial markets	618	1064	797	1317	1302	912	675	953
Other private	30	24	21	18	28	40	58	78
II. Multilateral	669	650	911	1083	1005	993	1276	1277
of which: concessional	28	40	106	115	113	107	119	121
memo: IMF, total	319	258	381	437	270	280	444	390
III. Non-OECD creditor countries	5	6	6	33	6	8	8	17
Subtotal: Service payments, long term debt	*1867*	*2265*	*2644*	*3256*	*3172*	*2603*	*2489*	*3114*
of which: concessional	106	98	297	183	410	215	217	284
Amortization, long term debt	766	773	1419	1717	1523	966	1000	1730
Interest, long term debt	1101	1493	1225	1539	1649	1637	1489	1383
Interest, short term debt	1298	947	555	401	446	420	364	287
Total service payments	**3166**	**3212**	**3199**	**3657**	**3618**	**3023**	**2853**	**3401**

US $ Million

	1984	1985	1986	1987	1988	1989	1990	1991
GROSS DEBT								
Long term								
I. OECD countries and capital markets	163	214	266	362	328	341	305	376
ODA	88	125	164	241	221	229	253	270
Official/off. supported	74	88	100	121	107	112	37	81
Official export credits	74	88	100	121	107	112	37	81
Guaranteed supplier credits	–	–	–	0	–	–	–	0
Guaranteed bank credits	0	0	–	0	–	–	–	0
Financial markets	1	1	2	–	–	–	15	25
Banks	1	1	2	–	–	–	15	25
Bonds	–	–	–	–	–	–	–	–
Other private	–	–	–	–	–	–	–	–
II. Multilateral	1	1	1	4	4	5	6	6
of which: concessional	1	1	1	1	1	3	4	4
non-concessional	–	–	–	2	2	2	2	2
memo: IMF, total	–	–	–	–	–	–	–	–
III. Non-OECD Creditor countries	–	–	–	–	–	–	–	–
C.E.E.C.	–	–	–	–	–	–	–	–
Arab countries	–	–	–	–	–	–	–	–
Other countries and unspecified	–	–	–	–	–	–	–	–
Subtotal: Long term debt	*164*	*215*	*267*	*365*	*332*	*345*	*311*	*382*
of which: concessional	89	126	165	242	223	232	257	274
non-concessional	75	89	102	123	109	114	54	108
Short term								
Subtotal: Short term debt	*3*	*8*	*15*	*32*	*31*	*32*	*11*	*7*
Banks	1	4	9	24	26	26	2	–
Export credits	2	4	6	8	5	6	9	7
Other identified liabilities	–	–	–	–	–	–	–	–
Total identified debt	**167**	**223**	**282**	**397**	**363**	**378**	**322**	**390**
SERVICE PAYMENTS								
Long term								
I. OECD countries and capital markets	18	11	16	9	38	32	20	45
ODA	8	7	8	3	18	14	10	20
Official/off. supported	10	3	7	6	20	18	10	24
Financial markets	0	0	0	0	–	–	–	1
Other private	–	–	–	–	–	–	–	–
II. Multilateral	1	0	0	0	0	1	1	1
of which: concessional	0	0	0	0	0	0	0	0
memo: IMF, total	–	–	–	–	–	–	–	–
III. Non-OECD creditor countries	–	–	–	–	–	–	–	–
Subtotal: Service payments, long term debt	*19*	*11*	*16*	*10*	*39*	*32*	*21*	*46*
of which: concessional	8	7	8	3	18	14	10	20
Amortization, long term debt	13	4	9	0	22	21	8	38
Interest, long term debt	6	7	7	10	17	11	13	8
Interest, short term debt	0	0	1	2	3	3	2	1
Total service payments	**20**	**11**	**16**	**11**	**41**	**35**	**23**	**46**

US $ Million

	1984	1985	1986	1987	1988	1989	1990	1991
GROSS DEBT								
Long term								
I. OECD countries and capital markets	200	197	222	122	93	172	308	368
ODA	–	–	–	–	–	–	–	–
Official/off. supported	108	135	89	83	20	48	71	87
Official export credits	–	–	–	–	–	–	–	25
Guaranteed supplier credits	52	75	46	1	0	3	18	16
Guaranteed bank credits	57	60	43	82	19	45	53	46
Financial markets	91	62	134	39	73	123	237	281
Banks	91	62	134	39	73	123	237	281
Bonds	–	–	–	–	–	–	–	–
Other private	–	–	–	–	–	–	–	–
II. Multilateral	–	–	–	–	–	–	–	–
of which: concessional	–	–	–	–	–	–	–	–
non-concessional	–	–	–	–	–	–	–	–
memo: IMF, total	–	–	–	–	–	–	–	–
III. Non-OECD Creditor countries	–	–	–	–	–	–	–	–
C.E.E.C.	–	–	–	–	–	–	–	–
Arab countries	–	–	–	–	–	–	–	–
Other countries and unspecified	–	–	–	–	–	–	–	–
Subtotal: Long term debt	*200*	*197*	*222*	*122*	*93*	*172*	*308*	*368*
of which: concessional	–	–	–	–	–	–	–	–
non-concessional	200	197	222	122	93	172	308	368
Short term								
Subtotal: Short term debt	*308*	*403*	*417*	*608*	*815*	*756*	*1058*	*1458*
Banks	273	354	366	547	761	711	1006	1398
Export credits	35	49	51	61	54	45	52	60
Other identified liabilities	–	–	–	–	–	–	–	–
Total identified debt	**508**	**600**	**639**	**730**	**908**	**928**	**1366**	**1826**
SERVICE PAYMENTS								
Long term								
I. OECD countries and capital markets	181	99	108	60	18	108	24	44
ODA	–	–	–	–	–	–	–	–
Official/off. supported	137	84	102	48	14	100	12	26
Financial markets	44	15	6	12	4	8	13	18
Other private	–	–	–	–	–	–	–	–
II. Multilateral	–	1	–	–	–	–	–	–
of which: concessional	–	1	–	–	–	–	–	–
memo: IMF, total	–	–	–	–	–	–	–	–
III. Non-OECD creditor countries	–	–	–	–	–	–	–	–
Subtotal: Service payments, long term debt	*181*	*101*	*108*	*60*	*18*	*108*	*24*	*44*
of which: concessional	–	1	–	–	–	–	–	–
Amortization, long term debt	161	76	90	37	13	89	12	22
Interest, long term debt	20	24	19	24	5	18	13	22
Interest, short term debt	38	29	28	35	56	70	75	76
Total service payments	**219**	**130**	**136**	**96**	**74**	**178**	**99**	**120**

RWANDA

	1984	1985	1986	1987	1988	1989	1990	1991
GROSS DEBT								
Long term								
I. OECD countries and capital markets	44	51	70	110	112	126	141	155
ODA	20	34	55	90	91	101	115	121
Official/off. supported	13	14	12	9	11	8	16	19
Official export credits	1	1	1	0	2	2	3	5
Guaranteed supplier credits	10	11	7	4	5	3	6	3
Guaranteed bank credits	2	2	4	5	4	3	7	11
Financial markets	11	3	3	10	9	17	11	15
Banks	11	3	3	10	9	17	11	15
Bonds	–	–	–	–	–	–	–	–
Other private	–	–	–	–	–	–	–	–
II. Multilateral	188	242	306	398	440	479	542	613
of which: concessional	187	241	304	396	439	478	541	612
non-concessional	2	2	2	2	1	1	1	0
memo: IMF, total	11	10	9	7	4	1	0	13
III. Non-OECD Creditor countries	35	38	55	68	74	65	75	78
C.E.E.C.	–	–	–	–	–	–	–	–
Arab countries	15	22	29	33	37	36	50	53
Other countries and unspecified	20	16	26	35	37	28	26	24
Subtotal: Long term debt	*268*	*331*	*431*	*575*	*626*	*670*	*759*	*845*
of which: concessional	207	275	359	486	530	579	656	733
non-concessional	61	56	72	89	96	91	103	112
Short term								
Subtotal: Short term debt	*37*	*27*	*28*	*44*	*41*	*43*	*45*	*30*
Banks	8	6	11	18	18	28	20	10
Export credits	29	21	17	26	23	15	25	20
Other identified liabilities	15	22	–	8	11	6	7	7
Total identified debt	**320**	**379**	**459**	**627**	**678**	**719**	**811**	**882**
SERVICE PAYMENTS								
Long term								
I. OECD countries and capital markets	12	14	9	10	14	16	20	17
ODA	1	2	2	3	5	4	6	2
Official/off. supported	4	6	6	7	5	4	4	6
Financial markets	7	6	2	0	3	8	10	8
Other private	–	–	–	–	–	–	–	–
II. Multilateral	5	6	8	10	10	13	10	10
of which: concessional	4	6	7	10	9	13	10	10
memo: IMF, total	0	2	3	3	3	3	1	0
III. Non-OECD creditor countries	2	3	2	3	2	5	4	7
Subtotal: Service payments, long term debt	*19*	*23*	*19*	*23*	*25*	*34*	*34*	*34*
of which: concessional	5	8	9	12	14	17	16	12
Amortization, long term debt	14	18	14	17	15	24	23	23
Interest, long term debt	5	5	5	7	10	10	11	11
Interest, short term debt	4	4	3	3	4	5	4	2
Total service payments	**24**	**27**	**22**	**26**	**29**	**39**	**38**	**36**

SAO TOME & PRINCIPE

US $ Million

	1984	1985	1986	1987	1988	1989	1990	1991
GROSS DEBT								
Long term								
I. OECD countries and capital markets	13	13	18	18	17	20	22	25
ODA	–	–	–	–	–	3	6	9
Official/off. supported	12	12	18	17	15	17	16	16
Official export credits	8	8	16	16	13	15	15	16
Guaranteed supplier credits	0	–	–	–	1	1	1	0
Guaranteed bank credits	5	4	2	2	1	1	1	0
Financial markets	1	1	0	0	2	–	–	–
Banks	1	1	0	0	2	–	–	–
Bonds	–	–	–	–	–	–	–	–
Other private	–	–	–	–	–	–	–	–
II. Multilateral	20	21	24	32	42	58	75	83
of which: concessional	20	21	24	31	41	56	74	82
non-concessional	–	–	0	1	1	1	1	1
memo: IMF, total	–	–	–	–	–	1	1	1
III. Non-OECD Creditor countries	48	51	62	66	49	47	47	46
C.E.E.C.	25	32	33	35	35	35	35	35
Arab countries	1	1	1	1	1	1	1	1
Other countries and unspecified	23	18	29	29	13	11	10	10
Subtotal: Long term debt	*82*	*85*	*105*	*115*	*108*	*124*	*144*	*154*
of which: concessional	20	21	24	31	41	60	80	91
non-concessional	62	64	81	84	67	65	64	64
Short term								
Subtotal: Short term debt	*1*	*1*	*1*	*4*	*4*	*13*	*8*	*8*
Banks	1	1	1	3	3	12	7	7
Export credits	0	–	–	1	1	1	1	1
Other identified liabilities	–	–	–	–	–	–	–	–
Total identified debt	**83**	**86**	**106**	**119**	**112**	**137**	**152**	**162**
SERVICE PAYMENTS								
Long term								
I. OECD countries and capital markets	1	2	1	1	1	1	0	0
ODA	–	–	–	–	–	–	0	0
Official/off. supported	1	2	1	1	1	1	–	–
Financial markets	0	0	0	0	0	0	–	–
Other private	–	–	–	–	–	–	–	–
II. Multilateral	0	0	0	2	1	1	1	1
of which: concessional	0	0	0	2	1	1	1	1
memo: IMF, total	–	–	–	–	–	–	0	0
III. Non-OECD creditor countries	2	2	1	1	0	0	0	–
Subtotal: Service payments, long term debt	*3*	*4*	*2*	*4*	*2*	*2*	*1*	*1*
of which: concessional	0	0	0	2	1	1	1	1
Amortization, long term debt	2	2	1	2	1	1	1	0
Interest, long term debt	1	2	1	1	1	1	0	1
Interest, short term debt	0	0	0	0	0	1	1	0
Total service payments	**3**	**4**	**2**	**4**	**3**	**3**	**2**	**2**

SAUDI ARABIA

US $ Million

	1984	1985	1986	1987	1988	1989	1990	1991
GROSS DEBT								
Long term								
I. OECD countries and capital markets	3289	4106	3203	3746	1919	2185	2045	2892
ODA	–	106	146	187	4	–	–	–
Official/off. supported	1729	1962	1915	2264	698	950	1011	1352
Official export credits	97	94	0	1	0	0	0	6
Guaranteed supplier credits	1371	1666	1746	2031	582	161	129	480
Guaranteed bank credits	261	202	169	232	116	788	881	865
Financial markets	1560	2038	1142	1295	1217	1235	1035	1541
Banks	1410	1738	992	1145	1067	1085	935	1491
Bonds	150	300	150	150	150	150	100	50
Other private	–	–	–	–	–	–	–	–
II. Multilateral	–	–	–	–	–	–	–	–
of which: concessional	–	–	–	–	–	–	–	–
non-concessional	–	–	–	–	–	–	–	–
memo: IMF, total	–	–	–	–	–	–	–	–
III. Non-OECD Creditor countries	1	1	1	1	1	1	1	1
C.E.E.C.	1	1	1	1	1	1	1	–
Arab countries	–	–	–	–	–	–	–	–
Other countries and unspecified	–	–	–	–	–	–	–	–
Subtotal: Long term debt	*3290*	*4107*	*3203*	*3747*	*1919*	*2186*	*2046*	*2893*
of which: concessional	1	107	146	188	4	1	1	1
non-concessional	3289	4000	3057	3559	1915	2185	2045	2892
Short term								
Subtotal: Short term debt	*10578*	*10024*	*10857*	*12929*	*13093*	*14498*	*13020*	*14216*
Banks	8528	8272	8922	11052	11657	12769	10852	11767
Export credits	2050	1752	1936	1877	1436	1730	2168	2449
Other identified liabilities	41	51	37	38	30	30	84	65
Total identified debt	**13908**	**14182**	**14098**	**16714**	**15042**	**16714**	**15151**	**17174**
SERVICE PAYMENTS								
Long term								
I. OECD countries and capital markets	2375	1786	1574	1238	1744	868	691	522
ODA	0	1	2	3	–	0	–	–
Official/off. supported	2044	1472	1205	1119	1593	726	566	431
Financial markets	331	313	367	116	152	142	125	92
Other private	–	–	–	–	–	–	–	–
II. Multilateral	–	–	–	–	–	–	–	–
of which: concessional	–	–	–	–	–	–	–	–
memo: IMF, total	–	–	–	–	–	–	–	–
III. Non-OECD creditor countries	–	–	–	–	–	0	0	–
Subtotal: Service payments, long term debt	*2375*	*1786*	*1574*	*1238*	*1744*	*868*	*692*	*522*
of which: concessional	0	1	2	3	–	0	0	–
Amortization, long term debt	2181	1610	1380	1137	1604	734	539	440
Interest, long term debt	195	176	194	101	140	134	152	82
Interest, short term debt	1159	844	707	814	1032	1231	1125	806
Total service payments	**3535**	**2630**	**2281**	**2052**	**2776**	**2099**	**1816**	**1328**

US $ Million

	1984	1985	1986	1987	1988	1989	1990	1991
GROSS DEBT								
Long term								
I. OECD countries and capital markets	737	962	1154	1520	1596	1722	1657	1569
ODA	202	287	445	669	731	951	972	942
Official/off. supported	407	529	603	754	648	600	633	626
Official export credits	240	340	423	527	495	517	540	555
Guaranteed supplier credits	15	23	8	6	97	4	23	15
Guaranteed bank credits	151	167	172	221	57	79	70	56
Financial markets	129	146	106	97	216	170	51	–
Banks	127	145	105	97	216	170	51	–
Bonds	1	2	1	–	–	–	–	–
Other private	–	–	–	–	–	–	–	–
II. Multilateral	681	799	1058	1493	1485	1511	1672	1786
of which: concessional	345	390	611	994	1066	1157	1365	1538
non-concessional	336	409	448	499	419	354	307	247
memo: IMF, total	230	268	289	343	318	316	314	327
III. Non-OECD Creditor countries	354	433	481	523	631	607	580	466
C.E.E.C.	2	3	3	3	3	3	2	2
Arab countries	281	331	398	434	436	435	421	323
Other countries and unspecified	71	99	80	86	192	170	157	141
Subtotal: Long term debt	*1771*	*2194*	*2693*	*3536*	*3712*	*3840*	*3909*	*3820*
of which: concessional	546	677	1056	1663	1798	2109	2338	2481
non-concessional	1225	1517	1637	1873	1914	1731	1571	1340
Short term								
Subtotal: Short term debt	*235*	*230*	*336*	*742*	*707*	*478*	*555*	*431*
Banks	169	116	221	596	543	291	362	252
Export credits	66	113	115	146	164	187	193	179
Other identified liabilities	42	43	62	65	71	142	84	60
Total identified debt	**2048**	**2467**	**3091**	**4342**	**4490**	**4460**	**4548**	**4311**
SERVICE PAYMENTS								
Long term								
I. OECD countries and capital markets	79	52	121	136	209	244	155	140
ODA	10	8	16	24	26	17	14	23
Official/off. supported	55	32	91	102	86	94	89	61
Financial markets	14	13	14	10	97	134	52	55
Other private	–	–	–	–	–	–	–	–
II. Multilateral	61	90	135	155	155	162	154	150
of which: concessional	13	17	23	39	43	44	43	49
memo: IMF, total	35	67	86	85	83	77	70	57
III. Non-OECD creditor countries	17	12	36	55	44	52	55	40
Subtotal: Service payments, long term debt	*158*	*154*	*293*	*346*	*408*	*459*	*364*	*329*
of which: concessional	23	25	39	64	69	60	57	72
Amortization, long term debt	66	92	159	223	266	285	228	201
Interest, long term debt	91	62	134	123	142	173	136	128
Interest, short term debt	33	21	21	39	60	58	47	30
Total service payments	**190**	**175**	**313**	**385**	**467**	**516**	**411**	**359**

SEYCHELLES

US $ Million

	1984	1985	1986	1987	1988	1989	1990	1991
GROSS DEBT								
Long term								
I. OECD countries and capital markets	38	59	67	92	96	81	115	171
ODA	17	23	33	47	48	48	69	70
Official/off. supported	14	14	25	32	32	25	43	102
Official export credits	5	6	6	7	6	6	18	6
Guaranteed supplier credits	4	3	2	2	5	3	4	2
Guaranteed bank credits	5	6	16	23	21	17	21	94
Financial markets	7	22	10	13	16	8	3	–
Banks	7	22	10	13	16	8	3	–
Bonds	–	–	–	–	–	–	–	–
Other private	–	–	–	–	–	–	–	–
II. Multilateral	13	19	30	39	39	42	45	46
of which: concessional	4	7	13	18	18	20	23	25
non-concessional	8	13	17	21	21	21	23	21
memo: IMF, total	–	–	–	–	–	–	–	–
III. Non-OECD Creditor countries	8	13	13	13	13	13	15	17
C.E.E.C.	–	–	–	–	0	0	0	0
Arab countries	6	10	10	11	11	11	14	14
Other countries and unspecified	2	3	3	2	2	1	1	2
Subtotal: Long term debt	*58*	*91*	*110*	*144*	*148*	*136*	*176*	*234*
of which: concessional	22	29	46	65	66	69	92	95
non-concessional	37	62	64	79	82	67	84	140
Short term								
Subtotal: Short term debt	*22*	*26*	*42*	*44*	*41*	*64*	*57*	*106*
Banks	20	18	33	32	32	54	43	16
Export credits	2	8	9	12	9	10	14	90
Other identified liabilities	–	–	–	–	–	–	–	–
Total identified debt	**80**	**117**	**152**	**188**	**189**	**200**	**233**	**340**
SERVICE PAYMENTS								
Long term								
I. OECD countries and capital markets	6	9	11	8	16	19	16	22
ODA	0	0	1	1	2	1	2	4
Official/off. supported	4	7	8	6	12	12	3	14
Financial markets	2	2	2	1	2	5	11	3
Other private	–	–	–	–	–	–	–	–
II. Multilateral	1	2	3	3	4	5	6	5
of which: concessional	0	0	0	0	1	1	1	1
memo: IMF, total	–	–	–	–	–	–	–	–
III. Non-OECD creditor countries	1	2	1	1	1	1	1	3
Subtotal: Service payments, long term debt	*8*	*13*	*15*	*12*	*21*	*25*	*22*	*29*
of which: concessional	0	1	1	2	3	2	3	5
Amortization, long term debt	4	6	9	6	12	17	16	21
Interest, long term debt	4	6	6	6	9	8	7	9
Interest, short term debt	2	2	2	3	3	4	4	2
Total service payments	**10**	**15**	**17**	**14**	**24**	**29**	**27**	**31**

SIERRA LEONE

US $ Million

	1984	1985	1986	1987	1988	1989	1990	1991
GROSS DEBT								
Long term								
I. OECD countries and capital markets	259	234	269	325	284	304	277	330
ODA	117	82	101	121	111	133	81	156
Official/off. supported	102	99	123	173	151	158	192	170
Official export credits	30	36	62	120	82	91	110	101
Guaranteed supplier credits	58	47	60	53	69	67	81	68
Guaranteed bank credits	14	16	1	0	–	1	1	1
Financial markets	40	53	45	31	22	12	4	3
Banks	40	53	45	31	22	12	4	3
Bonds	–	–	–	–	–	–	–	–
Other private	–	–	–	–	–	–	–	–
II. Multilateral	194	224	243	277	278	277	290	298
of which: concessional	106	130	155	175	188	189	199	216
non-concessional	89	95	89	102	91	87	91	83
memo: IMF, total	96	101	101	116	109	105	108	101
III. Non-OECD Creditor countries	41	47	43	43	48	42	49	50
C.E.E.C.	6	6	6	6	6	6	6	6
Arab countries	0	–	0	0	1	1	1	1
Other countries and unspecified	35	41	37	37	41	36	43	44
Subtotal: Long term debt	*495*	*505*	*555*	*645*	*610*	*623*	*616*	*678*
of which: concessional	222	212	256	296	299	323	280	372
non-concessional	272	293	299	349	311	300	336	307
Short term								
Subtotal: Short term debt	*182*	*150*	*76*	*110*	*111*	*106*	*127*	*117*
Banks	175	143	62	94	93	88	96	83
Export credits	7	7	14	16	18	18	31	34
Other identified liabilities	–	–	–	–	–	–	–	–
Total identified debt	**677**	**655**	**631**	**756**	**721**	**729**	**743**	**796**
SERVICE PAYMENTS								
Long term								
I. OECD countries and capital markets	15	19	11	17	12	22	11	4
ODA	1	5	4	4	2	10	3	1
Official/off. supported	8	9	3	8	7	9	6	2
Financial markets	6	5	4	4	3	3	1	0
Other private	–	–	–	–	–	–	–	–
II. Multilateral	25	10	51	5	8	4	9	11
of which: concessional	4	2	12	2	1	4	4	2
memo: IMF, total	17	8	47	3	1	4	5	8
III. Non-OECD creditor countries	–	–	0	0	–	0	–	–
Subtotal: Service payments, long term debt	*40*	*29*	*62*	*22*	*20*	*26*	*20*	*14*
of which: concessional	5	7	17	6	2	13	7	3
Amortization, long term debt	25	21	39	11	10	16	12	10
Interest, long term debt	16	9	23	11	9	10	8	4
Interest, short term debt	20	13	7	5	8	8	8	6
Total service payments	**60**	**43**	**69**	**27**	**28**	**34**	**28**	**20**

SINGAPORE

US $ Million

	1984	1985	1986	1987	1988	1989	1990	1991
GROSS DEBT								
Long term								
I. OECD countries and capital markets	3302	3632	3075	3468	3460	3763	3379	3824
ODA	22	77	87	102	29	100	101	84
Official/off. supported	908	1035	631	606	451	376	419	365
Official export credits	264	236	9	166	131	111	112	79
Guaranteed supplier credits	453	584	426	127	86	46	26	26
Guaranteed bank credits	190	216	197	313	234	219	281	259
Financial markets	2173	2320	2156	2460	2630	2937	2483	3000
Banks	1679	1780	1514	1557	1728	1808	1880	2287
Bonds	494	540	642	903	902	1129	603	713
Other private	200	200	200	300	350	350	375	375
II. Multilateral	151	147	138	121	97	96	57	57
of which: concessional	11	11	12	12	12	12	10	10
non-concessional	141	136	127	109	85	85	47	47
memo: IMF, total	–	–	–	–	–	–	–	–
III. Non-OECD Creditor countries	1	27	27	32	32	32	32	32
C.E.E.C.	–	–	–	–	6	6	6	–
Arab countries	–	–	–	–	–	–	–	–
Other countries and unspecified	1	27	27	32	26	26	26	26
Subtotal: Long term debt	*3455*	*3806*	*3239*	*3620*	*3588*	*3892*	*3468*	*3913*
of which: concessional	33	115	125	146	73	144	144	127
non-concessional	3421	3691	3114	3474	3516	3748	3324	3786
Short term								
Subtotal: Short term debt	*673*	*601*	*548*	*576*	*603*	*683*	*736*	*912*
Banks	550	420	360	360	400	421	450	550
Export credits	123	181	188	216	204	263	286	362
Other identified liabilities	–	–	–	–	–	–	–	–
Total identified debt	**4128**	**4407**	**3787**	**4196**	**4192**	**4575**	**4204**	**4825**
SERVICE PAYMENTS								
Long term								
I. OECD countries and capital markets	555	1230	830	860	475	775	480	464
ODA	8	7	9	11	11	9	15	28
Official/off. supported	288	545	576	627	218	202	154	125
Financial markets	239	652	221	210	225	529	249	245
Other private	20	26	24	12	21	35	63	66
II. Multilateral	32	33	39	42	35	25	46	16
of which: concessional	2	2	2	3	0	0	2	0
memo: IMF, total	–	–	–	–	–	–	–	–
III. Non-OECD creditor countries	1	1	7	8	–	–	1	14
Subtotal: Service payments, long term debt	*588*	*1264*	*875*	*910*	*509*	*800*	*526*	*494*
of which: concessional	11	10	18	21	11	10	17	42
Amortization, long term debt	295	982	642	712	276	505	226	260
Interest, long term debt	293	283	234	198	233	295	301	234
Interest, short term debt	69	52	39	39	47	58	59	49
Total service payments	**657**	**1317**	**914**	**949**	**556**	**858**	**586**	**543**

SOLOMON ISLANDS (BR)

US $ Million

	1984	1985	1986	1987	1988	1989	1990	1991
GROSS DEBT								
Long term								
I. OECD countries and capital markets	20	26	29	62	55	55	68	105
ODA	9	6	7	11	21	25	29	30
Official/off. supported	6	10	15	37	31	27	28	67
Official export credits	6	9	11	33	27	24	25	64
Guaranteed supplier credits	–	1	4	4	3	3	3	3
Guaranteed bank credits	0	0	–	–	–	–	–	–
Financial markets	5	10	7	13	4	3	11	8
Banks	5	10	7	13	4	3	11	8
Bonds	–	–	–	–	–	–	–	–
Other private	–	–	–	–	–	–	–	–
II. Multilateral	27	32	38	46	51	56	63	66
of which: concessional	24	29	35	44	49	54	63	66
non-concessional	3	3	4	2	2	1	1	–
memo: IMF, total	3	3	4	2	2	1	1	–
III. Non-OECD Creditor countries	2	2	5	7	12	11	11	11
C.E.E.C.	–	–	–	–	–	–	–	–
Arab countries	2	2	4	6	5	5	5	4
Other countries and unspecified	–	–	2	2	7	6	6	6
Subtotal: Long term debt	*49*	*60*	*73*	*115*	*118*	*122*	*142*	*181*
of which: concessional	33	35	42	55	70	79	91	95
non-concessional	16	25	31	60	48	43	51	86
Short term								
Subtotal: Short term debt	*83*	*235*	*50*	*17*	*3*	*5*	*17*	*33*
Banks	82	233	48	16	1	3	15	31
Export credits	1	2	2	1	2	2	2	2
Other identified liabilities	–	–	–	–	–	–	–	–
Total identified debt	**132**	**295**	**123**	**132**	**121**	**126**	**158**	**214**
SERVICE PAYMENTS								
Long term								
I. OECD countries and capital markets	1	1	4	3	6	8	8	20
ODA	1	1	0	0	0	1	1	1
Official/off. supported	0	0	0	2	4	5	5	15
Financial markets	0	0	3	1	1	2	3	4
Other private	–	–	–	–	–	–	–	–
II. Multilateral	1	1	2	3	2	1	2	3
of which: concessional	0	1	1	1	1	1	1	2
memo: IMF, total	0	1	2	2	1	0	1	1
III. Non-OECD creditor countries	–	–	0	0	0	1	0	1
Subtotal: Service payments, long term debt	*2*	*3*	*6*	*6*	*8*	*9*	*11*	*24*
of which: concessional	1	1	1	1	2	2	2	3
Amortization, long term debt	1	1	4	2	4	5	7	17
Interest, long term debt	1	2	2	3	4	4	4	7
Interest, short term debt	5	13	10	2	1	0	1	1
Total service payments	**7**	**16**	**16**	**8**	**8**	**10**	**12**	**26**

SOMALIA

US $ Million

	1984	1985	1986	1987	1988	1989	1990	1991
GROSS DEBT								
Long term								
I. OECD countries and capital markets	547	521	505	597	516	527	520	496
ODA	220	267	334	458	349	351	357	367
Official/off. supported	218	214	107	121	130	140	145	129
Official export credits	69	77	96	75	96	94	99	86
Guaranteed supplier credits	148	128	8	6	13	5	2	2
Guaranteed bank credits	1	9	3	41	21	41	44	41
Financial markets	109	40	65	18	37	36	17	–
Banks	109	40	65	18	37	36	17	–
Bonds	–	–	–	–	–	–	–	–
Other private	–	–	–	–	–	–	–	–
II. Multilateral	448	564	643	784	787	825	909	881
of which: concessional	340	412	484	615	627	683	759	729
non-concessional	108	153	159	169	159	142	151	151
memo: IMF, total	112	154	156	175	165	150	159	160
III. Non-OECD Creditor countries	715	690	704	766	757	728	744	743
C.E.E.C.	323	329	340	385	381	365	378	378
Arab countries	310	280	281	287	283	280	280	283
Other countries and unspecified	81	81	83	94	93	82	86	83
Subtotal: Long term debt	*1709*	*1775*	*1853*	*2147*	*2059*	*2080*	*2173*	*2120*
of which: concessional	560	679	818	1073	977	1034	1116	1096
non-concessional	1149	1097	1034	1074	1082	1046	1057	1024
Short term								
Subtotal: Short term debt	*109*	*108*	*146*	*295*	*198*	*263*	*222*	*234*
Banks	104	105	57	185	60	80	12	3
Export credits	5	3	89	110	138	183	210	230
Other identified liabilities	–	–	–	–	–	–	–	–
Total identified debt	**1819**	**1883**	**1998**	**2442**	**2257**	**2343**	**2395**	**2354**
SERVICE PAYMENTS								
Long term								
I. OECD countries and capital markets	30	28	21	17	42	42	22	16
ODA	6	10	3	5	13	20	9	4
Official/off. supported	13	9	16	7	27	19	9	11
Financial markets	11	10	3	5	1	3	3	1
Other private	–	–	–	–	–	–	–	–
II. Multilateral	17	17	60	35	5	23	10	0
of which: concessional	5	3	7	7	4	9	6	0
memo: IMF, total	13	15	55	30	1	15	4	–
III. Non-OECD creditor countries	14	2	2	2	–	–	–	–
Subtotal: Service payments, long term debt	*61*	*47*	*83*	*53*	*47*	*65*	*32*	*16*
of which: concessional	10	12	10	12	17	29	15	4
Amortization, long term debt	29	19	42	30	25	34	10	4
Interest, long term debt	32	28	41	24	22	31	22	11
Interest, short term debt	11	9	6	9	11	8	5	1
Total service payments	**73**	**56**	**89**	**62**	**57**	**74**	**38**	**17**

SRI LANKA

US $ Million

	1984	1985	1986	1987	1988	1989	1990	1991
GROSS DEBT								
Long term								
I. OECD countries and capital markets	1726	2288	2589	3015	2904	2869	3129	3331
ODA	1040	1404	1784	2180	2278	2329	2614	2870
Official/off. supported	272	436	499	740	520	493	514	461
Official export credits	20	138	173	295	187	173	164	134
Guaranteed supplier credits	71	70	53	64	49	39	33	30
Guaranteed bank credits	180	229	273	381	284	281	316	298
Financial markets	414	448	306	95	105	47	2	–
Banks	414	448	306	95	105	47	2	–
Bonds	–	–	–	–	–	–	–	–
Other private	–	–	–	–	–	–	–	–
II. Multilateral	964	1091	1200	1327	1498	1619	2030	2323
of which: concessional	587	704	836	1001	1130	1320	1759	2149
non-concessional	377	387	363	326	368	299	271	174
memo: IMF, total	405	397	347	277	359	366	410	401
III. Non-OECD Creditor countries	155	167	173	174	175	149	121	104
C.E.E.C.	21	20	19	17	9	5	3	1
Arab countries	42	49	69	72	75	70	64	59
Other countries and unspecified	91	98	85	84	90	74	54	44
Subtotal: Long term debt	*2844*	*3546*	*3962*	*4516*	*4577*	*4638*	*5279*	*5758*
of which: concessional	1627	2108	2620	3181	3409	3649	4373	5019
non-concessional	1217	1438	1342	1335	1168	988	907	739
Short term								
Subtotal: Short term debt	*373*	*178*	*398*	*345*	*586*	*612*	*476*	*423*
Banks	267	152	366	325	554	579	440	393
Export credits	106	26	32	20	32	32	36	30
Other identified liabilities	110	150	178	205	229	278	318	407
Total identified debt	**3327**	**3874**	**4537**	**5066**	**5392**	**5527**	**6074**	**6588**
SERVICE PAYMENTS								
Long term								
I. OECD countries and capital markets	162	187	210	248	304	297	273	257
ODA	39	42	51	68	88	98	107	119
Official/off. supported	75	82	91	119	178	176	151	125
Financial markets	48	62	68	61	38	23	15	12
Other private	–	–	–	–	–	–	–	–
II. Multilateral	75	97	141	164	163	128	107	147
of which: concessional	20	27	37	42	44	34	31	33
memo: IMF, total	58	77	114	134	128	94	68	104
III. Non-OECD creditor countries	32	28	32	33	31	32	26	28
Subtotal: Service payments, long term debt	*269*	*312*	*383*	*445*	*498*	*456*	*406*	*431*
of which: concessional	59	69	88	110	132	133	138	152
Amortization, long term debt	149	178	249	300	345	299	251	296
Interest, long term debt	121	134	134	144	153	158	154	135
Interest, short term debt	58	33	31	39	54	76	69	48
Total service payments	**327**	**345**	**414**	**484**	**552**	**532**	**475**	**479**

SUDAN

US $ Million

	1984	1985	1986	1987	1988	1989	1990	1991
GROSS DEBT								
Long term								
I. OECD countries and capital markets	2405	2731	2860	3417	3223	3501	3720	3354
ODA	320	426	510	587	643	631	638	660
Official/off. supported	1385	1749	1782	2000	1741	1953	2108	2069
Official export credits	1134	1306	1453	1686	1578	1808	1963	1952
Guaranteed supplier credits	96	80	169	170	68	67	52	35
Guaranteed bank credits	155	363	159	144	95	78	92	81
Financial markets	701	556	568	831	840	917	974	626
Banks	701	556	568	831	840	917	974	626
Bonds	–	–	–	–	–	–	–	–
Other private	–	–	–	–	–	–	–	–
II. Multilateral	1545	1698	1895	2189	2279	2364	2679	2776
of which: concessional	857	932	1041	1197	1340	1430	1665	1757
non-concessional	687	766	854	992	939	934	1015	1019
memo: IMF, total	664	739	823	954	905	884	956	961
III. Non-OECD Creditor countries	2697	2876	2806	2886	2997	3137	3168	3169
C.E.E.C.	161	165	153	152	199	288	290	290
Arab countries	2143	2220	2224	2310	2369	2374	2410	2416
Other countries and unspecified	394	491	429	424	430	476	467	463
Subtotal: Long term debt	*6647*	*7305*	*7561*	*8493*	*8500*	*9002*	*9567*	*9299*
of which: concessional	1177	1358	1551	1784	1982	2062	2303	2417
non-concessional	5470	5946	6010	6709	6517	6940	7264	6882
Short term								
Subtotal: Short term debt	*711*	*1041*	*1178*	*1361*	*1310*	*1424*	*1752*	*1891*
Banks	525	784	762	783	710	782	936	777
Export credits	186	257	416	578	600	642	816	1114
Other identified liabilities	–	–	–	–	–	–	–	–
Total identified debt	**7358**	**8346**	**8739**	**9854**	**9809**	**10426**	**11320**	**11191**
SERVICE PAYMENTS								
Long term								
I. OECD countries and capital markets	154	153	145	153	202	188	135	119
ODA	5	4	13	10	5	10	14	14
Official/off. supported	79	85	93	100	105	96	38	34
Financial markets	70	64	39	43	93	81	82	70
Other private	–	–	–	–	–	–	–	–
II. Multilateral	96	56	125	48	40	67	25	23
of which: concessional	16	14	100	32	35	51	22	20
memo: IMF, total	61	40	22	14	1	29	1	–
III. Non-OECD creditor countries	36	17	93	19	38	17	–	–
Subtotal: Service payments, long term debt	*286*	*226*	*363*	*220*	*280*	*272*	*160*	*142*
of which: concessional	21	18	112	43	40	62	36	35
Amortization, long term debt	126	34	158	42	82	64	19	16
Interest, long term debt	161	192	205	177	198	208	141	125
Interest, short term debt	58	56	54	54	60	69	73	53
Total service payments	**344**	**282**	**416**	**273**	**340**	**341**	**233**	**195**

SURINAME

US $ Million

	1984	1985	1986	1987	1988	1989	1990	1991
GROSS DEBT								
Long term								
I. OECD countries and capital markets	14	26	23	23	35	26	49	35
ODA	1	1	1	1	1	1	0	0
Official/off. supported	0	16	9	9	9	6	14	10
Official export credits	–	–	1	–	–	–	–	–
Guaranteed supplier credits	0	8	–	–	0	1	–	–
Guaranteed bank credits	0	9	8	9	9	5	14	10
Financial markets	13	8	13	13	26	20	35	25
Banks	13	8	13	13	26	20	35	25
Bonds	–	–	–	–	–	–	–	–
Other private	–	–	–	–	–	–	–	–
II. Multilateral	6	6	7	10	11	17	22	22
of which: concessional	6	6	7	9	9	15	16	16
non-concessional	–	–	–	1	2	2	6	6
memo: IMF, total	–	–	–	–	–	–	–	–
III. Non-OECD Creditor countries	10	11	11	11	11	11	11	11
C.E.E.C.	–	–	–	–	–	–	–	–
Arab countries	10	11	11	11	11	11	11	11
Other countries and unspecified	–	–	–	–	–	–	–	–
Subtotal: Long term debt	*29*	*43*	*40*	*43*	*57*	*54*	*82*	*68*
of which: concessional	16	18	19	21	20	26	27	27
non-concessional	13	25	22	22	37	28	55	41
Short term								
Subtotal: Short term debt	*30*	*14*	*19*	*30*	*14*	*24*	*28*	*102*
Banks	27	8	15	23	4	13	16	96
Export credits	3	6	4	7	10	11	12	6
Other identified liabilities	–	–	–	–	–	–	–	–
Total identified debt	**59**	**57**	**60**	**73**	**71**	**77**	**110**	**170**
SERVICE PAYMENTS								
Long term								
I. OECD countries and capital markets	3	3	3	9	3	7	13	10
ODA	0	0	0	0	0	0	0	0
Official/off. supported	0	1	1	8	1	1	8	6
Financial markets	3	3	1	1	2	6	4	4
Other private	–	–	–	–	–	–	–	–
II. Multilateral	0	1	0	1	1	0	0	1
of which: concessional	0	1	0	1	0	0	0	1
memo: IMF, total	–	–	–	–	–	–	–	–
III. Non-OECD creditor countries	0	0	1	1	0	0	0	1
Subtotal: Service payments, long term debt	*4*	*4*	*4*	*11*	*4*	*7*	*14*	*12*
of which: concessional	1	1	1	2	1	1	1	2
Amortization, long term debt	2	2	1	6	1	4	11	7
Interest, long term debt	2	3	3	5	2	4	3	6
Interest, short term debt	4	2	1	2	1	1	1	3
Total service payments	**7**	**6**	**5**	**12**	**5**	**8**	**15**	**16**

US $ Million

	1984	1985	1986	1987	1988	1989	1990	1991
GROSS DEBT								
Long term								
I. OECD countries and capital markets	99	147	126	148	190	109	116	110
ODA	64	58	70	88	146	70	81	79
Official/off. supported	20	34	34	51	30	25	28	27
Official export credits	12	13	18	36	16	15	19	22
Guaranteed supplier credits	3	8	2	1	0	–	1	0
Guaranteed bank credits	5	13	14	14	14	10	8	6
Financial markets	15	55	22	9	13	14	7	4
Banks	15	55	22	9	13	14	7	4
Bonds	–	–	–	–	–	–	–	–
Other private	–	–	–	–	–	–	–	–
II. Multilateral	103	115	138	160	140	134	121	121
of which: concessional	30	32	37	43	41	45	52	55
non-concessional	73	83	101	118	98	89	69	65
memo: IMF, total	14	14	11	6	2	0	0	–
III. Non-OECD Creditor countries	1	16	17	17	13	11	11	9
C.E.E.C.	–	–	–	–	–	–	–	–
Arab countries	–	–	–	–	–	–	–	–
Other countries and unspecified	1	16	17	17	13	11	11	9
Subtotal: Long term debt	*202*	*279*	*281*	*326*	*342*	*254*	*248*	*240*
of which: concessional	95	91	107	131	188	115	133	134
non-concessional	108	188	175	195	155	139	115	106
Short term								
Subtotal: Short term debt	*37*	*14*	*17*	*12*	*25*	*21*	*2*	*4*
Banks	36	13	17	12	17	17	1	3
Export credits	1	1	0	0	8	4	1	1
Other identified liabilities	–	–	–	–	–	–	–	–
Total identified debt	**239**	**292**	**298**	**338**	**367**	**275**	**249**	**244**
SERVICE PAYMENTS								
Long term								
I. OECD countries and capital markets	8	19	33	31	20	16	21	13
ODA	4	4	1	4	10	5	7	6
Official/off. supported	3	5	9	11	9	10	9	6
Financial markets	1	10	22	15	1	2	4	2
Other private	–	–	–	–	–	–	–	–
II. Multilateral	13	15	21	27	26	21	40	15
of which: concessional	1	2	4	5	5	3	2	2
memo: IMF, total	1	2	6	6	4	1	0	0
III. Non-OECD creditor countries	0	1	3	3	3	3	2	2
Subtotal: Service payments, long term debt	*21*	*35*	*57*	*62*	*49*	*40*	*63*	*30*
of which: concessional	5	6	5	9	14	8	10	7
Amortization, long term debt	9	24	42	44	33	26	50	20
Interest, long term debt	12	11	15	18	16	14	13	10
Interest, short term debt	4	2	1	1	1	2	1	0
Total service payments	**25**	**37**	**58**	**63**	**50**	**42**	**64**	**30**

US $ Million

	1984	1985	1986	1987	1988	1989	1990	1991
GROSS DEBT								
Long term								
I. OECD countries and capital markets	345	393	400	772	968	1033	1177	1293
ODA	105	133	195	557	674	757	857	993
Official/off. supported	168	187	167	182	219	166	208	142
Official export credits	0	1	1	4	53	44	46	48
Guaranteed supplier credits	106	109	88	93	121	87	124	66
Guaranteed bank credits	62	77	78	85	45	36	38	28
Financial markets	72	73	38	33	76	110	112	158
Banks	72	73	38	33	76	110	112	158
Bonds	–	–	–	–	–	–	–	–
Other private	–	–	–	–	–	–	–	–
II. Multilateral	393	504	727	954	997	1014	1069	1045
of which: concessional	118	129	176	225	245	254	265	262
non-concessional	275	375	551	729	752	760	804	783
memo: IMF, total	–	–	–	–	–	–	–	–
III. Non-OECD Creditor countries	6037	7991	10123	12713	13284	13751	12685	11560
C.E.E.C.	5442	7336	9072	11648	12243	12738	11686	10598
Arab countries	568	556	521	530	507	480	473	442
Other countries and unspecified	27	99	529	535	535	533	527	521
Subtotal: Long term debt	*6776*	*8888*	*11249*	*14440*	*15249*	*15798*	*14932*	*13898*
of which: concessional	224	262	371	782	919	1011	1122	1255
non-concessional	6552	8625	10879	13658	14330	14787	13810	12643
Short term								
Subtotal: Short term debt	*1016*	*1307*	*1359*	*1479*	*1125*	*1037*	*948*	*822*
Banks	879	1070	1040	1061	861	822	797	632
Export credits	137	237	319	418	264	215	151	190
Other identified liabilities	–	–	–	–	–	–	–	–
Total identified debt	**7792**	**10195**	**12609**	**15919**	**16374**	**16834**	**15880**	**14719**
SERVICE PAYMENTS								
Long term								
I. OECD countries and capital markets	77	87	109	164	147	123	125	152
ODA	10	10	12	9	18	10	39	61
Official/off. supported	60	69	74	77	18	35	37	22
Financial markets	7	7	23	78	111	77	49	69
Other private	–	–	–	–	–	–	–	–
II. Multilateral	56	59	54	40	44	71	88	86
of which: concessional	10	11	13	13	14	20	28	27
memo: IMF, total	–	–	–	–	–	–	–	–
III. Non-OECD creditor countries	179	189	177	207	321	826	1202	438
Subtotal: Service payments, long term debt	*311*	*335*	*340*	*411*	*512*	*1020*	*1415*	*677*
of which: concessional	19	22	25	22	32	30	67	88
Amortization, long term debt	228	248	256	323	404	906	1274	529
Interest, long term debt	83	87	83	88	107	114	141	148
Interest, short term debt	102	94	89	95	100	90	73	44
Total service payments	**413**	**429**	**429**	**506**	**611**	**1110**	**1488**	**720**

TAIWAN

US $ Million

	1984	1985	1986	1987	1988	1989	1990	1991
GROSS DEBT								
Long term								
I. OECD countries and capital markets	6134	5530	4117	3060	2958	2637	2708	3109
ODA	81	86	33	37	55	14	13	12
Official/off. supported	2880	2637	2012	828	516	310	317	334
Official export credits	1511	1269	972	6	3	2	1	–
Guaranteed supplier credits	1017	1061	797	616	441	277	272	201
Guaranteed bank credits	353	307	242	206	72	31	44	133
Financial markets	2772	2332	1522	1495	1488	1413	1277	1663
Banks	2520	2065	1257	1193	1063	908	877	993
Bonds	253	267	266	302	425	505	400	670
Other private	400	475	550	700	900	900	1100	1100
II. Multilateral	146	142	135	5	–	–	–	–
of which: concessional	–	–	–	–	–	–	–	–
non-concessional	146	142	135	5	–	–	–	–
memo: IMF, total	–	–	–	–	–	–	–	–
III. Non-OECD Creditor countries	103	114	105	105	105	105	135	135
C.E.E.C.	–	–	–	–	–	–	–	–
Arab countries	103	114	105	105	105	105	135	135
Other countries and unspecified	–	–	–	–	–	–	–	–
Subtotal: Long term debt	*6383*	*5786*	*4357*	*3170*	*3063*	*2742*	*2843*	*3244*
of which: concessional	185	200	138	142	160	119	148	147
non-concessional	6199	5586	4220	3028	2903	2623	2695	3097
Short term								
Subtotal: Short term debt	*3262*	*3360*	*8400*	*16932*	*15532*	*15148*	*15616*	*16656*
Banks	3140	3171	8124	16640	15173	14784	15421	16392
Export credits	122	189	276	292	359	364	195	264
Other identified liabilities	–	–	–	–	–	–	–	–
Total identified debt	**9645**	**9146**	**12757**	**20102**	**18595**	**17890**	**18459**	**19900**
SERVICE PAYMENTS								
Long term								
I. OECD countries and capital markets	2058	2004	1310	1813	497	510	557	949
ODA	6	5	3	2	3	3	2	2
Official/off. supported	813	1285	925	1517	322	273	213	526
Financial markets	1202	642	309	261	123	144	129	145
Other private	37	72	73	33	49	90	213	277
II. Multilateral	27	25	30	140	9	7	9	1
of which: concessional	–	–	–	–	–	–	–	–
memo: IMF, total	–	–	–	–	–	–	–	–
III. Non-OECD creditor countries	3	12	17	6	2	2	20	9
Subtotal: Service payments, long term debt	*2088*	*2041*	*1357*	*1960*	*508*	*519*	*586*	*960*
of which: concessional	9	17	20	9	5	5	22	11
Amortization, long term debt	1537	1520	974	1675	298	260	383	750
Interest, long term debt	551	521	384	285	210	260	203	210
Interest, short term debt	339	271	399	873	1298	1380	1277	968
Total service payments	**2427**	**2312**	**1757**	**2833**	**1806**	**1899**	**1862**	**1928**

TANZANIA

US $ Million

	1984	1985	1986	1987	1988	1989	1990	1991
GROSS DEBT								
Long term								
I. OECD countries and capital markets	765	795	1035	1208	1077	1326	1550	1427
ODA	369	464	461	704	580	682	629	565
Official/off. supported	324	285	568	496	490	638	915	863
Official export credits	134	129	305	267	267	486	767	726
Guaranteed supplier credits	99	35	156	76	122	92	94	85
Guaranteed bank credits	92	120	107	153	100	60	54	52
Financial markets	71	46	6	7	7	6	6	–
Banks	67	40	–	–	–	–	–	–
Bonds	5	6	6	7	7	6	6	–
Other private	0	0	0	0	0	0	0	0
II. Multilateral	937	1089	1253	1464	1554	1617	1894	2038
of which: concessional	709	807	913	1050	1192	1286	1589	1791
non-concessional	228	283	340	413	362	331	305	247
memo: IMF, total	59	58	71	113	141	129	140	113
III. Non-OECD Creditor countries	979	1033	1093	1150	1150	1128	1196	1192
C.E.E.C.	258	286	326	369	486	507	584	584
Arab countries	190	223	252	259	206	201	204	216
Other countries and unspecified	531	524	515	522	457	420	408	392
Subtotal: Long term debt	*2680*	*2917*	*3381*	*3821*	*3781*	*4071*	*4641*	*4657*
of which: concessional	1078	1271	1374	1754	1772	1968	2218	2356
non-concessional	1602	1647	2007	2067	2009	2103	2423	2301
Short term								
Subtotal: Short term debt	*328*	*509*	*658*	*674*	*529*	*458*	*523*	*503*
Banks	73	130	197	242	108	112	116	65
Export credits	255	379	460	432	421	346	407	437
Other identified liabilities	–	–	–	545	621	–	–	–
Total identified debt	**3009**	**3426**	**4038**	**5040**	**4931**	**4529**	**5164**	**5160**
SERVICE PAYMENTS								
Long term								
I. OECD countries and capital markets	25	34	38	48	35	49	42	42
ODA	4	8	9	21	17	22	32	11
Official/off. supported	12	10	26	21	14	22	20	29
Financial markets	10	16	3	6	5	5	–	2
Other private	–	–	–	–	–	–	–	0
II. Multilateral	75	60	105	99	92	89	116	122
of which: concessional	15	15	31	33	32	31	35	39
memo: IMF, total	33	9	36	19	13	15	34	29
III. Non-OECD creditor countries	8	2	–	2	10	13	12	1
Subtotal: Service payments, long term debt	*109*	*95*	*143*	*150*	*137*	*151*	*169*	*164*
of which: concessional	19	23	40	55	49	53	57	50
Amortization, long term debt	62	59	81	79	62	77	97	103
Interest, long term debt	46	36	62	71	75	73	73	61
Interest, short term debt	20	18	17	37	63	40	10	6
Total service payments	**128**	**113**	**160**	**186**	**200**	**190**	**180**	**170**

THAILAND

US $ Million

	1984	1985	1986	1987	1988	1989	1990	1991
GROSS DEBT								
Long term								
I. OECD countries and capital markets	8538	10595	10707	12517	11693	13254	16476	20002
ODA	1187	1758	2331	3164	3317	3244	3877	4463
Official/off. supported	1419	1689	1788	2452	1383	1547	2492	2773
Official export credits	719	878	982	1013	817	825	1037	1337
Guaranteed supplier credits	398	452	428	1078	339	391	970	683
Guaranteed bank credits	302	360	378	361	228	331	485	753
Financial markets	5432	6648	6088	6301	6293	7762	9357	12016
Banks	5020	6150	5623	5842	5753	7211	7981	10840
Bonds	412	498	465	459	540	551	1376	1177
Other private	500	500	500	600	700	700	750	750
II. Multilateral	3298	4218	4849	5388	4291	3585	3708	3523
of which: concessional	336	354	365	348	303	273	298	315
non-concessional	2963	3864	4484	5040	3989	3313	3410	3208
memo: IMF, total	903	1122	1069	972	662	273	1	–
III. Non-OECD Creditor countries	80	1290	1350	1905	1896	1880	1873	1868
C.E.E.C.	–	–	–	–	–	–	–	–
Arab countries	80	94	101	101	92	83	77	71
Other countries and unspecified	–	1196	1249	1804	1804	1797	1797	1797
Subtotal: Long term debt	*11916*	*16103*	*16906*	*19810*	*17880*	*18719*	*22057*	*25394*
of which: concessional	1522	2112	2697	3512	3620	3517	4174	4778
non-concessional	10394	13991	14209	16298	14261	15202	17883	20616
Short term								
Subtotal: Short term debt	*2243*	*1204*	*1374*	*2227*	*3681*	*3619*	*7657*	*11174*
Banks	2163	1073	1234	2084	3490	3465	7472	10986
Export credits	80	131	140	144	191	154	185	188
Other identified liabilities	325	467	478	641	667	948	933	1070
Total identified debt	**14484**	**17774**	**18758**	**22678**	**22228**	**23286**	**30648**	**37637**
SERVICE PAYMENTS								
Long term								
I. OECD countries and capital markets	2086	2231	2551	2362	2301	2789	3571	2741
ODA	75	81	102	134	183	189	216	268
Official/off. supported	445	492	617	850	774	621	820	810
Financial markets	1484	1618	1797	1348	1302	1909	2386	1511
Other private	83	40	35	30	42	70	149	153
II. Multilateral	402	628	843	902	1346	1157	1025	764
of which: concessional	30	38	52	59	52	37	29	22
memo: IMF, total	145	312	380	316	319	412	302	1
III. Non-OECD creditor countries	5	5	9	10	11	10	10	10
Subtotal: Service payments, long term debt	*2493*	*2864*	*3403*	*3275*	*3658*	*3956*	*4606*	*3515*
of which: concessional	104	119	155	193	235	226	245	290
Amortization, long term debt	1487	1880	2326	2142	2486	2789	3324	2321
Interest, long term debt	1006	984	1077	1132	1171	1167	1282	1194
Interest, short term debt	483	174	120	163	288	401	545	624
Total service payments	**2976**	**3038**	**3523**	**3437**	**3946**	**4357**	**5150**	**4139**

TOGO

US $ Million

	1984	1985	1986	1987	1988	1989	1990	1991
GROSS DEBT								
Long term								
I. OECD countries and capital markets	514	448	413	493	478	419	487	493
ODA	137	43	72	102	135	148	203	211
Official/off. supported	302	326	286	341	284	229	247	246
Official export credits	266	302	242	317	258	203	219	218
Guaranteed supplier credits	6	5	32	21	20	19	23	24
Guaranteed bank credits	31	19	12	3	6	7	6	4
Financial markets	75	79	55	50	59	41	36	36
Banks	75	79	55	50	59	41	36	36
Bonds	–	–	–	–	–	–	–	–
Other private	–	–	–	–	–	–	–	–
II. Multilateral	294	367	455	523	552	578	653	673
of which: concessional	209	258	328	389	432	488	582	620
non-concessional	85	108	127	134	120	90	71	53
memo: IMF, total	62	74	90	85	78	75	87	79
III. Non-OECD Creditor countries	14	21	25	29	27	23	22	19
C.E.E.C.	–	–	–	–	–	–	–	–
Arab countries	7	16	22	27	25	23	22	19
Other countries and unspecified	7	5	3	2	2	–	–	–
Subtotal: Long term debt	*822*	*836*	*893*	*1044*	*1056*	*1020*	*1162*	*1186*
of which: concessional	346	301	400	490	567	637	785	831
non-concessional	476	535	493	554	489	383	377	355
Short term								
Subtotal: Short term debt	*92*	*135*	*188*	*255*	*190*	*289*	*291*	*140*
Banks	24	47	66	115	90	180	201	61
Export credits	68	88	122	140	100	109	90	79
Other identified liabilities	13	14	29	38	28	32	39	39
Total identified debt	**927**	**985**	**1111**	**1337**	**1275**	**1342**	**1492**	**1365**
SERVICE PAYMENTS								
Long term								
I. OECD countries and capital markets	79	38	77	44	80	54	54	40
ODA	13	5	8	5	25	9	9	5
Official/off. supported	57	24	53	31	48	37	40	28
Financial markets	9	9	16	8	7	8	5	6
Other private	–	–	–	–	–	–	–	–
II. Multilateral	22	29	28	46	56	55	44	33
of which: concessional	7	7	9	12	12	12	11	10
memo: IMF, total	10	16	12	24	32	28	20	11
III. Non-OECD creditor countries	4	3	4	3	3	5	1	4
Subtotal: Service payments, long term debt	*104*	*70*	*109*	*92*	*139*	*114*	*99*	*76*
of which: concessional	20	13	16	17	37	21	20	16
Amortization, long term debt	54	33	71	50	88	76	64	46
Interest, long term debt	50	37	38	42	52	38	35	31
Interest, short term debt	9	8	9	13	16	20	24	14
Total service payments	**113**	**78**	**118**	**105**	**155**	**134**	**123**	**90**

TRINIDAD AND TOBAGO

US $ Million

	1984	1985	1986	1987	1988	1989	1990	1991
GROSS DEBT								
Long term								
I. OECD countries and capital markets	1432	1744	1774	1989	2140	1821	1646	1352
ODA	9	8	25	65	59	56	62	52
Official/off. supported	581	616	590	592	704	631	666	508
Official export credits	301	306	265	238	280	244	282	317
Guaranteed supplier credits	107	128	141	126	284	205	222	62
Guaranteed bank credits	174	183	184	227	139	182	162	128
Financial markets	842	1120	1159	1331	1378	1135	919	792
Banks	591	717	692	637	628	496	432	319
Bonds	251	402	467	695	750	638	487	473
Other private	–	–	–	–	–	–	–	–
II. Multilateral	51	57	66	73	183	277	440	556
of which: concessional	22	23	24	27	23	20	25	28
non-concessional	29	34	42	46	160	257	415	528
memo: IMF, total	–	–	–	–	115	205	329	385
III. Non-OECD Creditor countries	–	–	0	1	1	1	1	1
C.E.E.C.	–	–	–	–	–	–	–	–
Arab countries	–	–	–	–	–	–	–	–
Other countries and unspecified	–	–	0	1	1	1	1	1
Subtotal: Long term debt	*1484*	*1801*	*1840*	*2062*	*2323*	*2098*	*2088*	*1909*
of which: concessional	31	31	49	92	81	76	87	80
non-concessional	1453	1770	1791	1970	2242	2022	2001	1829
Short term								
Subtotal: Short term debt	*157*	*149*	*284*	*166*	*178*	*170*	*272*	*363*
Banks	113	91	220	130	133	129	183	275
Export credits	44	58	64	36	45	41	89	88
Other identified liabilities	72	42	30	30	27	27	27	23
Total identified debt	**1713**	**1992**	**2154**	**2258**	**2528**	**2295**	**2387**	**2295**
SERVICE PAYMENTS								
Long term								
I. OECD countries and capital markets	195	301	321	334	274	245	293	213
ODA	1	1	1	2	4	7	2	11
Official/off. supported	112	166	154	190	104	108	89	156
Financial markets	82	134	166	142	165	130	202	47
Other private	–	–	–	–	–	–	–	–
II. Multilateral	9	10	13	16	15	29	40	49
of which: concessional	3	4	5	5	6	6	4	5
memo: IMF, total	–	–	–	–	–	13	24	29
III. Non-OECD creditor countries	–	–	0	0	2	0	2	2
Subtotal: Service payments, long term debt	*204*	*311*	*333*	*350*	*291*	*274*	*335*	*264*
of which: concessional	4	5	6	6	11	13	7	16
Amortization, long term debt	93	183	219	229	169	112	191	154
Interest, long term debt	111	128	114	121	122	162	144	111
Interest, short term debt	37	17	17	17	15	16	17	17
Total service payments	**241**	**328**	**350**	**367**	**306**	**290**	**352**	**281**

US $ Million

	1984	1985	1986	1987	1988	1989	1990	1991
GROSS DEBT								
Long term								
I. OECD countries and capital markets	3180	3684	3565	3857	4127	3540	3725	3729
ODA	1026	1268	1521	1859	1816	1931	2113	2277
Official/off. supported	1570	1686	1636	1613	1727	1150	1498	1117
Official export credits	786	809	674	634	406	286	299	313
Guaranteed supplier credits	150	164	176	132	645	205	397	111
Guaranteed bank credits	634	714	786	847	676	658	802	693
Financial markets	585	729	408	386	584	460	114	335
Banks	524	669	348	326	524	400	114	335
Bonds	60	60	60	60	60	60	–	–
Other private	–	–	–	–	–	–	–	–
II. Multilateral	608	826	1316	1808	1843	2081	2423	3021
of which: concessional	118	136	174	210	218	239	332	418
non-concessional	490	691	1142	1598	1625	1841	2091	2603
memo: IMF, total	–	–	183	271	277	270	176	258
III. Non-OECD Creditor countries	527	533	547	543	545	542	534	557
C.E.E.C.	79	91	102	100	94	77	74	66
Arab countries	401	401	410	403	412	432	428	458
Other countries and unspecified	47	41	36	40	39	33	31	33
Subtotal: Long term debt	*4315*	*5043*	*5429*	*6208*	*6515*	*6163*	*6682*	*7307*
of which: concessional	1144	1404	1695	2069	2034	2170	2445	2694
non-concessional	3171	3639	3733	4139	4481	3993	4236	4612
Short term								
Subtotal: Short term debt	*317*	*419*	*991*	*1058*	*1037*	*1044*	*1199*	*894*
Banks	175	251	835	870	773	757	812	519
Export credits	142	168	156	187	264	287	387	374
Other identified liabilities	377	439	398	398	516	528	655	1250
Total identified debt	**5009**	**5901**	**6818**	**7664**	**8068**	**7735**	**8536**	**9450**
SERVICE PAYMENTS								
Long term								
I. OECD countries and capital markets	531	613	496	542	669	789	848	747
ODA	54	57	76	109	103	122	183	165
Official/off. supported	407	493	357	394	331	369	407	351
Financial markets	69	63	63	40	235	297	258	231
Other private	–	–	–	–	–	–	–	–
II. Multilateral	102	111	172	243	285	284	450	516
of which: concessional	5	6	8	11	13	13	17	26
memo: IMF, total	–	–	–	13	17	23	135	153
III. Non-OECD creditor countries	67	71	68	102	84	95	68	54
Subtotal: Service payments, long term debt	*699*	*796*	*737*	*888*	*1038*	*1169*	*1366*	*1317*
of which: concessional	59	63	84	120	116	135	200	191
Amortization, long term debt	442	515	432	553	685	795	977	969
Interest, long term debt	257	281	304	335	353	374	390	348
Interest, short term debt	69	63	76	98	119	139	140	117
Total service payments	**769**	**859**	**813**	**986**	**1157**	**1308**	**1506**	**1434**

US $ Million

	1984	1985	1986	1987	1988	1989	1990	1991
GROSS DEBT								
Long term								
I. OECD countries and capital markets	10884	13177	16423	21272	24646	27123	31556	32702
ODA	3170	3588	4266	5117	4950	4936	5795	6058
Official/off. supported	4367	5335	6404	7973	8399	8483	10474	10125
Official export credits	2856	3209	3377	3723	3066	2994	3179	3104
Guaranteed supplier credits	569	795	1021	1252	1142	911	587	603
Guaranteed bank credits	942	1330	2006	2998	4192	4578	6708	6419
Financial markets	3347	4254	5753	8183	11296	13704	15287	16518
Banks	3324	4158	5536	7621	8556	9160	10093	10834
Bonds	23	97	217	562	2741	4543	5194	5684
Other private	–	–	–	–	–	–	–	–
II. Multilateral	4951	6273	7793	9766	9105	8673	9630	9929
of which: concessional	542	647	949	1257	1294	1267	1400	1390
non-concessional	4408	5626	6844	8509	7812	7407	8231	8539
memo: IMF, total	1426	1326	1085	770	299	48	–	–
III. Non-OECD Creditor countries	1704	2016	2153	2109	1791	1661	1419	1201
C.E.E.C.	934	1019	1055	945	853	942	857	760
Arab countries	727	915	1007	1101	871	673	530	407
Other countries and unspecified	44	82	91	63	67	45	32	33
Subtotal: Long term debt	*17539*	*21466*	*26369*	*33148*	*35543*	*37458*	*42606*	*43831*
of which: concessional	3712	4235	5215	6374	6244	6203	7195	7447
non-concessional	13827	17231	21154	26774	29298	31255	35411	36384
Short term								
Subtotal: Short term debt	*2670*	*4042*	*5136*	*6306*	*4363*	*4582*	*7978*	*7631*
Banks	2181	3388	4509	5261	3727	4009	7234	6927
Export credits	489	654	627	1045	636	573	744	704
Other identified liabilities	492	551	366	398	670	362	668	709
Total identified debt	**20701**	**26059**	**31871**	**39852**	**40575**	**42402**	**51253**	**52171**
SERVICE PAYMENTS								
Long term								
I. OECD countries and capital markets	1714	2584	2441	3148	4428	5076	4566	5303
ODA	208	187	276	232	391	461	505	464
Official/off. supported	1122	1076	1224	1558	2106	2466	1927	1973
Financial markets	384	1321	942	1358	1931	2150	2133	2866
Other private	–	–	–	–	–	–	–	–
II. Multilateral	812	929	1248	1517	1744	1549	1546	1521
of which: concessional	34	33	43	65	80	104	81	69
memo: IMF, total	395	412	499	534	486	250	53	–
III. Non-OECD creditor countries	223	259	312	535	604	556	468	295
Subtotal: Service payments, long term debt	*2750*	*3771*	*4002*	*5200*	*6776*	*7181*	*6580*	*7119*
of which: concessional	241	220	319	297	471	565	587	533
Amortization, long term debt	1381	2400	2439	3252	4170	4707	4128	4811
Interest, long term debt	1369	1371	1563	1948	2607	2474	2453	2308
Interest, short term debt	246	307	329	394	442	436	558	507
Total service payments	**2996**	**4078**	**4331**	**5595**	**7218**	**7617**	**7138**	**7626**

UGANDA

US $ Million

	1984	1985	1986	1987	1988	1989	1990	1991
GROSS DEBT								
Long term								
I. OECD countries and capital markets	158	150	114	120	255	305	274	216
ODA	29	32	32	43	53	66	67	61
Official/off. supported	107	102	63	34	168	226	169	128
Official export credits	40	46	41	29	142	183	112	87
Guaranteed supplier credits	43	32	0	5	26	17	21	12
Guaranteed bank credits	24	24	22	0	–	25	36	29
Financial markets	18	15	15	38	30	10	10	–
Banks	18	6	6	27	19	–	–	–
Bonds	–	9	9	11	11	10	10	–
Other private	3	1	4	5	4	4	27	27
II. Multilateral	651	760	830	1107	1149	1232	1579	1874
of which: concessional	272	390	487	692	796	969	1342	1681
non-concessional	379	370	343	415	353	264	237	193
memo: IMF, total	337	305	249	274	252	225	282	330
III. Non-OECD Creditor countries	193	209	215	313	388	472	485	461
C.E.E.C.	46	51	53	100	78	93	101	101
Arab countries	39	39	44	40	32	119	117	118
Other countries and unspecified	108	119	117	173	278	260	267	243
Subtotal: Long term debt	*1002*	*1118*	*1158*	*1540*	*1792*	*2010*	*2338*	*2551*
of which: concessional	301	422	519	735	849	1035	1409	1742
non-concessional	701	696	639	805	944	975	929	809
Short term								
Subtotal: Short term debt	*34*	*40*	*90*	*106*	*117*	*123*	*151*	*125*
Banks	19	16	41	34	44	52	62	24
Export credits	15	23	49	72	73	71	90	102
Other identified liabilities	–	–	–	–	–	–	–	–
Total identified debt	**1035**	**1158**	**1248**	**1645**	**1909**	**2133**	**2490**	**2677**
SERVICE PAYMENTS								
Long term								
I. OECD countries and capital markets	48	40	16	5	22	32	31	38
ODA	2	2	4	2	3	2	4	2
Official/off. supported	33	15	9	2	9	8	25	10
Financial markets	12	23	2	1	9	22	1	24
Other private	–	–	1	–	–	–	0	2
II. Multilateral	79	113	138	122	119	130	88	80
of which: concessional	4	10	14	17	19	17	18	20
memo: IMF, total	69	97	112	91	83	90	58	42
III. Non-OECD creditor countries	45	13	19	12	37	21	8	27
Subtotal: Service payments, long term debt	*171*	*166*	*172*	*139*	*178*	*182*	*127*	*145*
of which: concessional	7	12	17	19	22	19	21	22
Amortization, long term debt	106	119	126	99	149	143	96	110
Interest, long term debt	65	47	47	41	29	39	32	36
Interest, short term debt	2	2	2	3	3	5	5	3
Total service payments	**174**	**168**	**174**	**142**	**181**	**187**	**132**	**148**

UNITED ARAB EMIRATES

US $ Million

	1984	1985	1986	1987	1988	1989	1990	1991
GROSS DEBT								
Long term								
I. OECD countries and capital markets	1451	1244	1211	1426	1332	1439	1126	1033
ODA	1	1	35	166	131	126	128	110
Official/off. supported	663	348	323	382	236	353	265	253
Official export credits	2	2	0	–	1	1	1	0
Guaranteed supplier credits	392	138	90	72	66	7	–	85
Guaranteed bank credits	269	209	233	310	168	346	264	167
Financial markets	787	895	853	878	966	959	732	670
Banks	787	895	833	838	926	919	712	670
Bonds	–	–	20	40	40	40	20	–
Other private	–	–	–	–	–	–	–	–
II. Multilateral	13	14	15	17	17	17	17	17
of which: concessional	–	–	–	–	–	–	–	–
non-concessional	13	14	15	17	17	17	17	17
memo: IMF, total	–	–	–	–	–	–	–	–
III. Non-OECD Creditor countries	16	17	17	17	17	17	17	17
C.E.E.C.	–	–	–	–	–	–	–	–
Arab countries	16	17	17	17	17	17	17	17
Other countries and unspecified	–	–	–	–	–	–	–	–
Subtotal: Long term debt	*1480*	*1276*	*1243*	*1460*	*1367*	*1473*	*1160*	*1067*
of which: concessional	17	18	52	183	149	143	146	127
non-concessional	1463	1257	1192	1277	1218	1330	1014	940
Short term								
Subtotal: Short term debt	*8598*	*7658*	*7425*	*6705*	*8696*	*8731*	*9721*	*8307*
Banks	8371	7409	7120	6388	8419	8302	9326	8054
Export credits	227	250	305	317	277	429	395	253
Other identified liabilities	339	709	472	634	797	856	752	720
Total identified debt	**10416**	**9643**	**9140**	**8799**	**10860**	**11060**	**11633**	**10094**
SERVICE PAYMENTS								
Long term								
I. OECD countries and capital markets	617	693	384	464	262	244	356	378
ODA	0	0	0	2	10	13	18	17
Official/off. supported	378	464	284	358	148	106	182	245
Financial markets	238	229	100	104	103	125	155	116
Other private	–	–	–	–	–	–	–	–
II. Multilateral	–	–	–	1	–	1	1	1
of which: concessional	–	–	–	–	–	–	–	–
memo: IMF, total	–	–	–	–	–	–	–	–
III. Non-OECD creditor countries	1	1	1	1	0	0	0	1
Subtotal: Service payments, long term debt	*617*	*693*	*386*	*466*	*262*	*246*	*357*	*381*
of which: concessional	1	1	1	3	11	13	19	18
Amortization, long term debt	490	577	300	359	169	129	244	282
Interest, long term debt	127	116	86	107	92	116	113	98
Interest, short term debt	940	705	549	520	666	850	822	576
Total service payments	**1557**	**1399**	**934**	**987**	**928**	**1095**	**1180**	**957**

URUGUAY

US $ Million

	1984	1985	1986	1987	1988	1989	1990	1991
GROSS DEBT								
Long term								
I. OECD countries and capital markets	2098	2151	2323	2283	2381	2365	2215	2706
ODA	63	61	61	61	58	57	65	77
Official/off. supported	119	109	91	95	76	88	138	140
Official export credits	36	38	30	31	27	31	33	28
Guaranteed supplier credits	37	27	29	34	24	26	29	27
Guaranteed bank credits	46	44	32	30	25	32	76	85
Financial markets	1916	1980	2171	2127	2247	2219	2013	2489
Banks	1655	1630	1739	1687	1757	1638	1411	1030
Bonds	261	350	432	440	490	581	601	1459
Other private	–	–	–	–	–	–	–	–
II. Multilateral	461	654	788	943	874	827	800	915
of which: concessional	18	18	17	17	18	20	22	25
non-concessional	443	636	771	927	856	808	778	890
memo: IMF, total	222	350	395	392	309	202	101	58
III. Non-OECD Creditor countries	325	310	314	311	305	297	264	228
C.E.E.C.	9	6	5	4	4	4	3	2
Arab countries	–	–	–	–	–	–	–	–
Other countries and unspecified	317	304	309	306	302	294	262	227
Subtotal: Long term debt	*2885*	*3116*	*3425*	*3537*	*3560*	*3489*	*3279*	*3850*
of which: concessional	81	79	78	77	76	77	86	103
non-concessional	2803	3036	3348	3459	3485	3412	3193	3747
Short term								
Subtotal: Short term debt	*360*	*683*	*574*	*642*	*1529*	*917*	*1105*	*1447*
Banks	346	659	547	609	1498	887	1060	1402
Export credits	13	24	28	32	32	29	45	44
Other identified liabilities	443	439	523	821	1280	1808	2168	2329
Total identified debt	**3687**	**4238**	**4523**	**4999**	**6369**	**6214**	**6552**	**7625**
SERVICE PAYMENTS								
Long term								
I. OECD countries and capital markets	299	334	229	308	451	387	615	259
ODA	5	5	4	5	4	3	3	4
Official/off. supported	31	45	37	43	23	27	24	31
Financial markets	263	284	187	260	424	357	587	225
Other private	–	–	–	–	–	–	–	–
II. Multilateral	60	82	147	205	177	214	255	168
of which: concessional	1	1	1	1	1	1	1	1
memo: IMF, total	17	29	84	134	88	120	140	50
III. Non-OECD creditor countries	55	53	27	25	27	32	59	63
Subtotal: Service payments, long term debt	*414*	*469*	*402*	*539*	*655*	*633*	*929*	*491*
of which: concessional	6	6	5	6	5	5	4	5
Amortization, long term debt	152	204	163	263	375	319	620	290
Interest, long term debt	263	264	239	276	279	314	309	201
Interest, short term debt	87	79	75	88	170	249	249	211
Total service payments	**502**	**548**	**478**	**627**	**825**	**882**	**1178**	**702**

US $ Million

	1984	1985	1986	1987	1988	1989	1990	1991
GROSS DEBT								
Long term								
I. OECD countries and capital markets	59	105	135	122	154	172	225	356
ODA	2	3	4	7	8	9	12	15
Official/off. supported	20	61	51	33	22	20	23	21
Official export credits	2	3	2	3	5	5	10	10
Guaranteed supplier credits	10	37	32	18	13	9	5	2
Guaranteed bank credits	8	21	17	12	4	6	8	8
Financial markets	36	40	80	82	124	142	190	320
Banks	36	40	80	82	124	142	190	320
Bonds	–	–	–	–	–	–	–	–
Other private	–	–	–	–	–	–	–	–
II. Multilateral	1	1	2	6	8	13	17	21
of which: concessional	1	1	2	6	7	12	16	20
non-concessional	–	–	–	0	1	1	1	1
memo: IMF, total	–	–	–	–	–	–	–	–
III. Non-OECD Creditor countries	–	–	–	0	–	–	2	4
C.E.E.C.	–	–	–	–	–	–	–	–
Arab countries	–	–	–	–	–	–	–	–
Other countries and unspecified	–	–	–	0	–	–	2	4
Subtotal: Long term debt	*59*	*106*	*137*	*129*	*162*	*184*	*244*	*381*
of which: concessional	3	5	6	13	15	21	28	35
non-concessional	56	101	131	116	147	163	216	346
Short term								
Subtotal: Short term debt	*34*	*22*	*42*	*42*	*63*	*71*	*101*	*161*
Banks	32	20	40	40	61	69	100	160
Export credits	2	2	2	2	2	2	1	1
Other identified liabilities	–	–	–	–	–	–	58	17
Total identified debt	**93**	**128**	**179**	**171**	**225**	**255**	**403**	**560**
SERVICE PAYMENTS								
Long term								
I. OECD countries and capital markets	14	15	57	20	27	31	38	47
ODA	0	1	1	1	1	1	3	0
Official/off. supported	7	10	49	13	11	11	9	8
Financial markets	7	4	8	7	16	19	26	39
Other private	–	–	–	–	–	–	–	–
II. Multilateral	0	0	0	0	0	0	1	1
of which: concessional	0	0	0	0	0	0	1	1
memo: IMF, total	–	–	–	–	–	–	–	–
III. Non-OECD creditor countries	–	–	–	0	–	–	–	–
Subtotal: Service payments, long term debt	*14*	*15*	*58*	*21*	*27*	*31*	*39*	*48*
of which: concessional	0	1	1	1	1	1	4	1
Amortization, long term debt	9	11	49	10	18	17	23	32
Interest, long term debt	6	4	9	11	9	14	15	16
Interest, short term debt	3	2	2	3	4	6	9	10
Total service payments	**18**	**17**	**60**	**23**	**32**	**37**	**48**	**58**

VENEZUELA

	1984	1985	1986	1987	1988	1989	1990	1991
GROSS DEBT								
Long term								
I. OECD countries and capital markets	13353	12211	18481	22081	21864	20865	17591	16553
ODA	12	12	13	13	1	1	57	56
Official/off. supported	1233	838	782	1124	1101	1556	1603	2839
Official export credits	267	218	163	147	149	225	340	815
Guaranteed supplier credits	379	313	179	545	415	450	254	194
Guaranteed bank credits	587	308	440	432	537	881	1008	1830
Financial markets	11708	10960	17287	20545	20363	18908	15501	13228
Banks	10677	9909	16239	19465	18872	17398	14100	11288
Bonds	1030	1051	1048	1080	1491	1510	1401	1940
Other private	400	400	400	400	400	400	430	430
II. Multilateral	100	84	98	161	296	1558	4651	5459
of which: concessional	50	41	29	21	18	15	12	9
non-concessional	50	43	70	140	278	1543	4639	5450
memo: IMF, total	–	–	–	–	–	998	3012	3249
III. Non-OECD Creditor countries	1	19	58	83	101	91	44	15
C.E.E.C.	1	1	0	–	–	–	–	–
Arab countries	–	–	–	14	–	–	–	–
Other countries and unspecified	–	18	58	69	101	91	44	15
Subtotal: Long term debt	*13455*	*12314*	*18638*	*22325*	*22262*	*22514*	*22286*	*22028*
of which: concessional	62	53	41	34	19	16	69	66
non-concessional	13393	12261	18597	22291	22243	22498	22217	21962
Short term								
Subtotal: Short term debt	*15755*	*17253*	*9579*	*5839*	*6965*	*6377*	*4641*	*5139*
Banks	15430	16925	9147	5210	5765	5806	3986	4379
Export credits	325	328	432	629	1200	571	655	760
Other identified liabilities	–	–	–	–	–	–	–	–
Total identified debt	**29210**	**29567**	**28217**	**28164**	**29227**	**28891**	**26927**	**27166**
SERVICE PAYMENTS								
Long term								
I. OECD countries and capital markets	2799	2306	2808	3460	4209	2757	2919	2870
ODA	0	0	0	0	0	0	0	2
Official/off. supported	342	506	475	570	536	428	468	406
Financial markets	2418	1767	2304	2865	3645	2289	2383	2382
Other private	40	32	28	24	28	40	68	80
II. Multilateral	34	35	43	35	58	78	104	472
of which: concessional	16	15	16	8	4	4	4	3
memo: IMF, total	–	–	–	–	–	35	37	338
III. Non-OECD creditor countries	–	7	8	17	11	21	63	36
Subtotal: Service payments, long term debt	*2833*	*2348*	*2860*	*3512*	*4278*	*2856*	*3086*	*3378*
of which: concessional	16	15	16	9	4	4	4	5
Amortization, long term debt	1258	966	1955	2092	2410	740	1149	1850
Interest, long term debt	1575	1382	905	1419	1868	2116	1937	1528
Interest, short term debt	1614	1343	901	520	501	590	446	282
Total service payments	**4447**	**3690**	**3761**	**4032**	**4779**	**3446**	**3532**	**3661**

US $ Million

	1984	1985	1986	1987	1988	1989	1990	1991
GROSS DEBT								
Long term								
I. OECD countries and capital markets	553	688	692	839	788	743	659	737
ODA	308	363	401	486	475	444	480	495
Official/off. supported	76	75	54	89	50	53	140	63
Official export credits	16	16	5	6	1	10	13	13
Guaranteed supplier credits	30	34	7	3	1	–	65	–
Guaranteed bank credits	29	25	42	80	48	43	62	50
Financial markets	169	250	237	264	263	245	38	180
Banks	169	250	237	264	263	245	38	180
Bonds	–	–	–	–	–	–	–	–
Other private	–	–	–	–	–	–	–	–
II. Multilateral	264	302	339	382	373	321	324	314
of which: concessional	236	270	305	342	334	284	283	274
non-concessional	28	31	35	40	38	37	40	41
memo: IMF, total	115	129	144	167	158	108	112	102
III. Non-OECD Creditor countries	8382	9123	10011	12778	13542	14071	15143	15643
C.E.E.C.	8367	9106	9990	12757	13521	14043	15115	15615
Arab countries	16	17	21	21	21	28	28	28
Other countries and unspecified	–	–	–	–	–	–	–	–
Subtotal: Long term debt	*9199*	*10112*	*11043*	*13999*	*14703*	*15134*	*16125*	*16694*
of which: concessional	8926	9756	10717	13606	14351	14799	15907	16412
non-concessional	273	356	326	393	351	336	219	283
Short term								
Subtotal: Short term debt	*153*	*233*	*370*	*452*	*545*	*527*	*1223*	*1018*
Banks	95	128	163	181	275	245	878	677
Export credits	58	105	207	271	270	281	344	341
Other identified liabilities	–	–	–	–	–	–	–	–
Total identified debt	**9352**	**10345**	**11413**	**14451**	**15248**	**15661**	**17348**	**17713**
SERVICE PAYMENTS								
Long term								
I. OECD countries and capital markets	32	31	73	41	38	50	138	56
ODA	0	0	5	5	2	3	5	5
Official/off. supported	9	7	27	4	1	4	87	13
Financial markets	23	24	41	32	34	43	46	38
Other private	–	–	–	–	–	–	–	–
II. Multilateral	4	31	3	17	4	5	13	16
of which: concessional	1	29	1	15	1	5	10	16
memo: IMF, total	3	2	2	2	2	–	7	10
III. Non-OECD creditor countries	1	93	172	301	170	178	281	156
Subtotal: Service payments, long term debt	*37*	*156*	*248*	*359*	*212*	*233*	*432*	*228*
of which: concessional	2	122	178	321	174	186	296	177
Amortization, long term debt	13	15	72	56	13	27	113	49
Interest, long term debt	24	141	176	303	199	206	319	179
Interest, short term debt	11	9	10	13	19	24	48	47
Total service payments	**47**	**165**	**259**	**372**	**231**	**258**	**480**	**275**

US $ Million

	1984	1985	1986	1987	1988	1989	1990	1991
GROSS DEBT								
Long term								
I. OECD countries and capital markets	862	1054	1477	1465	1648	1930	1218	1433
ODA	83	75	103	140	295	323	181	207
Official/off. supported	420	380	449	620	338	511	312	392
Official export credits	78	115	174	217	119	316	237	271
Guaranteed supplier credits	111	79	46	65	14	18	8	12
Guaranteed bank credits	231	186	229	338	205	176	66	109
Financial markets	359	599	925	705	1015	1097	725	834
Banks	359	598	924	705	1015	1097	725	834
Bonds	1	1	1	1	0	0	0	0
Other private	–	–	–	–	–	–	–	–
II. Multilateral	299	322	377	454	463	533	302	308
of which: concessional	222	248	304	371	390	466	263	269
non-concessional	77	74	73	83	74	67	39	39
memo: IMF, total	35	29	25	28	20	14	6	5
III. Non-OECD Creditor countries	37	39	40	40	23	27	29	32
C.E.E.C.	13	13	13	13	–	4	4	4
Arab countries	19	19	19	19	13	13	6	6
Other countries and unspecified	5	7	7	8	10	10	18	21
Subtotal: Long term debt	*914*	*1057*	*1321*	*1523*	*2135*	*2491*	*1549*	*1772*
of which: concessional	289	309	384	477	693	797	445	476
non-concessional	625	748	937	1046	1441	1694	1104	1296
Short term								
Subtotal: Short term debt	*788*	*1388*	*1710*	*1828*	*2396*	*2454*	*1679*	*1913*
Banks	756	1323	1632	1704	2278	2243	1532	1742
Export credits	32	65	78	124	118	210	148	171
Other identified liabilities	87	96	123	138	76	98	73	76
Total identified debt	**2225**	**3063**	**3915**	**4168**	**4606**	**5042**	**3301**	**3762**
SERVICE PAYMENTS								
Long term								
I. OECD countries and capital markets	132	232	424	252	153	172	182	135
ODA	4	4	4	11	5	4	4	5
Official/off. supported	90	167	293	88	71	47	100	64
Financial markets	38	61	126	153	77	121	78	66
Other private	–	–	–	–	–	–	–	–
II. Multilateral	16	25	22	35	28	26	19	20
of which: concessional	5	12	12	23	17	19	14	15
memo: IMF, total	10	12	10	7	9	1	2	1
III. Non-OECD creditor countries	3	1	3	2	1	1	1	1
Subtotal: Service payments, long term debt	*109*	*174*	*321*	*208*	*182*	*199*	*201*	*155*
of which: concessional	8	15	15	31	21	23	17	20
Amortization, long term debt	51	99	234	131	74	52	118	62
Interest, long term debt	58	75	87	77	108	146	82	93
Interest, short term debt	57	93	109	126	156	216	119	104
Total service payments	**216**	**365**	**567**	**432**	**338**	**415**	**319**	**260**

WESTERN SAMOA

US $ Million

	1984	1985	1986	1987	1988	1989	1990	1991
GROSS DEBT								
Long term								
I. OECD countries and capital markets	7	7	6	7	8	7	5	3
ODA	0	0	0	1	0	0	0	0
Official/off. supported	3	4	4	4	6	5	2	1
Official export credits	3	4	4	4	5	4	2	1
Guaranteed supplier credits	0	–	–	0	1	0	0	–
Guaranteed bank credits	–	0	0	–	–	–	–	–
Financial markets	4	3	2	2	1	2	2	1
Banks	2	1	1	1	–	1	1	–
Bonds	2	2	1	2	1	1	1	1
Other private	–	–	–	–	–	–	–	–
II. Multilateral	60	63	65	67	63	63	82	97
of which: concessional	52	54	56	60	60	61	81	97
non-concessional	8	9	9	7	3	2	1	0
memo: IMF, total	10	11	10	8	4	2	1	0
III. Non-OECD Creditor countries	5	3	3	6	7	6	6	6
C.E.E.C.	–	–	–	–	–	–	–	–
Arab countries	–	–	1	3	3	4	4	4
Other countries and unspecified	5	3	3	3	3	2	2	2
Subtotal: Long term debt	72	74	75	80	77	76	93	106
of which: concessional	52	54	56	61	60	62	82	97
non-concessional	20	20	18	19	17	15	11	9
Short term								
Subtotal: Short term debt	0	0	0	0	0	0	0	1
Banks	–	–	–	–	–	–	–	1
Export credits	0	0	0	0	0	0	0	0
Other identified liabilities	–	–	–	–	–	–	–	–
Total identified debt	72	74	75	80	78	77	93	107
SERVICE PAYMENTS								
Long term								
I. OECD countries and capital markets	1	2	2	1	1	3	1	1
ODA	0	0	0	0	0	0	0	0
Official/off. supported	1	0	1	1	1	2	1	1
Financial markets	0	1	1	0	0	1	0	0
Other private	–	–	–	–	–	–	–	–
II. Multilateral	3	4	4	6	7	5	4	4
of which: concessional	1	2	2	3	3	3	3	3
memo: IMF, total	2	2	3	4	4	2	1	1
III. Non-OECD creditor countries	2	2	1	0	0	1	0	0
Subtotal: Service payments, long term debt	6	7	7	7	8	8	6	5
of which: concessional	1	2	2	3	3	3	3	3
Amortization, long term debt	4	5	5	6	7	6	4	4
Interest, long term debt	2	2	2	2	2	1	1	1
Interest, short term debt	0	0	0	0	0	0	0	0
Total service payments	6	7	7	7	9	8	6	5

YEMEN

	1984	1985	1986	1987	1988	1989	1990	1991
GROSS DEBT								
Long term								
I. OECD countries and capital markets	293	401	483	515	568	555	590	513
ODA	89	126	165	232	248	301	324	345
Official/off. supported	138	146	192	240	285	222	225	134
Official export credits	14	8	3	4	3	4	6	8
Guaranteed supplier credits	66	64	125	163	192	140	157	120
Guaranteed bank credits	58	74	64	73	90	79	62	6
Financial markets	66	129	126	43	35	32	37	34
Banks	66	129	126	43	35	32	37	34
Bonds	–	–	–	–	–	–	–	–
Other private	–	–	–	–	–	–	–	–
II. Multilateral	693	799	864	1259	1345	1447	1025	1114
of which: concessional	575	668	756	1201	1273	1365	989	1098
non-concessional	118	131	109	59	73	82	36	16
memo: IMF, total	49	48	32	15	6	1	–	–
III. Non-OECD Creditor countries	3056	3678	4267	5353	6278	6743	6582	6571
C.E.E.C.	2241	2734	3330	4400	5130	5556	5761	5801
Arab countries	708	733	729	737	887	897	664	660
Other countries and unspecified	106	210	208	215	262	289	118	111
Subtotal: Long term debt	*4042*	*4878*	*5614*	*7127*	*8191*	*8744*	*8193*	*8198*
of which: concessional	2041	2547	2994	4126	4729	5141	5093	5142
non-concessional	2001	2331	2620	3001	3462	3603	3100	3055
Short term								
Subtotal: Short term debt	*362*	*274*	*410*	*334*	*389*	*448*	*524*	*390*
Banks	287	196	313	290	329	381	462	330
Export credits	75	78	97	44	60	66	62	59
Other identified liabilities	86	167	102	117	139	134	10	–
Total identified debt	**4490**	**5319**	**6127**	**7578**	**8719**	**9326**	**8727**	**8588**
SERVICE PAYMENTS								
Long term								
I. OECD countries and capital markets	74	79	70	151	234	257	54	55
ODA	3	3	6	8	12	14	16	16
Official/off. supported	59	63	33	128	85	142	7	35
Financial markets	12	13	30	15	137	101	30	5
Other private	–	–	–	–	–	–	–	–
II. Multilateral	41	62	104	135	108	62	56	69
of which: concessional	23	31	50	58	65	55	39	44
memo: IMF, total	4	9	22	22	8	4	1	0
III. Non-OECD creditor countries	93	108	125	169	229	225	31	5
Subtotal: Service payments, long term debt	*208*	*250*	*299*	*455*	*570*	*544*	*141*	*130*
of which: concessional	85	102	119	155	208	239	55	60
Amortization, long term debt	161	193	208	340	455	409	108	97
Interest, long term debt	47	56	91	115	116	134	33	33
Interest, short term debt	42	36	32	32	38	48	35	25
Total service payments	**249**	**286**	**331**	**488**	**609**	**592**	**176**	**155**

US $ Million

	1984	1985	1986	1987	1988	1989	1990	1991
GROSS DEBT								
Long term								
I. OECD countries and capital markets	13204	15403	13017	14034	13726	12844	10831	7753
ODA	344	428	542	677	601	634	718	761
Official/off. supported	3290	3625	3929	4716	3772	3986	3694	3159
Official export credits	1023	1225	1266	1924	1779	1961	1850	1817
Guaranteed supplier credits	411	376	419	649	390	454	289	367
Guaranteed bank credits	1856	2025	2245	2143	1604	1570	1556	975
Financial markets	9570	11349	8546	8641	9353	8224	6419	3832
Banks	9566	11347	8545	8641	9353	8224	6419	3832
Bonds	4	2	1	–	–	–	–	–
Other private	–	–	–	–	–	–	–	–
II. Multilateral	3715	4458	4956	5409	4297	3669	3559	3091
of which: concessional	94	94	94	92	58	38	25	15
non-concessional	3621	4364	4861	5317	4239	3631	3534	3075
memo: IMF, total	1947	2108	2069	1852	1310	686	467	307
III. Non-OECD Creditor countries	1436	1213	1281	1080	1036	1657	1644	1596
C.E.E.C.	474	478	652	570	614	1075	1066	1062
Arab countries	963	735	629	510	423	582	578	534
Other countries and unspecified	–	–	–	–	–	–	–	–
Subtotal: Long term debt	*18356*	*21075*	*19254*	*20524*	*19060*	*18170*	*16034*	*12439*
of which: concessional	438	522	637	770	659	672	743	777
non-concessional	17917	20552	18617	19754	18401	17498	15291	11662
Short term								
Subtotal: Short term debt	*2318*	*3465*	*3138*	*2731*	*1949*	*1803*	*3149*	*2367*
Banks	1853	2772	2043	1859	988	694	1572	703
Export credits	465	694	1095	872	961	1109	1577	1664
Other identified liabilities	–	–	–	–	–	–	–	–
Total identified debt	**20674**	**24540**	**22391**	**23255**	**21009**	**19973**	**19183**	**14806**
SERVICE PAYMENTS								
Long term								
I. OECD countries and capital markets	2564	2274	2475	1810	1842	2570	2669	1940
ODA	13	5	50	23	15	18	45	24
Official/off. supported	676	1296	1083	904	637	873	846	323
Financial markets	1875	973	1343	884	1190	1679	1777	1593
Other private	–	–	–	–	–	–	–	–
II. Multilateral	781	866	1057	1232	1540	1202	1092	866
of which: concessional	22	24	27	27	30	22	17	11
memo: IMF, total	483	537	618	664	750	595	419	196
III. Non-OECD creditor countries	217	374	167	176	107	67	99	569
Subtotal: Service payments, long term debt	*3561*	*3514*	*3699*	*3218*	*3489*	*3839*	*3860*	*3375*
of which: concessional	34	29	76	50	44	39	62	35
Amortization, long term debt	1919	1910	2110	1805	1951	2294	2316	2255
Interest, long term debt	1642	1604	1589	1413	1538	1545	1544	1121
Interest, short term debt	234	227	206	178	155	118	143	104
Total service payments	**3795**	**3741**	**3905**	**3395**	**3643**	**3957**	**4004**	**3479**

US $ Million

	1984	1985	1986	1987	1988	1989	1990	1991
GROSS DEBT								
Long term								
I. OECD countries and capital markets	3249	3771	4458	5321	5123	5553	6374	5679
ODA	640	781	1011	1273	1367	1522	1906	1557
Official/off. supported	2246	2573	3000	3478	3152	3481	3877	3652
Official export credits	1914	2279	2742	3216	2966	3294	3700	3457
Guaranteed supplier credits	158	193	136	181	151	142	132	110
Guaranteed bank credits	174	101	122	81	35	45	45	85
Financial markets	363	417	447	570	604	550	590	470
Banks	360	413	442	565	599	545	585	465
Bonds	3	4	4	5	5	4	5	5
Other private	–	–	–	–	–	–	–	–
II. Multilateral	1151	1415	1650	2187	2183	2214	2388	2562
of which: concessional	485	577	716	1093	1187	1425	1612	1700
non-concessional	666	839	934	1094	997	789	776	862
memo: IMF, total	675	808	856	967	786	628	521	472
III. Non-OECD Creditor countries	260	240	234	292	318	415	407	418
C.E.E.C.	–	–	–	–	–	–	–	–
Arab countries	200	190	177	235	256	339	339	339
Other countries and unspecified	60	50	57	57	62	76	68	79
Subtotal: Long term debt	*4660*	*5426*	*6341*	*7801*	*7625*	*8182*	*9169*	*8659*
of which: concessional	1125	1358	1726	2366	2554	2947	3519	3257
non-concessional	3535	4068	4615	5435	5071	5235	5650	5401
Short term								
Subtotal: Short term debt	*291*	*421*	*727*	*980*	*1110*	*1243*	*1184*	*1296*
Banks	213	281	304	387	436	518	423	290
Export credits	78	140	423	593	674	725	761	1006
Other identified liabilities	–	–	–	–	–	–	–	–
Total identified debt	**4951**	**5846**	**7068**	**8781**	**8735**	**9426**	**10352**	**9954**
SERVICE PAYMENTS								
Long term								
I. OECD countries and capital markets	340	408	486	346	344	402	787	204
ODA	46	18	68	36	49	60	98	19
Official/off. supported	169	284	361	262	271	171	558	123
Financial markets	125	106	56	48	24	170	131	62
Other private	–	–	–	–	–	–	–	–
II. Multilateral	132	204	232	307	252	455	257	127
of which: concessional	18	28	34	42	39	30	22	20
memo: IMF, total	105	175	195	247	181	391	190	60
III. Non-OECD creditor countries	19	20	24	21	20	26	8	4
Subtotal: Service payments, long term debt	*491*	*632*	*742*	*674*	*617*	*884*	*1052*	*335*
of which: concessional	64	46	103	78	88	91	121	39
Amortization, long term debt	202	299	361	345	319	519	554	112
Interest, long term debt	289	333	381	329	297	364	498	223
Interest, short term debt	24	23	22	29	40	20	45	26
Total service payments	**515**	**654**	**765**	**703**	**657**	**904**	**1098**	**361**

US $ Million

	1984	1985	1986	1987	1988	1989	1990	1991
GROSS DEBT								
Long term								
I. OECD countries and capital markets	1375	1620	1957	2266	2276	2174	1841	1688
ODA	575	677	872	1082	1129	1139	870	865
Official/off. supported	674	816	986	1099	952	936	866	735
Official export credits	396	468	678	788	591	767	599	564
Guaranteed supplier credits	131	176	163	199	299	115	213	126
Guaranteed bank credits	147	172	145	112	62	54	53	45
Financial markets	126	126	99	85	195	99	106	88
Banks	126	126	99	85	195	99	106	88
Bonds	–	–	–	–	–	–	–	–
Other private	–	–	–	–	–	–	–	–
II. Multilateral	1237	1533	1846	2223	2146	2140	2366	2200
of which: concessional	181	283	403	517	527	540	622	665
non-concessional	1055	1250	1444	1706	1620	1600	1744	1535
memo: IMF, total	739	801	858	991	940	900	949	918
III. Non-OECD Creditor countries	721	730	728	768	729	778	714	705
C.E.E.C.	288	297	345	375	326	402	332	332
Arab countries	117	117	113	113	113	113	113	113
Other countries and unspecified	315	316	271	279	290	263	269	259
Subtotal: Long term debt	*3332*	*3883*	*4532*	*5257*	*5152*	*5092*	*4921*	*4592*
of which: concessional	756	960	1274	1599	1655	1679	1491	1530
non-concessional	2576	2922	3257	3658	3496	3413	3429	3063
Short term								
Subtotal: Short term debt	*588*	*719*	*864*	*904*	*787*	*830*	*1109*	*1011*
Banks	515	578	674	608	577	531	725	700
Export credits	73	141	190	296	210	299	384	311
Other identified liabilities	20	11	9	13	12	10	9	9
Total identified debt	**3940**	**4613**	**5405**	**6174**	**5951**	**5932**	**6038**	**5613**
SERVICE PAYMENTS								
Long term								
I. OECD countries and capital markets	87	61	144	82	131	154	141	144
ODA	4	5	24	11	25	20	16	21
Official/off. supported	66	45	119	66	48	121	105	86
Financial markets	17	11	1	5	58	14	20	37
Other private	–	–	–	–	–	–	–	–
II. Multilateral	190	105	314	69	45	47	99	516
of which: concessional	5	13	15	10	7	15	13	36
memo: IMF, total	131	50	230	5	1	18	27	100
III. Non-OECD creditor countries	3	3	10	13	16	17	1	1
Subtotal: Service payments, long term debt	*279*	*169*	*469*	*164*	*191*	*217*	*242*	*661*
of which: concessional	9	18	39	21	32	34	29	57
Amortization, long term debt	129	74	288	65	103	133	149	337
Interest, long term debt	151	95	181	99	88	84	93	324
Interest, short term debt	67	49	46	41	35	34	20	44
Total service payments	**346**	**218**	**515**	**206**	**226**	**252**	**262**	**705**

ZIMBABWE

US $ Million

	1984	1985	1986	1987	1988	1989	1990	1991
GROSS DEBT								
Long term								
I. OECD countries and capital markets	1403	1516	1683	1861	1606	1654	1907	2061
ODA	204	276	378	541	538	590	690	748
Official/off. supported	378	485	555	652	536	558	620	733
Official export credits	107	116	107	117	90	83	103	117
Guaranteed supplier credits	12	22	42	68	83	43	69	58
Guaranteed bank credits	258	347	406	467	363	432	448	558
Financial markets	821	754	750	668	532	507	598	581
Banks	458	354	262	170	106	152	305	317
Bonds	363	401	487	498	426	355	293	263
Other private	–	–	–	–	–	–	–	–
II. Multilateral	423	532	620	677	606	598	645	751
of which: concessional	39	54	80	100	121	144	165	203
non-concessional	385	478	539	577	485	455	480	548
memo: IMF, total	256	264	234	157	70	29	7	–
III. Non-OECD Creditor countries	144	162	161	160	162	129	101	77
C.E.E.C.	–	–	–	–	–	–	–	–
Arab countries	41	41	39	40	39	36	35	34
Other countries and unspecified	103	121	122	120	123	93	66	42
Subtotal: Long term debt	*1970*	*2210*	*2463*	*2697*	*2374*	*2381*	*2653*	*2889*
of which: concessional	243	330	459	641	660	733	854	951
non-concessional	1728	1880	2005	2056	1715	1648	1799	1938
Short term								
Subtotal: Short term debt	*112*	*96*	*162*	*259*	*378*	*326*	*375*	*587*
Banks	92	63	121	228	338	266	322	547
Export credits	20	33	42	31	40	60	53	41
Other identified liabilities	19	24	40	–	–	–	–	–
Total identified debt	**2101**	**2330**	**2666**	**2956**	**2752**	**2707**	**3028**	**3476**
SERVICE PAYMENTS								
Long term								
I. OECD countries and capital markets	248	272	287	295	280	199	222	239
ODA	6	8	8	11	17	19	25	23
Official/off. supported	70	95	117	139	114	158	116	111
Financial markets	171	169	162	145	150	23	81	105
Other private	–	–	–	–	–	–	–	–
II. Multilateral	55	89	146	160	157	120	115	95
of which: concessional	1	1	2	1	7	7	6	7
memo: IMF, total	41	72	116	121	87	43	26	7
III. Non-OECD creditor countries	4	10	14	31	31	29	30	26
Subtotal: Service payments, long term debt	*307*	*372*	*447*	*487*	*468*	*348*	*366*	*360*
of which: concessional	7	9	9	13	24	25	32	30
Amortization, long term debt	187	234	311	334	342	233	248	250
Interest, long term debt	120	138	137	153	126	115	118	111
Interest, short term debt	44	10	11	16	25	32	29	29
Total service payments	**350**	**382**	**458**	**503**	**493**	**380**	**395**	**389**

TOTAL LDCS

US $ Million

	1984	1985	1986	1987	1988	1989	1990	1991
GROSS DEBT								
Long term								
I. OECD countries and capital markets	547559	598290	638373	698311	684795	686094	682789	705495
ODA	60158	73812	89870	111776	113520	115447	127376	136223
Official/off. supported	136247	158102	174208	198282	171583	181522	194158	201799
Official export credits	61347	71996	79865	95440	88941	94891	96637	103516
Guaranteed supplier credits	29830	32108	30504	29780	23375	22396	22778	21680
Guaranteed bank credits	45070	53999	63839	73062	59267	64235	74743	76604
Financial markets	339052	353055	361152	373258	383745	372088	343523	349235
Banks	310305	314357	316851	324828	331338	313211	279549	274622
Bonds	28748	38698	44301	48430	52407	58877	63974	74613
Other private	12102	13320	13142	14994	15947	17036	17728	18238
II. Multilateral	118560	146313	177778	215762	210724	218113	244591	261996
of which: concessional	37093	42380	48694	58233	61847	67641	76200	85179
non-concessional	81468	103933	129083	157529	148877	150472	168391	176817
memo: IMF, total	33792	38211	40314	41162	34465	31947	32315	33483
III. Non-OECD Creditor countries	106752	115956	128290	153472	161326	167678	166695	165427
C.E.E.C.	74068	81125	91085	114076	122012	128086	130902	132625
Arab countries	18859	19093	19797	20128	20270	21082	17824	14877
Other countries and unspecified	13825	15738	17407	19268	19045	18510	17929	17905
Subtotal: Long term debt	*772587*	*860200*	*943867*	*1067109*	*1056845*	*1071885*	*1094070*	*1132917*
of which: concessional	142602	164654	192062	237324	248468	258700	281121	300818
non-concessional	629985	695547	751805	829785	808377	813186	812949	832099
Short term								
Subtotal: Short term debt	*179467*	*207292*	*221511*	*242764*	*246946*	*255721*	*300918*	*317654*
Banks	154726	176060	183354	197803	199694	205008	237158	250606
Export credits	24740	31232	38157	44961	47252	50713	63760	67048
Other identified liabilities	20278	22454	21568	26652	29918	27236	32962	34232
Total identified debt	**972767**	**1090468**	**1187707**	**1337204**	**1333709**	**1354843**	**1427950**	**1484803**
SERVICE PAYMENTS								
Long term								
I. OECD countries and capital markets	88823	98908	93472	96064	103106	101154	93197	90428
ODA	3050	3125	3998	4416	5773	5649	6321	6218
Official/off. supported	33629	40833	42045	43819	36766	39990	35557	33702
Financial markets	50440	53538	45867	46397	59029	53804	48912	47046
Other private	1784	1412	1562	1432	1538	1712	2418	3463
II. Multilateral	12963	16468	23458	30293	31985	30005	34676	36001
of which: concessional	1153	1514	2131	2349	2422	2264	2406	2420
memo: IMF, total	4891	6691	9579	12222	10683	9964	10427	8785
III. Non-OECD creditor countries	3997	5232	4701	4987	4932	5390	6282	5845
Subtotal: Service payments, long term debt	*105962*	*120824*	*121773*	*131634*	*140523*	*137249*	*134255*	*132274*
of which: concessional	4582	5230	7003	7754	8974	8732	10123	9837
Amortization, long term debt	51870	65810	70515	80264	79452	79193	80407	82645
Interest, long term debt	54092	54914	51258	51370	61071	58056	53848	49629
Interest, short term debt	21401	17112	15367	16401	20078	22765	21721	17943
Total service payments	**127413**	**138034**	**137377**	**148133**	**160601**	**160014**	**155976**	**150217**

Annex 2

Developing Countries and Territories by Income Group as of 31 December 1992[a] and Selected Creditor Groups (OPEC, Arab Donors)

LICs: Low-Income		*UMICs: Upper Middle-Income*[b]	
*Afghanistan	*Madagascar	Antigua & Barbuda	Macao
Angola	*Malawi	Argentina	Malta
*Bangladesh	*Maldives	Aruba	Mexico
*Benin	*Mali	Bahamas	Montserrat
*Bhutan	*Mauritania	Bahrain	Netherlands Antilles
Bolivia	Mayotte	Barbados	New Caledonia
*Botswana	*Mozambique	Bermuda	Niue
*Burkina Faso	*Myanmar	Brazil	Oman
*Burundi	*Nepal	Brunei	Polynesia, French
*Cambodia	Nicaragua	Cayman Islands	Qatar
*Cape Verde	*Niger	Cyprus	Saudi Arabia
*Central African Republic	Nigeria	Falkland Islands	Seychelles
*Chad	Pakistan	Gabon	Singapore
China (P.R.)	Philippines	Gibraltar	Saint Kitts-Nevis
*Comoros	*Rwanda	Greece	Suriname
Côte d'Ivoire	*Sao Tome & Principe	Hong Kong	Taiwan
*Djibouti	Senegal	Iraq	Trinidad & Tobago
Egypt	*Sierra Leone	Israel	United Arab Emirates
*Equatorial Guinea	*Solomon Islands	Korea, Republic	Uruguay
*Ethiopia	*Somalia	Kuwait	Venezuela
*Gambia	Sri Lanka	Lebanon	Virgin Islands
Ghana	Saint Helena	Libya	Yugoslavia
*Guinea	*Sudan		
*Guinea-Bissau	*Tanzania		
Guyana	*Togo		
*Haiti	*Tuvalu		
Honduras	*Uganda		
India	*Vanuatu		
Indonesia	*Western Samoa		
Kenya	*Yemen		
*Kiribati	*Zaire		
*Laos PDR	*Zambia		
*Lesotho	Zimbabwe		
*Liberia			

LMICs: Low Middle-Income		*OPEC: Organisation of Petroleum Exporting Countries*	
Albania	Mauritius	+Algeria	+Libya
Algeria	Mongolia	Ecuador	Nigeria
Anguilla	Morocco	Gabon	+Qatar
Belize	Namibia	Indonesia	+Saudi Arabia
Cameroon	Nauru	Iran	+United Arab Emirates
Chile	Panama	+Iraq	Venezuela
Colombia	Pacific Islands (US)	+Kuwait	
Congo	Papua New Guinea		
Cook Islands	Paraguay		
Costa Rica	Peru		
Cuba	Saint Lucia		
Dominica	Saint Vincent		
Dominican Republic	Swaziland		
Ecuador	Syria		
El Salvador	Thailand		
Fiji	Tokelau Islands		
Grenada	Tonga		
Guatemala	Tunisia		
Iran	Turkey		
Jamaica	Turks & Caicos Islands		
Jordan	Vietnam		
Korea, Democratic	Wallis & Futuna		
Malaysia			

*   LLDC (47 Least-developed countries).
+   Arab donors.
a) The criterion for classifying a country as a LIC is a 1991 per capita GNP of under $765, as shown in the World Bank Atlas, or calculated on that basis; as a LMIC a per capita GNP between $765 and $2 555; and as a UMIC a per capita GNP above $2 556.
b) Includes also ''High-Income'' countries.

Glossary of Abbreviations and Signs Used

Abbreviations

BIS	Bank for International Settlements
CEECs	Central and Eastern European Countries
DAC	Development Assistance Committee of OECD
DRS	Debtor Reporting System (operated by IBRD)
FDI	Foreign Direct Investment
IBRD	International Bank for Reconstruction and Development (the World Bank)
IDA	International Development Association
IMF	International Monetary Fund
LDC	Developing Country
MDBs	Multilateral Development Banks
NFT	Net Financial Transfer
NGOs	Non-governmental Organisations
ODA	Official Development Assistance
ODF	Official Development Finance

Main Income Groups (see also Annex 2)

LICs	Low-income countries and territories
LMICs	Low middle-income countries and territories
UMICs	Upper middle-income countries and territories
LLDCs	Least-developed countries

Signs used

()	Secretariat estimate in whole or in part
– or 0.00	Nil or negligible
..	Not available
...	Not available separately but included in total
X	Less than half the smallest unit shown
n.a.	Not applicable
.	Incomplete
p	Provisional

MAIN SALES OUTLETS OF OECD PUBLICATIONS
PRINCIPAUX POINTS DE VENTE DES PUBLICATIONS DE L'OCDE

ARGENTINA – ARGENTINE
Carlos Hirsch S.R.L.
Galería Güemes, Florida 165, 4° Piso
1333 Buenos Aires   Tel. (1) 331.1787 y 331.2391
Telefax: (1) 331.1787

AUSTRALIA – AUSTRALIE
D.A. Information Services
648 Whitehorse Road, P.O.B 163
Mitcham, Victoria 3132   Tel. (03) 873.4411
Telefax: (03) 873.5679

AUSTRIA – AUTRICHE
Gerold & Co.
Graben 31
Wien I   Tel. (0222) 533.50.14

BELGIUM – BELGIQUE
Jean De Lannoy
Avenue du Roi 202
B-1060 Bruxelles   Tel. (02) 538.51.69/538.08.41
Telefax: (02) 538.08.41

CANADA
Renouf Publishing Company Ltd.
1294 Algoma Road
Ottawa, ON K1B 3W8   Tel. (613) 741.4333
Telefax: (613) 741.5439
Stores:
61 Sparks Street
Ottawa, ON K1P 5R1   Tel. (613) 238.8985
211 Yonge Street
Toronto, ON M5B 1M4   Tel. (416) 363.3171
Telefax: (416)363.59.63

Les Éditions La Liberté Inc.
3020 Chemin Sainte-Foy
Sainte-Foy, PQ G1X 3V6   Tel. (418) 658.3763
Telefax: (418) 658.3763

Federal Publications Inc.
Suite 103, 388 King Street W
Toronto, ON M5V 1K2   Tel. (416) 581.1552
Telefax: (416) 581.1743

Les Publications Fédérales
1185 Université
Montréal, QC H3B 3A7   Tel. (514) 954.1633
Telefax : (514) 954.1635

CHINA – CHINE
China National Publications Import
Export Corporation (CNPIEC)
16 Gongti E. Road, Chaoyang District
P.O. Box 88 or 50
Beijing 100704 PR   Tel. (01) 506.6688
Telefax: (01) 506.3101

DENMARK – DANEMARK
Munksgaard Book and Subscription Service
35, Nørre Søgade, P.O. Box 2148
DK-1016 København K   Tel. (33) 12.85.70
Telefax: (33) 12.93.87

FINLAND – FINLANDE
Akateeminen Kirjakauppa
Keskuskatu 1, P.O. Box 128
00100 Helsinki
Subscription Services/Agence d'abonnements :
P.O. Box 23
00371 Helsinki   Tel. (358 0) 12141
Telefax: (358 0) 121.4450

FRANCE
OECD/OCDE
Mail Orders/Commandes par correspondance:
2, rue André-Pascal
75775 Paris Cedex 16   Tel. (33-1) 45.24.82.00
Telefax: (33-1) 45.24.81.76 or (33-1) 45.24.85.00
Telex: 640048 OCDE

OECD Bookshop/Librairie de l'OCDE :
33, rue Octave-Feuillet
75016 Paris   Tel. (33-1) 45.24.81.67
(33-1) 45.24.81.81
Documentation Française
29, quai Voltaire
75007 Paris   Tel. 40.15.70.00
Gibert Jeune (Droit-Économie)
6, place Saint-Michel
75006 Paris   Tel. 43.25.91.19
Librairie du Commerce International
10, avenue d'Iéna
75016 Paris   Tel. 40.73.34.60
Librairie Dunod
Université Paris-Dauphine
Place du Maréchal de Lattre de Tassigny
75016 Paris   Tel. (1) 44.05.40.13
Librairie Lavoisier
11, rue Lavoisier
75008 Paris   Tel. 42.65.39.95
Librairie L.G.D.J. - Montchrestien
20, rue Soufflot
75005 Paris   Tel. 46.33.89.85
Librairie des Sciences Politiques
30, rue Saint-Guillaume
75007 Paris   Tel. 45.48.36.02
P.U.F.
49, boulevard Saint-Michel
75005 Paris   Tel. 43.25.83.40
Librairie de l'Université
12a, rue Nazareth
13100 Aix-en-Provence   Tel. (16) 42.26.18.08
Documentation Française
165, rue Garibaldi
69003 Lyon   Tel. (16) 78.63.32.23
Librairie Decitre
29, place Bellecour
69002 Lyon   Tel. (16) 72.40.54.54

GERMANY – ALLEMAGNE
OECD Publications and Information Centre
August-Bebel-Allee 6
D-53175 Bonn 2   Tel. (0228) 959.120
Telefax: (0228) 959.12.17

GREECE – GRÈCE
Librairie Kauffmann
Mavrokordatou 9
106 78 Athens   Tel. (01) 32.55.321
Telefax: (01) 36.33.967

HONG-KONG
Swindon Book Co. Ltd.
13–15 Lock Road
Kowloon, Hong Kong   Tel. 366.80.31
Telefax: 739.49.75

HUNGARY – HONGRIE
Euro Info Service
POB 1271
1464 Budapest   Tel. (1) 111.62.16
Telefax : (1) 111.60.61

ICELAND – ISLANDE
Mál Mog Menning
Laugavegi 18, Pósthólf 392
121 Reykjavik   Tel. 162.35.23

INDIA – INDE
Oxford Book and Stationery Co.
Scindia House
New Delhi 110001   Tel.(11) 331.5896/5308
Telefax: (11) 332.5993
17 Park Street
Calcutta 700016   Tel. 240832

INDONESIA – INDONÉSIE
Pdii-Lipi
P.O. Box 269/JKSMG/88
Jakarta 12790   Tel. 583467
Telex: 62 875

IRELAND – IRLANDE
TDC Publishers – Library Suppliers
12 North Frederick Street
Dublin 1   Tel. (01) 874.48.35
Telefax: (01) 874.84.16

ISRAEL
Electronic Publications only
Publications électroniques seulement
Sophist Systems Ltd.
71 Allenby Street
Tel-Aviv 65134   Tel. 3-29.00.21
Telefax: 3-29.92.39

ITALY – ITALIE
Libreria Commissionaria Sansoni
Via Duca di Calabria 1/1
50125 Firenze   Tel. (055) 64.54.15
Telefax: (055) 64.12.57
Via Bartolini 29
20155 Milano   Tel. (02) 36.50.83
Editrice e Libreria Herder
Piazza Montecitorio 120
00186 Roma   Tel. 679.46.28
Telefax: 678.47.51
Libreria Hoepli
Via Hoepli 5
20121 Milano   Tel. (02) 86.54.46
Telefax: (02) 805.28.86
Libreria Scientifica
Dott. Lucio de Biasio 'Aeiou'
Via Coronelli, 6
20146 Milano   Tel. (02) 48.95.45.52
Telefax: (02) 48.95.45.48

JAPAN – JAPON
OECD Publications and Information Centre
Landic Akasaka Building
2-3-4 Akasaka, Minato-ku
Tokyo 107   Tel. (81.3) 3586.2016
Telefax: (81.3) 3584.7929

KOREA – CORÉE
Kyobo Book Centre Co. Ltd.
P.O. Box 1658, Kwang Hwa Moon
Seoul   Tel. 730.78.91
Telefax: 735.00.30

MALAYSIA – MALAISIE
Co-operative Bookshop Ltd.
University of Malaya
P.O. Box 1127, Jalan Pantai Baru
59700 Kuala Lumpur
Malaysia   Tel. 756.5000/756.5425
Telefax: 757.3661

MEXICO – MEXIQUE
Revistas y Periodicos Internacionales S.A. de C.V.
Florencia 57 - 1004
Mexico, D.F. 06600   Tel. 207.81.00
Telefax : 208.39.79

NETHERLANDS – PAYS-BAS
SDU Uitgeverij
Christoffel Plantijnstraat 2
Postbus 20014
2500 EA's-Gravenhage   Tel. (070 3) 78.99.11
Voor bestellingen: Tel. (070 3) 78.98.80
Telefax: (070 3) 47.63.51

OECD PUBLICATIONS, 2 rue André-Pascal, 75775 PARIS CEDEX 16
PRINTED IN FRANCE
(43 93 03 1) ISBN 92-64-14007-7 - No. 46577 1993